'This heady brew of fourteen studies of "the social supernatural" from all across Europe (in a cauldron stirred by two skilled editors) promises to become a standard reference work for anthropologists, folklorists, and cultural historians seeking to expose the darker strata underlying the prettified fairies that Disney has foisted on us.'

—Richard Firth Green, Academy Professor,
The Ohio State University

'From Swedish neighbourhood trolls to the dangerously erotic *bohyni* of Ukraine to the terrifying *Witte Wieven* of Dutch folklore, Young and Ermacora have pulled together an exciting collection of essays on the social supernatural in European folk narrative. Some chapters upend earlier conceptions of these creatures and their sociality, while others provide new and nuanced insight into less well-known traditions. Here is an exquisite volume of rigorous, engaging contributions that provides a wealth of evidence for broad reassessments of the social supernatural.'

—Timothy R. Tangherlini, Professor of Scandinavian Folklore,
University of California, Berkeley

'*The Exeter Companion To Fairies, Nereids, Trolls And Other Social Supernatural Beings* will serve for many years as the definitive study of these assorted entities. From oral tradition spanning countless generations to more recent efforts of folklorists, there has been a fascination with these incredible figures of legend and folktale. Most analysis has remained on a local level. Comparative studies are rare. With this volume, those wishing to understand fairies and similar supernatural beings will benefit from the insights of distinguished experts as they consider the possibilities across a geographic expanse.'

—Ron James, author of *The Folklore of Cornwall:
The Oral Tradition of a Celtic Nation*

'This accessible and fascinating volume presents a consortium of supernatural communities from across Europe, with representatives travelling to the page from the Norse north, the Latin south, the Celtic west, and the Slavic east. The international authors explore the personalities, passions, plottings, and pecking orders of the diverse societies of elves, trolls, fairies, and spirits, which sometimes mirror—and sometimes distort—our own.'

—Ceri Houlbrook, Senior Lecturer, University of Hertfordshire

'Taking the reader on a richly detailed tour though European folk traditions having to do with "social" otherworldly beings, the *Companion* demonstrates the inestimable value of collecting and analyzing folklore for a deeper understanding of cultures, their similarities, and their differences. It is a reference work that will be enjoyable to read and fruitful to consult for many years to come.'

—Joseph Falaky Nagy, Henry L. Shattuck
Professor of Irish Studies, Harvard University

# The Exeter Companion to Fairies, Nereids, Trolls and Other Social Supernatural Beings

# Exeter New Approaches to Legend, Folklore and Popular Belief

*Series Editors:*
**Simon Young**, University of California (Accent), Florence
**Davide Ermacora**, University of Turin

Exeter New Approaches to Legend, Folklore and Popular Belief provides a venue for growing scholarly interest in folklore narratives, supernatural belief systems and the communities that sustain them. Global in scope, the series encompasses milieus ranging from ancient to contemporary times and encourages empirically grounded, source-rich studies. The editors favour the broad multidisciplinary approach that has characterized the study of folklore and the supernatural, and which brings together insights from historians, folklorists, anthropologists and researchers from many other branches of the humanities and social sciences.

# The Exeter Companion to Fairies, Nereids, Trolls and Other Social Supernatural Beings

*European Traditions*

EDITED BY
SIMON YOUNG AND DAVIDE ERMACORA

UNIVERSITY
*of*
EXETER
PRESS

First published in 2024 by
**University of Exeter Press**
Reed Hall, Streatham Drive
Exeter EX4 4QR
UK

www.exeterpress.co.uk

Copyright © 2024 Simon Young, Davide Ermacora and the various contributors

The right of the individual contributors to be identified as the authors of this work has been asserted by them in accordance with the Copyright, Designs and Patents Act 1988.

*Exeter New Approaches to Legend, Folklore and Popular Belief*

ISSN 3049-7329 Print
ISSN 3049-7337 Digital

https://doi.org/10.47788/RPLR2812

**British Library Cataloguing in Publication Data**
A catalogue record for this book is available from the British Library

ISBN 978-1-80413-104-6 Hardback
ISBN 978-1-80413-105-3 ePub
ISBN 978-1-80413-106-0 PDF

Typeset by S4Carlisle Publishing Services Ltd, Chennai, India

Cover image: *A Dance around the Moon* (watercolour on paper) by Charles Altamont Doyle (1832–1893), 24.7 × 38.7 cm. Private Collection. Photo: The Maas Gallery, London

# Contents

|  | *Contributors* | ix |
|---|---|---|
|  | *Acknowledgements, Conventions and Abbreviations* | xiii |
| 1. | Introducing the Social Supernatural<br>*Simon Young and Davide Ermacora* | 1 |
| 2. | Ireland: The Tribes of the Gods and the People of the Hills<br>*John Carey* | 18 |
| 3. | The Isle of Man: 'They Call Them the Good People'<br>*Stephen Miller* | 32 |
| 4. | England: Small Fairies Are Beautiful Fairies<br>*Jeremy Harte* | 51 |
| 5. | Iceland: The Elves of Strandir<br>*Matthias Egeler* | 71 |
| 6. | Scandinavia: My Neighbour the Troll<br>*Tommy Kuusela* | 87 |
| 7. | The Netherlands: *Witte Wieven* and Other White Apparitions<br>*Yseult de Blécourt* | 107 |
| 8. | Iberia: Moors, *Gentiles* and *Encantadas*<br>*José Manuel Pedrosa* | 122 |
| 9. | France: Humanlike Societies and Spaces among the *Fées*<br>*Andrea Maraschi* | 138 |
| 10. | German-Speaking Europe: *Moosweiblein*, *Wichtel* and *Nixen*<br>*Janin Pisarek and Florian Schaefer* | 155 |
| 11. | The Hungarians: Heavenly and Earthly Fairy Societies<br>*Éva Pócs* | 173 |

12. Western Balkans: 'A *Vila* Like a *Vila*'  196
    Dorian Jurić

13. Greece (and Italy): The Nereids, 'Those from Outside'  217
    Tommaso Braccini

14. The Balts: *Laumės* and *Laimės*  233
    Francis Young and Saulė Kubiliūtė

15. Ukraine: Courtship Rituals and Legends of the *Bohyni*  243
    Natalie Kononenko

Index  261

# Contributors

**Yseult de Blécourt** is a historical anthropologist specializing in the study of witchcraft, werewolves, and fairy tales in Europe from the Late Middle Ages to the twentieth century. He is an Honorary Research Fellow at the Meertens Institute (Amsterdam), and an editor of the series Palgrave Historical Studies in Witchcraft and Magic.

**Tommaso Braccini** is Associate Professor of Classical Philology at the University of Siena. He is interested in folk creatures and folk tales from antiquity to the present day. His books include *Prima di Dracula: archeologia del vampiro* (2011); *Indagine sull'orco: miti e storie del divoratore di bambini* (2013); *Lupus in fabula: fiabe, leggende e barzellette in Grecia e a Roma* (2018); *Miti vaganti: leggende metropolitane tra gli antichi e noi* (2021); *Folklore* (2021); and *La nave di Caronte: visioni dall'Aldilà a Bisanzio* (with L. Silvano; 2022).

**John Carey** is Professor of Early and Medieval Irish at University College Cork; earlier, he held an appointment at Harvard University, and research fellowships at the Warburg Institute (University of London), the Institute of Irish Studies (Queen's University Belfast), and the School of Celtic Studies (Dublin Institute for Advanced Studies). His recent publications include *The Mythological Cycle of Medieval Irish Literature* (2018); and he has acted as coordinating editor for the collection *Apocrypha Hiberniae II: Apocalyptica* (2010–2024), published as three volumes in the Corpus Christianorum Series: Apocryphorum. He is a Fellow of the Temenos Academy, and general editor of the *Temenos Academy Review*.

**Matthias Egeler** has studied Scandinavian Studies, Celtic Studies, and the History of Religions in Munich and Oxford and has held scholarships and fellowships in Oxford, Cambridge, Berlin, and Cork. Since 2014, he has been principal investigator of several projects at LMU Munich, Germany, where he was appointed Supernumerary Professor in 2022. His research interests include the Nordic and Celtic literatures of the Middle Ages, the history of religions, and nineteenth-century folk belief. He currently directs a research project on landscape-related folk belief and storytelling in the Icelandic Westfjords, and teaches at Goethe University, Frankfurt am Main, Germany.

**Davide Ermacora** earned his joint doctorate in Anthropology from the University of Turin and Université Lumière Lyon 2. He currently lectures on the Anthropology of Religion at the University of Turin. His research interests include the history of religions, supernatural belief systems, and both traditional and contemporary legends. He is the author of numerous publications in these fields, the latest of which is 'The Reptile-Twin in Insular Southeast Asian Folklore', published in *Anthropos* (2023).

**Jeremy Harte** is a researcher into folklore and archaeology, with a particular interest in landscape legends and tales of encounters with the inhabitants of other worlds. His book *Explore Fairy Traditions* (2004) won the Katharine Briggs award of the Folklore Society for 2005, and his other publications include *The Green Man*, *Cloven Country: The Devil and the English Landscape* (2022) and *Fairy Encounters in Medieval England: Landscape, Folklore and the Supernatural* (forthcoming from UEP). Currently he is working on a book of British treasure traditions. He sits on the Council of the Folklore Society and organises the Society's Legendary Weekends. Since 1989 he has been curator of Bourne Hall Museum at Ewell in Surrey.

**Saulė Kubiliūtė** holds a BA degree in Political Science and graduated from the Institute of Political Science and International Relations at Vilnius University. Her thesis covered the national identities of the Baltic states. Currently, Saulė is studying in the MA program in Languages and Cultures of Northern Europe at the Faculty of Philology of Vilnius University.

**Natalie Kononenko** was Kule Chair in Ukrainian ethnography at the University of Alberta until her retirement in 2019. Prior to that she taught at the University of Virginia where she also served as Assistant Dean and Department Chair. Kononenko's publications included *Ukrainian Minstrels: And the Blind Shall Sing* (1998), winner of the Kovaliv and the American Association for Ukrainian Studies best book awards, *Slavic Folklore: A Handbook*, *Ukrainian Epic and Historical Song: Folklore in Context* (2019), winner of the Barbara Heldt best translation award, and *Ukrainian Ritual on the Prairies* (2023), nominated for the Kobzar Literary Award. Kononenko has conducted fieldwork in Ukraine, Canada, Kazakhstan, and Turkey and written numerous articles. Her interests extend to digital humanities and the presentation of folklore online.

**Tommy Kuusela** has a PhD in the History of Religions. Since 2016 he has been working as a researcher in the Folklore archive at the Institute for

Language and Folklore in Uppsala. He has written more than seventy articles on his research interests—magic, supernatural beings, and Old Norse religion. Kuusela regularly appears in the mass media and on podcasts and is one of the hosts of Sweden's biggest podcast on folklore: *När man talar om trollen* (Speaking of the trolls).

**Dorian Jurić** is a Visiting Assistant Professor in the Department of Folklore and Ethnomusicology at Indiana University Bloomington and the Vice President of the Slavic, East European, and Eurasian Folklore Association. His writings on oral epic, supernatural legends, nineteenth-century academic paradigms, and the political life of folklore in the contemporary and historical Western Balkans can be found in the journals *Folklore*, *The Journal of American Folklore*, *Oral Tradition*, *The Slavic and East European Journal*, *The Journal of Indo-European Studies*, and *Folklorica*.

**Andrea Maraschi** has a PhD in Medieval History (University of Bologna) and has been a postdoctoral fellow at the University of Iceland and at the University of Bari. Currently he is adjunct lecturer of the Anthropology of Food at the Department DISTAL of the University of Bologna. His research interests touch on, among other things, the history of food, the history of magic, and the history of medicine in medieval times. His latest monograph, co-authored with Francesca Tasca, is entitled *Food, Heresies, and Magical Boundaries in the Middle Ages* (2024).

**Stephen Miller**'s research covers the folklore and folk song of the Isle of Man, the institutional history of the Folklore Society, and the Scottish folklorists the Rev. Walter Gregor and William George Black. Current research is on Edward Lovett and Manx fairy beliefs for which a compendium of source material is close to completion. Manx research materials can be found at www.chiollaghbooks.com.

**José Manuel Pedrosa** is Professor of the Theory of Literature and Comparative Literature at the University of Alcalá, Spain. He has published numerous books and articles on oral and popular literature, comparative literature, and cultural anthropology. He has supervised more than twenty doctoral theses on these subjects. He has done fieldwork in various countries in Europe, America, and Africa and worked on many ethnographic projects.

**Janin Pisarek** is a narrative researcher and cultural scientist from Thuringia (Germany). She is a member of the Commission for Narrative Research in the Deutsche Gesellschaft für Empirische Kulturwissenschaft: Europäische Märchengesellschaft and is on the scientific advisory board for the Schweizerische

Märchengesellschaft. Pisarek's main interest are European fairy tales, demonological legends, and the mythical figures of the German-speaking world, as well as biographical storytelling. She has published in journals like *Märchenspiegel*, *Märchenforum*, and *Fabula*. Since 2018, she has been editor of the magazine *Heimat Thüringen*. Since 2019, she has been part of the interdisciplinary project Forgotten Creatures.

**Éva Pócs** is Professor Emeritus at the University of Pécs, Hungary, and she has been principal investigator on the European Research Council project 'Vernacular Religion on the Boundary of Eastern and Western Christianity'. She has written thirteen books, and she has been the editor or co-editor of thirty-five volumes on religious anthropology and folklore. Her works include *Fairies and Witches at the Boundary of South-Eastern and Central Europe* (1989), *Between the Living and the Dead: a Perspective on Witches and Seers in the Early Modern Age* (1998), *Body, Soul, Spirits and Supernatural Communication* (ed., 2019), and *Spirit Possession: Multidisciplinary Approaches to a Worldwide Phenomenon* (ed. with A. Zempléni, 2022).

**Florian Schäfer** studied Biology and International Nature Conservation at the Universities of Gießen, Göttingen (Germany), and Christchurch (New Zealand). Fascinated by the regional folklore and legends of Central Europe, he, from an early age, independently studied folklore and European ethnology. In 2017, he founded the project Forgotten Creatures with the aim of conveying cultural history surrounding mythical beings to a wider audience. In 2020, his first book, *Hausgeister!*, was published. As an artist, he creates lifelike sculptures of mythological beings based on historical texts, which are displayed in numerous museums and exhibitions.

**Francis Young** obtained his PhD in History from the University of Cambridge and is a Fellow of the Royal Historical Society. He is the author, editor or translator of twenty-four books in the area of the history of religion and belief with a particular focus on Britain and the Baltic region. His recent books include *Pagans in the Early Modern Baltic* (2022) and *Twilight of the Godlings and Pagans in the Early Modern Baltic* (2023). Francis teaches for Oxford University's Department for Continuing Education and is a lay canon of St Edmundsbury Cathedral. He lives in Peterborough, UK.

**Simon Young** is a British historian based in Italy. Simon teaches at the University of California program in Florence. His recent books include *The Boggart: Folklore, History, Place-names and Dialect* (2022) and *Nail in the Skull and Other Victorian Urban Legends* (2022). *Nail in the Skull* was winner of the Brian McConnell Book Award for 2023.

# Acknowledgements, Conventions and Abbreviations

The editors would like to thank all contributors, but particularly Francis Young and Saulė Kubiliūtė for stepping in at the last minute when considerably less space was available. We also wish to thank the University of Exeter Press, Exeter's peer reviewers and Anna Henderson for support and advice throughout. The editors dedicate their work on this volume to Ron James, a mentor, a friend and an inspiration.

Folklore motif references are to Stith Thompson, ed., *Motif-Index of Folk-Literature: A Classification of Narrative Elements in Folktales, Ballads, Myths, Fables, Medieval Romances, Exempla, Fabliaux, Jest-Books, and Local Legends*, 6 vols (Bloomington, IN: Indiana University Press, 1955–58).

ML numbers are taken from Reidar Th. Christiansen, ed., *The Migratory Legends: A Proposed List of Types with a Systematic Catalogue of the Norwegian Variants* (Helsinki: Academia Scientiarum Fennica, 1958).

ATU numbers refer to Hans-Jörg Uther, ed., *The Types of International Folktales: A Classification and Bibliography Based on the System of Antti Aarne and Stith Thompson. Animal Tales, Tales of Magic, Religious Tales, and Realistic Tales, with an Introduction*, 3 vols (Helsinki: Academia Scientiarum Fennica, 2004).

CHAPTER ONE

# Introducing the Social Supernatural

Simon Young (UCEAP, Florence) and Davide Ermacora (University of Turin)

## Tinker Bell and Her Forebears

The fairy is, today, a universal in Western culture: a small 'cute' Tinker Bell with wings, typically associated with natural processes (plant growth, flowering, even photosynthesis). She (and the modern fairy is almost always a 'she') can certainly be found throughout Europe. At one end of the continent in Iceland there are lyrical descriptions of 'flower fairies'. At the other, in Greece, there are children's colouring books of supernatural beings that, in the words of one of our authors, Tommaso Braccini, 'perfectly comply with Disney's fairies'.[1] But the fluttering hegemonic fairy is a relatively recent arrival. She was produced in anglophone popular culture in the eighteenth and nineteenth centuries. We still have the newspaper stories, the soap tins, the paintings and the theatrical reviews that mark her progress.[2]

The Tinker Bell fairy has, of course, little to do with the traditional supernatural of Britain, let alone with that of Iceland or Greece. Consequently, she is often abused by historians and folklorists who see her as an intolerable parvenu. Carlo Donà, for instance, in a moment of understandable pique, went so far as to call her the *fatina cretina* ('cretinous little fairy').[3] But whether we like it or not, the Tinker Bell fairy has wedged herself in the continent's unconscious. Many modern fairy sightings involve encounters with SWFs (small winged fairies) and this is the fairy that European schoolchildren draw.[4] She is also aligned with contemporary ecological consciousness. Spiritualists and more importantly theosophists greened Tinker Bell by including 'elementals' and 'nature spirits' in their theologies in the late 1800s.[5]

The time will come for Tinker Bell's history to be written. But in this volume we turn, instead, to Tinker Bell's forebears. There had been in Europe, from our earliest records, different regional and national traditions of the 'social supernatural': magical hierarchical communities of supernatural beings living in symbiosis with their human neighbours. These traditions are fossilized in language. The Icelandic flower fairy may be, in the words of Matthias Egeler, in his chapter on Iceland in this volume, 'an invasive species'. But she is the *blómálfur*, the flower *elf*, recalling in her name an older order of supernatural beings from the north. The Greek colouring books mentioned above are full of Tinker Bell clones, but they are called νεράιδες (nereids), a name with a similarly illustrious genealogy.[6] Then, in some cases, social supernatural traditions still survive on the ground: there have been recent encounters with the *szépasszony* of Hungary, the *daoine maithe* of Ireland and even the traditional (unwinged) British fairy.[7]

We bring together here fourteen studies of national and regional traditions of the social supernatural from across Europe, by scholars who know these traditions well. No other collection of this kind has been attempted and, in some cases, these entities have never been described extensively in English. We have covered as much of Europe as possible in the space available. Chapters range from the Norse north (Scandinavia and Iceland) to the Latin south (Spain and southern Italy), from the Celtic west (Ireland and the Isle of Man) to the Slavic east (Ukraine and Croatia). Some of the versions of the social supernatural covered here include well-known names: the trolls of Norway and Sweden, for instance. But others have been neglected: among them the white wives of the east Netherlands, the moss women of Germany and the *vile* of the Western Balkans.

The social supernatural is, as many of our authors suggest, 'a fantastic, distorted, but revelatory mirror to human society'.[8] After all, just over the hill we have a parallel 'closely knit society' that reflects the conditions (and desires) of rural society.[9] So in an isolated part of Iceland there are both human and elf farms dotting a lonely landscape: human homesteads with their equivalent elf homestead.[10] In medieval France stories are told of the feudal *dracs* living in their underwater castles: indeed, sometimes these castles were glimpsed by those peering into the Rhône. *Dracs* have families and visit human markets.[11] This mirroring, of course, is useful in narrative terms. Stories about the social supernatural can actually be about the stresses and strains in human society. Sometimes there are tales kicked up by national experiences: the tales around the *daoine maithe* in Ireland at the time of the Great Hunger, say.[12] At other times, these alternative worlds are given a literary spin. In the courtly writing of the High Middle Ages the fairy realm became Europe's utopia of choice: an imagined world of wonder and enchantment.[13]

## The Scholarly Tradition

A number of folklore writers have noticed this mirroring. There is, indeed, a convention in folklore studies, best established in north-western Europe, of differentiating between the social supernatural and the solitary supernatural. Social supernatural beings are usually much richer in terms of character, actions and behaviour than their solitary equivalents. The earliest attempt to distinguish between the social and the solitary came in 1870 in John O'Hanlon's *Irish Folk Lore*. O'Hanlon (aka Lageniensis) entitled his twenty-eighth chapter 'The Solitary Fairy', and he used this term for a number of Irish solitary supernatural beings 'to be discriminated from the wandering *sighes*, or trooping fairies'.[14] The distinction became influential. It was picked up by the Irish-American writer David Rice McAnally,[15] and by the Irish poet and folklore writer W.B. Yeats, most likely *via* McAnally. Yeats was obsessed with the classification of Irish fairies: 'an impulse stemming from nineteenth-century developments in scientific codification'.[16]

Yeats elaborated his classification of the Irish supernatural world in the late 1880s. In 1892, he edited *Irish Fairy Tales*, arguably 'the first Irish folklore collection to schematize and present the fairies in this way'.[17] Yeats favoured the phrase 'sociable fairies' there; he picked up the term 'trooping fairies' directly or indirectly from O'Hanlon, for the socials.[18] The distinction was to prove among the most influential ideas to come out of Irish folklore studies. It was borrowed into British folklore writing, particularly through the authoritative works of Katharine Briggs: a late beneficiary of what we might call the O'Hanlon–McAnally–Yeats nexus. In fact, the distinction has arguably been used more in relation to British than Irish tradition. Briggs only conformed to 'trooping' and 'solitary fairies' relatively late in her career. Earlier, she had used a more complex set of divisions with frequent references to 'trooping fairies' and only occasional references to 'solitary fairies'.[19]

A parallel analytical division began in Scandinavian and Finnish folklore in the mid-1920s with a short Swedish essay by Carl Wilhelm von Sydow.[20] It is possible that the inspiration came ultimately from Irish writing; note that von Sydow was already familiar with Irish folklore (and fluent in Irish Gaelic) at this date.[21] But his immediate inspiration for the social versus solitary concept seems to have been a reading of James MacDougall's 1910 posthumous collection of folktales from the Scottish Highlands.[22] Von Sydow's division of solitary and social beings got picked up, in any case, by some of the greatest northern folklore writers of that generation. Elisabeth Hartmann employed it in her seminal study of trolls in 1936: 'the solitary beings, as their name suggests, are in a sense absolutely supernatural, in contrast to the social ones, whose life is, on the whole, a faithful reflection of human life'.[23] Then Martti Haavio, the celebrated Finnish folklorist, underlined the importance of the solitary–social divide in the introduction to his *Finnish House Elves* in 1942.[24]

## Lumping and Splitting

The social–solitary distinction has become less common in the folklore writing of Ireland, Britain, Finland and Scandinavia in the last half-century.[25] This is, in part, because the distinction does not sit easily with our two most important folklore schools relating to supernatural terminology: schools that Michael Ostling and Richard Forest efficiently called 'lumpers' and 'splitters'.[26] Lumpers prefer to downplay differences between different supernatural beings, pointing to the amorphous and chaotic nature of folk traditions. For a lumper the difference between the solitary and the social tradition is another illusory attempt to classify the non-existent and the unclassifiable.[27] Splitters go, instead, to the other extreme and offer lists of different magical beings, each given a neat paragraph in a fairy dictionary or a supernatural encyclopaedia.[28] For the splitter the solitary–social distinction is a distraction because theirs is a flat form of classification (like that of a medieval bestiary). There is no need for taxonomic ranks.

Perhaps the easiest 'out' from the splitter–lumper binary is to say that the study of supernatural taxonomy should depend on the quantity and quality of evidence to hand. In a contemporary or exceptionally well-documented past society the folklore writer would be well advised to look for native folk taxonomies as the key to the supernatural.[29] In a poorly documented society (medieval, early modern or even some nineteenth- and twentieth-century societies where folklore collection was patchy) then the best way forward is to provide etic classifications based on function. 'If we find, under various terms, the same type, it also happens that the same term designates very different beings [...] Often the function is more important than the type'.[30] We are interested in this book in a more modest question though: were the intuitions of folklorists like Yeats and von Sydow correct? Is the social versus solitary division helpful for understanding European supernatural systems?

## Solitary versus Social

As we will see, the best answer is: 'it depends where, and it depends when'. In some parts of Europe, the division is stark; in others it is more nuanced, with smudged lines.[31] Unsurprisingly, there are a series of culture-specific variants: the supernatural—social and solitary—all too often changes not only from nation to nation but from region to region and, indeed, from parish to parish. Most interestingly we will see there are not only variations between the social and solitary, but *among* different types of the social supernatural, sometimes in the same folklore tradition. We will introduce below the concept of the 'supernatural society' and the 'supernatural collective' to give some sense of just how radically different supernatural groups can be.

Let us start, though, with the division between the social and the solitary supernatural. If we take the broadest possible definition for the solitary supernatural, we have beings like the unquiet dead, the demon and the amorphous shape-changer. These dwell alone and interact with humanity alone: 'many of the solitaries also hold associations with people'.[32] But these associations have a distinct character. The social human (often separated from their community at night) encounters the solitary supernatural being and typically the solitary supernatural being terrifies, harms or kills the human; sometimes it tricks; occasionally it tempts.[33] The social supernatural comes into contact with human beings in groups or as individuals. These meetings can involve terror, harm, death and trickery: in fact, they often do. But there is a wider range of possibilities. Sometimes the social supernatural being asks for or offers assistance. Sometimes they give or are compelled to give love. Sometimes there is a spectacle. The experience tends to be more layered.

The point that the social supernatural is not always met in groups is worth stressing. For instance, the midwife is woken late at night by a mysterious man (ATU 476** 'Midwife in the Underworld'; ML 5070 'Midwife to the Fairies'). The yokel falls hopelessly in love with a beautiful woman he sees bathing or dancing (ML 4080 'The Seal Wife'; ML 6010 'The Capture of a Fairy'). 'Midwife to the Fairies' is the quintessential social supernatural tale as there is a sense of a community behind the interactions:[34] it is by far the story most often cited by our authors. The midwife may have been woken by an emissary from elf-land, but she is brought to a house where there is another: a woman in her birthing pains. She is then, in some cases, paid by a third individual (or sometimes by the man that brought her). Likewise, in the tale of the man who falls in love with the bather, there is the tussle of desire, segueing to marriage and children. But the object of his desire may bring chattels from her own people as a dowry. Sometimes, the audience will only understand that she is supernatural because of clues dropped gradually into the text: luxurious clothes, preternatural beauty, hints of magic…[35] The supernatural woman may visit her own family (or miss them), and she will eventually return to her realm when the husband foolishly breaks her taboos. Even when encountered alone the social supernatural is still social.[36]

## Characteristics of the Social Supernatural

We gave above this definition for the social supernatural: 'magical hierarchical communities of supernatural beings living in symbiosis with their human neighbours'. But can we be more exact? We would itemize five characteristics that often cluster together: i) choral actions; ii) hierarchies; iii) visitable shared homes; iv) symbiotic relationship with human neighbours; and crucially v) distinct personalities. As so often in folklore classifications, these are polythetic: 'combinations of attributes, none of which are sufficient in isolation to indicate membership and, potentially, none of which are necessary'.[37]

> *Choral actions*: Social supernatural beings frequently carry out human-style actions in groups—the kind of pedestrian day-to-day actions you would find in any human society. These supernatural groups hunt, they bake and churn butter in teams, they hold markets, they attend funerals, they spin, they fight battles, they wash linen together... Above all, they dance, particularly in circles. The reader will see many examples in the next pages: *bohyni* caught up in their wild celebrations in the woods of Ukraine; a troll wedding procession in Norway; *Wichtel* migrating on their boats in Germany; *szépasszony* feasts in the Hungarian east; and, charmingly, *fée* women observed leaning out of their windows and gossiping with each other in southern France.[38]
>
> *Hierarchies*: Supernatural societies have hierarchies. The Irish raths had their petty *síd* kings. There was the 'Rois de Bois' in Marie-Catherine d'Aulnoy's writings, which 'shows [...] interesting continuities with medieval French folklore traditions'. Alice West, a seventeenth-century English confidence trickster, reeled in her dupes (as many of her kind) with constant reference to her friend 'the Queen of the Fairies'.[39] Sometimes we learn the name of these fairy monarchs. It was, for instance, Hacka, a Swedish troll queen, who gave humans a complimentary hoe when they settled around her mountain. Then there are supernatural clans. For instance, the *Nixen* of Germany appear in family units ruled over by a patriarchal *Noeck* (male water spirit): the *Noeck* often kills daughters for infractions of his iron laws. The *vila* troupes in the Balkans, meanwhile, 'invariably include an elder *vila* (often theorized as a remnant of Balkan Diana/Artemis/Bendis cults) and a younger *vila*'.[40]
>
> *Visitable shared homes*: The homes of social supernatural beings are typically striking sites in the wilds: a rock palace, an unusually shaped hill, a labyrinth of caves or an underwater castle—'noble places', in the words of Richard Jenkins.[41] There is also, in some traditions, associated infrastructure: chapels and churches, kitchens, defences

and even trading stations.[42] Taken together the homes are greater in size and sophistication than the lairs of the solitary supernatural: the underside of a bridge, a fetid pool, a stair closet…[43] Humans, we are assured, on occasion stumble into these social supernatural mansions or are brought there as guests or captives. What are the interiors like? Here, as in all visits to supernatural realms, there is a veil of ineffable wonder that means the experience can barely be processed, never mind communicated.[44] But we read of lights reflecting on precious stones, of carousing, of happiness, of human slaves and, pointedly, of glamour.[45]

*Symbiosis*: In many cases human and supernatural societies cannot, according to popular belief, survive without the other. As Jeremy Harte writes in his chapter below on England, 'some kind of dependence on human beings is a constant in fairy tradition'.[46] Its members steal human children to enrich their bloodlines or musicians to play at their feasts. Fairies (and their equivalents in other lands) borrow adult males to fight in their battles or to play in their games. Social supernatural beings also take human food for their tables and ask humans to fix their tools.[47] Humans, of course, for their part need the supernatural societies on their doorstep. A supernatural society is connected to fertility and good crops: poor relations with the supernatural community might lead to poor harvests and starvation. The social supernatural teaches skills: particularly music—bagpipes in Scotland, the lyre in Greece.[48] The social supernatural is often also associated with the provision of power to sorcerers and healers in the human community. A privileged relationship with magical neighbours permits cures, curses, lovers and wealth.[49]

*Distinct personalities*: A society is made up of individuals, who have their own distinct personalities and roles. This is true, too, of supernatural societies. In the fairy hill there is the queen, the warrior, the pregnant mother, the servant… They are often individuals with rich and complex personalities, very different from the flat personalities of most solitary supernatural beings. There is a developed internal life within the groupings.[50] These personalities come out of the larger supernatural society in one-to-one relations with humans: particularly in terms of the symbiotic relations between a human and a supernatural society. This distinction is worth making because, as we will now see, individuals do not always emerge from supernatural groups.

## Supernatural Societies versus Supernatural Collectives

Not all supernatural groups conform—as our authors discovered while writing their chapters—to this five-point model. Some are solidly social, resolutely ticking all five boxes offered above: others, instead, manage a couple of weak checks. To be social the supernatural needs a group, that much is obvious: how can you be social without a plurality? But not all groups, it transpires, are 'social'.[51] To illustrate just how wide the gap can be between the most social and the least social groups let us put side by side the two communities that bookend our volume: the *aos sí* of Ireland from the far west as analysed by John Carey; and the *bohyni* of Ukraine from the eastern margins of Europe. The *aos sí* are a textbook supernatural society: the paranormal equivalent of rural Irish life. The *bohyni* might be better described as a 'collective', to use a word from our contributor Natalie Kononenko. They are an aggregate from which individuals rarely emerge and which are more shadow than reflection of pre-industrial Ukraine.

We will start in Ireland... The *aos sí*, medieval and modern, are associated with raths (ring forts) in the Irish countryside.[52] They take part in a wide range of collective activities. There are cavalcades, feasts, hunts, dancing, washing, battles and even games of hurley. There is a hierarchy that takes inspiration from the Irish kingship of the Middle Ages with the fairy monarchs of Connacht, of Munster and the other quarters. There is the suspicion that the local fairy lords were the penumbra of Ireland's early medieval microkingdoms, the *tuatha*. The *aos sí* are connected with the fertility of human crops and give magic powers to 'fairy doctors'. But they also depend on humans for babies, nursing women, pipers and occasional adult males to fight in their battles. Personalities regularly emerge from these societies as the *aos sí* interact with humankind.

Compare this now with the *bohyni*. These Ukrainian spirits are female (there are no male *bohyni*) and they are associated, above all, with dancing and deadly erotic entanglements. Their range of group activities is limited— perhaps in part because there is only one sex—and their personalities are flatter than those of the *aos sí*: it is only rarely that an individual emerges from the morass. We have no *bohyni* markets or hunts or funerals, though there is one very awkward *bohyni* baby-making ceremony recorded.[53] We never get a glimpse of the *bohyni* base: is there even such a thing, or are they just associated with a stretch of woodland? There is no discernible hierarchy among the women. Nor is there any obvious co-dependence between humanity and the *bohyni*. The *bohyni* seem to feed off humanity, which could very well do without these troublesome neighbours who seduce, maim and kill. Their utility is to feature in folktales and folk legends where,

Kononenko suggests, they teach listeners, and particularly young women, life lessons.

## A Social Supernatural Spectrum?

The *aos sí* are a useful example of a supernatural society, and the *bohyni* prove to be a similarly useful example of a supernatural collective—not so very distinct from the solitary supernatural in terms of their behaviour. The two are entirely different in the way they are imagined among their human neighbours. But what of the other supernatural groupings described in this volume and, indeed, those many others in European folklore? Clearly, each tradition needs to be looked at on its own merits and within its own wider supernatural system. However, it is worth insisting here that there is not a simple binary division between supernatural societies and what we have called supernatural collectives. Rather there is a range of different possibilities across a social supernatural spectrum.

To get a sense of these different possibilities, let us turn to other all-female European groups: for instance, the *anguane* of northern Italy; the *vile* of the Balkans; and the more palatable *Moosweiblein* of Germany. In many respects these 'hyper-feminized' groupings[54] resemble the *bohyni*: there is a predilection for dancing and there are no men. But the literature suggests that these three groups are more social than their Ukrainian sisters. We have, for instance, traces of hierarchies. There is an elder *Moosweiblein* and there are, as noted above, elder *vile*. Personalities also start to emerge, particularly when these women are involved in seducing their human neighbours. There are records, too, of a symbiotic relationship with nearby human communities: for instance, the *anguane* in the Alps preside over many agricultural operations and direct the weather.[55]

## The Geography of the Social Supernatural

If we acknowledge that there is a social supernatural spectrum, can we usefully generalize about the types and the geography of these supernatural societies and collectives? Dorian Jurić, in his chapter, suggests a threefold division for Europe: the north-west, the east and the south.[56] It is true that supernatural societies seem more dominant in north-western Europe: 'Northern European cultures share the tradition that there is a world parallel to this world, whose inhabitants on the whole resemble humans in most respects.'[57] Indeed, English fairylore and Irish *aos sí*-lore are almost indistinguishable in our sources despite coming from different linguistic traditions, whereas other types of supernatural traditions were notably different between the two nations.[58] Nor is it an accident, as we have seen above, that the folklorists who have tried hardest to establish a division between the social and the solitary supernatural come from Scandinavia and insular Europe. It is also true that all-female supernatural societies/collectives are more dominant in the east than in the west of Europe. From the *rusalki* to the *laimės* and the *bohyni*, female supernatural groups are a commonplace in Slavic folklore primers.

But, in the same way that folklore tears up binaries, it quickly makes a mockery of generalizations, especially when carried out on a continent-wide scale. There may be a concentration of supernatural societies in the north-west. But there are also supernatural societies in the south and the east of the continent. One recent book is dedicated entirely to comparing the fairy traditions of Ireland and Romania. It is difficult to disagree with the author that there are many similarities.[59] Likewise the *szépasszony* of Hungary, as we see in Éva Pócs's chapter, share important features with the supernatural societies of Scandinavia and Britain and Ireland. Is it the case then that supernatural collectives are more typical among the Slav-speaking east? Very possibly, but there, too, there are important exceptions such as the forest spirits of northern Russia with their wedding and funeral ceremonies, their need for human midwives and human children, their supernatural cattle and their monarchs.[60]

Nor should we think that the all-female society is only the prerogative of the Slavic east, for there are a number of exclusively female societies in the west and in the south. We have already mentioned the *Moosweiblein* (of Germany), and the *anguane* of the Alps. But there are also the *witte wieven* (of the Netherlands): the last, as outlined in Yseult de Blécourt's chapter, stand as an example of a supernatural collective with a sideline in spinning.[61] The Breton *kannerezed-noz* is, likewise, a supernatural collective but of ghostly 'washing-women'.[62] Then there are the mermaids of the Atlantic coast (where mermen are usually offstage or non-existent), the *donni di fora* (of Sicily) and many, many others.[63] There are, too, some all-male societies including the 'swart fairy of the mine' (knockers, etc.) and the all-male *gentiles* of Iberia, introduced in this volume by José Manuel Pedrosa.[64]

These failures of symmetry are not, of course, a reason to give up on bolder generalizations. They point, rather, to the need for more comparative research into the European social supernatural and the need to look at supernatural groups on a case-by-case basis, contextualized within local supernatural ecosystems. Our authors have, in the pages that follow, taken up that challenge and shown that the key to an emic understanding of the social supernatural in a given area is the terminology of folk taxonomies as reflected in beliefs and narratives. They have written from different perspectives: some are historians, some philologists, some ethnologists and some folklorists. They also come from very different national traditions with different scholarly values and different interests. Any progress that has been made is thanks to the diversity of their methodologies. We hope that, in these overviews and case studies, the reader will start to glimpse the richness, the variety and the complexities of the European social supernatural.

## Notes

1. See *infra* 71–72 for Iceland and 232, n. 53 for Greece. We thank John Carey, Csenge Virág Zalka, Ron James, Tommy Kuusela, Stephen Miller and Ülo Valk for help with this chapter.
2. For the development of modern fairy culture, see C.G. Silver, *Strange and Secret Peoples: Fairies and Victorian Consciousness* (Oxford: Oxford University Press, 2000); N. Bown, *Fairies in Nineteenth-Century Art and Literature* (Cambridge: Cambridge University Press, 2001); A. Chassagnol, *La renaissance féerique à l'ère victorienne* (Berlin: Peter Lang, 2010); S. Young, 'Fairy Ain't What It Used to Be: Traditional vs Contemporary Fairies', *Deep Weird: The Varieties of High Strangeness Experience*, ed. J. Hunter (n.p.: August Night Press, 2023), 189–210.
3. 'La fata-bestia e la bestia fatata: note per una definizione della "fata"', *Fate: Madri-amant-streghe*, ed. S.M. Barillari (Alessandria: Edizioni dell'Orso, 2012), 3–31 at 4; *La fata serpente: indagine su un mito erotico e regale* (Rome: Writeupbooks, 2020), 14.
4. Young, 'Fairy', 201–02, for SWFs; for schoolchildren, see R. Sugg, *Fairies: A Dangerous History* (London: Reaktion, 2018), 237–38, 240–41.
5. For theosophy, occultism and fairies, see Silver, *Strange and Secret Peoples*, 38–41, 295–99; Chassagnol, *La renaissance féerique*, 295–99. For 'green' fairies, see A. Letcher, 'The Scouring of the Shire: Fairies, Trolls and Pixies in Eco-Protest Culture', *Folklore* 112 (2001), 147–61.
6. For Iceland see *infra* 72, and for Greece 232, n. 53.
7. For some modern experiences from Britain, Ireland and many other parts of the world, see *The Fairy Census, 2014–2017*, freely available online at https://www.fairyist.com/survey/.
8. For the quotation, see, 209 in the current volume and also 21, 72, 80, 97, 132, 140, 168, 203.
9. G.H. Heide, *Dwarfs in German Folk Legends: An Inquiry into the Human Quality of These Creatures*, PhD thesis (Los Angeles: University of California, 1976), 58.
10. See *infra* 144.
11. Gervase of Tilbury, *Otia imperialia*, ed. S.E. Banks and J.W. Binns (Oxford: Oxford University Press, 2002), 716–20; see also *infra* 144.
12. E.g. W.-Y. Evans Wentz, *The Fairy Faith in Celtic Countries* (London: Oxford University Press, 1911), 43, a subject, note, that cries out for a wider study.
13. A. Varvaro, *Apparizioni fantastiche: Tradizioni folcloriche e letteratura nel medioevo: Walter Map* (Bologna: Il Mulino, 1994); L. Guyenot, *La Mort féerique: anthropologie du merveilleux (XII$^e$–XV$^e$ siècle)* (Paris: Gallimard, 2011).

14. *Irish Folk Lore: Traditions and Superstitions of the Country, with Humorous Tales* (Glasgow: Cameron and Ferguson, 1870), 237, applied to the leprechaun. See also [T.C. Croker], *Fairy Legends and Traditions of the South of Ireland* (London: John Murray, 1825), 162: 'But the main point of distinction between the Cluricaune and the Shefro arises from the sullen and solitary habits of the former who are never found in troops or communities'. Croker implicitly pits the solitary against the social, but it is a chance sentence and he makes nothing of it: E. Hirsch, '"Contention Is Better than Loneliness": The Poet as Folklorist', *Genre* 12 (1979), 423–37 at 427; M.H. Thuente, 'W.B. Yeats and Nineteenth-Century Folklore', *The Journal of Irish Literature* 6 (1977), 64–79 at 72; *W.B. Yeats and Irish Folklore* (Totowa, NJ: Barnes and Noble, 1981), 84.
15. *Irish Wonders* (Boston: Houghton Mifflin, 1888), 92–93. For O'Hanlon's 'echoes' in McAnally, see F. Kinahan, 'Armchair Folklore: Yeats and the Textual Sources of "Fairy and Folk Tales of the Irish Peasantry"', *Proceedings of the Royal Irish Academy* 83C (1983), 255–67 at 257.
16. P. Muldoon, 'Foreword', *Irish Fairy Tales*, ed. W.B. Yeats (New York: The Modern Library, 2003), xi. Sarcastically, H. Orel, *The Development of William Butler Yeats: 1885–1900* (Lawrence: University of Kansas Publications, 1968), 25: Yeats established supernatural taxonomies 'with the precision of a Buffon [the great naturalist Georges-Louis Leclerc, Comte de Buffon]'. For more on Yeats's penchant for classification, see S.D. Putzel, 'Towards an Aesthetic of Folklore and Mythology: W.B. Yeats, 1888–1895', *Southern Folklore Quarterly* 44 (1980), 105–30 at 118.
17. Hirsch, '"Contention Is Better than Loneliness"', 426. See W.B. Yeats, *Fairy and Folk Tales of the Irish Peasantry* (London: Scott, 1888), 80–127; 'Irish Fairies, Ghosts, Witches, etc.', *Lucifer* 3 (1889), 401–04; ed., *Irish Fairy Tales* (London: T. Fisher Unwin, 1892).
18. The first scholar who pointed this out was Kinahan, 'Armchair Folklore', 257, *pace* Thuente, *W.B. Yeats and Irish Folklore*, 84: '[Yeats's distinction] is not found in any of his predecessors in Irish folklore'. It is worth noting that F. Kinahan, *Yeats, Folklore and Occultism: Contexts in the Early Work and Thought* (London: Unwin Hyman, 1988), 56–57, wondered whether Yeats adapted a slightly earlier (1887) 'Manichean view' between good and bad (demonic) fairies by Lady Wilde.
19. Compare 'The English Fairies', *Folklore* 68 (1957), 270–87, and *An Encyclopedia of Fairies* (New York: Pantheon, 1976), 375–76. See further Thuente, *W.B. Yeats and Irish Folklore*, 85; B. Bramsbäck, *Folklore and W.B. Yeats: The Function of Folklore Elements in Three Early Plays* (Stockholm: Almqvist and Wiksell, 1984), 27; H.R. Ellis Davidson, *Katharine Briggs: Story-Teller* (Cambridge: Lutterworth, 1986), 114; C. Gallant, *Keats and Romantic Celticism* (Houndmills: Palgrave, 2005), 146.
20. 'Naturväsen: en översikt till ledning för samlare', *i Folkminnen och folktankar* 11 (1924), 33–48.
21. B. Almqvist, 'C.W. von Sydow agus Éire: scoláire Sualannach agus an léann Ceilteach', *Béaloideas* 70 (2002), 3–49; N.-A. Bringéus, *Carl Wilhelm von Sydow: A Swedish Pioneer in Folklore* (Helsinki: Academia Scientiarum Fennica, 2009), 165–67. Silver, *Strange and Secret Peoples*, 220, ventured—wrongly—that Yeats used von Sydow as 'one of the authorities cited': this is based on a mistaken reading of P. Alderson Smith, *W.B. Yeats and the Tribes of Danu: Three Views of Ireland's Fairies* (Gerrards Cross: Colin Smythe, 1987), 143.

22. *Folk Tales and Fairy Lore in Gaelic and English*, ed. G. Calder (Edinburgh: J. Grant, 1910): the fairy stories are grouped under the headings 'The social fairies', 'Solitairies' and 'Water sprites'. Neither MacDougall nor his editor quote Yeats. G. Granberg, *Skogsrået i yngre nordisk folktradition* (Uppsala: Gustaf Adolfs Akademien för folklivsforskning, 1935), 13, compared Nordic and Celtic fairies, mentioned the social versus solitary classification in Scottish folklore and thanked von Sydow for having pointed out MacDougall's book to him.
23. *Die Trollvorstellungen in den Sägen und Märchen der skandinavischen Völker* (Berlin: Tübinger germanistische, 1936), 194.
24. *Suomalaiset kodinhaltiat* (Helsinki: SKS Kirjat, 2021), 11.
25. As evidenced by a recent discussion between Julian Goodare and Ronald Hutton: J. Goodare, 'Seely Wights, Fairies and Nature Spirits in Scotland', *Body, Soul, Spirits and Supernatural Communication*, ed. É. Pócs (Cambridge: Cambridge Scholars Publishing, 2019), 218–37 at 218–19.
26. M. Ostling and R. Forest, '"Goblins, Owles and Sprites": Discerning Early-Modern English Preternatural Beings through Collocational Analysis', *Religion* 44 (2014), 547–72 at 548–49.
27. E.g. T.M.G. Löfstedt, *Russian Legends about Forest Spirits in the Context of Northern European Mythology*, PhD thesis (Berkeley: University of California, 1993); 'How to Define Supernatural Beings', *Studies in Folklore and Popular Religion* 1 (1996), 107–12; Á. Jakobsson, 'The Taxonomy of the Non-Existent: Some Medieval Icelandic Concepts of the Paranormal', *Fabula* 54 (2013), 199–213.
28. The best modern example (and the most influential) is Briggs, *An Encyclopedia*—ground zero for the scores of supernatural bestiaries that have come out in the last forty years. The open nature of this kind of work can be clearly seen in Leander Petzoldt's *Kleines Lexikon der Dämonen und Elementargeister*, now in its fifth edition (München: C.H. Beck, 2014).
29. Two useful introductions to folk taxonomies are G. Cardona, *I linguaggi del sapere*, ed. C. Bologna (Bari: Laterza, 1990), 102–14; B. Berlin, *Ethnobiological Classification: Principles of Categorization of Plants and Animals in Traditional Societies* (Princeton: Princeton University Press, 1992). For examples where folk taxonomies have been applied to supernatural systems, see C.H. Brown et al., 'Some General Principles of Biological and Non-Biological Folk Classification', *American Ethnologist* 3 (1976), 73–85 at 79; G.L. Beccaria, *Santi, demoni, folletti e le parole perdute* (Torino: Einaudi, 1995); R. Bracchi, *Nomi e volti della paura nelle valli dell'Adda e della Mera* (Tübingen: Niemeyer, 2009); M. Hengsuwan and A. Prasithrathsint, 'A Folk Taxonomy of Terms for Ghosts and Spirits in Thai', *Manusya* 17 (2014), 29–49; S. Young, *The Boggart: Folklore, History, Place-Names and Dialect* (Exeter: Exeter University Press, 2022), 4–9.
30. C. Rager, ed., *Dictionnaire des fées et du peuple invisible dans l'occident païen* (Turnhout: Brepols, 2003), vi.
31. Several scholars have noted the division is not clear-cut: e.g. J. Simpson and S. Roud, eds, *A Dictionary of English Folklore* (Oxford: Oxford University Press, 2000), s.v. 'Fairies'.
32. G. MacLellan, 'Entertaining Faeries', *White Dragon* 19 (1998), 4–7 at 5, commenting on Yeats and the social versus solitary distinction.

33. Arguably, the suave Devil is the most flexible solitary: he interacts with people with an imposing personality and can appear, say, in the shape of a black gentleman. See Ü. Valk, *The Black Gentleman: Manifestations of the Devil in Estonian Folk Religion* (Helsinki: Academia Scientiarum Fennica, 2001).
34. As emphasized by Å. Campbell and Å. Nyman, 'Som jordemoder hos de underjordiska', *Atlas över svensk folkkultur* II, 2: *Sägen, tro och högtidssed: kommentar* (Uppsala: Almqvist och Wiksell, 1976), 58–64 at 62: 'The supernatural beings that appear in midwife legends differ in a characteristic way from the solitary and usually demonic nature spirits such as the water sprite and the forest spirit. Regardless of the names, the beings in question are thought to live much like humans, with families, children, servants, livestock, agriculture, and so on. Their abode is underground or beneath human dwellings, in mountains and hills, or elsewhere in the hidden world, which, although invisible to ordinary people, still exists all around us' (translation ours). See also Heide, *Dwarfs in German Folk Legends*, 58–61; Löfstedt, *Russian Legends about Forest Spirits*, 215, 227–28.
35. In France, humans married social supernatural beings and only discovered the fairy nature of their spouse long after their wedding: see *infra* 143. For a striking example from medieval literature, taken from *Richard the Lionheart*, see R. Green, *Elf Queens and Holy Friars: Fairy Belief and the Medieval Church* (Philadelphia: University of Pennsylvania Press, 2016), 69–70.
36. For these legends: C. Mac Cárthaigh, 'Midwife to the Fairies (ML 5070): The Irish Variants in Their Scottish and Scandinavian Perspective', *Béaloideas* 59 (1991), 133–43; B. Almqvist, 'Midwife to the Fairies (ML 5070) in Icelandic Tradition', *Legends and Landscape: Articles Based on Plenary Papers Presented at the 5th Celtic-Nordic-Baltic Folklore Symposium, Reykjavík 2005*, ed. T. Gunnell (Reykjavík: University of Iceland Press), 273–342. Note that the wide presence of 'Midwife to the Fairies' in the narrative tradition of the Near East, where the negative traits abound (instead of fairies there are demons), still awaits to be examined: demonization is not only found in Eastern Europe. For this problem in the light of Heda Jason's Jewish tale-type 476*-* 'A Midwife to Demons', see Campbell and Nyman, 'Som jordemoder hos de underjordiska', 62; H. Jason, ed., *Types of Oral Tales in Israel: Part 2* (Jerusalem: Israel Ethnographic Society, 1975), 16; O. Abenójar, 'El cuento tradicional de *La comadrona en el otro mundo* a la luz de nuevas versiones ibéricas y saarianas', *Revista de Literaturas Populares* 15, 2 (2015), 375–401. There is a massive literature on Melusine, fairy wives and the 'Melusinian scheme': C. Steinkämper, *Melusine—vom Schlangenweib zur 'Beauté mit dem Fischschwanz': Geschichte einer Aneignung* (Göttingen: Vandenhoeck & Ruprecht, 2007); A.M. Babbi, ed., *Melusine: atti del convegno internazionale (Verona, 10–11 novembre 2006)* (Verona: Fiorini, 2009); M. Morris and J.-J. Vincensini, eds, Écriture et réécriture du merveilleux féerique: autour de Mélusine (Paris: Classiques Garnier, 2012); S.M. Barillari, *Protostoria della strega: le fonti medievali latine e romanze* (Aicurzio: VirtuosaMente, 2014), 125–58; M. Urban et al., eds, *Melusine's Footprint: Tracing the Legacy of a Medieval Myth* (Leiden–Boston: Brill, 2017); Donà, *La fata serpente*.
37. B.J. Day et al., 'Attentional Meta-Learners for Few-Shot Polythetic Classification', *Proceedings of the 39th International Conference on Machine Learning* 162 (2022), 4867–89 at 4867.

38. *Infra* 254, 101, 161, 179 and 142.
39. *Infra* 21, 51–52 and 147 (for the quotation): for more on the Queen of the Fairies and criminal activities, see T. Willard, 'Pimping for the Fairy Queen: Some Cozeners in Shakespeare's England', *Crime and Punishment in the Middle Ages and Early Modern Age: Mental-Historical Investigations of Basic Human Problems and Social Responses*, eds A. Classen and C. Scarborough (Berlin: De Gruyter, 2012), 491–508.
40. *Infra* 100, 163–168 and 204 (for the quotation). In all-female social supernatural communities, the senior woman tends to be very much, in the style of British cabinet government, 'first among equals' rather than a monarch.
41. 'Witches and Fairies: Supernatural Aggression and Deviance among the Irish Peasantry', *The Good People: New Fairylore Essays*, ed. P. Narváez (Lexington, KT: University Press of Kentucky, 1991), 302–35 at 314; via Jurić in Chapter 12 of the current volume.
42. *Infra* 73, 163, 204, 147 and, again, 73.
43. Young, *The Boggart*, 98–104.
44. For the ineffable otherworld, see H. Levin, 'Paradises, Heavenly and Earthly', *Huntington Library Quarterly* 29 (1966), 305–24.
45. There is an obvious parallel with fairy gatherings involving beauty, delicious meals and all kinds of delights and pleasures. In Gustav Henningsen's words, the 'white sabbaths': '"The Ladies from Outside": An Archaic Pattern of the Witches' Sabbath', *Early Modern European Witchcraft: Centres and Peripheries*, eds G. Henningsen and B. Ankarloo (Oxford: Clarendon, 1990), 191–215; 'White Sabbath and Other Archaic Patterns of Witchcraft', *Acta Ethnographica Hungarica* 37, 1–4 (1991–92), 293–304 (for Sicily). See 206 for the Balkan *vile*.
46. *Infra* 63.
47. Changelings and abduction: P.M. Rojcewicz, 'Between One Eye Blink and the Next: Fairies, UFOs, and Problems of Knowledge', in *The Good People*, ed. Narváez, 479–514 at 492–95; R.A. Sawyer, *The Medieval Changeling: Health, Childcare, and the Family Unit* (Cambridge: D.S. Brewer, 2023). Fairy meals: Barillari, *Protostoria della strega*, 110–23; A. Maraschi, 'Þórgunna's Dinner and Other Medieval Liminal Meals: Food as Mediator between This World and the Hereafter', *Paranormal Encounters in Iceland 1150–1400*, eds Á. Jakobsson and M. Mayburd (Berlin: De Gruyter, 2020), 49–70.
48. F262.2 'Fairies teach bagpipe-playing' and *infra* 225–226.
49. The literature on cunning folk and the social supernatural in Europe is extensive: see Z. Čiča, 'Vilenica and Vilenjak: Bearers of an Extinct Fairy Cult', *Narodny Umjetnost* 39 (2002): 31–63; J. Goodare, 'The Cult of the Seely Wights in Scotland', *Folklore* 123, 2 (2012), 198–219; R.F. Green, 'Refighting Carlo Ginzburg's *Night Battles*', *Prowess, Piety, and Public Order in Medieval Society: Studies in Honor of Richard W. Kaeuper*, eds C.M. Nakashian and D.P. Franke (Leiden: Brill, 2017), 381–401; R. Hutton, *The Witch: A History of Fear, from Ancient Times to the Present* (New Haven, CT: Yale University Press, 2017), 215–42; P.L.J. Mannella, 'Toccati dalle *donni*: patogenesi preternaturali e mediatori terapeutici in Sicilia', *La Ricerca Folklorica* 75 (2020), 43–57.
50. We owe this phrase to Francis Young.
51. Think, also, of the case of many ancestral deities in Europe who 'have a strong tendency to appear in the plural as a collective group of beings instead of easily

distinguished individuals': K. Bek-Pedersen, *The Norns in Old Norse Mythology* (Edinburgh: Dunedin, 2011), 82. For the Greco-Roman sylvan deities who are found sometimes conceived of as plural (e.g. Pan/Pani, Silvanus/Silvani or Silvanae), see K. Vuković, *Wolves of Rome: The Lupercalia from Roman and Comparative Perspectives* (Berlin–Boston: De Gruyter, 2023), 195–96. The process of *interpretatio indigena* should not be overlooked here.

52. For medieval Ireland, see Chapter 2 of the current volume (18–31); and L. Bitel, 'Secrets of the *Síd*: The Supernatural in Medieval Irish Texts', *Fairies, Demons, and Nature Spirits: 'Small Gods' at the Margins of Christendom*, ed. M. Ostling (London: Palgrave Macmillan, 2018), 79–101. The literature for modern Ireland is larger. Important works include Wentz, *Fairy Faith*, 23–84; Lady Gregory, *Visions and Beliefs in the West of Ireland*, 2 vols (New York: Putnam's Sons, 1920); D. Mac Manus, *The Middle Kingdom: The Faerie World of Ireland* (Gerrards Cross: Smythe, 1973 [1959]); S. Ó hEochaidh, M. Ní Néill and S. Ó Catháin, eds, *Síscéalta ó Thír Chonaill: Fairy Legends of Donegal* (Dublin: Comhairle Bhéaloideas Éireann, 1977); A. Smith, *W.B. Yeats and the Tribes of Danu*.
53. See *infra* 256–257.
54. *Infra* 203.
55. D. Perco, 'Le *Anguane*: mogli, madri e lavandaie', *La Ricerca Folklorica* 36 (1997), 71–81; D. Ermacora, 'Due libri recenti sulle *Agane*', *Ce Fastu?* 1 (2011), 71–82; F. Guariglia, 'Le Krivapete delle Valli del Natisone: convergenze folkloriche e letterarie', *Stregoneria nelle Alpi: malefici, processi, inquisitori e roghi*, ed. L. Giarelli (Tricase: Youcanprint, 2022), 207–30; F. Chiocchetti, ed., *Letres da Larcioné: Amadio Calligari a Tita Cassan (1887–1897). Lingua e tradizioni dei tempi antichi* (Vigo di Fassa: Istitut Cultural Ladin 'Majon di Fascegn', Union di Ladins de Fascia, 2023), 224–25, 240.
56. See *infra* 199–200.
57. Löfstedt, *Russian Legends about Forest Spirits*, 214. Influenced by Granberg (see above n. 22), Löfstedt posited a distinction for his materials between 'social otherwordly beings' and 'the generally solitary nature spirits'. See also Heide, *Dwarfs in German Folk Legends*, 3, stressing the importance of the social–solitary distinction for German folklore: 'The concept of a dwarf society is the only criterion that I can use with certainty to differentiate dwarfs from other diminutive spirits that are believed to haunt forest, pond, air, and house.'
58. A striking example of this is the English tradition of house helping spirits, also found in Wales, lowland Scotland and, to some extent, in the Scottish Highlands. In Ireland household helping spirits are not common and when they appear in nineteenth-century sources it is often in an Anglo-Irish context: [Croker], *Fairy Legends and Traditions of the South of Ireland*, 149–64; in one case the helper serves the Mac Carthies, in another the Harris family. B. Almqvist, 'Irish Migratory Legends on the Supernatural: Sources, Studies and Problems', *Béaloideas* 59 (1991), 1–43 at 8, wrote on ML 7020 'Vain Attempt to Escape from the Nisse' (the most common household helper spirit legend from northern Europe). This legend is, Almqvist acknowledged, 'extremely rare' in Ireland.
59. D. Simina, *Where Fairies Meet: Parallels between Irish and Romanian Fairy Traditions* (Alresford: Pagan Portals, 2023).
60. Löfstedt, *Russian Legends about Forest Spirits*, 213, 217–35.

61. See also B. Roling, 'Our White Ladies on the Graves: Historicisations of Nymphs in Early Modern Antiquarianism', *The Figure of the Nymph in Early Modern Culture*, eds K.A.E. Enenkel and A. Traninger (Leiden: Brill, 2018), 445–62. For a more traditional form of the social supernatural in the Netherlands we need to look to gnomes: L. Modderman, 'Gnomes: A View from the Netherlands', *The Wollaton Gnomes: A Nottingham Fairy Mystery*, ed. S.R. Young (n.p.: Pwca Books 2023), 169–82.
62. F. Kurzawa, 'Kannerezed noz ou Les lavandières de la nuit', *Le pouvoir et la foi au Moyen Âge en Bretagne et dans l'Europe de l'Ouest : mélanges en mémoire du professeur Hubert Guillotel*, eds J. Quaghebeur and S. Soleil (Rennes: Presses Universitaires de Rennes, 2010), 327–36; D. Giraudon, *Sur les chemins de l'Ankou : croyances et légendes autour de la mort en Bretagne* (Fouesnant: Yoran Embanner, 2012), 250–85.
63. Mermaids: G. Benwell and A. Waugh, *Sea Enchantress* (London: Hutchinson, 1961); V. Scribner, *Merpeople: A Human History* (London: Reaktion Books, 2020). *Donni*: Henningsen, '"The Ladies from Outside"'; 'White Sabbath'; A. Borghini, 'Le "Donne di fuora"/"Padroni del luogo": un presumibile corrispondente antico e una proposta etimologica', *Le Apuane* 55 (2008), 113–45; P.L.J. Mannella, 'Trizzi di donna, tra etnopatia e virtù', *Etnografie del contemporaneo* 2, 2 (2019), 49–66; 'Toccati dalle donni'.
64. For the Cornish and other European mine spirits, see R.M. James, 'Knockers, Knackers, and Ghosts: Immigrant Folklore in the Western Mines', *Western Folklore* 51 (1992), 153–76; *The Folklore of Cornwall: The Oral Tradition of a Celtic Nation* (Exeter: University of Exeter Press, 2018), 136–80; for *gentiles*, see *infra* 131–132.

CHAPTER TWO

# Ireland: The Tribes of the Gods and the People of the Hills

John Carey (University College Cork)

The supernatural beings who have come to be called 'fairies' in English are known by many names in Irish,[1] the most common of these in recent times being *daoine maithe* or 'good people'. In medieval sources, they are most frequently called áes *síde* ('people of the *síde* or hollow hills'),[2] *Túath(a) Dé* ('Tribe(s) of Gods') or *Túath(a) Dé Donann/Danann* (usually interpreted as meaning 'Tribe(s) of the Goddess Donu/Danu').[3] It is these terms that I will employ when discussing the medieval evidence, both to avoid the potentially distracting connotations that the word 'fairy' has attracted in English usage, and to acknowledge the evident derivation of these entities from the divinities of the pre-Christian Irish.

In considering depictions of the society of the áes *síde*, it should be borne in mind that almost every aspect of the life of human society was regarded as being to a great extent dependent on the supernatural race. Thus they controlled the fertility of crops and herds,[4] were regarded as the originators and/or patrons of various arts,[5] presided over the frenzy and horror of battle,[6] and provided to kings the confirmation of their right to rule.[7] This close association on the part of the immortals with the structure and workings of the mortal community is surely relevant to the ways in which their own communities are portrayed. Having noted these general points, we can proceed to a consideration of some of the literary evidence, beginning with texts assigned to the Old Irish period (*c.*600–900).

A frequent theme, not surprisingly, is the splendour and perfection of the life of the immortals: this is expressed among other respects in the harmony of their communal life. In *Echtrae Chonnlai*, generally regarded as one of the oldest surviving Irish tales (*c.*700?), a woman who says that her people are

John Carey, "Ireland: The Tribes of the Gods and the People of the Hills" in: *The Exeter Companion to Fairies, Nereids, Trolls and Other Social Supernatural Beings: European Traditions.* University of Exeter Press (2024). © John Carey. DOI: 10.47788/OFEV8836 'in a great *síd*' describes them as existing in 'concord without strife [...] so that we are called *áes síde*'.[8] Here there is a play on words, as the word *síd* can mean both 'hollow hill' and 'peace': *áes síde*, accordingly, can be taken to mean 'people of peace' as well as 'people of the hollow hills'. Tomás Ó Cathasaigh, in the course of a sensitive exploration of this homonymy, has proposed that peace in the human realm was regarded as an assimilation to the realm of the supernatural, observing that 'the connection between the Otherworld and conditions in this world, as mediated in the person of the king, is deeply embedded in the very ground-rock of Irish mythology and literature'.[9] The woman in *Echtrae Chonnlai* goes on to speak of her *síd* as being ruled over by 'Bóadach the eternal: a king without lament, without sorrow in his land since he took sovereignty'.[10]

Often it is only the ruler of an individual *síd* who figures in a tale, together sometimes with his immediate family. This is the case, for instance, in *Compert Con Culainn*, when the warriors of Ulster spend the night in a supernatural dwelling where they are made welcome by a 'couple', but no attendants are mentioned.[11] In *Scél Mongáin*, similarly, a young poet who is sent to various *síde* is simply said to have been received by a couple in each of them; and in the ninth-century *Baile in Scáil* the earthly king Conn of the Hundred Battles comes to an Otherworldly hall, the only occupants of which to be mentioned are its lord, Lug, and a young woman who personifies the sovereignty of Ireland.[12] In *Cath Maige Mucrama*, which has also been dated to the ninth century, Eógabul is called 'king of the *síd*' of Áine Chlíach, but when he appears he is accompanied only by his daughter.[13] Yet another example apparently from this period is afforded by *Táin Bó Dartada*, in which a woman and a warrior from the *síd* of Cuilenn appear in a dream to the local king.[14]

This frequent failure to mention any inhabitants of a *síd* other than its rulers need reflect no more than the aristocratic bias of medieval Irish literature in general: accounts of mortal households likewise frequently mention only rulers and nobles. On the other hand, it may in at least some instances be the case that the effortless and inexhaustible abundance of the *síd* was imagined to render servants unnecessary, as when the woman in *Echtrae Chonnlai* says that her people enjoy 'feasts without service'; or when the *síd* of the Dagda is said to contain an ever-full cauldron, a tree perpetually bearing fruit, and two pigs of which one is always cooked and the other always alive.[15] In the tale *Tochmarc Becfola*, even though no one seems to inhabit the magical feasting hall of Inis Fedaig, 'the meal of a hundred, both food and drink, is what it provides every evening, without service by anyone'.[16]

Like an earthly king, though, the lord of a *síd* can also be portrayed as having many followers and servants. In the tale *Tochmarc Étaíne*, Midir of the *síd* of

Brí Léith usually appears alone, but it is evident that he presides over a magnificent establishment. At one point we are told that he had 150 foster sons, and as many foster daughters; and when he assembles his people for a great task, the 'company of the *síd*' (*lucht an tsídha*) are likened to 'the men of the world from the rising of the sun to its setting'.[17] In *Táin Bó Fraích*, 150 richly attired women emerge from the *síd* of Crúachan in Connacht: we are given to understand that they are the female retinue (*bantrocht*) of the *síd* woman Bé Find. The same tale speaks of the 'kings of the *síde* of Ireland', implying (as does *Cath Maige Mucrama* above) that each *síd* is ruled by its own king.[18]

More ambiguous is the reference to a supernatural king in the tenth-century tale *Togail Bruidne Da Derga*. Here Conaire, the protagonist, is conceived when his mother is impregnated by a stranger who comes to her in the form of a bird; subsequently, he encounters a flock of birds which change into armed men. Their leader identifies himself as Nemglan, 'the king of the bird-flock of your father'; he instructs Conaire how to become king of Tara, and teaches him the *geisi* or prohibitions which he must observe henceforth.[19] The wording leaves the relationship between Nemglan and Conaire's father uncertain. Is the latter an over-king, with Nemglan a subordinate king to whom authority over his birds has been delegated? Or does Conaire's father simply belong to the magical bird-flock of which Nemglan is the king?

A clear reference to a servile dweller in the *síd* is given elsewhere in the same story, when Nár Túathcháech is said to be the swineherd of Bodb of Síd ar Femin.[20] In *De Chophur in Dá Muccida*, Bodb is again said to rule over this *síd*, and is moreover called 'king of the *síde* of Munster'; here too he is said to have a swineherd, in this case named Friuch. The same tale speaks of Ochall Ochne, king of Síd Crúachan and more generally of the *síde* of Connacht, whose swineherd is Rúcht.[21]

Bodb is again called 'king of the *síde* of Munster' in the tale *Aislinge Óenguso*; in the same passage, the Dagda is said to be king of the *síde* of Ireland as a whole.[22] This is also evidently the Dagda's role in *De Gabáil int Śída*, where he is described as 'king over the Túatha Dé' who distributed the *síde* among the lords of his people; and he is similarly portrayed in *Tochmarc Étaíne*.[23] There are accordingly kings of individual *síde*, over-kings of the *síde* of the various provinces, and a king over all the *síde* of Ireland: a hierarchy parallel to that which was postulated for mortal Irish kingship.

The tale *Echtra Nerai* provides further details concerning life in a *síd*. Nera, a member of the household of the king and queen of Connacht at Ráith Chrúachan, follows an 'army' into the nearby Síd Crúachan after they have destroyed the royal stronghold and massacred its inhabitants.[24] The *síd*'s king (here unnamed), to whom Nera identifies himself only as someone who had come into the *síd* accompanying the warriors, instructs him to dwell with a single woman who lives in the vicinity, and to come to his hall every day with a load of firewood. Eventually the woman bears a son to Nera, and gives him the task of herding cattle.[25]

This highly selective synopsis omits many of the most important elements in the story, but highlights aspects relevant to the present discussion. The *síd* of Crúachu, like other *síde* already mentioned, is ruled over by a king—in this case one who remains at home while his troops carry out a raid. Most interesting is the treatment of Nera, who arrives in the *síd* as a friendless stranger; he is attached to the household of a woman, whose cattle he eventually herds, and he is given the task of carrying firewood. This is just what the provisions of early Irish law would lead us to expect in a non-supernatural context: a stranger without kin would have no place in society apart from that which he might have as the spouse of a woman of the community;[26] and carrying firewood was regarded as one of the most degrading forms of work, appropriate to a slave or someone without status.[27] That Nera is given his wife's cattle to herd is appropriate to the term *ambue* by which such an outsider was known, if Kim McCone is correct in arguing that the word's original meaning was 'one without cows'.[28]

The social mechanics within the *síd*, in other words, seem precisely to mirror those of human society. This is all the more striking in that *Echtra Nerai* is a tale which in other respects gives close attention to the mysterious differences between the natural and the supernatural realms, in particular the discrepancy between this-worldly and Otherworldly time.[29] The idea that earthly kingship has its basis in the realm of the *síd* also finds expression in this story, although here the context is one of antagonism between the two realms. In a raid of their own, the men of Connacht carry off the crown of the king of the *síd*: this is called the 'crown of Brión', indicating that it becomes part of the regalia of the principal dynasty of Connacht kings in historical times, the Uí Briúin or 'Descendants of Brión'.

One of the attributes of a 'chief stronghold' (*prímdún*) could be a sacred tree, or *bile*, growing in the open space in front of it;[30] as A.T. Lucas observed, 'there is ground for believing that a *bile* was regarded as an appropriate adjunct to a chiefly or kingly residence'.[31] Such trees might also grow at royal inauguration sites, and to cut them down was an attack on the kingdom's sovereignty.[32] It is in this context that we can understand the 'golden *bile*' in front of the hall of Lug; and the Otherworldly court in the related tale *Tucait Baile Mongáin* is said to be *bilech*, meaning perhaps 'having a *bile*'.[33] When Cú Chulainn's charioteer Lóeg describes to him the court of the king of the Otherworldly realm of Mag Mell, in the tale *Serglige Con Culainn*, he speaks of it as being adorned with a radiant tree of silver, sixty trees abounding with nuts, and 'three *bili* of purple glass' before its eastern door.[34]

Despite the homonymy of the words *síd* 'hollow hill' and *síd* 'peace', *Echtra Nerai* shows that the people of the *síde* could be fierce warriors. Besides attacking mortals, they sometimes warred against one another; and humans could be drawn into these conflicts. Thus Lóegaire mac Crimthainn, son of the king of Connacht, assisted the king of the Otherworldly realm of Mag Dá Cheó against the king of Mag Mell ('the Plain of Delights'); and in *Serglige Con Culainn*, Cú Chulainn similarly allied himself with Labraid Lúathlám ar Chlaidiub, who is also described as reigning in Mag Mell, against three enemy kings.[35]

Legendary accounts of Irish origins came to incorporate the idea that Ireland had been ruled by the Túatha Dé before the coming of the Gaels: sometimes they were said to have been spirits, sometimes euhemeristically regarded as humans with magical powers. Perhaps the earliest attestation of their inclusion in the sequence of settlements is the statement in *Scél Tuáin maic Cairill* that Ireland was settled by 'the Túatha Dé ocus Andé, whose origin the learned do not know; but they thought it likely that they are some of the exiles who came to them from heaven'.[36] The phrase *Túatha Dé ocus Andé* appears to mean 'Tribes of Gods and Un-gods', and considerable ingenuity has been devoted to attempts to interpret its background;[37] here, I shall limit myself to its use in the literature.

In the saga *Táin Bó Cúailnge*, where it occurs in the formulaic utterance *Bennacht dé ocus andé fort* ('The blessing of gods and un-gods on you'), this is accompanied by the comment 'They considered the folk of power (*áes cumachta*) to be gods, but the folk of agriculture to be un-gods'.[38] Even apart from the possibility that no more may be involved here than an ad hoc guess, without real roots in the tradition, aspects of the statement are ambiguous. Does it mean that the pagan Irish in the saga imagined their own society to consist of 'folk of power', whom they called 'gods', and the 'un-gods' of the peasantry; or did they assign such a dichotomy to the *áes síde*? That the blessing of 'gods and un-gods' is invoked suggests the latter. And was the 'power' wielded by the 'gods' the political and military power of a ruling class, or was it magical power—it being the latter to which the word *cumachta* frequently refers?[39] If it is in fact the *áes síde* who are being referred to, this distinction may not be an essential one, as their rulers were both wizards and warriors. Whatever the details, the phrase is most easily understood as reflecting a view of the immortals as having a hierarchical society, divided between an elite and commoners: a picture already indicated by other sources that we have considered.

The best-known early tale concerning the Túatha Dé is probably *Cath Maige Tuired*, generally regarded as having been first composed in the ninth century, but extensively revised some centuries later. This relates how, led by the young hero Lug, the Túatha Dé defeated an invading army of the hostile race of the Fomoiri; and it is exceptionally rich in information regarding the workings of society: the virtues and failings of kings, the functions and capacities of the different classes and professions, structures and duties of kinship. Elizabeth A. Gray's extended examination of the story is, in fact, primarily an exploration of its vision of society.[40] It would seem, accordingly, to be a text of primary importance to the present study.

While there can be no doubt of this importance, the special nature of *Cath Maige Tuired* is such that its evidence for conceptions of the supernatural race can only be used with considerable caution. I have argued elsewhere that the tale was composed as a parable, in the context of challenges posed to traditional Irish society by increasing Scandinavian cultural influence in the course of the ninth century.[41] If this analysis is correct, its portrayal of the workings of community would have more to tell us about mortal than about immortal norms. And indeed the Túatha Dé of *Cath Maige Tuired*, although possessed of various magical powers, and occasionally said to be of extraordinary size,[42] lack the alluring uncanniness of the people of the *síde* as they appear in other sources. In fact, any connection with the *síde* themselves is barely mentioned. We are told that the 'men of the three gods' chose the musician Abcán 'in the *síde*', and that victory in the battle is proclaimed 'to the royal strongholds of Ireland and to its *síd*-troops and to its lofty waters and to its estuaries';[43] but these references do not make any clear connection between the *síde* and the Túatha Dé (or 'men of Ireland', as they tend to be called in *Cath Maige Tuired*) as a people. Where such a connection is made, it is with the sinister Fomoiri: it is they who are called 'the champions of the *síde*'.[44]

Some developments to the picture sketched above can be discerned in sources belonging to the Middle Irish (*c*.900–1200) and Early Modern Irish (*c*.1200–1650) periods. Besides being portrayed as dwelling underground or underwater, or on islands, the Túatha Dé were also thought of as inhabiting lands that had no specified relationship with earthly geography: thus Lóegaire mac Crimthainn, following his Otherworld ally, finds himself suddenly in another country; and Conn of the Hundred Battles wanders through a mist in *Baile in Scáil*, which clears to reveal the plain in which stands the hall of Lug.[45] Alternatively, these countries were thought to lie far off across the sea, as when an immortal woman in the early voyage tale *Immram Brain* speaks of thrice fifty islands, each of them greater than Ireland, 'in the ocean to the west of us'.[46] Such regions are given various names: one of the earliest attested, mentioned above, is Mag Mell or 'the Plain of Delights', a designation already found in *Echtrae Chonnlai*.[47]

From about the year 1000 onward, one such name is Tír Tairngire, 'the Land of Promise'. This phrase is already found in Old Irish, where it is used to render the biblical *terra repromissionis* or 'promised land'. Its application to a non-ecclesiastical Otherworld appears to have had its basis in the ancient apocalyptic text known as the *Vision of Paul*, where the visionary passes from the ocean to a paradise, inhabited by the souls of the righteous, which he is told is the *terra repromissionis*. This in turn was one of the inspirations of the *terra repromissionis sanctorum*, the island paradise in the ocean which is the object of the quest of Saint Brendan in the Hiberno-Latin *Nauigatio Sancti Brendani*.[48] The whereabouts of Tír Tairngire are magically obscure in the Middle Irish story of how Cormac mac Airt arrives there after going astray in a mist, as had his grandfather Conn;[49] but even here its ruler is said to be Manannán, who is consistently associated with the sea. In other later tales, the location of Tír Tairngire beyond the sea is clearly indicated (*Acallam na Senórach*, *Eachtra Airt*) or strongly implied (*Altram Tighe Dá Mheadar*).[50]

A consequence of the increasing prominence of Tír Tairngire in the later Middle Irish period and thereafter is that the Túatha Dé come to comprise two populations: those who inhabit Ireland, primarily dwelling in the *síde*; and the inhabitants of Tír Tairngire beyond the sea. In *Acallam na Senórach*, these populations seem simply to coexist—although there can be sharing between them, as when Úaine Buide is both linked with a *síd* in Munster, and said to be 'female musician of all Tír Tairngire';[51] or when the garments of immortals (and indeed of mortal princes) in Ireland are said to be made of wool from Tír Tairngire.[52] In *Altram Tighe Dá Mheadar*, however, Manannán as ruler of Tír Tairngire is 'high king' of the Túatha Dé: after the defeat of the Túatha Dé by the invading Gaels, it is Manannán who guides them in their selection of Bodb as their king, Manannán who apportions the *síde* among them as the Dagda is said to have done in earlier sources, and Manannán who gives them their magical powers of invisibility, immortality and perpetual youth.[53] Such a hegemony may also be implicit in *Eachtra Airt*, where it is stated that after banishing a woman of their own people, the rulers of Tír Tairngire send messengers to ensure that she should not find shelter 'in (any) *síd* of the *síde* of Ireland'.[54]

*Acallam na Senórach*, the longest medieval Irish narrative text, not only celebrates the memory of the hero Finn mac Cumaill and his war-band or *fían*, but also gives considerable attention to the Túatha Dé, making it a rich source for the present discussion. At the same time, the author's inventive and often playful relationship with his sources renders it risky to use the *Acallam* as evidence for the tradition as a whole.[55] Acknowledging this caveat, the tale's testimony is well worth our attention.

At the outset, we noted the extent to which, inevitably, the worlds of mortals and of the *síde* are parallel; and we have seen this illustrated in the tales that we have considered, particularly vividly perhaps in *Echtra Nerai*. This parallelism is palpable in the *Acallam*, being even rendered formulaically explicit in the statement that 'there are only two aristocracies of equal weight in Ireland: the sons of Míl [i.e. the Gaels] and the Túatha Dé Danann'.[56] In a kind of counterpoint, the patchwork of human kingdoms throughout Ireland, great and small, coexists with a network of *síde*, each with its own ruler.

The descriptions of the conditions of existence within the *síde* are in keeping with those that are to be found in earlier sources;[57] theirs is a world of inexhaustible abundance, of opulent beauty and of youthful immortality. When three princes petition the lords of the *síde* for gifts, they receive not only wives, gold, weapons and territory, but also vessels which can transmute water into mead and wine, a cook who can provide endless food, a musician who can bring sleep even to those in agonizing pain, and three apple trees each in a different season.[58] With all its supernatural traits, the social world of the *síde* appears closely to parallel that of mortal humanity. Besides kings and aristocratic warriors, we read of druids (male and female), poets, prophets, physicians (male and female), musicians (male and female), cooks, an array of household functionaries (stewards, cupbearers, porters and grooms), jesters and slaves.[59]

Just as in the earlier literature, the people of the *síde* sometimes engage in internecine warfare in the *Acallam*: one such war is between the lords of two *síde*, Ilbrecc of Síd Essa Rúaid and Lir of Síd Finnachaid.[60] In another conflict, Bodb Derg son of the Dagda, to whom the Túatha Dé Danann have collectively granted the kingship, wages war on his nephews the sons of Midir because they will not yield hostages to him; although vastly outnumbered, the sons of Midir at length prevail with the aid of Finn's *fían*, and it is Donn son of Midir who takes the sovereignty.[61] At the beginning of the Early Modern Irish tale *Oidheadh Chloinne Lir*, it is Lir who refuses to accept the overlordship of Bodb Derg, but he is eventually placated by receiving women of Bodb's household as wives.[62] The people of the *síde* also attack the human world, but—although these attacks can be highly destructive—it is here a matter of ones and threes, not of armies;[63] there is also some raiding in the other direction.[64]

The principal relations between the 'two aristocracies', however, are not military but sexual: mortal rulers and lords find partners among the Túatha Dé. Such relationships figure repeatedly in medieval Irish literature, from the earliest period. The consequence may be that the man vanishes forever into the Otherworld;[65] it may be only a matter of a temporary liaison;[66] or the Otherworld woman may join the mortal world through marriage, usually as the consort of a king.[67] According to a poem on Gaelic origins from the late ninth century, all of the first Gaelic settlers took their wives from the Túatha Dé, so that the subsequent population of Ireland in fact belongs to both races.[68] It is generally held that the basis of such stories is the concept, fundamental to all of the Celtic peoples, that a king's authority and legitimacy are conferred by his union with a supernatural woman, who personifies the land and the right to rule over it.[69]

The theme of what Mark Williams has called 'romance across the border between worlds' is well represented in the *Acallam*.[70] Various of Finn's followers have lovers from the *síd*;[71] and Finn himself, whose stepmother and mother belong to the same realm,[72] includes *síd* women among his many wives and mistresses.[73] In a rare instance of a man of the *síd* pairing with a mortal woman, the musician Cas Corach marries the sister of the king of Connacht.[74] The king of Connacht himself marries one of the daughters of Bodb Derg: of all the marriages in the *Acallam*, this is probably the one that receives the most narrative emphasis. It is one of the culminating events of the entire text, and is said to be the first marriage celebrated by Patrick in Ireland.[75] Besides sexual unions, the two communities are linked by ties of fosterage, a mode of relationship that is also attested in later tales.[76] Such, then, is the portrayal of the collective life of the people of the *síde* in the medieval sources, which are literary and aristocratic. A comparable survey of the communal life of the 'fairies', in the popular, oral accounts that have been recorded in more recent times, would also be full of interest; but it must await another occasion, and another author.[77]

## Notes

1. For the modern period, a generous selection of terms attested in County Donegal alone is provided in *Síscéalta ó Thír Chonaill: Fairy Legends of Donegal*, eds S. Ó hEochaidh, M. Ní Néill and S. Ó Catháin (Dublin: Comhairle Bhéaloideas Éireann, 1977), 34–37.
2. A *síd* is a height of land, whether natural or artificial, believed to be inhabited by supernatural beings; even when they are not portrayed as dwelling underground, such beings can be referred to in this way. As *aos sí*, the phrase *áes síde* survives in the modern language.
3. For some of the difficulties attaching to this term see J. Carey, 'The Name "Tuatha Dé Danann"', *Éigse* 18, 2 (1981), 291–94.
4. This power is explicitly attributed to them in the Old Irish tale *De Gabáil int Śída*: V. Hull, '*De Gabáil in t-Śída*: The Seizure of the Fairy Mound', *Zeitschrift für celtische Philologie* 19 (1931), 53–58. See the late Middle Irish or Early Modern Irish *Tochmarc Treblainne*: K. Meyer, 'Mitteilungen aus irischen Handschriften', *Zeitschrift für celtische Philologie* 13 (1921), 3–30, 166–84, 371–82 at 167.

5. Thus poets, blacksmiths and physicians appear all to have revered the goddess (*dea*) Brigit: *Sanas Cormaic*, ed. K. Meyer (Halle: Niemeyer, 1912), §150.
6. An early study, which retains its value as a collection of evidence, is W.M. Hennessy, 'The Ancient Irish Goddess of War', *Revue celtique* 1 (1870), 32–55. For a recent and comprehensive treatment, see M. Egeler, *Walküren, Bodbs, Sirenen: Gedanken zur religionsgeschichtlichen Anbindung Nordwesteuropas an den mediterranen Raum* (Berlin–New York: De Gruyter, 2011), 116–72.
7. Thus the Túatha Dé Danann were said to have brought with them to Ireland the oracular stone that confirmed the authority of the kings of Tara: R.A.S. Macalister, *Lebor Gabála Érenn: The Book of the Taking of Ireland*, vol. 4 (London: Irish Texts Society, 1938–56), 106–7, 110–13, 142–45, 168–69, 174–75.
8. K. McCone, *Echtrae Chonnlai and the Beginnings of Vernacular Narrative Writing in Ireland* (Maynooth: Department of Old and Middle Irish, 2000), 121. Here and in what follows, translations are my own unless otherwise noted.
9. 'The Semantics of *Síd*', *Éigse* 17, 2 (1977–78), 137–55 at 148.
10. McCone, *Echtrae Chonnlai*, 121.
11. R. Thurneysen, 'Compert Con Culainn nach der Handschrift von Druim Snechta', *Zu irischen Handschriften und Litteraturdenkmälern*, *Abhandlungen der Königlichen Gesellschaft der Wissenschaften zu Göttingen, Philologisch-historische Klasse* 14, 2 (1912), 31–41.
12. N. White, *Compert Mongáin and Three Other Early Mongán Tales* (Maynooth: Department of Old and Middle Irish, 2006), 75; K. Murray, *Baile in Scáil: The Phantom's Frenzy* (London: Irish Texts Society, 2004), 34.
13. M. O Daly, *Cath Maige Mucrama: The Battle of Mag Mucrama* (Dublin: Irish Texts Society, 1975), 38.
14. E. Windisch, 'Táin Bó Dartada', *Irische Texte* 2, 2 (1887), 185–205 at 189–90.
15. McCone, *Echtrae Chonnlai*, 121; Hull, '*De Gabáil in t-Śída*'.
16. M. Bhreathnach, 'A New Edition of *Tochmarc Becfhola*', *Ériu* 35 (1984), 59–91 at 74, citing the oldest version of the tale.
17. O. Bergin and R.I. Best, 'Tochmarc Étaíne', *Ériu* 12 (1934–38), 137–96 at 142–43, 178–79.
18. W. Meid, *Táin Bó Fraích* (Dublin: Dublin Institute for Advanced Studies, 1974), 9–10. See the reference to 'the men of the *síde*, both kings and nobles' in E. Knott, *Togail Bruidne Da Derga* (Dublin: Stationery Office, 1936), 2.
19. Knott, *Togail Bruidne Da Derga*, 5–6.
20. Ibid., 42.
21. U. Roider, *De Chophur in Dá Muccida: Wie die beiden Schweinehirten den Kreislauf der Existenzen durchwanderten* (Innsbruck: Institut für Sprachwissenschaft, 1979), 24–27.
22. W. Meid, *Die Suche nach der Traumfrau. Aislinge Óenguso: Oengus' Traum* (Innsbruck: Institut für Sprachen und Litteraturen, 2017), 54.
23. Hull, '*De Gabáil in t-Śída*'. In Bergin and Best, 'Tochmarc Étaíne', the Dagda is 'a wondrous king over Ireland, his race of the Túatha Dé' (142), and is said to be 'in the kingship of Ireland' (144).
24. That the courts of kings might be threatened by Otherworld attack is also suggested in *Baile in Scáil*, where it is stated that the king, accompanied by his druids and poets, would stand on the rampart of Tara every day before sunrise 'so that the

men of the *síde* ['and the Fomoiri', one manuscript adds] should not conquer Ireland without being detected' (Murray, *Baile in Scáil*, 33, 103, 113).

25. K. Meyer, 'The Adventures of Nera', *Revue celtique* 10 (1889), 212–28.
26. F. Kelly, *A Guide to Early Irish Law* (Dublin: Dublin Institute for Advanced Studies), 5–6.
27. Thus fetching firewood is described as typical work for a slave in legal commentary: D.A. Binchy, *Corpus Iuris Hibernici* (Dublin: Dublin Institute for Advanced Studies, 1978), 265. That Ogma, one of the greatest of the Túatha Dé, is made to carry firewood by the unjust king Bres is to be understood as an extreme degradation: E. Gray, *Cath Maige Tuired: The Second Battle of Mag Tuired* (Naas: Irish Texts Society, 1982), 32–33.
28. 'Werewolves, Cyclopes, *Díberga*, and *Fíanna*: Juvenile Delinquency in Early Ireland', *Cambridge Medieval Celtic Studies* 12 (1986), 1–22 at 11.
29. I have discussed this dimension of the story in 'Sequence and Causation in *Echtra Nerai*', *Ériu* 39 (1988), 67–74.
30. E.g. C. O'Rahilly, *Táin Bó Cúalnge from the Book of Leinster* (Dublin: Dublin Institute for Advanced Studies, 1970), line 1581.
31. A.T. Lucas, 'The Sacred Trees of Ireland', *Journal of the Cork Historical and Archaeological Society* 68 (1963), 16–54 at 20 (with supporting discussion at 20–22). See further A. Watson, 'The King, the Poet and the Sacred Tree', *Études celtiques* 18 (1981), 165–80.
32. Thus the wars between the Ulaid and the Cenél nEógain involved their cutting down one another's *bili*: S. Mac Airt and G. Mac Niocaill, *The Annals of Ulster (to A.D. 1131)* (Dublin: Dublin Institute for Advanced Studies, 1983), *s.aa.* 1099, 1111, with further references in Lucas, 'Sacred Trees', 25–26.
33. Murray, *Baile in Scáil*, 34; White, *Compert Mongáin*, 77.
34. M. Dillon, *Serglige Con Culainn* (Dublin: Dublin Institute for Advanced Studies, 1953), 17–18.
35. K. Jackson, 'The Adventure of Laeghaire mac Crimhthainn', *Speculum* 17 (1942), 377–89; Dillon, *Serglige Con Culainn*. Both of these tales were believed by their editors to have been first composed in the ninth century; both also contain extended poetic descriptions of the splendours of the Otherworld (and, in the former, of the prowess of its fighters), dating from the later Middle Irish period.
36. J. Carey, '*Scél Tuáin meic Chairill*', *Ériu* 35 (1984), 93–11 at 102; I have discussed some of the implications of this wording in *A Single Ray of the Sun: Religious Speculation in Early Ireland* (Aberystwyth: Celtic Studies Publications, 2011), 19–20.
37. Overview and references in J. Carey, 'A Tuath Dé Miscellany', *Bulletin of the Board of Celtic Studies* 39 (1992), 24–45 at 37–39.
38. Thus C. O'Rahilly, *Táin Bó Cúailnge: Recension I* (Dublin: Dublin Institute for Advanced Studies, 1976), lines 2043–45.
39. This was the interpretation of the Middle Irish tract which I have edited as the 'Túath Dé Miscellany', where *áes dáno* 'folk of skill' is substituted for *áes cumachta*: Carey, 'A Tuath Dé Miscellany', 28 (§11).
40. '*Cath Maige Tuired*: Myth and Structure', *Éigse* 18 (1981), 183–209; 19 (1982), 1–35; 19 (1983), 230–62.
41. 'Myth and Mythography in *Cath Maige Tuired*', *Studia Celtica* 24–25 (1989–90), 53–69.

42. Discussion by M. Williams, *Ireland's Immortals: A History of the Gods of Irish Myth* (Princeton: Princeton University Press, 2016), 95–96 and n. 70; he is correct that this aspect of the story is often given scant attention. I do not however regard this as being necessarily a supernatural characteristic: as Williams also points out, exaggerated dimensions are often attributed to ancient heroes in premodern narrative.
43. Gray, *Cath Maige Tuired*, 38, 70.
44. Ibid., 34; see the reference to hostile 'sons of Tethra from the *síde*' on 48. On the overlap between Túatha Dé and Fomoiri see J. Carey, 'The Nature of the Fomoiri: The Dark Other in the Medieval Irish Imagination', *Myth and History in Celtic and Scandinavian Traditions*, ed. E. Lyle (Amsterdam: Amsterdam University Press, 2021), 25–48.
45. Jackson, 'Adventure of Laeghaire', 382–83; Murray, *Baile in Scáil*, 33–34.
46. S. Mac Mathúna, *Immram Brain: Bran's Journey to the Land of the Women* (Tübingen: Niemeyer, 1985), 37. On the question of the location of the Irish Otherworld(s), see J. Carey, 'The Location of the Otherworld in Irish Tradition', *Éigse* 19 (1982), 36–43; 'Time, Space, and the Otherworld', *Proceedings of the Harvard Celtic Colloquium* 7 (1987), 1–27; W. Sayers, 'Netherworld and Otherworld in Early Irish Literature', *Zeitschrift für celtische Philologie* 59 (2012), 201–30.
47. McCone, *Echtrae Chonnlai*, 121, 140.
48. For some discussion of these developments, see J. Carey, 'The End of the World at the Ends of the Earth: Apocalyptic Thought in Medieval Ireland', *The Cambridge Companion to Apocalyptic Literature*, ed. C. McAllister (Cambridge: Cambridge University Press, 2020), 156–71 at 165–68; also J. Carey, 'The Old Gods of Ireland in the Later Middle Ages', *Understanding Celtic Religion: Revisiting the Pagan Past*, eds K. Ritari and A. Bergholm (Cardiff: University of Wales Press, 2015), 51–68 at 54–56. The unnamed western paradise in the late tale *Eachtra Thaidhg mheic Céin* is described as a dwelling for the souls of the righteous, but is also the home of Otherworldly women: S.H. O'Grady, *Silva Gadelica (I.-XXXI.): A Collection of Tales in Irish*, vol. 1 (London: Williams and Norgate, 1892), 346–53.
49. W. Stokes, 'The Irish Ordeals, Cormac's Adventure in the Land of Promise, and the Decision as to Cormac's Sword', *Irische Texte* 3, 1 (1891), 183–229 at 195.
50. W. Stokes, 'Acallamh na Senórach', *Irische Texte* 4 (1900), 107–09; R.I. Best, 'The Adventures of Art Son of Conn, and the Courtship of Delbchæm', *Ériu* 3 (1907), 149–73. In *Altram Tighe Dá Mheadar*, Tír Tairngire is paired with Eamhain Abhlach: L. Duncan, 'Altram Tige Dá Medar', *Ériu* 11 (1932), 184–225 at 188. The latter is referred to as an overseas Otherworld already in *Immram Brain*, and is sometimes identified with the Isle of Man; discussion in B. Ó Cuív, 'A Poem in Praise of Raghnall, King of Man', *Éigse* 8 (1957), 283–301 at 297–98.
51. Stokes, 'Acallamh na Senórach', 200.
52. Ibid., 11, 143, 202.
53. Duncan, 'Altram Tige Dá Medar', 184–225 at 188. Contrast the Middle Irish version of *Mesca Ulad*, which simply states that following their defeat 'the Túath Dé Danann went into hills and *síd*-dwellings, so that they dug *síde* for themselves beneath the earth': J. Carmichael Watson, *Mesca Ulad* (Dublin: Dublin Institute for Advanced Studies, 1967), 1.
54. Best, 'Adventures of Art', 152–53.

55. See the discussion of the *Acallam*'s portrayal of the people of the *síde* in Williams, *Ireland's Immortals*, 199–234, esp. 211–14. I have considered the paradoxically untraditional character of the author's celebration of the past in '*Acallam na Senórach*: A Conversation between Worlds', *In Dialogue with the Agallamh: Essays in Honour of Seán Ó Coileáin*, eds A. Doyle and K. Murray (Dublin: Four Courts, 2014), 76–89 at 76–79.
56. Stokes, 'Acallamh na Senórach', 12.
57. Besides the poems in the story of Lóegaire mac Crimthainn and in *Serglige Con Culainn*, cited in n. 34 above, evocative accounts of the magnificence of the Otherworld are to be found for instance in Mac Mathúna, *Immram Brain*, 33–43; and in Bergin and Best, 'Tochmarc Étaíne', 180–83.
58. Stokes, 'Acallamh na Senórach', 12–13.
59. Ibid., 22, 139, 208, 213 (druids); 200 (poets); 195 (prophets); 49, 108, 142, 189 (physicians); 13, 18, 22, 95, 137, 139, 200 (musicians); 13 (cooks); 22 (household functionaries); 108 (jesters); 201 (slaves).
60. Ibid., 46.
61. Ibid., 138–39, 147. Mark Williams has made the interesting suggestion that the kingship was originally held by Midir, from whom it had been seized by Bodb (*Ireland's Immortals*, 232); but in the scene in which both first appear, although Midir is called the one who was 'loftiest and most lordly' in the council of the Túatha Dé Danann, it is already Bodb who appears to preside (Stokes, 'Acallamh na Senórach', 12).
62. S. Ua Ceallaigh, *Trí Truagha na Scéaluidheachta* (Baile Átha Cliath: M.H. MacGuill agus a Mhac, 1927), 42–44. Here, as in the *Acallam*, the kingship is granted to Bodb by the Túatha Dé Danann assembled in council; in this case, they choose among five candidates. Both tales differ in this regard from *Altram Tighe Dá Mheadar*: here, as we saw above, the selection was guided by Manannán in his capacity as 'high king'.
63. E.g. Stokes, 'Acallamh na Seórach', 47, 170, 213–15.
64. E.g. ibid., 197.
65. This is for instance the case with Connlae, Lóegaire and Nera, whose stories we have considered above.
66. Cú Chulainn has a brief affair with the Otherworld woman Fann, but returns to his wife thereafter: Dillon, *Serglige Con Culainn*, 24–29. A negative example, with disastrous consequences, is Ailill Ólomm's rape of Áine of the *síd* of Áine Chlíach: O Daly, *Cath Maige Mucrama*, 38–39.
67. A particularly clear-cut instance of this is the union, in *Togail Bruidne Da Derga*, between Eochaid Feidlech king of Ireland and Étaín, 'daughter of Étar king of Echraide from the *síde*': Knott, *Togail Bruidne Da Derga*, 1–2.
68. R.I. Best et al., *The Book of Leinster formerly Lebar na Núachongbála*, vol. 3 (Dublin: Dublin Institute for Advanced Studies, 1954–83), 520.
69. There is an extensive scholarly literature on this 'king and goddess' theme. A particularly useful contribution is M. Herbert, 'Goddess and King: The Sacred Marriage in Early Ireland', *Women and Sovereignty*, ed. L.O. Fradenberg, *Cosmos* 7 (Edinburgh: Edinburgh University Press, 1992), 264–75.
70. *Ireland's Immortals*, 205.

71. Stokes, 'Acallamh na Senórach', 22–24 (Cáel), 111 (Caílte), 156–57 (Oscar).
72. Ibid., 35 (Alma), 181 (Muirne).
73. Ibid., 2 (Blaí), 68 (Úaine), 78 (Sadb). Dairenn daughter of Bodb Derg seeks to form a union with Finn, but he rejects her (ibid., 135).
74. Ibid., 210.
75. Ibid., 219. Discussion in Carey, '*Acallam na Senórach*', 86–87; Williams, *Ireland's Immortals*, 206–08.
76. Williams, *Ireland's Immortals*, 204. As he notes, the fostering of the young of the *síde* by mortal kings is described in *Tocmarc Treblainne* (Meyer, 'Mitteilungen', 167). The mortal warrior Díarmait is foster son of Óengus of Síd in Broga; see, for example, Kuno Meyer, 'Uath Beinne Etair', *Revue celtique* 11 (1890), 125–34 at 131.
77. Editors' note: for a short bibliography on modern Irish fairylore, see page 16, n. 52 of the current volume.

CHAPTER THREE

# The Isle of Man: 'They Call Them the Good People'

Stephen Miller (independent scholar)

## Introduction: The Isle of Man—'Between Great Britain and Ireland'

'Between Great Britain and Ireland is stretched out a considerable Island from North to South, about thirty Italian Miles in Length; but where widest, not above Fifteen in Breadth',[1] recounted George Waldron in his posthumously published *A Description of the Isle of Man* (1731), one of the major sources for Manx fairylore. The Isle of Man is 571 square kilometres in extent and located in the north of the Irish Sea. The last remnant of the Norse-ruled Kingdom of Man and the Isles, which ended in 1265, brought into the English orbit in 1414, it retains its self-governance, and today is a Crown Dependency of the United Kingdom. Evidence for the Norse period on the Island is seen in place- and surnames, and Tynwald, the Manx parliament. The economy was one of subsistence farming and fishing in the main, until lead mining and the Irish mackerel fishing developed in the nineteenth century, though soon to collapse by the turn of the century. This period saw large-scale emigration to America. As regards population, 1726 saw a figure of 14,426, while the 1901 census counted 54,752, with 4,419 returned as being Manx and English speakers. Manx Gaelic was the community language until the middle of the nineteenth century, the last reputed native speaker dying only in 1974.

## 'Sundry legends which are to be found in Waldron': The Major Sources for Manx Fairylore

'Sundry legends which are to be found in Waldron' was one response to Henry Jenner's postal questionnaire in 1874–75, enquiring about Manx and its

Stephen Miller, "The Isle of Man: 'They Call Them the Good People'" in: *The Exeter Companion to Fairies, Nereids, Trolls and Other Social Supernatural Beings: European Traditions*. University of Exeter Press (2024). © Stephen Miller. DOI: 10.47788/YFYX8175 vernacular culture.² Waldron had resided on the island from 1724 to 1728, as a Commissioner for the British Crown. Whilst there he became fascinated with its vernacular Gaelic expressive culture and within the *Description* is a remarkably early—and, moreover, extensive—account of its fairylore.³ Walter Scott employed Waldron for background in writing *Peveril of the Peak* (1822), a novel part-set on the Island, and so drew attention to him. Writers of guidebooks to the Island in the nineteenth century regularly picked over Waldron to fill out their passages on Manx folklore. The consequence of this was that the numerous guidebooks and directories produced contain little, if any, direct observations of Manx folklore of any value. Waldron's continuing impact can be shown in A.W. Moore's *The Folk-Lore of the Isle of Man* (1891). In his chapter on fairylore, material from Waldron is reproduced on twelve occasions, with seven other printed sources drawn on twice, but with oral sources numbering just three.⁴

Karl Roeder (1848–1911) was a German national living in Manchester. At some date, he encountered Edward Faragher (1831–1908), a fisherman from Cregneash in the south of the island. Faragher was a Manx speaker, but unusual in being literate in Manx, and developed a close friendship with Roeder. There are over forty letters from Faragher to Roeder, many of which relate fairylore. 'I have not gotten many things put in the book yet', he wrote to Roeder in 1896,⁵ referring to notebooks compiled for Roeder on folklore. Six are extant, one from 1897, two from 1898 and 1901, the other undated.⁶ One other is known from a contemporary transcript.⁷ Roeder's principal publication is *Manx Notes and Queries* (1904), a reprint of his column from the *Isle of Man Examiner* (1901–03).⁸ The fairylore material is drawn from Faragher's notebooks and, as a consequence, it provides a contemporary collection of Manx folklore.

The Manx Folk Life Survey initiated by the Manx Museum in 1948, modelled along the lines of the Irish Folklore Commission, provides a key source of fairylore reminiscences. Finally, the digitization of the insular newspapers provides access to a further body of material. That said, this rich source material, stretching remarkably from the 1720s to the 1950s, has yet to be systematically gathered and edited. Nor, for that matter, is there any literature on Manx fairylore to notice bar this source material.

## 'In the companie of the ffary Elves':
## The Names of the Manx Fairies

The first reference to Manx fairies comes in 1665, in a presentment from Andreas parish: 'Phillip ffarcher [i.e. Faragher], for Confessing that he himselfe was in the companie of the ffary Elves that night they came to Knock Doony when the good Wiffe was strucken with the ffairyes.'⁹ The first printed mention

(1702) comes from William Sacheverell, where he refers to Cronk Mooar in Rushen as the 'Fairy Hill'.[10] It is in Waldron that vernacular names are recorded for fairies (though in English), namely the 'little people' (still current on the Island), 'the good people' and the 'little Gentry'.[11] As regards Manx, there are two dictionaries to draw on, the earliest compiled by the Rev. John Kelly (1750–1809), published in 1866, and the later *A Dictionary of the Manks Language* (1835 [but 1837]) by Archibald Cregeen (1774–1841).[12] These introduce the trio of *ferrish*, *lhiannan-shee* and *phynnodderee*.

Kelly glosses *ferrish* as 'a fairy, an elf'. Kelly also has two further names: *mooinjer-ny-gione-veggey*, glossed as 'fairies; the existence of which is still firmly believed by the ignorant', literally, 'people of the small heads'; and *mooinjer-veggey*, 'fairies', literally, 'little people' (also used in another sense to mean children).[13] These are vernacular names in Manx for fairies, rather than the borrowing from English that *ferrish* represents. Cregeen's glosses are minimal, with *ferish* simply 'a fairy', and *mooinjer-veggey*, 'little ones about one', with the same sense as Kelly.[14] Edward Faragher uses only *ferish* when referring to fairies and not any of the vernacular names. Turning to a later source, Sophia Morrison (1859–1917) has 'little people', or *mooinjer-veggey* (glossed by her as 'little family'), 'or in a more familar mood', as she writes, the following: 'Themselves', the *guillyn veggey* ('little boys') and 'Lil Fellas'.[15]

For Kelly, the *lhiannan-shee* is 'a genius, a sprite or spirit, a familiar spirit, a guardian angel', with *lhiannan* 'a sweetheart, a mistress, a lover, a bosom friend, an importunate person', and further, *fer-lesh-lhiannan-shee* 'a person with a familiar spirit'.[16] Cregeen has *lhiannan-shee*, 'a familiar spirit'.[17] Phynnodderee was spelt by Kelly as *fenodyree*, and glossed as 'a satyr, wild man of the woods, elf'.[18] Cregeen took the spelling *phynnodderee*, 'a satyr', as used in translating the usage of *satyr* in the passages Isaiah 13:21 and Isaiah 34:14 in the Manx Bible.[19] The *English Dialect Dictionary* has a gloss that reflects the role played by the *phynnodderee* in Manx folklore, namely '[a] useful sprite, said to dislike clothing'.[20]

## 'Besides the common-place fairies': The Manx Otherworld of Land, Sea and Water

In 1893, someone said that they had seen 'a fairy which had come from the other world, which "other" he did not mention'.[21] That Otherworld contained more than just fairies, as the *Mona's Herald* reminded its readers in 1847: 'we have even here among us, besides the common-place fairies, and every day mermaids, the wonderful Tarro Ushtey, the Doinney Oie, the Phynnodderee, the Lhiannan-shee, and the big Boghane'.[22] First and foremost from this list was the *buggane*, essentially a shape-shifting creature.[23] The *glashtin* or ogre when met would challenge you to a strength contest.[24] Haunting and guarding churchyard stiles was the *keimagh*.[25] The *moddey dhoo* or black dog was seen on the roads at night, and the *arc-vuc-sonney* or the pig of plenty could be spotted on a moonlit night crossing one's path.[26] The *foawr* or giant was no longer seen,[27] but the *scaan* or ghost was still ever-present,[28] as well as the *scaa goanlyssagh* or malicious ghost, who could cut the clothes off a person without being seen or felt.[29] The *dooiney oie* or night-man was a nocturnal spirit heard but not seen, helpful to mortals by warning farmers and fishermen of coming storms. The *cabbyl ushtey* or water horse, often referred to as a *glashtyn*, sought to drown its rider who mistook it at night for a regular mount.[30] The *tarroo ushtey* or water bull came amongst cattle at night.[31] The *nikessen* was a river spirit, the *cughtagh* a sea cave-dwelling spirit,[32] and finally as regards the sea, there was the *ben-varrey* or mermaid,[33] and the *pohllinagh* or merman.[34] There was a major difference between the fairies and these other supernatural figures, as William Cashen pointed out:

> The fairies differed from the *bugganes* and other evil things in that the fairies might be in any place, and at any time, and would not covet a full-grown person, but only infants and children, whereas the *buggane*, *lhiannan-shee* and so on, kept to well-defined places beyond which they were not to travel.[35]

## 'The fairies here seem to be responsible for everything': The Manx Fairy World

'The fairies here seem to be responsible for *everything*' (1846).[36] The fairies pervaded the world of mortals on the island,[37] ever-present but rarely, if ever, seen. With limited space, only a selection of topics relating to Manx fairy beliefs can be discussed here—with a particular focus on interactions between fairies and mortals.

### Fairies and the household

'At every baking, and every churning, a bit of dough, and a bit of butter, is stuck upon the wall, *for the little folks*. This custom still prevails very much amongst the country folks; especially up in the mountains.'[38] Another account explains the reasoning behind this practice: 'to make sure of the butter and milk being good, some farmers used to put food and drink for them on the kitchen table before going to bed'.[39] The foodstuffs mentioned are bread, oatmeal, milk and barley bread.[40] In one case it was 'the more pretentious meal of *braghtan*, which consists of barley cake well buttered. Between two of these cakes is laid mashed potatoes and salt herring, the flesh being carefully picked from the bone.'[41] At Block Eary it was porridge in winter and *pinjean* in the summer.[42] As regards *bonnag*, 'the last cake was left behind the turf-flag for the little people'.[43] The fairies had to be thought of at harvest time, when they too would join in with the *mhellia*, the celebration of the end of harvesting.[44] Failure to provide food and drink would lead to fairy displeasure, from which harm followed—as happened to the servant girl who was too busy during the harvest to leave out their supper, who was then abducted and found in the stable yard the next morning: '[s]he was taken up insensible, but fortunately some recovered from the effects of the little people's vengeance.'[45] At the Corrody the oatmeal was left outside so the fairies would not come in and the girls would be safe.[46] At another farmhouse, if nothing was left out, 'you would find the doorstep scratched and marked with the fairies scraping it. That was because they weren't pleased'.[47] As for the fairies cooking for themselves, they seemingly made broth, baked and cooked up beef.[48]

'A Person would be thought impudently profane, who should suffer his Family to go to Bed without having first set a Tub, or Pail full of clean Water, for these Guests to bathe themselves in, which the Natives aver they constantly do, as soon as ever the Eyes of the Family are closed, wherever they vouchsafe to come.'[49] By guests Waldron means the fairies. This water by a later account 'was never used for any other purpose, but thrown away each morning'.[50] Whilst described in 1874 as a passing custom,[51] the Folk Life Survey shows that it continued much later: '[t]hey always put the crock full of water filled every night for the fairies. My people never minded that very much, but I knew others that did mind.'[52] There was a particular motive behind this kindness, as described by the Folk Life Survey: '*Would they do anything to keep them on their side?* Well, the water was always put out.'[53] Should clean house-water not be left out, the fairies would cause a commotion—as a man in Colby found out one night, who then had to go to the well to draw water for them.[54] This neglect of hospitality could bring one to harm. The fairies wanted to bake one night but on finding there was no water left out, they punished the servant girl by 'bleeding her under the big toe until they had enough to wet the dough and finish their baking'. The girl fell ill, and it was only when an old beggar woman who had heard the fairies talking called again that the farmer went to a herb doctor and she was cured.[55]

## Mortals receiving harm from the fairies

'On the road they passed a man, bent double as with rheumatism. The farmer told how the cripple was quite a young man, who in some way had angered the fairies, who in a single night had struck him helpless.'[56] There were numerous ways in which mortals could fall foul of the fairies. A woman complained when the fairies helped themselves to her food and drink, and was blinded in one eye.[57] A boy stealing money from a healing well sickened and died.[58] Cursing the fairies when drunk led one man to death.[59] A mean farmer begrudged the fairies taking potatoes from his field and died soon after.[60] Spying on the fairies through the keyhole caused another man to lose his eye from a poke with a fiddle stick.[61] Complaining of the smell of the fairies caused one woman to lose her sense of smell.[62] Illness followed after looking in on the fairies at the kiln.[63] Being angry with the fairy dogs met at night left a man bedridden for six months.[64] Illness again followed when answering a fairy's whistle.[65] A drunk man threw a stick at the fairies who were crowding the road, only to have it thrown back at him with such force that he was lamed and bedridden.[66] 'My daughter went over a stile once and came in with a crooked mouth.'[67] These sorts of things could happen simply by being around the fairies: 'The old Manx people used to believe that if people walked on ground where the fairies had been, they would be injured—became halt or lame or crippled.'[68] The fairies, however, 'had no power to hurt anyone who was on an errand of mercy or charity'.[69]

## Fairies mislead at night

'I went astray in a field on Ballamoddey one night. I knew the field well enough, but I couldn't get out. I walked around until I came to a gorse fence and I found the gate and got out.'[70] On Ballamooar in Jurby was a field that was 'haunted by fairies' and where a servant girl was unable to find her way out until dawn came.[71] There were other fields of this nature, such as 'the Gravel Field where a man walked around all night and couldn't find his house until the morning',[72] and another one, 'where somebody was once *took* by the fairies—he went round and round in it and couldn't find the gate'.[73] For some the true cause was spirits of a human nature: 'he also remembered a man who told a story of being carried by the fairies across the fields, when the obvious explanation was that he had lost his way through emptying a rum bottle'.[74]

## Fairy abduction of mortals

Young or old, male or female, day or night, all were at risk from fairy abduction. Waldron related how the daughter of the family's butter seller was once abducted by the fairies when sent on an errand.[75] Others were whisked away without harm: 'I have heard many of them protest they have been carried insensibly great Distances from home, and, without knowing how they came there, found themselves on the Top of a Mountain.'[76] A man from Kirk Andreas 'was absent from his people for four years, which he spent with the fairies'.[77] It was three years for a woman who met two fairy armies at South Barrule before she managed to escape.[78] From 1895: '[a] superstition is still extant that fairies will take children who are out alone after sunset, unless they are marked on their faces with soot.'[79]

Two young men once called in at a fairy house where there was a party going on. One danced away and took a drink, while the other tired of waiting for him and left. When the second man visited the house exactly one year later, his friend was still dancing away and on leaving did not realize that a year had passed.[80] In another version the fairy house disappears after the man goes outside and urinates against its wall. It then reappears seven years later and the man goes in to collect his friend, who is oblivious that he has been dancing away all those years.[81] A mortal was once lured by fairy music into a barn and 'though it and the neighbouring fields were thoroughly searched, that man has never been seen or heard of to this day'.[82] 'Once a woman was living down the Howe, and she was taken away in her confinement, and a dead carcass left in her place.' However, it was discovered that 'she was with the fairies'.[83]

The bride of Magher-y-Breck was stolen away on her wedding night but when the fairies were threatened with their hill being dug up, '[s]he returned home the same day, but did not know she had been away at all'.[84] Sometimes it was simply bad luck, as when '[t]he fairies took you if you lose your way over the mountains'.[85] 'If a person had a fit of the shivers or came out in a rash, then the old people would say "Oh, he's been took by the fairies." Meaning that he had been out in the meadows and got mixed up with these little folk.'[86] As one respondent to the Folk Life Survey in 1950 said: '"Mind the fairies don't get you" is a phrase we still hear when a person goes out alone at night.'[87]

Waldron was told the story of a man led by fairy music to a feast around a table in the open air. Some of the faces seemed familiar but he thought nothing of it, but upon 'the little People offering him Drink', someone tugged at his coat and told him not to drink anything as if he did, then 'you will be as I am, and return no more to your Family'. When a large silver cup was put into his hands, he threw its contents on the ground when suddenly the music stopped and those there all disappeared, leaving him standing alone and holding the cup. The next day he went to see the Vicar of Malew to ask his advice on what to do with the drinking vessel, and 'this very Cup, they tell me, is that which is now used for the consecrated Wine in Kirk-Merlugh'.[88]

This is recognizably ML 6045 'Drinking Cup Stolen from the Fairies'. Later versions extend Waldron's narrative and describe a flight from the fairies after tipping the drink on the ground. One from 1894 has the man fleeing from the Fairy Hill with the cup in his hand; when making his way through the bog he stepped in the water and '[t]he fairies were calling out to him to keep on the stones and not in the water, but he was careful not to obey them'. He made it to a barn and locked the door against them, and '[t]he next morning it was said that the ground was strewed about with fairies' blood'.[89] It was Donagher Lowy who took the cup, according to Karl Roeder in 1897, and when the fairies gave chase they shouted, '*Donagher Lowy, cur dty chass er cloch, as na cur 'sy phoyll*' ('Donagher Lowy, put thy foot on the stone, don't put it in the puddle of water'). Reaching the cow-house, he threw out the cow's urine, which the fairies could not cross.[90]

## *Mortals going with the fairies at night*

Philip Faragher was charged in 1665, 'for Confessing that he himselfe was in the companie of the ffary Elves that night they came to Knock Doony when the good Wiffe was strucken with the ffairyes'.[91] He was not the only one— in the nineteenth century there was *Nan y wyllar vollagh* ('Nan the Daughter of the Rough Miller'),[92] who went with them at night, and '[n]ext day she would tell who had offended the Fairies by not leaving plenty of flour cake and fresh water for their midnight repast'.[93] Another account from 1958 recalls a man who said 'he'd been bothered all night with the fairies pestering him for rides. They'd been riding on his back round the field all night and he hadn't been able to get rid of them till then.'[94]

## *Fairies and the newborn child*

'It was common for fairies to substitute fairy babies for human infants. [...] It was not uncommon for women expecting to be confined to see troops of seven or eight little women come into the chamber at night bearing a baby.'[95] Waldron recounts at length attempts made on one woman for each of her two newborn children.[96] In a later account, two fairy women tried to seize the baby from the mother's arms when she exclaimed, '*Jee jean myghin orrym*' ('God have mercy on me'), and they disappeared. However, visible were 'marks made on the baby's heel made by the fairy fingers. They were quite clearly printed, though at that time the baby had become an old woman.'[97] Children were at danger until they were baptized, a peril that persisted even on the way to the church. '[A] piece of bread and cheese' was carried 'to give to the first person she met, for the purpose of saving the child from witchcraft or the fairies.'[98]

When at home, the child needed to be protected: 'her mother said they wouldn't go out of the house, without putting a pair of trousers or else the tongs cross the cradle that the fairies wouldn't come and take the child'.[99] Some tied a red thread around the neck or put a *crosh cuirn*, made from the mountain ash, in the cradle.[100] Others used a Bible, put under the pillow, or the *Book of Common Prayer* (either in Manx or English), and 'with the great prevalence of Wesleyanism, the use of a copy of Wesley's *Hymns* was just beginning to creep in'.[101] Many of the Folk Life Survey informants were succinct in their recollections: '[t]ongs were put across a baby's cradle to keep the fairies away'.[102] They were also used outside the house when necessary: 'I remember hearing of them taking the babies down to the fields and leaving them in the corners of the fields while they worked and putting the tongs across them so the fairies would leave them alone.'[103]

### Fairy changelings

'The old Story of Infants being changed in their Cradles, is here in such Credit, that Mothers are in continual Terror at the Thoughts of it.'[104] This is Waldron from 1731, and the belief was still current in 1953: 'There is a fairy child down at Maughold today [...] His mother was busy and went to work and they came and changed him.'[105] As it was simply put a century earlier, '[f]airies change children; a woman had one for eighteen years, and could not make it walk or speak.'[106] Harvest and haymaking times were dangerous periods for children left unattended in the fields, when the fairies would take them.[107] On one occasion, just leaving the house to draw water from the well was sufficient time for the fairies. The fairies could be forced to take back the changeling, however. The most common solution was simply not to attend to the crying child, and then the fairies would be forced to take it back.[108] Placing it across a pot of urine was another method,[109] or leaving the changeling out on the doorstep at midnight.[110] Nevertheless, some children lived out their lives as changelings and one such living in the Ballaugh Curraghs was remembered as late as 1964.[111]

## '[T]hese days people are getting enlightened': Edward Faragher and Manx Fairy Belief

'I think I cannot pick up any more fairies tales as the old people who knew about them are all gone and few of the young ones that believe in fairies but the world is gone to be very unfaithful and there are many that dont believe even the bible in these days people are getting enlightened.'[112] So wrote Edward

Faragher in 1897. Fluent in Manx and English, written as well as spoken, and an insider to his own vernacular expressive culture, he possesses a singular voice. It is, moreover, as can be seen above, a reflective one, and Faragher had much more to say about the fairies.

Not only were people becoming more enlightened, but also 'not so simple as the people used to be but I believe they are more wicked and are not so friendly as the people were in the past'.[113] And as evidence of this, 'I remember when I was a boy when the season for setting the potatoes was come the whole of Cregnaish people were all helping one another until every one had their crops down but now no one will help the other and they have to get others to help and pay for it.'[114] The cash nexus had replaced the bonds of mutual obligation. There were other wider changes too, and 'I fancy the old farmers wives that used to provide for the fairies was far kinder to the poor than they farmers wives of our days even my own Mother kept a bed for the poor that came our way to lodge them but beggars get very little nowadays.'[115] Left out for the fairies at night was clean house-water and food and as the fairies were once cared for, so too were those mortals who begged around the farmhouses.

There was an element of self-interest in dealing with the fairies, as one had to be careful not to cross them since they could bring harm to mortals. Faragher recounts the sudden death of a young girl and says 'whither it was the fairies that charmed the little girl away or not I cannot tell but the old folks when I was young would have blamed the fairies for all thing of that description'.[116] The fairies were capricious, 'some of them were very mischeiviou [sic] and others very kind but I think we are much better without their company'.[117] Faragher was also to write that 'the fairy days are over and I dont think many people wish them to come back again'.[118] The fairies spoke Manx: 'The woman that keeps the shop in C[regneash] was telling me this morning that she heard the fairies in the garden again but not understand their language very likely they are speaking the manx language yet and there is very few can understand them I never heard them talking mysel I spose they would not like me to hear them for I might understand them if they speak manx and might expose them.'[119]

But not all spoke that language, it must be added, as 'I am told they are heard often but I dont hear of any one that can understand their language I sopose it will be the language of fairy land and whither that land is under the earth or above it nobody knows and nobody can tell.'[120] Fairies from outside the Island were also encountered. A man, when coming home on Christmas Eve to his cottage at Perwick, 'heard great talking at the house when he came near but could not understand one word of them so it must have been some foreigh fairies that could not speak manx'.[121] Whilst the fairies were still around—'[o]ne of my neighbours has been telling me about hearing the fairies very often but very seldom getting a peep at them'[122]—they were on the wane: '[b]ut it seems the ghosts are like the fairies and dont like to shew themselves as they did formerly.'[123] Faragher had little personal contact with them: '[t]here are some folks very good for seeing fairies I have not come across myself but very little and I dont want neither to get among them for I think I am too fainthearted.'[124]

One fairy figure which did fascinate him was that of the *lhiannan-shee*, a fairy woman dressed in white or yellow silk, who was encountered at night, either alone or in a pair. Talking to her turned her into one's sweetheart, and that bond was for life. Faragher when a young man was once spotted in the company of a *lhiannan-shee*, although unbeknown to him. As he crested the top of the Cronk at Glenchass on the way home to Cregneash, some men there stopped to stare. 'I was alone and had no one with me but they all said they saw some person beside me dressed in white but I did not believe them although they all affirmed it was the truth', he related, going on to add 'that Glenchass is a likely place for fairies with its deep glen and running stream'.[125] He was later to come across a *lhiannan-shee* when coming back from a meeting at the Methodist chapel in Port Erin, though he did not recognize her as being one. 'I met a young lady in a yellow silk dress rustling as she past me by she had a white parasol in her left hand hanging down by her side but neither of us spoke so the people were telling me it was a llananshee and I would have spoken to her she would have followed me.'[126] Despite the dangers of a fairy woman and knowing full well what talking to her would lead to, 'the next sunday night I went across the hill at the same hour intending to speak to her but she was not there'.[127]

The fairies were once widespread, Faragher said, '[b]ut it appears they have deserted all the countries round about us as well as our little Island there is a shetland woman living at glenshass and she has great yarns about shetland fairies, it appear the fairies were all over Europe in old times.'[128] And not just fairies but mermaids as well: 'I sopose the mermaids and their families are gone to fairy land with the fairies for mermaids and fairies have disappeared.'[129] The reason for mermaids in particular no longer being seen was climate change: 'Though mairmaids are very seldom seen in our days I have no doubd but such things exist still but may have gone to some fairer clime for this climate has changed in my own days and not like it was when I was a boy there are far more storms and changeable weather and not at all like old times.'[130] The spirits of those murdered were now fewer due to increased detection of those responsible—'hence it is that the boganes are all gone away as there is no murders in the Island now that the murderers has not been found out and punished'.[131] In 1898, Faragher sent one of his notebooks on to Roeder with this comment at the end: 'I send you this book as I am not likely to get anymore fairy yarns and they are only foolish things to make the best of them yet the may amuse children.'[132]

## Endnote: 'The nature & probable origin of the Manx fairy-creed?'

'I wonder what is your own general point of view in respect to the nature & probable origin of the Manx fairy-creed?'[133] So wrote Sophia Morrison in 1910 to Josephine Kermode. David Robertson, earlier in 1794, when stranded on the Island and having sought refuge overnight, put fairy beliefs down to the 'pensive and melancholy aspect' of his narrator. For one of Her Majesty's Inspectors of Schools in 1851, it was due to the Manx having 'nothing to interest their thoughts, and rouse them to constant activity, and [so] an injurious sluggishness is superinduced. One of the consequences which might be expected from such a state of mind is certainly prevalent, I mean *superstition*.'[134] For those who did believe in fairies:

> It seems to have occasioned no surprise that at one time the fairies were dwarfish; at another, indistinguishable from human beings. Nor did any seek to enquire why full grown fairies lived under alder trees, nor yet how they reduced their size. Being supernatural they defied the laws of nature.[135]

Fairies live both in their own world and that of the mortal world. They are moral beings, as Waldron remarked, living not in the cities because of the 'Wickedness acted therein', and 'all the Houses are blessed where they visit'. The fairies place standards upon mortals, expecting that the farmer provides hospitality of a night, such that food and water is left out for them, and only then is the house 'blessed'. They also pass judgement on the behaviour of mortals 'for they fly Vice',[136] and their displeasure can turn to harm. An angry gesture such as throwing a stick at them has the stick coming back with such force as to make one lame. Failing to leave out water for the fairy christening leads to punishment for the servant girl, whose death is only adverted by the beggar woman, the former only being able to sleep through the night due to the obligation to offer a bed to the poor of the community.

'[T]hey live in Wilds and Forests, and on Mountains'[137]—in other words, in liminal spaces. The night belongs to the fairies, and as the Rev. J.G. Cumming wrote in 1848, '[t]he superstition has with them [i.e. Manx people] its use, it causes them to keep good hours; and in some parts of the Island it would be difficult to prevail on a native to stir out after dark alone.'[138] For those who did 'stir out', there was the chance of an encounter with the *lhiannan-shee*, whose temptations led unsuspecting mortals into fairy houses where the boundary between the mortal and fairy worlds is blurred. The fairies are at their most dangerous in those liminal moments in the mortal life cycle, such as childbirth, when there is the utmost danger of the newborn child being stolen and a changeling being substituted. As we have seen, fairies want from us—but mortals should not take from them:

> Though so considerately treated by mortals, to partake of fairy hospitality is dangerous in the extreme, showing that the good people do not appreciate as they ought the kindness shown them; and bitter experience has proved to many that to accept money, food, or drink from these sprites is always followed by misfortune.[139]

But even then, misfortunes due to the fairies also served a purpose, explaining away the ills that mortals faced in their day-to-day lives:

> Those terrible creatures are only euphemistically named 'Good-folk'. If offended in the slightest degree they proved themselves vindictive in the extreme. [...] There are thousands of legends illustrating the deadly vengeance of the fairies—their good deeds have scarcely a single record. It may be that prosperity was attributed to a Divine Providence, while the insulted gnome got the benefit of ill-fortune. Child-stealing, bodily hurt, and destruction to property were the works of these ill-mannered fairies. Nor had the provocation to be great—never was there much, often none.[140]

The fairy world also served another purpose: 'the people in those days were all going to each other's houses, and talking and telling stories about the fairies—it was all the entertainment they had'.[141] And here one fond recollection from Bride of those storytelling sessions:

> I remember when I was a young boy at home down at Cranstal the old people were very fond of talking about the fairies and about signs, and whenever a neighbour came into that house at night, it was always this kind of talk that was going. I've been too frightened to stir from the fire after listening to their talk all night. It was wonderful the things that would be happening to them.[142]

**Figure 3.1:** The road sign mentioning Fairy Hill in Rushen.

On a final note, where are *the good people* of Waldron today? According to the Folk Life Survey in 1961, '[t]hey say that the fairies all went over the mountain to Laxa fair, and after that they never came back. They were never seen much about after that time. That must have been the time they went away and left the Island.'[143] From 1949, the fairies all shouted '"Hi! for Ireland!" and they were gone.'[144] But they still exist, and should they ever return to the Island, the Fairy Hill in Rushen is still there and now conveniently signposted for them.

## Notes

1. G. Waldron, 'A Description of the Isle of Man', *The Compleat Works, in Verse and Prose, of George Waldron*, ed. T. Waldron (n.p. [but London]: 1731), 93. We follow Manx convention here in capitalizing Island.
2. H. Jenner, *Information Respecting the State of the Manx Language in the Years 1874–5 Obtained from the Clergy of the Diocese of Sodor & Man*, British Library, Add MS 29894, fol. 30.
3. S. Miller, 'George Waldron and the Good People', *Magical Folk: British & Irish Fairies 500 AD to the Present*, eds S. Young and C. Houlbrook (London: Gibson Square, 2018), 165–80.

4. A.W. Moore, 'Fairies and Similar Spirits', *The Folk-Lore of the Isle of Man* (Douglas–London: David and Son & David Nutt, 1891).
5. Edward Faragher to Karl Roeder, 18 Sep 1896, Manx National Heritage Library (MNHL), MS 11064, Box 2.
6. Four are to be found amongst the Karl Roeder Papers at MNHL, MS 09447, one in the Sophia Morrison Papers, MNHL, MS 09495, Box 5, and one is deposited as MNHL, MD 999.
7. MNHL, MS 09469/2. The other manuscript, MS 09469/1, is a copy of one of the notebooks at MNHL, MS 09447.
8. S. Miller, ed., *Ghosts, Bugganes & Fairy Pigs: Karl Roeder's Manx Notes & Queries (1904)* (St John's: Culture Vannin, 2019).
9. Anon. [but D. Craine], 'Unpublished Documents in the Manx Museum, No 139. 1665. Church Presentments: KK Andreas', *Journal of the Manx Museum* 3, 44 (1935).
10. W. Sacheverell, *An Account of the Isle of Man* (London: J. Hartley, R. Gibson and Tho. Hodgson, 1702).
11. Waldron, 'A Description', 101, 26, 33.
12. Rev. W. Gill, ed., *The Manx Dictionary in Two Parts* (Douglas: Manx Society, 1866); A. Cregeen, ed., *A Dictionary of the Manks Language* (Douglas–London–Liverpool: J. Quiggin; Whittaker, Treacher, and Arnot; Evans, Chegwin, and Hall, 1835 [but 1837]).
13. Gill, ed., *The Manx Dictionary in Two Parts*, 83a (*ferrish*); 135a (*mooinjer-ny-gione-veggey* and *mooinjer-veggey*).
14. Cregeen, *A Dictionary of the Manks Language*, 66b (*ferish*); 117a (*mooinjer-veggey*).
15. S. Morrison, 'Manx Dialect Connected with the Fairies', *Proceedings of the Isle of Man Antiquarian and Natural History Society* 1, 9 (1914), 561.
16. Gill, ed., *The Manx Dictionary in Two Parts*, 120a (*lhiannan-shee* and *lhiannan*); 82b (*fer-lesh-lhiannan-shee*).
17. Cregeen, *A Dictionary of the Manks Language*, 106a.
18. Gill, ed., *The Manx Dictionary in Two Parts*, 81b.
19. Cregeen, *A Dictionary of the Manks Language*, 130a.
20. J. Wright, ed., *The English Dialect Dictionary: M–Q*, vol. 4 (London: Henry Frowde, 1905), 481b.
21. Anon., 'Mr W.J.C. Joughin…', *Manx Sun* (23 Dec 1893).
22. Anon., 'Walls and Boundaries Still', *Mona's Herald* (5 Sep 1847).
23. Cregeen, *A Dictionary of the Manks Language*, 30b.
24. Ibid., 79a, Gill, ed., *The Manx Dictionary in Two Parts*, 96b.
25. Gill, ed., *The Manx Dictionary in Two Parts*, 111b.
26. W. Cashen, *William Cashen's Manx Folk-Lore*, ed. S. Morrison (Douglas: Manx Language Society, 1912), 23.
27. Cregeen, *A Dictionary of the Manks Language*, 67b; Gill, ed., *The Manx Dictionary in Two Parts*, 85b.
28. Cregeen, *A Dictionary of the Manks Language*, 140a; Gill, ed., *The Manx Dictionary in Two Parts*, 158b.
29. Cashen, *William Cashen's Manx Folk-Lore*, 22–23; Cregeen, *A Dictionary of the Manks Language*, 80b; Gill, ed., *The Manx Dictionary in Two Parts*, 98a.
30. Gill, ed., *The Manx Dictionary in Two Parts*, 96b.

31. Cregeen, *A Dictionary of the Manks Language*, 165b.
32. Gill, ed., *The Manx Dictionary in Two Parts*, 59b.
33. Cregeen, *A Dictionary of the Manks Language* 25a; Gill, ed., *The Manx Dictionary in Two Parts*, 22a.
34. Cregeen, *A Dictionary of the Manks Language*, 131a.
35. Cashen, *William Cashen's Manx Folk-Lore*, 18–19.
36. J. Platt, *Letters from the Isle of Man in 1846* (London: Saunders and Otley, 1847), 62.
37. See n. 1 above.
38. R. Townley, *A Journal Kept in the Isle of Man*, vol. 1 (Whitehaven: J. Ware and Son, 1791), 208, fn. [1].
39. Anon. [initialled as 'M.L.Q.'], 'Manx Superstitions', *The Cushag* 2, 7 (1907), 149.
40. Anon., '[Local News] A Ghost Story in Anticipation of Christmas', *Manx Sun* (15 Nov 1856) (bread); Rev. J.G. Cumming, *A Guide to the Isle of Man* (London: Edward Standford, 1861), 23–24 (oatmeal); Anon., 'Recollections of Manxland', *The Monthly Packet* 10 (1870), 189 (milk); MNHL, FLS KB J/1 (1949) (barley bread).
41. I.H. Leney, *Shadowland in Ellan Vannin* (London: Elliot Stock, 1890), 146–47.
42. MNHL, FLS Q/32 B/2 (1957).
43. J.W. Thomas, 'Propitiating the Fairies', *Notes & Queries (1st ser.)* 8 (1853), 618a.
44. K. Roeder, 'Contributions to the Folk Lore of the Isle of Man', *Yn Lioar Manninagh* 3, 4 (1897), 153.
45. Flaxney Stowell [as 'Flaxney'], *Castletown A Hundred Years Ago* (Douglas: Manx Sun Office, n.d. [but 1902]), 20.
46. MNHL, FLS C/104, 1 (1960).
47. MNHL, FLS C/153 A/1–2 (1963).
48. Note 168, K. Roeder, 'Manx Notes and Queries: Nos 165–73', *Isle of Man Examiner* (13 Sep 1902) (broth); Note 237, K. Roeder, 'Manx Notes and Queries: No. 237', *Isle of Man Examiner* (20 Jun 1903) (baking); Notebook (1897), [6]–[7], MNHL, MS 09447 (beef).
49. Waldron, 'A Description', 126.
50. W. Harrison, *Mona Miscellany: A Selection of Proverbs, Sayings, Ballads, Customs, Superstitions, and Legends Peculiar to the Isle of Man, 2nd Series*, vol. 21 (Douglas: Manx Society, 1873), 194–95.
51. Henry Irwin Jenkinson, *Jenkinson's Practical Guide to the Isle of Man* (London: Edward Stanford, 1874), 75.
52. MNHL, FLS KJR B/10 (1948).
53. MNHL, FLS C/15 A/3 (1949).
54. Roeder, 'Contributions to the Folk Lore of the Isle of Man', 152–53.
55. Note 237, Roeder, 'Manx Notes and Queries: No. 237'.
56. Anon., 'Benighted Manxland!', *Mona's Herald* (31 May 1916).
57. M. Lee, *Clara Lennox; or, The Distressed Widow*, 2 vols (London: Adlard, 1797), 199.
58. Miss ('Nelly') Weeton to Miss Ann Winkley, 15 Jun (concluded 5 Jul) 1812, *Miss Weeton: Journal of a Governess 1811–1825, with an Epilogue*, ed. E. Hall (London: Oxford University Press, 1939), 35–40 at 39–40.
59. Lord Teignmouth, *Sketches of the Coasts and Islands of Scotland, the Isle of Man*, vol. 2 (London: John W. Parker, 1836), 262.

60. A.M. Crellin, 'Folklore', *Yn Lioar Manninagh* 1, 8 (1891), 222–23.
61. K. Roeder, 'Manx Folk-Lore, 1882 to 1885', *Yn Lioar Manninagh* 1, 11 (1892), 324.
62. A.M. Crellin, 'Report of the Folklore and Place-Name Section [= Report for 1894]', *Yn Lioar Manninagh* 2 (1901), 196.
63. Roeder, 'Contributions to the Folk Lore of the Isle of Man', 150.
64. Note 178, Karl Roeder, 'Manx Notes and Queries: Nos 174–82', *Isle of Man Examiner* (20 Sep 1902).
65. Anon., 'Manx Folklore and Superstition', *The Barrovian* 72 (1903), 14.
66. S. Morrison, untitled and undated single sheet, MNHL, MS 09495, Box 5.
67. MNHL, FLS C/33 C/1 (1949).
68. MNHL, FLS T/33, 3 (1977).
69. Cashen, *William Cashen's Manx Folk-Lore*, 18.
70. MNHL, FLS G/2 A/1 (1949).
71. MNHL, FLS PCI A/7 (1948).
72. MNHL, FLS WA E/18 (1950–51).
73. MNHL, FLS R/19, 2 (1975).
74. Anon., '"A Night with the Lil Fellas": London Manx Society', *Ramsey Courier* (21 Mar 1919).
75. Waldron, 'A Description', 131.
76. Ibid., 126.
77. J. Rhys, 'Manx Folk-Lore and Superstitions (i)', *Folklore* 2, 3 (1891), 288–89.
78. Pseud. [initialled 'A.C.'], 'Isle of Man Folk Lore', *Notes & Queries* (1st ser.) 5 (1852), 341a.
79. A.W. Moore, 'Further Notes on Manx Folklore: Chapter Three, Fairies and Familiar Spirits (Continued)', *The Antiquary* 31, 66 (1895), 178b.
80. Roeder, 'Contributions to the Folk Lore of the Isle of Man', 146.
81. Ibid., 147.
82. Anon., 'The Supernatural in the South of the Island', *Isle of Man Examiner* (3 Jun 1899).
83. Roeder, 'Contributions to the Folk Lore of the Isle of Man', 149.
84. W.W. Gill, *A Manx Scrapbook* (London and Bristol: Arrowsmith, 1929), 415–16.
85. MNHL, FLS QK B/17 (1951).
86. MNHL, FLS KJ A/31 (1950).
87. MNHL, FLS KJ A/31 (1950).
88. Waldron, 'A Description', 126–27.
89. Anon., 'Isle of Man Natural History and Antiquarian Society: Visit to Fairy Hill […]', *Isle of Man Times* (1894), [4]f.
90. Roeder, 'Contributions to the Folk Lore of the Isle of Man', 145.
91. Anon. [but David Craine], 'Unpublished Documents in the Manx Museum, No 139. 1665. Church Presentments: KK Andreas'.
92. Roeder, 'Contributions to the Folk Lore of the Isle of Man', 151.
93. Stowell, *Castletown A Hundred Years Ago*, 20.
94. MNHL, FLS C/123 9–10 (1958).
95. *Ward & Lock's Descriptive and Pictorial Guide to the Isle of Man* (London: Ward, Lock and Co., 1883), 13.
96. Waldron, 'A Description', 129.

97. S. Morrison, [Envelope labelled 'Manx Plant Names Lore'] Disbound notebook, unpaginated, undated, ['Nan Wade…'], undated, [9], MNHL, MS 09495, Box 6.
98. Thomas, 'Propitiating the Fairies', 617b.
99. MNHL, FLS C/86 C/4 (1971).
100. 'Notes by the Editor', 49 ('Infants being changed in their cradles'); G. Waldron, *A Description of the Isle of Man*, Manx Society, vol. 11, ed. W. Harrison (Douglas: Manx Society, 1865), 108.
101. Anon., 'Recollections of Manxland', 189.
102. MNHL, FLS FCE A/4 (1957).
103. MNHL, FLS W/11 A/2 (1953).
104. S. Schoon Eberly, 'Fairies and the Folklore of Disability: Changelings, Hybrids and the Solitary Fairy', *Folklore* 99 (1988), 58–77; S. MacPhilib, 'The Changeling (ML 5058): Irish Versions of a Migratory Legend in Their International Context', *Béaloideas* 59 (1991), 121–31, here 128.
105. MNHL, FLS W/11 A/2 (1953).
106. Pseud. [initialled 'A.C.'], 'Isle of Man Folk Lore', 314b.
107. For late printed accounts, see E. Stubbs, 'Manannan: The Fairy Lore of the Isle of Man', *Oldham Chronicle* (10 Sep 1932); Anon., 'In Romantic Agneash', *Isle of Man Weekly Times* (10 Jun 1939).
108. Roeder, 'Contributions to the Folk Lore of the Isle of Man', 154.
109. Ibid., 154.
110. MNHL, FLS QK B/18 (1951).
111. MNHL, FLS K/22, 2 (1964).
112. Notebook (1897), [61], MNHL, MS 09447. All quotes from Faragher are diplomatic.
113. Notebook (1897), [62], MNHL, MS 09447.
114. Ibid.
115. Notebook (1897), [62]–[63], MNHL, MS 09447.
116. Notebook (1897), [60]–[61], MNHL, MS 09447.
117. Notebook (1897), [13], MNHL, MS 09447.
118. Notebook (1898), [79], MNHL, MS 09495, Box 5.
119. Notebook (1898), [43], MNHL, MS 09495, Box 5.
120. Notebook (1898), [4]–[5], MNHL, MS 09495, Box 5.
121. Edward Faragher to Karl Roeder, 18 Apr 1897, MNHL, MS 09447.
122. Notebook (1897), [57], MNHL, MS 09447.
123. Notebook (1898), [7], MNHL, MS 09495, Box 5.
124. Notebook (1897), [57], MNHL, MS 09447.
125. Notebook (1897), [14]–[15], MNHL, MS 09447.
126. Edward Faragher to Karl Roeder, 20 Jul 1896, MNHL, MS 1246/1 A.
127. Ibid
128. Notebook (1897), [13], MNHL, MS 09447.
129. Notebook (1901), [68], MNHL, MS 09447.
130. Notebook (1898), [13], MNHL, MS 09495, Box 5.
131. Notebook (1898), [28], MNHL, MS 09495, Box 5.
132. Notebook (1898), [113]–[114], MNHL, MS 09495, Box 5.
133. Sophia Morrison to Josephine Kermode, 26 Jun 1910, MNHL, MS 08979, [Box] Josephine Kermode ('Cushag').

134. Anon., 'Manx Education', *Mona's Herald* (3 September 1851).
135. Anon., 'Manx Folklore and Superstition', 14.
136. Waldron, 'A Description', 125–26.
137. Ibid.
138. Rev. J.G. Cumming, *The Isle of Man* (London: John Van Voorst, 1848), 29.
139. Leney, *Shadowland in Ellan Vannin*, 147.
140. Anon., 'Manx Folklore and Superstition', 12.
141. MNHL, FLS C/131 A/1 (1961).
142. MNHL, FLS C/117, 6 (1957).
143. MNHL, FLS C/24 C/2 (1961).
144. MNHL, FLS KB F/2 (1949).

CHAPTER FOUR

# England: Small Fairies Are Beautiful Fairies

Jeremy Harte (independent scholar)

## Fairy Fixers

Forget everything you ever knew, let your old life melt away; now you are in another world, strange, bright, full of marvellous possibilities. Mostly revolving around lust and gold, it is true, for even in scenes of unrationed wonder the human imagination runs on fairly predictable lines. Not that this troubled the fairy fantasists of the sixteenth and seventeenth centuries, for they knew what the client wanted and their supernatural drama provided it, right up to the point where a wise con artist slips offstage.

When Alice West had wormed her way into the household of Thomas Moore in the 1610s, she told 'how the fayrie King and Queene had appeared to her in a vision, saying they had a purpose to bestow great summes of gold upon this man and this woman'. All that the Moores need do was provide money for the rites, which they gladly did. Like all dupes, having ventured something, they didn't want to back out, and paid more; when Thomas expressed doubt, West and her husband

> brought him into a vault, where they showed him two attired like the King and Queene of Fayries, and by them little Elves and Goblings, and in the same place an infinite company of bags, and upon them written, 'this is for Thomas Moore', 'this is for his wife', but would not let him touch anything.[1]

This was convincing, for a while. For the trick to work, the Moores and the Wests must have held shared ideas about English social fairies: that

---

Jeremy Harte, "England: Small Fairies Are Beautiful Fairies" in: *The Exeter Companion to Fairies, Nereids, Trolls and Other Social Supernatural Beings: European Traditions*. University of Exeter Press (2024). © Jeremy Harte. DOI: 10.47788/ULSI6409 they have a king and queen, that they can capriciously bestow wealth, and that they enjoin strict secrecy about their doings—alas, a taboo which was eventually broken, leaving Alice in the dock at the Old Bailey. The same lack of faith landed Judith Phillips in court after she had acted on behalf of the queen of the fairies, who was to provide unlimited treasure in return for a little seed gold buried at a spot known only to those she loved.[2]

But there was more to fairy faith than a checklist of shared stories. It required trust—if not in the fairy queen, then at least in her representatives Alice and Judith. Not that this trust was necessarily misplaced, for the fairy cozener was simply the criminal twin of the service magician, who really did talk to the fairies—whatever that meant—and returned from their realm to heal illness, baffle crime and restore social order. As soon as the first detailed records of service magic become available late in the Middle Ages, we encounter the mother and daughter Agnes and Marion Clerk, friends of *les Gracyous Fayry* who taught these Suffolk girls what good or bad fortunes would fall to their querents, and sometimes revealed hidden treasure as well.[3] Until the end of the seventeenth century there were still specialists like the Gloucestershire woman who

> when any Person was sick, and she had a mind to know the Issue, a Jury of *Fairies* came to her in the Night time, who consider'd of the Matter; and if afterwards they look'd cheerful, the Party would recover; if they look'd sad, he would die.[4]

These gossipers with the fairies were mostly women. They may have found their clients by word of mouth and personal recommendation, not through the aggrandizing placards printed by contemporary cunning men; if so, that would explain why we know less about them than their male counterparts.[5] Listening to their promises, ordinary people could build up a picture of fairies. Their belief was credal, not propositional: the more they trusted in the fairy world, the more confidently they knew what it was like. We as folklorists have all sorts of tabulated lists—'fairies bring on sudden illness', 'fairy reveals name of healing plant', see motif N452 'Secret remedy overheard in conversation of animals (witches)'—but these catalogue the endpoint of belief as if it were the beginning. In real life it was the illness that came first, then the healer, and only then the healer's hints about fairies who can cause lameness or wasting or stroke, a suggestion at which people would snatch without reservations if it offered them hope. For those who inflict harm can also take it away, like the mysterious confidante of Susan Snapper at Rye:

> the woman in the greene petticoat saide unto her I would have you goe unto young Anne Bennett & call her & goe into her garden with her & digge and set sage and then you should be well.[6]

In just the same way, Joan Tyrry of Somerset prescribed herbs for the bewitched; she could see who the witches were because 'the fayre vayres' had taught her this lore, 'such knowledge that she getteth her living by it'.[7] When pressed for more, she told a confused story about walking through Taunton market and coming across a fairy man who held a white rod in his hand, and as she greeted him she lost the sight of one eye. She did not tell, and perhaps she didn't know, the rest of the story, which we recognize as ML 5070 'Midwife to the Fairies'. At some point in the chain of transmission, the narrative has been whittled down to its final episode: originally, Joan would have been called to the other world to deliver a fairy child, dabbing one eye with the ointment intended for baby imps only. That gave her the ability to see into the world of illusion. And *that* was resented as soon as her shady acquaintances found that they were being spied on in Taunton market, leaving her one eye poorer.[8] If this theme of anointed eyes had survived on its own, just one motif from the parent story, it was because it explained a woman's claim to see differently from other folk. Telling tales is itself a kind of midwifing—it brings something into existence that was not there before. Joan's fragment of story was not remembered by accident.[9]

## Seers and Storytellers

But while storytelling and magic may be allied crafts, the same person wasn't necessarily expert in them both. Instead, the imagery which made fairies so compelling as an imagined source of treasure or healing or love came from people who could tell the tales. They may not have been performance artists, like the gifted individuals who could tell wonder tales for hours and even nights on end, but they were living archives of lore, authorities on the supernatural as other people might be on genealogy or local rights. English fairy traditions are typically short narratives, ten or twenty minutes in delivery—the same length as historical local legends, and like them keyed into a particular place. It matters that Joan's fatal accident happened in Taunton market, a place familiar to all her listeners, and not in some fantastic otherwhere beyond the north wind.

Until recently, English scholarship was more interested in traditions than in the people who told them; by the time folklorists began to take an interest in their informants, there was little in the way of fairylore left to collect. But occasional hints slip through of those who supplied 'all the Faries evidence', like Richard Corbett's old servant from the seventeenth century:

> To William Chourne of Stafford shire
> Give laud and praises due,
> Who every meale can mend your cheare
> With tales both old and true.[10]

A repertoire was not built up at random: the storyteller chose or adjusted tale-types to exemplify certain recurrent features.[11] Wealth, for instance, is a fairy attribute which we have already met in the form of treasure, but its presence is also implied in the glittering splendours that characterize the fairy realm, and in the stories of how cleanliness might be rewarded by sixpence in the shoe. All these motifs illustrated the general principle, but each had different origins. Behind the limitless buried store of fairy wealth we can trace the subterranean hoards of demons, and perhaps of the dead. The jewelled walls of Faerie owe something to those universally experienced visions in which the Otherworld is bright with reflective surfaces. That theme also draws on the trope by which the supernatural world is simply the human social elite enlarged: people who live by rushlight are imagining something brighter even than a candlelit room. And both the wealth and the motive behind fairy rewards come very close, as contemporaries recognized, to the coercive incentives used by masters and adults—a distinction without a difference, in a world where most servants were adolescents.[12]

Origins are intricate, and as we trace them beyond their immediate context we soon lose any historical thread. The distant sources of these themes matter less than the art by which early modern storytellers put them together to imagine the English social fairy. They knew that mysterious ladies had been seen dancing in lonely places, like the elf-maidens from whom Wild Edric snatched his wife in the 1050s.[13] They had also seen the dark green circles found in close-cropped grass, an anomaly in a world where people 'attribute nearly everything for which they cannot account to the fairies'.[14] Put these two elements together and we have another story, that of the fairies who dance in a ring by moonlight and leave a trace that puzzles mortals the next day. Dancing, after all, was a signature pastime of the aristocracy since, like the hunt or the procession, it involved activity without work; once again, the supernatural is an idealized projection of the elite.

Not that everyone needed a storyteller to tell them about the fairies: some people could speak from experience. Mr Hart the curate was returning home across the Marlborough Downs in 1633,

> it being neere darke, and approaching one of the faiery dances, as the common people call them in these parts ... he all at once sawe an innumerable quantitie of pigmies or very small people, dancing rounde and rounde, and singing, and making all maner of small odd noyses ... They no sooner perceive him but they surround him on all sides, and what betwixt feare and amazement, he fell down scarcely knowing what he did; and thereupon these little creatures pinch'd him all over, and made a sort of quick humming noyse all the time.[15]

This is a typical narrative of personal experiences with the supernatural: a memorate in folkloristic terminology, an 'It Happened to Me' story such as appears in a modern setting in *Fortean Times*.[16] The scene is conventional—little dancers, and so on—but memorates show no sign of having been retrospectively worked up to cohere with folk belief. What we hear was what they really saw: all these stories have the same conjunction of the eerie and familiar, whether they are first-hand reports like the sighting of fairies at the White Wells in Ilkley, or have passed down through many hands like Jack Wilson's vision of the fairy ladder at Sandwick Rigg, or are something in-between like Mr Hart's encounter, which has come to us because among the pupils to whom he told it was the future founder of folklore, John Aubrey.[17]

So there were three channels from which people in early modern England could get their knowledge of fairies: ordinary people who had come across them like Mr Hart, seers like the Clerks who were in regular touch with them, and raconteurs like William Chourne who had a fund of stories about them. But when it came to advice on dealing with fairies, seers and storytellers spoke with one voice:

> These fairies ... are clean spirits desiring to be in houses, or else where, that are kept with cleanly people, to such they give Gifts of rewards which in respect of them brush, sweep, & garnish their rooms, setting faire & fresh water in place with faire fyer light.[18]

What was it like to meet a fairy? That varied according to which channel of tradition you trusted most. Plucked suddenly into another reality, the casual experiencer saw fairies as a pressing multitude, whereas seers, like the characters in stories, encountered them as individuals. They did not do this by going into a shamanic trance; instead they seem to have had the occultist's gift of projecting inner visualization into the external world.[19] Even the fairy cozeners, who were only playing at being seers, insisted that their fairies were present in the world like anyone else, only harder to get hold of. Mary Parish, who duped Goodwin Wharton for years with hopes of an unconsummated relationship with the fairy queen, was always arranging private meetings which never quite came off, just like someone with an elusive contact at court.[20]

The fairies might come from a realm of illusion, but they were solid enough to pinch and bruise mortals they did not like and have sex with those they did. Curiously for creatures so closely linked with the imagination, they did not appear in dreams, as supernatural beings often do in other contexts and cultures.[21] People learned of hidden treasures from the fairies, or in dreams, but not both at once. When people received a message from an enigmatic figure in a dream, they knew at once they were dealing with a saint, if they lived before the Reformation; later, such instructions came from a heavenly messenger. It is as if there was a supernatural economy, with different activities reserved to beings according to their higher or lower class: for the social fairies, however powerful or revered, always belong to a lesser mythology, the 'small gods'.[22] They have taken up the imaginative spaces that were not already reserved for God and his saints, for angels, ghosts and devils.[23] These spaces were already marginal at the beginning of the modern period; they would shrink further still.

## Where Fairies Haunt

It is not easy to track down the fairies—at least not in England, which lacks the central archives collected by more methodical nations.[24] The map of English fairylore looks colourful at a distance, but some areas are suspiciously blank.[25] As we move closer the broad shading reduces to a very few spots of systematic collecting, which must stand for the whole: for English fairylore, read the fairies of Stowmarket, Puttenham, Tavistock, Arlington, Danby, Moston, Alfrick and Leek.[26] At these favoured spots, the earlier accounts may represent the fortunate meeting of an attentive folklorist with a good informant, but the later ones look like the last areas of remnant tradition, pools left by a receding tide of belief.

Because fairy traditions were tied so specifically to places, the narrator's repertoire—even that of a William Chourne of Staffordshire, or a Master Fowington of Arlington, or a Mary Colling of Tavistock—was confined to scenes which their hearers would recognize, a social world perhaps some ten miles in diameter. No doubt they were sometimes tempted to take a story heard somewhere else and localize it in that little circle, otherwise migratory legends couldn't migrate at all. But to be plausible (and without plausibility the fairies have no power) the stories needed a recognizable geography.[27]

These places where fairies can be seen are overwhelmingly natural locations: at least a hundred of them, set against eight churches or churchyards, with a single mill and bridge.[28] Natural but not untouched by humanity, for a fairy presence is recorded just as often from slighted castles, Roman towns and hillforts as from a cliff or cave; like ragwort and rabbits, the secret people will colonize any area which humans have left untouched. This is not the numinous, wild nature of the Romantics but something much more prosaic. The outdoor places most frequently associated with fairies are hills, which make up 38% of the total—two-thirds of them small hillocks, mounds or barrows (either natural or artificial; the storytellers knew or cared less about this distinction than early folklorists) and the other hills large enough to be crowned with some kind of ruins or embankments. Rocks and stones make up 22%, caves 12%, and pits, holes and hollows 8%. That leaves 16% for water features, mostly wells and springs, and a final 4% for woods.

What is the common denominator here? The fairies like to be *hidden*. They live within the hill—this is why small mounds are preferred to larger eminences, because the imagination can more readily seize on the idea that there is something inside; they are under the rock, or down the cave. And many rocks overhang hollows, while hilltop ruins are full of unexplored crevices and cellars.[29] As for the holes, these vary in size but place-names always use this word for the sort of drop in the land where something can lie unseen, a robber or a recluse or a supernatural being. The theme of hiding does not apply universally, for some of the stones and most of the springs are supposed to be sites of assembly, places where fairies can gather to dance or play, but the abiding image is of a landscape where something can exist without you knowing that it's there.

Modern English tradition knows nothing of the fairy place as a gateway—a portal by which you can pass from this reality to something wholly other.[30] Nor does it have much to say about fairy-owned places. In Ireland you cannot travel more than a few miles without coming across a thorn tree that is dear to the fairies and must not be damaged, or a rath which cannot be ploughed at the risk of incurring their vengeance. In England the fairies do very little to protect their mounds or stones, and fairy trees are few, perhaps because you cannot hide in a tree. Instead, English traditions about fairy places suggest a certain ontological unease. To believe in fairies at all, we must place them in locations where their non-existence cannot be proved by looking.

## Names and Natures

In the twelfth and thirteenth centuries the belief in social fairies was less at risk from scepticism, but everywhere time has played down certain attributes and exaggerated others. The disparity of national and regional fairy traditions is reflected in the words that they use. As a rule, European languages have a very limited set of synonyms—often only one term—for social fairies, whereas there is a much more extensive terminology for the solitary fairies. The *Dictionary of Fairies* patiently distinguishes the brag from the brownie, the puck from the kow, the hob from the dob from the grim from the goblin.[31] But fairies (outside a circumscribed area of south-west Britain) are just fairies.[32]

The etymology of the word has long been known: it is a substantive use of *faierie*, a Middle English abstract term for the condition, or sometimes the realm or community, of the *fai*—where *fai* is a loanword from Old French with a dual sense of 'enchanted' and 'lady from the world of enchantment'. Beyond this is a Vulgar Latin original *fata*, both 'things said or fated' and also 'a Fate, a being who decrees futures at birth'.[33] Very gradually *faierie* like *fai* came to be used as a word for a particular being. The first attestation is usually credited to Chaucer, who wrote in the *Wife of Bath's Tale* how

> Al was this land fulfild of fayerye...

in the old sense, 'full of enchantment': these were the days when

> The elf-queene, with hir joly compaignye,
> Daunced ful ofte in many a grene mede...

but now you can't move for holy friars blessing everything in sight, and

> This maketh that ther ben no fayeryes.[34]

But even this last line does not require the new sense: while Chaucer may have meant 'all this has exorcized the fairies', he could just as well have intended 'and that put an end to these supernatural goings-on'. The first indisputable use of *faierie* as a count noun does not come until well into the fifteenth century, when a translation of the *Epistle of Othea* tells us bluntly 'Galathe was a fairye'.[35]

Chaucer wrote before Middle English *faierie* had become quite synonymous with *elf*.[36] The words were interchangeable down to Aubrey's time; he reports Mr Hart's adventure as an encounter with 'these elves or fayries'. *Elf* derived from Old English *ælf*, itself the reflex of an earlier Germanic term, but supernatural words can keep an outward form through many changes of meaning. The Anglo-Saxon *ælf* lacked most of the characteristics that define social fairies: a parallel world of homes, activities and governance like and yet magically other than that of humanity.[37] But by the twelfth century *ælf* had merged with its Scandinavian cognate *álfr*, used more confidently of a supernatural community, and in the north of England these people dwelt in or on hills, for we find it in hybrid compounds with Old Norse *haugr*, 'mound, barrow'.[38]

After the Norman Conquest, *ælf* came within the semantic orbit of *fai*. In the 1210s, Laȝamon's hero Arthur is the favourite of the *aluen*, who bestow on him nobility, strength and long life, just as the Fate-like *fais* might have done in a French romance.[39] This is a set-piece from the ideal world of epic, but the same equivalence appears in contemporary settings. A thirteenth-century charm, although headed in Anglo-Norman *pur faies*, addresses the spirits as 'you elves': and getting a name wrong in a charm can have serious consequences.[40] Equally serious, according to the *South English Legendary*, are the results of intimacy with the *eleuene* who dance on high hills and in the secret places of the woods:

> Heore membres to-swelleþ sone: and somme a-scapieth onneþe
> And some for-dwineþ al awei: for-to huy beon i-brouȝt to deþe.[41]

It was lucky for a hero like Sir Launfal that his tryst with a *fai* took place in the less censorious atmosphere of poetry.[42] Far from dwindling away or being brought to death, he gained honour, wealth and a willing bedmate; Mary Parish herself could not have offered anything more. Imagery from a medieval lay overlaps with the promises made centuries later by a fairy fraud, for fantasy has no fixed boundary with belief, or French and Latinate literature with English oral tradition.[43] Everyone agreed on the facts about fairies, at least in outline; if there was a difference between courtly romance and popular superstition, it lay in how much wish fulfilment was allowed to these thrilling contacts with the Otherworld.

One innovation was confined to the vernacular: the folk etymology linking *fairy* with *fair*. Joan Tyrry's 'fayre vayres' reflect this, and so does the Scots idiom *farefolkis*.[44] Two phrases in other languages seem to be calques on the phrase—*pulcher populus* in mid-fourteenth-century Latin, and *tylwyth teg* in fifteenth-century Welsh; both alliterate, like their presumed English original.[45] 'Folk' is typical of the convention that identifies the fairies as a social group, instead of by their regular name. The Welsh speak of the *plant Annwfn*, the Irish of the *daoine uisle*, while the English have known them as 'the little people'.[46]

In other languages these circumlocutions were used to avoid offending the ears of invisible hearers; even in Lowland Scots we are sternly warned to say 'seelie wight', not *fairy* or *elf*.[47] But Modern English had no such linguistic taboos. By 1500 *fairy* had become standard, at least in the south. It cannot have been meant as a euphemism for *elf* since that word continued in limited use, gradually losing ground until in the forms *aulf* and finally *oaf* it became the term first for a fairy changeling, and finally for the kind of disabled child who might have once been taken for a changeling.[48]

At the same time a rival term for fairies was springing up in the southwest. A Devon author writes in 1630 about wandering astray on a pixy-path, as if this was a regular local expression. The word is a curtailed form of *collepixie*, the name of a spirit or class of spirits, itself of unknown origin; but *pixy* suggested *pouke*, which had been the preferred term for solitary fairies throughout England up to the edge of the old Danelaw. Literary treatment had already blurred the boundaries between solitary and social fairies, between Puck and Oberon, and now *pixy* became the standard word for the secret people. In the eighteenth century it is attested in Devon and parts of Dorset.[49] By the nineteenth it had extended to Somerset; in Minehead, not far from the market where Joan Tyrry's eye had been put out by a fairy, the same story was now told of a pixy.[50]

From the seventeenth century onwards, metropolitan visitors found in Somerset and Devon the furthest limits of the West, counties where nature defied art and everyone spoke barbarous dialect. Instead of dismissing these perceptions, natives reworked them into a passionate regional patriotism, and they may have seized the chance to have their own supernaturals too—a rugged counterpart to the weak spirits of the Home Counties. For the pixies were dangerous in a way that fairies no longer were. They called Jan Coo of Rowbrook Farm near Dartmeet, and after following their summons he was never seen again.[51]

## The Stock of Tales

This story was still being told into the nineteenth century, at a time when tales of abduction had died out elsewhere in England. They had once been current here as in other countries. In 1725 'fairies, they tell you, have frequently been heard and seen—nay, that there are some living who were stolen away by them, and confined seven years'.[52] It was this same period, seven years, that Malekin the Suffolk changeling had to work out before she was free to rejoin the human world, and that was back in the twelfth century.[53] Here is a trace-motif going back to the early fairy mythology of abduction by the magical people, retention in their world, and rescue through the efforts of concerned kinsfolk.[54] Aubrey still knew of it: 'Some were led away by Fairies ... but never any afterwards enjoy themselves.'[55] Yet within two centuries this dark heart of the lore had dropped out altogether, diminishing the fairy tradition as it went. In 1711 the Earl of Shaftesbury could hardly contain his mirth that a clergyman educated at both Oxford and Cambridge, and Bishop of Gloucester to boot, was taking these tales seriously.[56] As the fairies became less credible, they did fewer things that might stretch belief, which in the end meant doing very little at all.

The innocuousness of English fairies has embarrassed folklorists. At a time when their counterparts abroad were authorizing murder and infanticide, fighting pitched gun battles and ripping people apart to spill their blood on the threshold, our native supernaturals showed little more than peevishness when their favourite flower beds were cleared.[57] Unsurprisingly anglophone writers on fairies, from Keightley to Purkiss, have preferred to mine the greater emotional depths found in neighbouring nations.[58] But late modern English fairylore has an atmosphere all of its own.[59]

We can put together a corpus of the migratory legends found at more than one place in England—the authorities agree on about seventy local stories.[60] Unexpectedly, the most popular of them is a tale seldom discussed: ML 7060 'The Disputed Site for a Church', in which stones of a new church are moved from the site intended by the human architects to one more pleasing to the fairies. 'The Disputed Site for a Church' makes up 19% of the total, perhaps because it is easily told of new places—any settlement with a church on a hill or at a distance from the village provides an opportunity. There are many different candidates for the role of mysterious architect, the Devil first amongst them, followed by other enigmatic agents with the same interest in the local church. Remember that in the lore of fairy-haunted places, churches were the only non-natural sites to appear more than once.

The second most popular story, at 17%, circulated in England as a fusion of what elsewhere are two separate types. A field worker, usually a ploughman, finds a broken spade or baker's peel or other tool, of fairy dimensions. Good-natured, he picks it up and mends it. On returning later to the same spot, he sees a cake or piece of bread or keg of fairy butter, eats it, and prospers forever afterwards, while a mate who turns down the offered food has bad luck.[61] The second part of the story ('Food from the Fairies' or 'A Cake in the Furrow') circulates in Norway as an independent tale-type (ML 5080 'Food from the Fairies') which suggests that the first half ('The Broken Peel') may have originated separately. If so, it was a clever move to have a peel as the broken tool of the fairies, since without it they could not have baked the cake which rewards the ploughman. But here the storytellers fail in their drive to harmonize different elements of the lore: eating fairy food is normally taboo.[62] Some commentators have proposed a subtle rule by which it is dangerous in their world, but lucky in ours.[63] It's more likely that by the time 'A Cake in the Furrow' was circulating in England, the stories that prohibited eating when captured by the fairies had been forgotten along with the rest of the abduction cycle.

Third in the popularity rankings, at 13%, was 'Midwife to the Fairies' (ML 5070), although the full story was often reduced, as in Joan Tyrry's recollections, to the episode where the woman hails a fairy and has her eye put out for this rashness. These versions lose the first part, in which the woman goes into the fairy realm to deliver a baby—typical of the English lack of interest in journeys from the human to the fairy world.

Next in frequency is 'The Changeling' (ML 5085), making up 9% of the total. This is a genuinely threatening story, about a baby snatched by the fairies who leave a substitute from their own race, which can only be exchanged through a cruel-seeming ritual. Story and magic practice are linked much more closely here than in other tale-types; there were children (the aulfs or oafs) who were identified as fairy substitutes in real life, and service magicians gladly took on the role of the friend who advises the mother on how to get rid of them and recover her own child. But by the eighteenth century the story seems to have circulated in England as pure narrative, since nobody carried out the protective rituals—putting a poker across the cradle, draping the father's trousers over its foot—which were still practised in neighbouring countries to ward off the chance that fantasy might become horribly real.[64]

But almost as popular (8%) as the internationally known changeling tale is a peculiarly English story in which a farmer realizes that his store of grain is dwindling inexplicably. He sits up to watch, and on the stroke of midnight sees a crowd of fairies enter the barn, each carrying away a single ear of wheat. The Scandinavian version is called 'The Heavy Burden' (ML 7005) but here the story title is more appropriately 'I Tweat, You Tweat', after the dialogue overheard by the farmer in which one fairy tells another how much he sweats ('tweats') hauling such a weight. It can end with the farmer chasing out the little pilferers, or go on to describe his descent into bad luck and poverty for disturbing them. The second ending restores something to the fairies' injured dignity but otherwise the story does not present them in a very splendid light; they are a kind of vermin, like John Clare's fairies, 'tiny things' that

> Crowd in cupboards as they please
> As thick as mites in rotten cheese
> To feast on what the cotter leaves.[65]

In the Nordic versions, the elves are still small but they haul their tiny burden towards the barn, not away: magically it carries the whole profit of the year, and when the farmer intervenes he loses his harvest.[66] Though some of the English tellers agreed that having fairies or pixies at work in your barn was lucky, they had forgotten the paradox by which tiny size is coupled with awesome powers. To the Sussex or Suffolk farmer, a little fairy is just a fairy that you can reach down and catch in your hand.

## Little People

Significantly, the plot in two of these five main narratives depends on the small size of fairies.[67] This had been a theme for storytellers since the 1210s, when Gervase of Tilbury wrote of *portuni* who were evidently tiny, although textual corruption may have confused their actual size; like Clare's fairies they came trooping into peasant houses at night.[68] *Pygmeus*, the standard Medieval Latin word for fairies, means literally a forearm in height, about one and a half feet. But size is not a constant in these fantasies. Even in *A Midsummer Night's Dream*, Cobweb is simultaneously tasked with bringing Bottom a honey-bag stolen from a bee and fetching him an apricot, which would be about a thousand times bigger.

Cobweb and Mustardseed may be tiny but they are still akin to Titania, 'a spirit of no common rate' whose quarrels can drown the land and dislocate the seasons, and who would command awe from anyone less bumptious than Bottom.[69] The Victorian fairies have lost this respect. Each small as a child, or smaller, they speak the broken English of children—'I tweat'—and like them rely on the benevolence of the adult human world. There are versions of 'The Broken Peel' where the ploughman assumes that the snapped tool is a child's toy, and mends it out of fatherly concern. It's true that some kind of dependence on human beings is a constant in fairy tradition. They need us, it seems, to deliver their children, fight their battles, even cook their food: the *portuni* were particularly fond of roast frog, which was why they gathered round the embers at night. But the older lore balances this need with a reciprocal power over human luck and fate. As the sense of awe before fairy strength dwindled away, the surviving motifs of their weakness began to align them with the children for whom most of these stories were now being told.

## A Farewell to Charms

Imagining fairies as children brought an end to the intimate relations which had once been common between mortals and the other world; at least one would hope so, although the twin project of infantilizing and feminizing the fairies may instead have made it easier to think they could be coerced into sex. Magicians, who were rarely interested in anyone's consent, had a ritual in which a table was spread with bread and water for the spirits Michel, Chicam and Burfee, one of whom would respond to the potent touch of the mage's sceptre. 'Ly on the righte side of the bed and she on the lyfte sid of the bede and do what yow wilt ... Then lycans hir in the morning to go and she will com again when thou callst hir'.[70] This was set down in 1600, and it is the last English report of successful fairy lust, reduced afterwards to the empty hopes of Bottom and Goodwin Wharton.

Occult names resist philology, but Michel the easy fairy may be the same being that was invoked by a London seer for William Lilly: *Micol o tu Micol regina pigmeorum!* If so, her demeanour when she came again may have been less complaisant than at first. Lilly himself obliged a friend by raising her in a wood outside London, where

> a gentle murmuring Wind came first; after that, amongst the Hedges, a smart Whirlwind; by and by a strong Blast of Wind blew upon the Face of the Friend,—and the Queen appearing in a most illustrious Glory. No more, I beseech you (quoth the Friend) my Heart fails.[71]

By the late eighteenth century occultists had transferred their attentions to angels, good or fallen. Meanwhile Titania and her doubles disappear from the narrative repertoire, except in the conservative idiom of place-names where a Queen of Fairies' Chair could be seen in the Yorkshire Dales as late as 1817.[72] And the fairy realm had lost more than its figureheads: the whole project of modelling a supernatural Otherworld on the human elite was at an end. For English storytellers, there would be no more cavalcades, jewelled costumes, great houses blazing with a thousand lights; their fairies were distinctly proletarian, more likely to be heard as they baked, brewed and washed clothes than on a hunt through the woods with dim cry and blowing. When Francis Newman painted a fairy ring for Vauxhall Gardens in the 1730s, he showed little dancers in robes and armour which, while dignified enough, owe more to theatrical costuming than upper-class dress.[73] From then on, the glamour of the fairies would be expressed through images taken from the theatre rather than the aristocracy.

Glamour still had its deceptive powers. As late as 1823 Agnes Lovell could persuade a London servant maid to hand over her clothes, money and necklaces as a bribe for the fairy queen, in a recapitulation of the trick played by

Judith Phillips and Alice West two centuries earlier.[74] An occult story which, with suitable stage management, had once deluded a well-connected City merchant was still capable of persuading a girl just up from the county to part with her hard-earned savings. But the world had changed, and the fairies were hard put to keep up with it. Democrats were already imagining a society without aristocracy, a social order not maintained by elite male violence, sources of wealth which bypassed capricious patronage, and power no longer based in mystery or ritual. Modernity was the acid which etched social fairies out of the collective imagination.

## Notes

1. *The seuerall notorious and lewd cousnages of Iohn West, and Alice West, falsely called the King and Queene of Fayries* (1613), accessible in *Early English Books Online*.
2. *The brideling, sadling and ryding, of a rich churle in Hampshire, by the subtill practise of one Iudeth Philips* (1594), accessible in *Early English Books Online*.
3. F. Young, *Suffolk Fairylore* (Norwich: Lasse Press, 2019), 51–54.
4. J. Beaumont, *An Historical, Physiological and Theological Treatise on Spirits, Apparitions, Witchcrafts and Other Magical Practices* (London: D. Browne, 1705), 104–05.
5. Among the top seven London cunning folk in 1549 there was one woman, 'and she only speaketh with the fayrayes': J. Gough Nichols, *Narrative of the Days of the Reformation* (London: Camden Soc 59, 1859), 334.
6. https://ryetext.thehedgepress.co.uk/rye-text/first-examination-of-susan-swapper-sheet-1-new2/; for the full story, see A. Gregory, *Rye Spirits: Faith, Faction and Politics in a Seventeenth Century English Town* (London: Hedge Press, 2013).
7. K. Thomas, *Religion and the Decline of Magic: Studies in Popular Beliefs in Sixteenth- and Seventeenth-Century England* (London: Weidenfeld and Nicolson, 1971), 220, 221, 296, 317, 727, 733.
8. The tale-type was first recognized by Edwin Sidney Hartland in Chapter 3 of *The Science of Fairy Tales: An Enquiry into Fairy Mythology* (London: Walter Scott, 1891).
9. Daniel Harms puts these ointment stories in a magical context: 'Hell and Fairy: The Differentiation of Fairies and Demons within British Ritual Magic of the Early Modern Period', *Knowing Demons, Knowing Spirits in the Early Modern Period*, eds M. Brock, R. Raiswell and D. Winter (London: Palgrave Macmillan, 2018), 55–78 at 73.
10. 'The Faeryes Farewell', *The Poems of Richard Corbett*, eds J. Bennett and H. Trevor-Roper (Oxford: Clarendon Press, 1955), 49.
11. Therefore the project of establishing what fairies were originally like—as in L. Spence, *The Fairy Tradition in Britain* (London: Rider & Co, 1948)—is invalid; they had many likenesses. Even Katharine Briggs sometimes tended, for example in *The Vanishing People: A Study of Traditional Fairy Beliefs* (London: Batsford, 1978), to write as if all tradition made up a single hypertext in which contradictions could be harmonized.
12. D. Purkiss, *Troublesome Things: A History of Fairies and Fairy Stories* (London: Penguin, 2000), 164–65.

13. W. Map, *De Nugis Curialium (Courtiers' Trifles)*, eds F. Tupper and M. Ogle (London: Chatto & Windus, 1924), 94–96. The lady is described in fine classical fashion as a dryad; but as their son was called Ælfnoð, the implication is that she was an *ælf*.
14. S. Oldall Addy, *Household Tales with Other Traditional Remains Collected in the Counties of York, Lincoln, Derby and Nottingham* (London: David Nutt, 1895), xxxiii.
15. Transcribed, apparently from the lost *Hypomnemata B*, in J. Orchard Halliwell-Phillips, *Illustrations of the Fairy Mythology of A Midsummer Night's Dream* (London: Shakespeare Society, 1845), 235–36.
16. C. von Sydow, *Selected Papers on Folklore* (Copenhagen: Rosenkilde & Bagger, 1948), 73. *Fortean Times*, the journal of strange phenomena, is now in its fiftieth year; published in London, it has featured a column of readers' experiences since 2009.
17. For Ilkley, see S. Young, 'Three Notes on West Yorkshire Fairies in the Nineteenth Century', *Folklore* 123 (2012), 223–30 at 225–26; for Sandwich Rigg, J. Sullivan, *Cumberland and Westmoreland, Ancient and Modern: The People, Dialect, Superstitions and Customs* (Kendal: Whittaker, 1857), 137. For later examples, see J. Bord, *Fairies: Real Encounters with Little People* (London: Michael O'Mara, 1997), 39–57.
18. A seer's report of the late seventeenth century in D. Harms, '"Of Fairies": An Excerpt from a Seventeenth-Century Magical Manuscript', *Folklore* 129 (2018), 192–98 at 196, its advice identical with that harvested from traditional tales in K.M. Briggs, *A Dictionary of Fairies* (London: Allen Lane, 1976), 421.
19. 'Manifesting before them in clearly defined, three-dimensional human or animal forms'—E. Wilby, *Cunning Folk and Familiar Spirits: Shamanistic Traditions in Early Modern British Witchcraft and Magic* (Eastbourne: Sussex Academic Press, 2005), 61—which is not what shamans experience: R. Hutton, *The Witch: A History of Fear, from Ancient Times to the Present* (New Haven, CT: Yale University Press, 2017), 225–26.
20. F. Timbers, *The Magical Adventures of Mary Parish: The Occult World of Seventeenth-Century London* (Kirksville, MO: Truman State University Press, 2016).
21. But in Shetland a human taken by the fairies could appear in a dream: B. Edmonston and J. Saxby, *The Home of a Naturalist* (London: Nisbet, 1888), 207–08.
22. M. Ostling, 'Where've All the Good People Gone?', *Fairies, Demons, and Nature Spirits: 'Small Gods' at the Margins of Christendom* (Palgrave Macmillan, London: 2018), 1–53 at 4–11.
23. The lines are much less clear-cut between witches and fairies. Hutton has shown (*The Witch*, 216–42) that the two traditions competed as different explanations of misfortune, but at the level of motif and tale-type fairies overlap substantially with witches, as they do with devils and the dead. D. Oldridge, 'Fairies and the Devil in Early Modern England', *The Seventeenth Century* 31 (2016), 1–15, looks at these correspondences from the perspective of the elite. The motives of the storytellers themselves have yet to be explored.
24. Here, and elsewhere in the chapter, I am excluding Cornwall from 'England'.
25. In J. Bord, *The Traveller's Guide to Fairy Sites: The Landscape and Folklore of Fairyland in England, Wales and Scotland* (Glastonbury: Gothic Image, 2004), all Kent, Lincolnshire and Norfolk are absent. That may be extreme, but a recent county survey admits that 'fairies seldom appear in Norfolk': P. Tolhurst, *This Hollow Land: Aspects of Norfolk Folklore* (Norwich: Black Dog, 2018), 268.

26. A. Hollingsworth, *The History of Stowmarket, The Ancient County Town of Suffolk* (Ipswich: F. Pawsey, 1844), 247–48; R. Dugmore, *Puttenham under the Hog's Back: A Social Study of a Surrey Village* (Chichester: Phillimore, 1972), 80–81; A. Bray, *Traditions, Legends, Superstitions and Sketches of Devonshire on the Borders of the Tamar and the Tavy*, vol. 1 (London: John Murray, 1838), 169–92; M.A. Lower, *Contributions to Literature: Historical, Antiquarian, and Metrical* (London: John Russell Smith, 1854), 156–63 (Arlington in Sussex); J. Atkinson, *Forty Years in a Moorland Parish: Reminiscences and Researches in Danby in Cleveland* (London: Macmillan, 1891), 51–57 (in the North Riding of Yorkshire); C. Roeder, 'Some Moston Folk-Lore', *Tr. of the Lancashire and Cheshire Antiquarian Society* 25 (1907), 65–78 at 73–75; J. Allies, *The Antiquities and Folk-Lore of Worcestershire* (Worcester: J. Grainger, 1852), 418–29; E. Cope, 'Some Local Fairies', *Memorials of Old Staffordshire*, ed. W. Beresford (London: George Allen, 1909), 88–93.
27. R. Suggett, *Fairies: A Dangerous History* (London: Reaktion, 2018), 26–39.
28. This analysis is based on Bord, *Fairy Sites*, 24–117 (her section on England, omitting the chapters for Cornwall and Man), and confined to the descriptions and place-names which specify social rather than solitary fairies.
29. 'Cumbrian fairies ... liked ... underground places', Simon Young concludes in a similar but much more detailed analysis: 'Fairy Holes and Fairy Butter', *Magical Folk: British and Irish Fairies 500 AD to the Present*, eds S. Young and C. Houlbrook (London: Gibson Square, 2018), 79–94 at 83.
30. The last detailed account is from a seer, apparently in the 1650s: J. Webster, *The Displaying of Supposed Witchcraft* (London: J.M., 1677), 300–02.
31. Briggs, *Dictionary of Fairies*, passim.
32. Allowing for dialect variations, such as *farisee* (often assimilated to the biblical *Pharisee*) which is found in the South-East, East Anglia and West Midlands: J. Wright, *The English Dialect Dictionary*, vol. 4 (Oxford: Henry Frowde, 1900–05), 480. Formally this is a reduplicated plural but it seems odd that it should be so widespread, and it may represent a subconscious desire to differentiate the folk idiom from Standard English.
33. T. Keightley, *The Fairy Mythology* (London: H.G. Bohn, 1850), 4–13, established the philological groundwork. Noel Williams argues for the influence of OE *fæge* on this process, but his deliberately iconoclastic paper supplements the standard etymology rather than replacing it: 'The Semantics of the Word *Fairy*: Making Meaning Out of Thin Air', *The Good People: New Fairylore Essays*, ed. P. Narváez (Lexington, KT: University Press of Kentucky, 1991), 457–78.
34. *The Complete Works of Geoffrey Chaucer*, ed. F.N. Robinson (Oxford: Oxford University Press, 1966), 84.
35. R.F. Green, 'Forms of the Marvelous: Fairy Stories, or Stories about Fairies?', *A Cultural History of Fairy Tales in the Middle Ages*, ed. S. Aronstein (London: Bloomsbury, 2021), 23–44 at 41.
36. When the Clerks named their supernatural contacts in 1499, the mother referred to *les Elves* but the daughter to *les Fayry*: Young, *Suffolk Fairylore*, 51–52.
37. A. Hall, *Elves in Anglo-Saxon England: Matters of Belief, Health, Gender and Identity* (Woodbridge: Boydell, 2007), 66–74.
38. A. Armstrong et al., *The Place-Names of Cumberland* (Cambridge: English Place-Name Society, 1950–52), vol. 1, 209, vol. 2, 397, 435; A.H. Smith, *The Place-Names of*

*Westmorland* (Cambridge: English Place-Name Society, 1967), vol. 1, 135, 133, 175, vol. 2, 5, and *The Place-Names of the West Riding of Yorkshire* (Cambridge: English Place-Name Society, 1961–63), vol. 5, 168, vol. 6, 180.

39. J. Church, '"The Play of Elves": Supernatural Peripheries and Disrupted Kingship in Layamon's *Brut*', *Philament* 24 (2018), 15–32.
40. T. Hunt, *Anglo-Norman Medicine II: Shorter Treatises* (Cambridge: D.S. Brewer, 1997), 224.
41. *The South English Legendary*, ed. C. Horstmann (London: Early English Texts Society, 1887), 306: 'Their limbs soon swell up: and some hardly escape / And some dwindle all away: because they have been brought to death'.
42. Fourteenth-century versions in English work up the eroticism that Marie de France hints at in her original *lai*: J. Wade, *Fairies in Medieval Romance* (London: Palgrave Macmillan, 2011), 112–14.
43. R.F. Green, *Elf Queens and Holy Friars: Fairy Beliefs and the Medieval Church* (Philadelphia, PA: University of Pennsylvania Press, 2016), 29–41, shows how much free movement there could be between literary expression and living fact.
44. J. Jamieson, *An Etymological Dictionary of the Scottish Language* (Edinburgh: Edinburgh University Press, 1808), s.v. '*farefolkis*'.
45. Green, *Elf Queens*, 22; R. Gwyndaf, 'Fairylore: Memorates and Legends from Welsh Oral Tradition', *The Good People*, ed. Narváez, 155–98 at 159.
46. First attested as a definite term for fairies ('these little people, as we call them here') in Cardiganshire in 1795: *Gentleman's Magazine* 65, 560.
47. I. Opie and M. Tatem, *A Dictionary of Superstitions* (Oxford: Oxford University Press, 1989), 146.
48. G. Edwards, *Hobgoblin and Sweet Puck* (London: Geoffrey Bles, 1974), 53–54.
49. P. Manning, 'Pixies' Progress: How the Pixie Became Part of the Nineteenth-Century Fairy Mythology', *The Folkloresque: Reframing Folklore in a Popular Culture World*, eds M.D. Foster and J. Tolbert (Boulder, CO: University Press of Colorado, 2016), 81–103; Harte, 'Fairy Barrows and Cunning Folk', *Magical Folk*, eds Young and Houlbrook, 65–78 at 71–72. The OED suggests derivation from *pouke* with a diminutive hypocoristic *-sy* but this is incompatible with the earlier evidence for *collepixie* and the absence of any forms in *-o-*, *-u-*.
50. F. Hancock, *The Parish of Selworthy in the County of Somerset: Some Notes on Its History* (Taunton: Barnicott & Pearce, 1897), 248.
51. W. Crossing, *Tales of the Dartmoor Pixies* (London: W.H. Hood, 1890), 74–79.
52. H. Bourne, *Antiquitates Vulgares* (Privately, 1725), 82.
53. Young, *Suffolk Fairylore*, 48–51. Aspects of the story—including 'Malekin' itself, a Flemish name—belong to the 1220s when it was written, rather than the 1190s when the events happened. Editor's note: see also pages 38, 144 and 145 in the current volume.
54. First clearly set out in three classic articles by W.B. Yeats, *Writings on Irish Folklore, Legend and Myth*, ed. R. Welch (London: Penguin, 1993), 138–88.
55. From a passage in *Hypomnemata Antiquaria A* published in J. Aubrey, *Three Prose Works: Miscellanies, Remaines of Gentilisme and Judaisme, Observations*, ed. J. Buchanan-Brown (Fontwell: Centaur, 1972), 204.
56. M. Hunter, *The Decline of Magic: Britain in the Enlightenment* (New Haven, CT: Yale University Press, 2020), 53.

57. For murder, see A. Bourke, *The Burning of Bridget Cleary: A True Story* (London: Pimlico, 1999); for infanticide, S. Young, 'Some Notes on Irish Fairy Changelings in Nineteenth-Century Newspapers', *Béascna* 8 (2013), 34–47; for battles, P. Sahlins, *Forest Rites: The War of the Demoiselles in Nineteenth-Century France* (Cambridge, MA: Harvard University Press, 1994); for blood, M. Killip, *The Folklore of the Isle of Man* (London: Batsford, 1975), 32; and for peevishness, Bray, *Traditions of Devonshire*, vol. 1, 190–92.

58. Keightley, *Fairy Mythology* (in his 1850 edition, rather than the first modest compilation of 1828) and Hartland, *Science of Fairy Tales*, were typical Victorian polyglots covering all Europe from Greece to Iceland. Katharine Briggs had intended something similar (*Dictionary of Fairies*, xv–xvi) but settled in the end for 'our small islands' (still a political unity when she was young). Purkiss, *Troublesome Things*, deals mostly—as might be expected from such a close reader of texts—with material accessible in English but takes it from throughout the British Isles. When folklorists work on English tradition, it is usually at a regional level, as in the six counties studied in Young and Houlbrook, *Magical Folk*, with another for Lancashire in A. Turner-Bishop, 'Fairy and Boggart Sites in Lancashire', *Lancashire's Sacred Landscape*, ed. L. Sever (Stroud: History Press, 2010), 94–107, and Young's book-length *Suffolk Fairylore*.

59. R. Hutton, 'The Making of the Early Modern British Fairy Tradition', *The Historical Journal* 57 (2014), 1157–75, broke new ground on the growth of fairy tradition 'by adopting a historical perspective on the subject, concerned with dynamism and change'; perhaps the present chapter could do the same for its attenuation and decline.

60. This analysis is based on a collation of K.M. Briggs, *A Dictionary of British Folk-Tales in the English Language* (London: Routledge & Kegan Paul, 1970–71), B1.176–411, with J. Westwood and J. Simpson, *The Lore of the Land* (London: Penguin, 2005) and Bord, *Fairy Sites*. As before, Cornwall and the Isle of Man have been omitted.

61. S. Menefee, 'A Cake in the Furrow', *Folklore* 91 (1980), 173–92 at 174, notes that this is one of the few tale-types more common in England than the adjoining countries.

62. The taboo was known in medieval England, for it features in *The Turk and Gowin*: R. Thompson, '"Muse on ði mirrore...": The Challenge of the Outlandish Stranger in the English Arthurian Verse Romances', *Folklore* 87 (1976), 201–08 at 203.

63. K.M. Briggs, *The Fairies in Tradition and Literature* (London: Routledge & Kegan Paul, 1967), 116–17.

64. In 1771 Smollett notes that horseshoes protected 'the good women that are in the straw' from fairies, but significantly he puts this in the mouth of a Welsh servant girl reporting Scottish superstitions: *The Expedition of Humphry Clinker*, 'Winifred Jenkins', letter of 7 Sep.

65. *The Shepherd's Calendar*, eds E. Robinson and D. Powell (Oxford: Oxford University Press, 1993), Jan lines 124–26.

66. R.Th. Christiansen, ed., *The Migratory Legends: A Proposed List of Types with a Systematic Catalogue of the Norwegian Variants* (Helsinki: Academia Scientiarum Fennica, 1958), 192–94. However, there are other versions, as the peer reviewer of this chapter reminds me, where 'the supernatural beings (not always elves) are human-sized and

then progressively become smaller until the last of them is carrying but one grain of wheat. The farmer who is watching the spectacle laughs at the sight of the theft of the single grain, but then learns that the entire substance—the entire value of the harvest—is contained in that one grain'.

67. A further five repeated types came in at under 8% each: these were 'Telling of Fairy Gifts', 'Borrowing from the Fairies', 'Bells Cause Departure of Fairies', variations on 'The Capture of a Fairy', and 'Cup Stolen from the Fairies'. A small cluster of 'Loss of Time in Faerie' stories is found in Herefordshire, but these are really the extension of a type more popular in Wales.
68. *Otia imperialia: Recreation for an Emperor*, eds S.E. Banks and J.W. Binns (Oxford: Clarendon, 2002), 675–77.
69. *A Midsummer Night's Dream* Act III scene 1; Act II scene 1.
70. F. Klaassen and K. Bens, 'Achieving Invisibility and Having Sex with Spirits: Six Operations from an English Magic Collection ca. 1600', *Opuscula* 3 (2013), 1–14 at 12–14.
71. *William Lilly's History of His Life and Times* (London: Charles Baldwin, 1822), 229, 230–31.
72. Smith, *Place-Names of the West Riding*, vol. 6, 241.
73. D. Coke and A. Bord, *Vauxhall Gardens: A History* (New Haven, CT: Yale University Press, 2011), 102.
74. J. Mori, 'Magic and Fate in Eighteenth-Century London: Prosecutions for Fortune-Telling, c.1678–1830', *Folklore* 129 (2018), 254–77 at 268.

CHAPTER FIVE

# Iceland: The Elves of Strandir

Matthias Egeler (Goethe University, Frankfurt am Main)

## Reykjavík Fairies

Icelanders' alleged belief in elves has in recent decades become firmly established in Icelandic tourism marketing, travel writing and film making.[1] This trope is, at one and the same time, not entirely wrong and yet deeply misleading. 'Elves' have long played a central role in Icelandic 'folk belief' and folk storytelling; yet often, the way that these 'elves' are presented to an international audience is far removed from traditional views and stories.

What Ármann Jakobsson has dubbed 'the Icelandic tourist elf' has since the late twentieth century emerged from an amalgamation of marketing interests, local storytelling motifs and international New Age representations of fairies.[2] These representations are deeply indebted to both Victorian fairy painting and Disney films. The resulting image has turned out to be attractive for an international audience, as it appears to give familiar literary and artistic tropes about fairies a place in the 'real world'. It offers a form of enchantment that counteracts the supposed disenchantment of modernity, at least for the duration of a holiday. This new fairy form is becoming naturalized even in Iceland. In the urbanized environment of Reykjavík, self-declared mediums and psychics have not only absorbed a general anglophone New Age fairy. They have also taken on many specifically theosophic ideas and have integrated them into their own thinking about such supernatural entities. Probably the most influential has been Erla Stefánsdóttir (1935–2015), who through books, the creation of 'elf maps' and numerous TV appearances established herself as the voice of modern reinterpretations of traditional elves.[3] The fairies that arose from this process are often imagined in ways that were entirely unknown to nineteenth- and early twentieth-century Iceland. Take flower fairies. These did not feature in the Icelandic imagination a century ago. But they have now become a stock element of urban fairy publications. Their Icelandic designation *blómálfar* is a calque on English 'flower fairies', and in all their main traits they are an invasive species owing more to Arthur Conan Doyle's *The Coming of the Fairies* than to any traditional Icelandic ideas.[4]

Modern 'Reykjavík fairies' define, for the world, the Icelandic belief in fairies. Yet these 'Reykjavík fairies' have to be viewed in strict separation from traditional rural elves. This chapter will focus on the traditional conceptualization of elves in the Icelandic countryside in the nineteenth and early twentieth centuries.[5] We will particularly look at how 'traditional rural elves' were imagined in the district of Strandir in the Icelandic Westfjords. After a short general overview of Strandir 'elves', I will focus on the example of the farm of Naustvík. The storytelling tradition there is both representative of wider patterns common throughout the region and has been documented in unusual detail.

## Traditional Rural Elves

Local variations in the conception of and storytelling about Icelandic elves have not yet been studied.[6] The following discussion will focus on the historical district of Strandir. This forms the eastern part of the Icelandic Westfjords, and while most of the ideas found there probably are representative of wider patterns, this may not be so for all aspects. Thus there are Icelandic stories about 'changelings' (*umskiptingar*),[7] but no example of a changeling story is attested in Strandir. It is difficult to say whether this simply reflects the general rarity of changeling stories or whether it is an instance of regional variation.[8]

In Strandir, two terms are commonly used for the supernatural beings here under discussion: *álfar* ('elves') and *huldufólk* ('hidden people'). These terms are used interchangeably with no discernible difference in meaning.[9] In the rural environment in the nineteenth and early twentieth centuries, *álfar* were viewed as a parallel society that directly mirrored human society. Just as the human population predominantly lived in scattered, more or less isolated farmsteads, the elves lived on their own scattered farms. They practised the same kinds of farming as their human neighbours, and their abodes were usually located in close proximity to human settlements.

Elf settlements were generally identified with features in the natural landscape, usually hills or rock formations. While individual cases vary, a typical elf settlement (*álfabyggð*) corresponds, in terms of scale, to a human residence, between the size of a small cabin and that of a multi-family house. Very small elf boulders or very large elf cliff faces are uncommon; generally, elf habitations have a similar order of magnitude to human ones. The landscape formations identified as such are typically set apart from their surroundings, such as a free-standing hill, and show at least a small cliff face on one side, maybe mirroring the wood-panelled facade of a well-to-do nineteenth-century Icelandic farmhouse. They tend to be located in close proximity to human homes, normally not more than a couple of minutes' walk from the farmhouse. A limited number of exceptions are located far from human habitations, but all instances of such remote locations that I am aware of are on roads or bridleways (though some are now disused). In these instances, closeness to human society was established through an integration into the human network of roads and paths.[10]

Not only their settlements but also elf economy and social organization are modelled closely on human equivalents. Like human farmers, elves essentially practise subsistence farming, but they are not entirely self-sufficient. Human farmers have to travel to trading posts to buy and sell essential commodities, and in the same way elves have their trading posts, which are scattered throughout the region. On Sundays and church holidays, the human population congregates at Lutheran Protestant churches, and in the same way elves have their churches where they celebrate divine service. Sometimes the singing of hymns and the ringing of bells are heard from elf churches. The elves not only have a Christian society mirroring their Christian surroundings, but elf churches by far outnumber human ones. The categories of elf churches and elf habitations are not kept strictly separate. The sounds of divine services can on occasion also be heard emanating from places otherwise known as elf dwellings, and not all storytellers agree on which elf hill is a dwelling place and which a church.

In their physical appearance, elves are virtually indistinguishable from human beings. It is a recurring pattern of stories about encounters with elves in Strandir that people while travelling encounter unknown individuals. They assume that these individuals come from farm X. When the travellers then reach the next farm, they tell of the encounter, but learn that the people they met could not have been from farm X. They were evidently elves. This type of story shows that even if one meets an elf face to face, there may be nothing that marks out the elf as a non-human.[11] The only thing that recurrently sets elves apart is their use of dyed clothing in red or blue, something too expensive for their poorer human neighbours to afford. Physically elves may look much the same as human beings and do the same kinds of animal husbandry and grass cutting in the hay meadows, but the society of the elves seems to be somewhat wealthier than their human counterpart. On some level, traditions about elves seem to have been characterized by an element of escapism or wish fulfilment. Wish fulfilment may also play a role in the comparatively common stories about love relationships between elves and human beings.

I am not aware of any story from Strandir that engages with the question of the origin of elves. In the mid-nineteenth century, Jón Árnason collected an origin story of the hidden people that identified them as children of Adam and Eve. According to this story, God wanted to visit Adam and Eve, and so Eve started washing her children to make them presentable. She did not manage to wash all of them before God's arrival, however, and when he came she was so embarrassed that she hid the ones who still were dirty. Yet nothing can be hidden from God, and he was not amused: he declared that what was hidden from him should henceforth be hidden also from human beings. Thus the hidden people came into being.[12] Another mid-nineteenth century story explains the elves as former angels who did not take sides when Lucifer revolted against God. As a punishment they were sent from Heaven down to earth to live in the hills, mountains, and stones, and henceforth were called *álfar* ('elves') or *huldumenn* ('hidden people').[13] The early modern author Jón the Learned Guðmundsson (1574–1658) mentioned the idea that the elves came into being when, before Eve arrived, Adam's semen fell on the earth.[14] It is difficult to say whether these kinds of ontological speculations ever had wide currency; in all storytelling from Strandir that I know of, the existence of the elves is simply taken for granted.

## The Farm of Naustvík: Traditional (Rural) Elves in Context

What traditional elves look like in their actual lived context only really becomes clear in the world of the everyday. There, they form an important part of farm life. Until well into the twentieth century, the individual farm was the basic unit of settlement and economy. In this section I will therefore present a concrete example of one such farm and its elves.

The farm of Naustvík overlooks the fjord of Reykjarfjörður in Árneshreppur, in the northernmost part of Strandir. It is rather isolated; its nearest neighbours are five kilometres and six kilometres distant. Naustvík was a working farm until 1967, when farming was given up and never resumed.[15] The last family to farm Naustvík had owned the farmstead since the mid-nineteenth century, and a family tradition connected their earliest years there with an elf incident. This family tradition was passed down by Guðrún Jónsdóttir, who in 1947 died at Naustvík, aged ninety-one. When, Guðrún told, her parents took over Naustvík, they had little money and no cattle. But then one day in early summer, Guðrún's mother saw a cow on the headland of Höfði, which juts out into the sea just east of the farmhouse. The cow was there for much of the day, but then in the late afternoon it disappeared. Guðrún's father went to investigate, but the only thing he found was a cowpat. Guðrún's parents decided that the cow must have been a cow of the elves, a 'hidden cow' (*huldukýr*).[16]

The cattle husbandry of the elves also affected the farm many years later, when Guðrún had grown up and taken over Naustvík. It then happened that a cow of hers that had just calved was giving milk so inconsistently that she was beginning to think that something must be wrong with the way the cow was being looked after. Guðrún then had a dream. In this dream a woman came to her whom she did not know. This woman told her that she should not blame anybody for the lack of milk. Both the dream woman's husband and son were ill and her own cow had not given birth to its calf yet, and therefore they had no milk in their home. She had taken the milk. That was the end of this dream. Later, Guðrún dreamt of the same woman again, and she looked happy. She said that her family had recovered from their illness and her cow had calved. She also said that their home was in Snoppa below Guðrún's farmhouse, but in spring they would move out to Höfði. The woman affectionately took her leave.[17]

This diptych of tales is representative of local storytelling about elves. For one thing, it illustrates how elven society resembles its human equivalent. Just like the human farmers at Naustvík, the elves are a single subsistence-farming family with cattle. These elves are a tad wealthier than human farmers, as they already have a cow when the humans do not. But they are not so wealthy that a streak of misfortune cannot make them dependent on human help. They communicate with their human neighbours through dreams, a very common motif in storytelling about elves. It is also typical that the communication with the elves runs through an older woman: in the first story it is Guðrún's mother who sees the elf cow, and in the second story, which is set much later, Guðrún herself, by now the senior woman on the farm, communicates with the elf woman in her dreams.

Elves explain and thus rationalize misfortune: the dream appearance gives a reason for Guðrún's cow giving so little milk, which in turn helps to maintain peace on the farm; by putting the blame on the elves, nobody else is blamed. In these tales, we also see the common mechanism at work by which somebody or something is identified as belonging to the hidden people: the cow is thought to be a 'hidden cow' (*huldukýr*) because it suddenly appears where no cow should be. It is no different from human cattle; it even leaves an unremarkable cowpat behind. It is just seen where it should not be and then later it is gone. So the 'simplest' explanation is used, which is that it belongs to the closest neighbours, the local elves. The nearest human neighbours live several kilometres away.

Just how closely the elves neighbour the humans becomes clear only when one sees the story places directly in Naustvík (Figure 5.1). Snoppa, where the elf woman in the dream says that the elf farmers are living, is a rock outcrop. It stands some 50 metres below the human farmhouse. It is a jagged wall of free-standing rock that protrudes from the mountainside and that has roughly the same dimensions as the farmhouse. The elf cow in the earlier story was seen on Höfði, and Höfði is also where the elves want to move from Snoppa; this Höfði ('Headland') is the small rocky promontory that juts into the fjord just next to the farm, only about 250 metres from the farmhouse. The elves of Iceland are never called 'good neighbours', as is often used in English, but they are neighbours indeed—and much closer neighbours than any human beings.

Naustvík is isolated in terms of human neighbours. But its elf population is very dense: Snoppa and Höfði are not the only elf places on the farm. Some 450 metres uphill from the farmhouse, the coastal road meets an old bridleway that formerly was a much-used route between the fjord of Reykjarfjörður and the bay of Trékyllisvík. Trékyllisvík is the closest centre of settlement to the north, and the local parish church was located there; so the farmers from Naustvík would have taken this bridle path every time they went to church. The bridleway also led to some hay meadows, an important part of the economy of Naustvík. Where this bridleway and the coastal road meet, a spur of land ends in a remarkably thin wall of rock. This rock wall is Kirkjuklettur, 'Church Rock' (Figure 5.2), and the Church Rock not only lay on the old

**Figure 5.1:** The farm of Naustvík. Snoppa, where the elves dwell at first, is a rock outcrop located directly below the farmhouse. Höfði, where the elf cow is seen and where the elves plan to move, is the headland jutting into the fjord directly behind the farm. Photo © M. Egeler, 2021.

**Figure 5.2:** Kirkjuklettur, 'Church Rock', seen from the side. From the front, it is a straight wall which in places has an almost masonry-like structure. In the background, note the coastal road which directly passes by Kirkjuklettur. The photograph was taken from the bridle path to Trékyllisvík. Photo © M. Egeler, 2021.

bridleway to the local human parish church, but it was also a church of the hidden people.[18] In a way typical of many elf places, it is not connected with a story in the sense of a narrative with a beginning, a middle and an end. In the words of Ingibjörg Guðmundsdóttir (1921–2010), an important Naustvík informant (see below): 'It was supposed to be a church of the elves'.[19]

Another 400 metres directly east of Kirkjuklettur, below a belt of cliffs, a spur of land juts out of the side of Sætrafjall mountain. The top of this spur of land is remarkably smooth and is covered in a dense carpet of good grass. Elsewhere, one would hardly find grassland of this quality outside the specially cared-for 'home fields' of local farms. Yet here, a perfect hay meadow has just evolved naturally—except that it is not used as a hay meadow, for this is Grænuflöt ('Green Meadow'), and it was viewed as an elf home and an *álagablettur* (Figure 5.3). The word *álagablettur* literally translates as 'place of enchantments', and it designates a specific class of Icelandic supernatural locale: an *álagablettur* is a place whose use is forbidden or subject to strict rules, the violation of which can mean supernatural punishment.[20] Details vary, but often such places can take the form of a meadow where it is forbidden to cut the grass, or of a rock formation where it is forbidden to mine for stone. Grænuflöt is an example of the common type of *álagablettur* where a piece of grassland is effectively withdrawn from intense agricultural use. In 1976, Ingibjörg Guðmundsdóttir gave an interview about the place-names and place-stories of Naustvík; she was a niece of Guðrún Jónsdóttir who told the stories of Snoppa and Höfði related above, and had also herself grown up at Naustvík. In this interview, Ingibjörg emphasized how unusually green Grænuflöt was, just like a well-tended hay meadow. However, the hidden people lived there and it was forbidden to meddle with it. Her father never cut the Grænuflöt grass, and when on one occasion the grass was cut, the hay caught fire and went up in flames. She also noted that the animals were particularly calm when they were there.[21]

As an *álagablettur* that was inhabited by the hidden people, Grænuflöt exemplifies a recurrent element of traditions about elves in Strandir. *Álagablettur*-type places are extremely common. In the early decades of the twentieth century, such places were probably still found on nearly every farm: they are attested for almost every one for which good documentation exists. Time and again, such sites are connected with the elves. These places were withdrawn from human use because they were the property of the hidden people. From an academic perspective, they have sometimes been interpreted as something like miniature nature reserves;[22] but on another level they may also have provided a way of coping with the uncertainties of life. An *álagablettur* is a place whose violation leads to accidents and ill-luck; and this may have

**Figure 5.3:** On Grænuflöt below the towering mountain of Sætrafjall.
Photo © M. Egeler, 2021.

suggested that, conversely, if one left the *álagablettur* alone, no mishaps would befall the farm. Thus elf-lore seems to have contributed towards creating a feeling of safety by making danger controllable.

Having encountered already the fourth elf place at Naustvík, we should have now some sense of the local landscape in terms of storytelling and 'folk belief'. The closest human neighbours are several kilometres away, but its invisible neighbours are ubiquitous. Already in 1940, the Icelandic medievalist and folklorist Einar Ólafur Sveinsson saw one of the core functions of the Icelandic *álfar* in coming to terms with the emptiness of the land: 'In very many stories of the hidden folk it is as if loneliness and longing for the society of men cried out to nature until hillocks and rocks and hillsides opened and were filled with hidden folk'.[23] At Naustvík, a farm that at first glance is surrounded by kilometres of rugged, empty landscape is encircled by supernatural neighbours that turn emptiness into community, imaginary though it may be.

It is also worth highlighting that the elves are not the only entities who fill the emptiness of the land: elf society is only a part of supernatural Iceland.[24] Some 400 metres or so east of the farmhouse of Naustvík, at the bottom of a small river valley beyond the promontory of Höfði, there is a small cluster of heavily eroded turf buildings. These ruins are called Flöskubakstóftir, 'Bottle Back's Ruins', and one tradition connects them with a ghost called Bottle Back who carried bottles on his back, whose jangling during the night alerted everybody to his presence.[25] Only a few hundred metres from there, on the coast below the cliff of Sætrakleif, there is a rock pillar. A troll turned to stone when he was overtaken by the light of day. The rock pillar is Tröllkarl, 'Troll Man', and he forever looks across the fjord towards the troll woman Kerling who has turned to stone there.[26] In the past, Tröllkarl used to have a strikingly human appearance, but since then his head has broken off;[27] even more recently, a chunk of the modern coastal road fell on top of him and blocked the former coastal bridleway that use to run behind him.[28] Yet in spite of all these tribulations, the remains of the petrified troll still stand magnificently erect.

Thus, within less than one kilometre as the crow flies, the farm of Naustvík is surrounded by half a dozen supernatural places—and this is if one looks at only the land (see Figure 5.4). If one looks out to and across the waters, the supernatural landscape becomes even denser. I have already mentioned that the troll man of Naustvík looks over the fjord to the troll woman on the other side of the water. In addition, the bay of Naustvík directly below the farm was said to be haunted by sea monsters, whose tracks could sometimes be made out in the bay.[29] And when the weather was clear, at the top of the fjord one could see even more elf places. The rock formations of the Kvíaklettar and the rocks at Lambhagi rise sharply out of the shoreline. Even though these places are almost five kilometres away from Naustvík, they lie across the open expanse of the fjord and so their bulk can be made out in the distance. According to local tradition, these two rock formations were respectively a church and a trading post of the hidden people.[30] Thus the storied landscape stretches as far as the eye can see—and the society of the hidden people again mirrors that of the human population. For the human inhabitants of Naustvík likewise had to undertake long treks to visit a trading post: until the middle of the twentieth century, the local trading post was located at Kúvíkur on the opposite shore of the fjord from Naustvík.[31] Humans and elves both had to go to the other end, or the other side, of the fjord to get provisions. Seen from Naustvík, the resulting landscape of trade and storytelling forms a panorama that encompassed the whole fjord.

## The Question of Belief

At places like Naustvík, we find an elf society which is tightly interwoven with human society in both storytelling and space: a rich folklore tradition

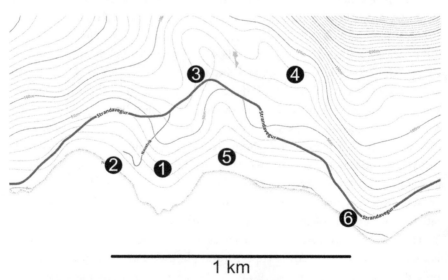

**Figure 5.4:** The story landscape of Naustvík. The former farmhouse is located at the end of the access road; its next neighbours on the fjord were respectively 5 km and 6 km distant. 1) Höfði, the headland where the elf cow was seen. 2) Snoppa, dwelling place of the hidden people. 3) Kirkjuklettur, church of the hidden people. 4) Grænuflöt, dwelling place of the hidden people and 'place of enchantment' (*álagablettur*). 5) Flöskubakstóftir, ruins belonging to the ghost 'Bottle Back'. 6) Tröllkarl, a half-collapsed troll forever looking towards the troll woman on the opposite side of the fjord. Base map created on Inkatlas.com; © OpenStreetMap contributors (openstreetmap.org), Inkatlas.

describes the elves as a society of hidden but otherwise very human-like farmers who lead much the same lives in precisely the same spaces as their human neighbours. Furthermore, we also see how this parallel society is just one of many components in a dense landscape of storytelling that uses a broad range of supernatural entities to fill an environment that is relatively deserted in terms of humankind. The elves are an important and even dominant part, but still only a part, of a strategy that appears to serve the purpose of combatting the emptiness of the land and the resulting social isolation of its inhabitants through the density of its intangible heritage.

But was this parallel society believed in as a reality, or was it merely a storytelling trope? In 1970, Sveinsína Ágústsdóttir (1901–1987) from Kjós on Reykjarfjörður—two farms south from Naustvík—noted during an interview a story which perhaps throws an interesting light on this question. In the course of this interview, Sveinsína was asked about sea monster traditions in the fjord. She then spoke about an occurrence that took place when she was nine years old. One day in autumn, only a few people were at home on the farm, because everybody was busy bringing the sheep to the slaughterhouse. After nightfall, she was sent to get the cows, and she was afraid of the dark and of the sea monsters that populated old stories. While she was on her way, she believed that she saw a sea monster on the shore, and ran back home. Her grandfather believed her, she remembered, and went out with the gun, and on the way they met the cows and drove them back.[32]

Does this story mean that everybody involved believed in the factual existence of sea monsters? Or did the old man simply choose to play along with the child's fears and make an event out of it? If he was playing along, he certainly succeeded, as Sveinsína still remembered that evening sixty years later; and he did no harm to his granddaughter's sense of reality, as in the interview she went on to conclude her story by suggesting that probably she had just seen a sheep on the shore. The point is, it is not clear who 'really believed' in which story at which point in their life. Nor is it clear that this matters. In the history of religions, it has long been emphasized that the concept of 'belief' is a very loaded one that in academic discourse has all too often been used in an overly simplistic manner. It hardly ever is clear what it really means 'to believe', and what role exactly such belief plays in a religious system, including systems of 'folk belief'. In the history of research, the assumption that belief can be taken for granted as a fact of life is based on a specific academic perspective. That perspective is deeply indebted to Protestant ideas about the nature of religions, ideas which have been increasingly questioned by recent research.[33]

In research on the Icelandic *álfar*, the problems inherent in the question of belief have even been explored empirically. In the 2000s, a group of Icelandic social scientists undertook a large-scale survey of 'beliefs' in Iceland, exploring both what people (said they) believed and how strongly they (said they) believed it. This survey also covered the question of whether people believed in elves, allowing for a range of answers: participants could specify whether they thought the existence of such beings 'impossible', 'unlikely', 'possible', 'likely' or 'certain'. The results showed a distribution that certainly highlighted how misleading it would be to think of 'belief' as a yes/no question. Among 602 replies, 15% professed to consider the existence of elves impossible, 24% unlikely, 35% possible, 18% likely and 9% certain (Figure 5.5).[34] So, yes, quite a few people actually (said that they) 'believed in' or 'disbelieved' in the existence of elves. But the vast majority of participants preferred the vagueness of possibility.

So did the inhabitants of Naustvík believe in the existence of a parallel society of hidden people that closely mirrored their own and inhabited the same land? We do not know. Even if they had told us what they 'really' believed, we would not know in what spirit those statements were made. Chances are that the answer might have been very different both between individuals and within the course of the life of these same individuals. Current studies of non-religion have highlighted how people's behaviour, their outlook on life and their view of the world are deeply influenced not only by 'beliefs', but also by stories that people do not believe in as factually true: a novel can influence behaviour and worldview, even while the reader remains fully conscious that the novel is a fiction. As Timothy Stacey said of a research

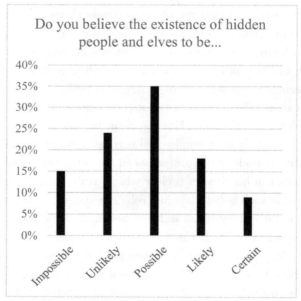

**Figure 5.5:** Icelandic belief in 'elves' according to a survey undertaken in 2006.[35]

approach that focused on the effect of stories rather than on the question of belief: 'It may well be, for example, that people recall a deed of Gandalf when confronted with a moral situation. For my purposes, it is just not all that interesting to stop them and ask, "but do you *actually believe* in Gandalf?"'.[36]

What is clear is that the parallel society of the hidden people was important for the family at Naustvík: over the course of several generations, they built up a dense local mythology that gave them the close neighbours they lacked in reality, and that maybe placed an enchantment on their land that on some level alleviated their isolation. In this, Naustvík can stand in for many farms in rural Iceland; it serves as an example that illustrates an 'ideal type' of farm whose land was densely filled with stories about the parallel lives of its human and not-so-human inhabitants. There the supernatural not only mirrored the life of its human inhabitants, but even became an intrinsic (if imaginary) part of the weft of their social life too.

## Funding acknowledgement

This research was funded by the Deutsche Forschungsgemeinschaft (DFG, German Research Foundation) – project numbers 453026744, 317340660, 495416732, and supported by Rannsóknasetur Háskóla Íslands á Ströndum – Þjóðfræðistofa as well as the Institut für Skandinavistik of the Goethe-Universität in Frankfurt am Main.

## Notes

1. See M. Egeler, 'Pilgrims to Thule: Religion and the Supernatural in Travel Literature about Iceland', *Marburg Journal of Religion* 22 (2020), 1–55. https://doi.org/10.17192/mjr.2020.22.8011.
2. Ármann Jakobsson, 'Beware of the Elf! A Note on the Evolving Meaning of Álfar', *Folklore* 126 (2015), 215–23 at 217.
3. For instance, Erla Stefánsdóttir, *Harfnarfjörður: Huldisheimakort* (Harfnarfjörður: Ferðamálanefnd Hafnarfjarðar, 1993); *Lífssýn mín: Lebenseinsichten der isländischen Elfenbeauftragten. Aus dem Isländischen von Hiltrud Hildur Guðmundsdóttir* (Saarbrücken: Neue Erde, 2007; the original was apparently self-published and I have not been able to trace it); *Erlas Elfengeschichten: Die „isländische Elfenbeauftragte" erzählt. Aus dem Isländischen von Hiltrud Hildur Guðmundsdóttir* (Saarbrücken: Neue Erde, 2011), original ed. *Örsögur* (n.p.: Sigrún Lilja, 2010).
4. For a wide-ranging study of the underlying historical developments and international entanglements, see M. Egeler, *Elfen und Feen: Eine kleine Geschichte der Anderwelt* (München: Beck, 2024).
5. Medieval elves are in many ways markedly different and will not be discussed here; see Ármann Jakobsson, 'Beware'; T. Gunnell, 'How Elvish Were the Álfar?',

*Constructing Nations, Reconstructing Myth: Essays in Honour of T.A. Shippey*, eds A. Wawn et al. (Turnhout: Brepols, 2007), 111–30.

6. For research on Icelandic elves, see for instance M. Egeler, Dagrún Ósk Jónsdóttir, and Jón Jónsson, 'Patterns in Icelandic Elf Hills,' *Folklore*, forthcoming; Ármann Jakobsson, 'Beware'; T. Gunnell, 'Álfar (Elves)', *The Pre-Christian Religions of the North: Histories and Structures*, vol. 3: *Conceptual Frameworks: The Cosmos and Collective Supernatural Beings*, eds J.P. Schjødt, J. Lindow and A. Andrén (Turnhout: Brepols, 2020), 1571–80; 'Introduction', *Hildur, Queen of the Elves and Other Icelandic Legends*, ed. T. Gunnell (Northampton, MA: Interlink Books, 2007), 1–26; 'The Álfar, the Clerics and the Enlightenment: Conceptions of the Supernatural in the Age of Reason in Iceland', *Fairies, Demons, and Nature Spirits: 'Small Gods' at the Margins of Christendom*, ed. M. Ostling (London: Palgrave Macmillan, 2018), 191–212; Gunnell, 'How Elvish Were the Álfar?'; Einar Ólafur Sveinsson, *The Folk-Stories of Iceland*, eds A. Faulkes et al. ([London]: Viking Society for Northern Research, University College London, 2003), esp. 170–83; Valdimar Tr. Hafstein, 'The Elves' Point of View: Cultural Identity in Contemporary Icelandic Elf-Tradition', *Fabula* 41 (2000), 87–104; K. Maurer, *Isländische Volkssagen der Gegenwart: Vorwiegend nach mündlicher Überlieferung gesammelt und verdeutscht* (Leipzig: J.C. Hinrichs'sche Buchhandlung, 1860), 2–29. Two recent and lavishly illustrated popular books on elf dwelling places are Símon Jón Jóhannsson, *Hulduheimar: Huldufólksbyggðir á Íslandi* (n.p.: Nýhöfn, 2020), and Bryndís Björgvinsdóttir and Svala Ragnarsdóttir, *Krossgötur: Álfatrú, álfabyggðir og bannhelgi á Íslandi* (Reykjavík: Bjartur, 2018). Stories about 'elves' are ubiquitous; the database *Sagnagrunnur: A Geographically Mapped Database of Icelandic Folk Legends*, by Terry Gunnell and Trausti Dagsson, https://sagnagrunnur.com, lists over a thousand even though it only catalogues instances in the major published collections; it is difficult to give even an estimate of the number of elf stories preserved in archives. The largest single published collection of elf narratives is still probably Jón Árnason, *Íslenzkar þjóðsögur og ævintýri*, eds Árni Böðvarsson and Bjarni Vilhjálmsson (Reykjavík: Bókaútgáfan Þjóðsaga, Prentsmiðjan Hólar, 1961), vol. 1: 3–124 and vol. 3: 3–200.

7. For examples see Jón Árnason, *Íslenzkar þjóðsögur*, vol. 1: 41–57.

8. The *Sagnagrunnur* database lists 1,002 stories of elves, but only 33 changeling stories. It is worth noting that these changeling stories at least partly represent international story-types; already Maurer in 1860 recorded Icelandic variants of the 'Brewery of Egg-Shells' (on which see page 199): Maurer, *Isländische Volkssagen*, 12–13. Theoretically, the absence of changeling stories in Strandir could also be due to a bias in the extant collections; I do not think that this is the most likely explanation, however, as changeling stories were a very prominent part of nineteenth-century folklore collections in a wider European context. This would lead one to expect Icelandic collectors to overemphasize rather than to underemphasize their local importance. No present-day inhabitant of Strandir that I talked to was aware of local changeling tales. But I did not pursue this question in a systematic fashion.

9. Today, probably in the wake of the rise of the 'Reykjavík fairies', some Icelanders ascribe different nuances of meaning to the different historical terms: Ásdís Aðalbjörg Arnalds et al., *Könnun á íslenskri þjóðtrú og trúarviðhorfum* ([Reykjavík]: Félagsvísindastofnun Háskóla Íslands, 2008), 91, 198. http://thjodfraedi.hi.is/sites/thjodfraedi.hi.is/files/null/konnun_a_islenskri_thjodtru_og_truarvidhorfum_0.pdf. There is no evidence,

however, that such distinctions have a historical basis or that they are anything other than recent. I have never encountered them in Strandir.
10. Cf. Egeler et al., 'Patterns in Icelandic Elf Hills'.
11. Outside of Strandir, one very occasionally finds the idea that elves have some physical features that distinguish them from human beings. For instance, they are said to have a ridge instead of a dent in their upper lip below their nose: Maurer, *Isländische Volkssagen*, 3; Jón Árnason, *Íslenzkar þjóðsögur*, vol. 1: 4; or—in a seventeenth-century account— there is no division between their nostrils: Gunnell, 'The Álfar, the Clerics', 201.
12. Jón Árnason, *Íslenzkar þjóðsögur*, vol. 1: 7.
13. Ibid. Editors' note: see further page 158.
14. Gunnell, 'The Álfar', 202.
15. Haukur Jóhannesson, 'Lesið í landið í Árneshreppi á Ströndum', *Ferðafélag Íslands: árbók 2000*, 44–117 at 62. For an archaeological survey of Naustavík see Birna Lárusdóttir, Guðrún Alda Gísladóttir and Uggi Ævarsson, *Fornleifaskráning í Árneshreppi II: fornleifar frá Kolbeinsvík til Kjörvogs og frá Seljanesi til Skjaldarbjarnarvíkur*. FS260-02053 (Reykjavík: Fornleifastofnun Íslands, 2005), https://www.vesturverk.is/docs/296/FS_-_Fornleifaskr%C3%A1ning_-__%C3%81rneshreppur_II.pdf, 112–23. Other documentary evidence about the farm, which also forms the basis of the following discussion, is found in the archives of the former Place-Name Institute of the Icelandic National Museum, now held by the Árni Magnússon Institute in Reykjavík and digitized at *nafnid.is*, and in the collection of audio recordings of folkloristic interviews from esp. the 1970s and digitized at *ismus.is*. There is also a limited amount of material in printed sources: Haukur Jóhannesson, 'Lesið', 62–64; Jóh. Örn Jónsson, *Sagnablöð hin nýju* (Reykjavík: Leiftur h.f., 1956), 204–5.
16. Jóh. Örn Jónsson, *Sagnablöð*, 204–5. Editors' note: for more on dreams and supernatural communication (and travel), see Chapter 11 in the current volume.
17. Jóh. Örn Jónsson, *Sagnablöð*, 204–5.
18. Birna Lárusdóttir et al., *Fornleifaskráning*, 114 (ST-007:007); Jóh. Örn Jónsson, *Sagnablöð*, 63; Guðrún S. Magnúsdóttir, 1976, 'Naustvík (Strandasýsla, Árneshreppur)'. Heimildamaður: Ingibjörg Guðmundsdóttir (1921–2010), https://nafnid.is/ornefnaskra/17387, 4.
19. Guðrún S. Magnúsdóttir, 'Naustvík', 4.
20. See T. Gunnell, 'The Power in the Place: Icelandic *Álagablettir* Legends in a Comparative Context', *Storied and Supernatural Places: Studies in Spatial and Social Dimensions of Folklore and Sagas*, eds Ü. Valk and D. Sävborg (Helsinki: Finnish Literature Society, 2018), 27–41; Dagrún Ósk Jónsdóttir and Jón Jónsson, *Álagablettir á Ströndum* (Strandir: Sauðfjársetur á Ströndum og Rannsóknasetur HÍ á Ströndum—Þjóðfræðistofa, 2021).
21. Guðrún S. Magnúsdóttir, 'Naustvík', 2; see Símon Jóh. Ágústsson, 'Álagablettir (Árneshreppur, Strandasýsla)', s.a., https://nafnid.is/ornefnaskra/17427; Símon Jóh. Ágústsson, 'Ørnefni. Naustvík (Árneshreppur, Strandasýsla)', Heimildarmaður: Guðmundur Árnason, 1964, https://nafnid.is/ornefnaskra/17390, 1; Birna Lárusdóttir et al., *Fornleifaskráning*, 112–13 (ST-007:003).
22. Ólína Þorvarðardóttir, 'Man and Nature in Icelandic Rural Narratives', *Rustica Nova: The New Countryside and Transformations in Operating Environment*, eds K. Pihlainen and E. Tirkkonen (Turku: University of Turku, 2002), 159–60.

23. Einar Ólafur Sveinsson, *Folk Stories*, 290.
24. For a detailed study of the supernatural landscape of Strandir that covers not only elves, but also a broad range of other traditional supernatural entities, see M. Egeler, *Landscape, Religion, and the Supernatural: Nordic Perspectives on Landscape Theory* (New York: Oxford University Press, 2024). https://doi.org/10.1093/oso/9780197747360.001.0001.
25. Haukur Jóhannesson, 'Lesið', 62. On the ruins see Birna Lárusdóttir et al., *Fornleifaskráning*, 113 (ST-007:004). Ingibjörg Guðmundsdóttir explained the name as being derived from a man who lived there and had the nickname 'Bottle Back': Guðrún S. Magnúsdóttir, 'Naustvík', 3.
26. Haukur Jóhannesson, 'Lesið', 62; Símon Jóh. Ágústsson, 'Ørnefni: Kjós (Árneshreppur, Strandasýsla)', 1964, https://nafnid.is/ornefnaskra/17354, 2.
27. Guðrún S. Magnúsdóttir, 'Naustvík', 1–2.
28. See Birna Lárusdóttir et al., *Fornleifaskráning*, 112.
29. Interview with Sveinsína Ágústsdóttir (1901–1987) from Kjós on Reykjarfjörður, held in the audio file collection of Stofnun Árna Magnússonar, recorded on 28 Sep 1970, SÁM 90/2329 EF – 18, https://www.ismus.is/i/audio/id-1012729; interview with Sigurður Guðjónsson (1886–1971) from Eyjar in Strandir, recorded on 09 Jul 1970, SÁM 91/2360 EF – 10, https://www.ismus.is/i/audio/uid-a27697b8-745e-435a-ad2c-8a1b4bfbc9aa.
30. Informant: Sveinsína Ágústsdóttir (1901–1987) from Kjós on Reykjarfjörður: Guðrún S. Magnúsdóttir, 'Kjós (Strandasýsla, Árneshreppur)', Athugasemdir og viðbætur, 1980, https://nafnid.is/ornefnaskra/17350, 2. Sveinsína made essentially the same statement in an interview held in the audio file collection of Stofnun Árna Magnússonar, recorded on 28 Sep 1970, inventory no. SÁM 90/2329 EF, https://www.ismus.is/i/audio/id-1012724. Her brother Símon Jóhannes Ágústsson described both as dwelling places of the elves: Guðrún Magnúsdóttir, 'Kjós (Strandasýsla, Árneshreppur)', 1974, https://nafnid.is/ornefnaskra/17350, 8, 9.
31. Haukur Jóhannesson, 'Lesið', 55–56.
32. Interview recorded on 28 Sep 1970, SÁM 90/2329 EF – 18, https://www.ismus.is/i/audio/id-1012729.
33. E.g. M. Ruel, 'Christians as Believers', *Belief, Ritual, and the Securing of Life* (Leiden: Brill, 1997), 36–59; B. Meyer and D. Houtman, 'Introduction: Material Religion—How Things Matter', *Things: Religion and the Question of Materiality* (New York: Fordham University Press, 2012), 1–23 at 2–3; T.M. Luhrmann, *How God Becomes Real: Kindling the Presence of Invisible Others* (Princeton–Oxford: Princeton University Press, 2020), 3–4.
34. Ásdís Aðalbjörg Arnalds et al., *Könnun*, 88–89.
35. Ibid.
36. T. Stacey, 'Imaginary Friends and Made-Up Stories: How to Explore (Non)Religious Imaginaries Without Asking Belief-Centred Questions', *Secularism and Nonreligion* 9, 3 (2020), 1–7 at 2.

CHAPTER SIX

# Scandinavia: My Neighbour the Troll

Tommy Kuusela (Institute for Language and Folklore, Uppsala)

## Introduction

Trolls are by far the most famous supernatural beings in Scandinavian folklore. If you type the word 'troll' into Google you will get more than 156 million hits in 0.63 seconds.[1] In popular culture they are portrayed as nasty, large, dumb and aggressive cave-dwellers, but this has little to do with older folk narratives and belief. The trolls of traditional Scandinavian folklore are supernatural beings, living in nature. They are to be found in stories told in the pre-industrial fishing and farming communities. Although common in folklore, descriptions of them differ depending on genre, and they also differ, I would argue, from Old Norse trolls. In the folklore sources, trolls could be violent and threatening; sometimes they were big, nasty and ugly. At other times, they were described as ambivalent, or in some cases, as beautiful and helpful. Their lifestyle was in many ways similar to that of humans, but it was for the most part an inversion of it. However, most accounts of trolls describe them as disruptive beings that threaten humans and their cattle. In this chapter, we will look at a rarer type of troll: the peaceful, even good, neighbour troll.

A brief overview of troll research is offered below. This is followed by a short summary of trolls in Old Norse sources; an exploration of how the word 'troll' has been interpreted; and then an outline of how trolls were depicted from the sixteenth to the twentieth centuries, predominantly in Sweden. The reason for mostly using Swedish material is that trolls are far more common in Swedish legends than in any other Scandinavian country. In Norway trolls are common in folktales. But in memorates, belief utterances and folk legends they are sporadic and when they do appear, this is usually in formulaic stories centring around trolls as enemies of the church or of the saint king Olav.[2] The material used for this research consists of folklore accounts representing the rural oral traditions and beliefs of Scandinavia.[3] My main

Tommy Kuusela, "Scandinavia: My Neighbour the Troll" in: *The Exeter Companion to Fairies, Nereids, Trolls and Other Social Supernatural Beings: European Traditions*. University of Exeter Press (2024). © Tommy Kuusela. DOI: 10.47788/LHEL2533 objective will be to understand in what way trolls can be said to be social beings. Do they live in families and interact in a way that can be said to be social? Do they mirror human life? If so, how? If they are hurtful and dangerous, does this fulfil a function at the societal level? How do they interact with human society?

## Earlier Research on Trolls

Trolls are the best-known of all the supernatural beings of Scandinavian folklore. But there is far less research on them than we might expect, with only a few book-length studies undertaken. In early research, the concept of the troll was used in describing people that were considered technologically and culturally less developed. Take the idea that trolls are a collectivized memory of an earlier, more primitive and heathen state or people. This theory was popular in seventeenth-century Scandinavia, a time when Old Norse literature was used for describing the nation's history in Sweden, Denmark and Norway.[4] Some argued that the trolls were actually the saga authors' interpretation of the Finnish and Sámi populations. One who particularly pushed this notion was the Swede Jacob Fredrik Neikter. In his *De gente antiqua troll* ('The Ancient Troll Nation'), published 1793–99, Neikter argued that trolls were the oldest inhabitants in the Nordic countries, in his view the Sámi and Finnish population. These populations were later subjugated by Óðinn and the Æsir, and were distorted, in the popular imagination, into the demonic trolls of folklore. Many others proposed similar euhemeristic views.[5] Naturally, this theory is as dated as it is flawed. Neikter was inspired by medieval authors who imagined a link between trolls and the 'Finns' (a word used for both Finns and Sámi); both the trolls and the 'Finns' were believed to be skilled in sorcery.[6]

There are four book-length studies on troll traditions worth mentioning; three of them consider both Old Norse material and later folklore. The last analyses later folklore accounts of trolls from a cultural and intertextual perspective in Swedish-speaking Finland.[7] One early work of 'trollology' is Elisabeth Hartmann's *Die Trollvorstellungen in den Sagen und Märchen der skandinavischen Völker* (1936).[8] Hartmann analysed troll traditions and identified distinctive characteristics of trolls in legends and folktales. She noticed that folk legends were primarily concentrated around the motifs of abductions by trolls and changeling traditions. The folktale types could be more diverse and included both trolls as opponents and trolls as helpers. In her view, the folk legends originated in real-life experiences, primarily as a result of fear, anxiety, depression, hallucinations, worries, dreams or altered states from disease or alcohol. The folktales, on the other hand, were unrealistic and purely fictive.[9]

But she also said that both genres built on some common traits, namely the size of the troll, its natural habitat and its hostility to man and to the church.

Another dissertation on trolls was written by Virgine Amilien: *Le troll et autres créatures surnaturelles dans les contes populaires norvégiens* (1996).[10] She interprets the Norwegian image of the troll and its habitat through the ages, from Old Norse sources to contemporary popular culture, and sees a link between the troll and the world of the dead. This was a place that in older Scandinavian traditions was located in the mountains. She says that the trolls inhabit the physical mountains, while the dead dwelt in the mountains of the imagination. She then adds the Christian Catholic division of the world of the dead into Paradise, Hell and Purgatory: the troll Otherworld is, she argues, where these three categories intermingle. The negative aspects of trolls are, Amilien claims, the folklore equivalent of the Devil. Earlier, trolls were associated with combat and sorcery. But she believes that other traits from pre-Christian times also survived the transition to Christianity. Amilien isolates four characteristics that are peculiar to the troll: the troll is noisy; it can have more or less than two eyes; it loves beauty and especially beautiful female humans; and it dies either by sunlight or by exploding through rage or anger.

In her dissertation *The Genre of Trolls* (2004), the folklorist Camilla Asplund Ingemark uses accounts from the folklore archive of the Swedish Literature Society in Helsinki to discuss nineteenth- and early twentieth-century trolls in Swedish-speaking Finland.[11] She examines the relationship between man and troll from different perspectives, and argues that interactions between trolls and humans are often characterized by conflict. This is, she continues, especially because trolls abduct women. But Asplund Ingemark also analyses more neutral interactions and even mutual assistance. She shows how conceptions of the troll can be related to Christian doctrine: both formed part of the same network of associations and could not be understood independently of one another. She also found that trolls, in her material, were more inclined to engage in dialogue with humans than vice versa. Genres are important and Asplund Ingemark uses theories of intertextuality to show a common store of expressions and the creation of supernatural images in folk belief. She argues that folk belief could be understood as a form of folk religion and that it is, therefore, misleading to separate official religion and folk belief when both deal with the same themes and structure them similarly.

The last book-length study to be mentioned here is folklorist and medievalist John Lindow's *Trolls: An Unnatural History* (2014).[12] *Trolls* is a cultural history arranged thematically by chapters, starting with 'The Earliest Trolls', moving on to 'Medieval Trolls', then 'Folklore Trolls' and 'Fairy-Tale Trolls and Trolls Illustrated'. After this, Lindow describes 'Trolls in Literature' and 'Trolls,

Children, Marketing, and Whimsy'. Lindow traces the development of trolls over time and space, and their relationship to specific cultural-historical moments and to specific media such as oral literature, medieval literature, folklore accounts and folk- and fairy tales, and then to artists' representation of trolls and trolls marketed for children and tourists. In his epilogue, Lindow discusses trolls as creatures of the social and virtual periphery and the general themes of what could be called 'trollishness', something that is disruptive, unpleasant and antisocial.

## The Word *Troll*

According to the *Oxford English Dictionary*, trolls did not enter the English language until the mid-nineteenth century. But *troll* was recorded before that in Shetland and Orkney dialects in the early seventeenth century, a legacy of the Viking Age.[13] If we look up the word 'troll' in *An Icelandic–English Dictionary* by Richard Cleasby and Gudbrand Vigfusson (1957), they give the following definition: 'A giant, fiend, demon, a generic term. The heathen creed knew of no "devil" but the troll; in mod. Dan[ish] *trold* includes any ghosts, goblins, imps and puny spirits, whereas the old Icel. *troll* conveys the notion of huge creatures, giants, Titans, mostly in an evil, but also in a good sense'. They go on to explain another connotation of the word relating to shape-shifting: 'a werewolf, one possessed by trolls or demons'. And then, they say the following about different types of trolls:

> In one single instance the trolls, strange to say, play a good part, viz. as being grateful and faithful; trolls and giants were the old dwellers on the earth, whom the gods drove out and extirpated, replacing them by man, yet a few remained haunting lonely places in wilderness and mountains; these trolls, if they meet with a good turn from man, are said to remain thankful for ever, and shew their gratitude [...] these milder notions chiefly apply to giantesses (*troll-konur*), for the troll-carles are seldom well spoken of: for trolls and giants are the older dwellers on earth.[14]

Their material is, as the title of the dictionary suggests, based on Old Norse sources. It is unclear what they mean be making the troll into a 'heathen' devil, as this is never explained.[15] Their inclusion of Danish as a modern point of reference is odd, as the word and the belief in trolls were far less common in Denmark than in Sweden or Norway. Trolls are one of the most common supernatural beings described in folklore accounts from central and southern

Sweden and from all Norway, as well as Iceland and the Swedish-speaking parts of Finland. The Danes knew of trolls, of course, but it was more common to speak of the *ellefolk* or the *bjærgfolk*, the hidden folk in general, or supernatural beings living in mountains.[16]

Trolls were well known as far back as the Viking Age. The word is found in Viking poetry and is found in many Icelandic sagas.[17] The word does not seem to appear in the oldest or Viking Age runic inscriptions.[18] However, trolls can be found on later, medieval runic inscriptions with magical formulas. One example found on a piece of wood from Bergen in Norway, dated to c.1335, had the following charm carved in runes: *Ríst ek bótrúnar, ríst ek bjargrúnar, einfalt við alfum, tvífalt við trollum, þrífalt við þurs[um]* ('I cut runes of help; I cut runes of protection; once against the elves, twice against the trolls, thrice against the ogres').[19]

But what does 'troll' mean? Is there a broadly accepted etymology? Sadly, no. Many theories have been proposed, including derivation from verbs such as 'tread', 'to rush away angrily', 'roll (as with ball lightning)' and 'enchant'. It has also been proposed that 'troll' is derived from nouns meaning 'stout person' or even 'whore'.[20] The word 'troll' could also be used for troublesome people and animals, as well as for many things associated with magic and sorcery. We might go so far as to say that a troll cannot be defined. It is in their nature to be elusive and indefinable. The word 'troll' certainly has different meanings in the Scandinavian languages, dialects and traditions. 'Troll' is still, and has been since medieval times, associated with magic and sorcery; *trollmannen* or *trollkarlen* (literally meaning 'the troll man') are, for example, the Norwegian and Swedish words for a wizard. To enchant or carry out magic is described with the verb *trolla/trylla*.[21] This link can be seen in medieval law texts, for example in Old Norse-Icelandic law codes indicating that it is forbidden to have supper with a troll. But it is also forbidden to sit out (a magical practice) for the sake of *vekja upp troll* ('evoking trolls').[22] A common word for a 'witch' in Sweden was *trollkäring* or *trollkona*, both meaning 'troll woman'. One clear example of this is the 1541 Swedish translation of the Bible. In the Book of Exodus 22:18, it is stated: *En trollkona skall du inte låta leva* ('Thou shall not suffer a troll woman to live'). In 1668 this became the law in Sweden and tragically led to the witch hunts and the execution of hundreds of women accused of being witches.

The word 'troll' could also be used for inedible berries, then called respectively *trollbär/trollbær* ('troll berry') in Sweden and Norway. Trolls are also to be found in some place-names, for example *Trollhättan* ('the troll cap'), *Trollekulla* ('the troll mound'), *Trollberget* ('the troll mountain') or *Trollfjorden* ('the troll fjord'). If we look at accounts from the folklore archives, describing folk life in Scandinavia in the nineteenth and early twentieth centuries, then 'troll' seems to be a generic term for different supernatural beings. These may be of different sizes, solitary or social, real or imagined. It could include anything from ghosts and *vättar/vittra/rå/huldrefolk/ellefolk* (hidden folk) to giants. In this chapter, I am using 'troll' to refer to supernatural beings inhabiting the wilderness with this name.

## A Brief Look at the Old Norse Sources

The word *troll/trǫll* is only mentioned twice in the *Poetic Edda*, in the poems *Vǫluspá*, stanza 40, and *Helgakviða Hiǫrvarðssonar* (prose introduction). It is also used in Snorri Sturluson's *Prose Edda*, and can be found in some skaldic poems. The trolls encountered in these mythological sources—concerning the divine world, heroes and some legendary kings—are normally female, or they are described as a group. They are hostile and if some of them can be described as skilled in magic or even wise, they are not positive beings. Martin Arnold argues that the 'mythico-legendary troll is an exotic, even erotic, social other, one that is instinctually and destructively magical'. He goes on to argue that they could be understood as the pre-patriarchal female.[23]

If we look at another type of material, the Icelandic saga literature of the thirteenth and fourteenth centuries, we are transported to events and interactions among humans. Here 'troll' is far more frequent, but it is usually found in insults or used as a signifier of danger, wrath, envy or contempt; the protagonists encounter few supernatural trolls. However, in the genre known as *fornaldarsögur* ('the legendary sagas'), trolls and their interaction with humans is a recurrent theme. This even led some eighteenth- and early nineteenth-century critics to use the derogative expression *trollsögur* ('troll sagas') for the *fornaldarsögur*. It seems, as Arnold points out, that trolls begin to occupy the imagination of the tradition bearers and authors of the sagas, just before and after the fall of the Icelandic Free State in 1262.[24] Social, political and economic realignment led to violence and upheavals, a suitable backdrop for the troll to come to centre-stage.

Trolls and their otherness reside in the margins, but they can also lurk at the heart of a story and be ascribed to certain individuals or disturbing occurrences. A troll was not positive in the Old Norse and medieval Scandinavian sources; it stands for disorder, tension and danger. The following categories can be discerned for trolls in the medieval literature: trolls as pejorative metaphor(s); folklore trolls; humans compared to trolls; trolls used for ghosts and evil spirits; trolls used for monsters and vile creatures; trolls for (supernatural) enemies of the church; strangers; and other miscellaneous cases.[25] The medieval literature of Sweden and Denmark includes more translations than the literature of medieval Norway or Iceland. In many of these Swedish and Danish translations, trolls are used for various Latin words such as *bestia*, *demonum* or *monstrum*.[26]

## Troll Traditions in Sixteenth- to Twentieth-Century Scandinavia

As I noted earlier, trolls can be found all over Scandinavia, from the Middle Ages and later in rural pre-industrial areas, with the biggest concentration of stories in Sweden and Norway. One early text that mentions trolls is *Historia de gentibus septentrionalibus* ('A Description of the Northern Peoples') by the exiled Swedish Catholic archbishop Olaus Magnus, printed in Rome in 1555. The collecting of folklore from oral traditions began sporadically in the sixteenth century in Scandinavia. It gained momentum and became a national endeavour in the nineteenth and early twentieth century when specialized folklore archives were established in the Nordic countries.[27] The collecting of folklore continues, though written texts (emails, digital questionnaires) are more common in contemporary collecting.[28] Trolls have been a part of the stories from the beginning, albeit under different forms.

Scandinavian folklore archives contain thousands of descriptions of and folk legends about trolls. These beings are sometimes helpful, sometimes neutral, and in most cases threatening or harmful. Trolls appear in different contexts. When someone encounters a troll, or says that they have, factors such as the weather, the landscape and time of day play an important part. Mental state also matters. Trolls are more likely to be encountered in moments of stress or fatigue. Trolls are typically not encountered during daylight or in the middle of a community; they are liminal beings, thriving at the edge of society, in the wilderness and under the cover of night.

As we have seen, troll traditions circulated in folk culture as early as the Middle Ages, but are better documented in later times. One crucial factor was the increased interest, and the documentation that followed the establishment of folklore archives. In her dissertation on trolls, Elisabeth Hartmann usefully distinguishes between eastern and western Nordic troll legends. By comparing folk legends and folktales, it seems clear that the western traditions, that is the Norwegian sources, contain more negative portrayals of trolls. In Norway, they can be interpreted, in the words of Hartmann, as *Schrek- und Dunkelheitswesen* ('Supernatural beings of horror and darkness').[29] Norwegians usually referred to more social supernatural beings like *huldrefolk*, the hidden folk: see Danish *ellefolk* and *bjærgfolk*, the Swedish *vättar* and *vittra* or the Icelandic *huldufólk*.

Many trolls are described as being old or ancient. Some helped form the landscape and have lived there from a bygone age. They inhabit caves, rocks and hills. Sometimes their dwellings are said to be the forests, the mountains or the wilderness. A few trolls live in buildings and castles. It is rare for trolls to inhabit lakes or the ocean, though there are stories of sea or lake trolls. If we were to generalize, the following places seem to be most common in the different parts of Scandinavia: mid-Sweden—mountains and forests; south Sweden and Denmark—barrows, hills and grave mounds; Norway—alpine areas and the high mountains. The legends also reflect economic differences between southern and northern Sweden. We find much about brewing, baking and grinding of flour in the agricultural south. In the north, stretching through mid-Sweden, pasture farming dominated: cattle (cows or goats) were taken to the shieling pastures every summer.[30] The same type of stock farming was common in Norway (*sætertradisjon*).[31] This is reflected in legends about the hidden folk's cattle. Stories of trolls stealing food and being killed by lightning are more typical of the south. In the north, many legends say that a person could become ill from contact with one of the hidden folk. In both the north and the south, legends of people being taken or spirited away are common; in the north it is usually into the hills (*vittertagen*) and in the south it is usually into a mountain (*bergtagen*).[32]

The physical appearance of trolls varies. Some are ordinary-looking, like human beings, some ugly or misshapen, some fair or enticing. Some are said to be as big as a giant and some are very small in stature like a child or infant. In the more wondrous folktales, trolls can have several heads (normally a magical number such as three or nine), one enormous eye, and are often described as large, clumsy and grotesque.[33] Trolls are shape-shifters and can appear as animals, natural phenomena or everyday objects. Many are invisible. Most trolls talk and interact with humans, even though their speech might be in verse or might contain paraphrases or strange and archaic words. In the following legend from Västergötland the word 'kneppa' is archaic and has to do with cutting something:

> There were many trolls at Bagle mountain in Hovs parish. When they were baking, they used to ask for yeast at the clergy house. The crofters, working at that clergy house, had a troubling autumn during harvest. Time went by and their grain were about to fall to the ground. They did not have time to cut it, because they had to work at the clergy house all through the weeks. One night, one of the crofters fell asleep and heard noises, as if someone was working, from the field, and he thought he heard someone saying, in a chanting

voice: 'Cut of and make bindings, cut of and make bindings' ('Kneppa å gôr bånn, kneppa å gôr bånn'). When morning came, he saw that the grain had been cut and was hung up in neat bindings. It was the trolls who had done so.[34]

If we look at the geographical distribution of troll legends, stories and beliefs in Sweden, it is clear that they are frequently found in Götaland and Svealand, and in Swedish-speaking Finland.[35] Bengt af Klintberg's catalogue of Swedish folk legends has 102 legend-types for Swedish trolls (K1–150; K171–180).[36] These are divided into the following main categories: friendly coexistence; bread from the trolls; breach of norms activates trolls; loans between trolls and humans; trolls and the sign of the cross; celebration and transportation among trolls; person can see invisible trolls; trolls suffer loss or damage; how to avoid being taken by trolls; taken into troll mountain (*bergtagen*); released from troll mountain; and trolls and thunder. In addition to af Klintberg's 102 troll types, there are seventeen changeling legend-types. These usually deal with trolls: having a changeling; changeling is treated badly; and changeling is tricked into revealing himself. The stories about abduction and changelings are, obviously, characterized by conflict between man and troll. But sometimes, albeit in very rare cases, someone who is taken into the troll mountain is on friendly terms with the trolls. One folk legend from Bohuslän offers an example:

> A girl, whom the mountain trolls had taken into the mountain, later returned to her home. She visited the mountain trolls on several occasions. One time, her mother decided to follow her. When she arrived at the mountain, she could hear how the girl talked with the mountain troll children, and that they answered, but she could not see anything. When the woman stood there her daughter suddenly disappeared. The priest could not do anything. But after eight days, the girl returned to her home. She said that she had a good time, because the trolls were wealthy and had much silver and copper. As soon as the girl had her confirmation (affirmation of baptism), she stopped visiting the trolls.[37]

In this folk legend it seems that the girl visited the trolls of her own free will. In Scandinavian folk belief, trolls are known to steal infants and replace them with one of their own.[38] The changeling is usually old and only seems to be a child. The stories rarely say that the troll changeling looks that much different in appearance from the normal infant. There are various ways in which the changeling is eventually deceived into betraying their age.

The fear of abduction by trolls actually served a function. Before baptism a person was considered unprotected. Even a mother who had just given birth was considered impure and had to be 'churched' in a special purificatory rite. Another important ritual was confirmation at the age of fourteen, when an adolescent became responsible for their Christian belief. These were church-sponsored rituals that instilled the importance of the church in individual and community life. They were meant to protect the individual from the Devil: supernatural beings such as trolls were a part of his host or worked, according to the church, as illusions that conspired against Christianity.[39] A belief in trolls and legends about them could be used to reinforce this notion and the importance of being a good member of society.

Occasionally the troll is thought of as a kindly helper, benevolent if perhaps stupid. But most often the troll is a vile creature. The same double nature may be found in stories of other supernatural beings such as giants or dwarfs. But the Otherworld can be interpreted as an embodiment of an ideal society used by people to redefine themselves and their own interactions with each other. Trolls are social beings and their own Otherworld reflects human society. I agree with Asplund Ingemark who, in her dissertation, argues that 'the troll and the supernatural sphere may be viewed as instruments for thinking about one's identity and place in the world, and for orienting oneself in a larger, complex reality. Simultaneously, the otherworld may represent an idealized version of the human community if it possesses qualities human society lacks but nevertheless needs'.[40]

In Norwegian folklore, trolls are frequently described as a group of solitary supernatural beings that are very large, similar to giants. In Norwegian folktales the trolls are depicted as grotesque and destructive. This is in contrast to the trolls usually described in Swedish and Danish folklore, who are social beings, living in families and typically not larger than humans. But we do find horrible trolls in Swedish and Danish folklore as well. One expression in Swedish is *ett stort, styggt troll* ('a large, nasty troll') and a common saying is *När man talar om trollen, så står de i farstun* ('When you speak about trolls, they will appear at your doorstep'). This is of course an equivalent of the English idiom 'Speak of the Devil, and he shall appear', and can be used when you are talking about someone and that person suddenly appears. In Scandinavia, those compared to a troll are those who with their arrival create an eerie, serendipitous interaction.

## Good Trolls: Social Beings and Friendly Neighbours

Some trolls gave advice about harvesting, brewing or handicraft. There are also stories about humans who help trolls, by providing food or firewood for troll children or by lending the trolls clothes, flour, beer or even silver. Trolls could be 'good to think with'. In the words of John Lindow and Timothy R. Tangherlini, 'The attributes of the supernatural outsiders contrast with those of human insiders and thereby help in the process of affirming group identity'.[41] Trolls as a category to think with offered the distinction between one's own group and everyone outside that group. In this section, I will look more closely at non-negative stories about troll–human interaction.

One category for trolls in Klintberg's catalogue is 'friendly coexistence'. This, together with some of the other legends, gives us a clear indication that many tales treat trolls as social beings. The whole 'K' section of the catalogue refers to trolls and hidden folk. The biggest difference between these groups is that trolls were predominantly believed to live in mountains and hills, while hidden folk lived in subterranean dwellings. Both trolls and hidden folk are nature spirits, who could form families and who (usually) live in larger groups, just as humans do. Both trolls and hidden folk could be human size and could make themselves invisible or change their appearance. Both are a mirror of human society. Some even have kings and therefore a hierarchical society. Sometimes they organize festivities where they sing and dance. Trolls marry and have children. Sometimes they are portrayed as smiths and farmers, sometimes they do textile work, sometimes they churn butter, brew beer and bake. In many stories about them, they have domesticated animals, dogs and cats and cattle. The cattle owned by hidden folk or trolls could be caught if someone threw iron over them. These animals were believed to be better than normal animals: stronger, with more milk and so on. But not all stories about troll cattle are good. Take the following example from Värmland in Sweden:

> Two maids happened to be out with their cattle late at night. A troll appeared and shouted, 'Kersti and Kari, you must go home, it is late in the evening!' Then it was time for the trolls to bring out their cattle. They went down to the stream and watered their cattle. After that, their cattle pastured in the fields and around. But it was not noticeable, that they had taken anything. The grain, where their cattle had pastured, was then of little use.[42]

This folk legend probably reinforced the notion that the cattle must be brought back home before night-time. It was a common belief that the night belonged to the supernatural. Many—but not all—trolls were turned to stone when touched by sunlight. Supernatural beings were for the most part believed to be a threat to human society. Therefore, the best protection against trolls or hidden folk were Christian symbols or words from the Bible, hymn books or other Christian words or names for Christ and God; in Catholic times, the names of saints and the Virgin Mary also served.

There is an unpublished collection of troll stories in the Uppsala folklore archive, with the label *Trollens bak* ('Trolls baking bread', though as we shall see, the file goes beyond this). The file consists of 270 accounts from the Swedish folklore archives in Uppsala, Lund, Gothenburg and Stockholm.[43] Trolls interact with and reward humans for assisting them or lending things. The most common form of reward is a loaf of bread, sometimes with butter on top, or a generous amount of wine or beer. But this is not only given as a reward, but also out of generosity. In nine accounts, trolls present bread for someone who is hungry and who wishes that they had some bread. Some stories mention a troll smith. If someone helped him, he could reward that person with wondrous smith work. A scythe or another tool made by a troll smith was always sharp. However, if one looked at its edge it became dull and worthless, as in the following story from Västergötland:

> A farm hand in Härna had received a scythe from a troll smith. It never became dull, even if the farmer cut with it in stone. But then he looked in its edge and it turned to bone.[44]

In unusual cases, trolls could be honourable. According to one belief utterance from Mark parish in Västergötland, a troll smith lived in Smedjeberg ('Smith mountain'). He worked for the humans in the area. If one placed a piece of iron and some coins outside a cave there, then the finished work was ready to pick up the following day. But if one placed too few coins, the smith wouldn't touch the iron. If one placed too much, the smith only took the coins needed for the work and left the rest.[45] When a troll returned with something they had borrowed, it was usually of greater value than what they had been lent. Occasionally they also gave a reward to the farmer with a valuable agricultural tip that increased their crops. The following example from Västergötland shows humans and trolls seemingly living in relative harmony:

> The trolls lived in a shed and bought bread from the folk. One day the troll woman asked: 'Can I do something else for you?' They asked the troll woman to spin flax. She asked if it should be plied two or three times. The farm wife said that it should be two. When she got the yarn back it was spun as fine as a spider's web.[46]

Six of the accounts in the aforementioned collection speak of trolls who borrow beer or brewing equipment (usually a kettle or wooden container) and later return with a reward. See for example the following from Värmland:

> The trolls in Vistbo mountain used to borrow drink from the farms. They used to get it in wooden containers with a wood band around. When they returned the containers, they always had an iron band around them and they were filled with good and strong brew.[47]

Another account informs us: 'In Botilsäter in Värmland, one informant said that at a certain location in the area, the door was opened late at night and a voice said: "Can I borrow the kettle, then place it outside". Within eight days the troll returned with the kettle and a jug of snaps [strong liquor]'.[48] Some accounts speak of humans who repair tools for the trolls. If, goes a well-known tale, a human helps a troll with something, usually by mending broken tools, a reward will be given. It is often a broken peel that is fixed, and freshly baked bread is given by the troll in thanks. Two accounts, the first from the island of Öland on the east coast of Sweden, the second from Västergötland, serve as examples of this kind of positive coexistence:

> An old woman in Lunda saw a hearth broom lying on a hill. She mended it and returned it. The next time she passed the hill, she found a good wheat cake lying there.[49]
>
> A farmhand ploughed outside a mountain when an old woman came out from the mountain and asked him if she could borrow a peel. When he complied with her request and later returned to get it back, he found a big, nice and freshly baked wheat cake as thanks for the loan.[50]

When a troll gives food as payment the food causes no harm and can be described as delicious. However, in some cases, the troll bread is just an illusion (coal, crumbs, wood shavings or similar), or can make the person or animal who ate it sick. In six of the accounts, a farmer says, to no one in particular, that he wishes for help and promises his cow or best ox as a reward. During the night he gets the work done and finds that the cow (or ox) is missing in the morning. This story, known already as 'The Old Man and Death' in Aesop's *Fables*, lives on in our 'be careful what you wish for'. In Aesop's version, an old man had chopped up wood and was carrying the heavy load on his back. Halfway back he felt exhausted and cried out in desperation that Death could come and take him. Death appears, ready to take the old man's life, but the man begs for mercy and is spared.

There are more miscellaneous examples from the collection mentioned above that describe trolls as social beings. They live close to and interact with humans:

> A small child was found in the fen and the farmers brought it with them to their house. Then they heard its mother calling, and brought it back. The morning after, they found a silver bell outside their door. (Värmland)[51]
>
> Queen Hacka [a legendary troll woman] had once farmed on the mountain Omberg. Those who wanted to settle there got four cups of grain and a hoe to farm with from her. (Östergötland)[52]
>
> A fine-looking woman came to a farmhouse and wanted to warm herself by the fire. The farmer gave her a slice of meat on his knife. She tried to take it three times, then he gave it to her on a piece of stick instead. She said, 'Tomorrow, you will shoot my big boar.' The day after, the farmer encountered and shot a great bear. (Trolls could refer to a bear as a pig or boar; Hälsingland)[53]

Another example of coexistence from Skåne in southern Sweden:

> The people of Fostorp village were on good terms with the trolls. The trolls used to borrow bread from the people. When a troll peel broke, they placed them outside their mounds. Someone in the village repaired it. The trolls then offered bread and other goods for the service.[54]

If there is a competition between humans and trolls or giants, humans usually win because they outsmart the supernatural being. In some cases, they get a little help from a rival. In the following example, collected in 1920 by Ola O. Hola in Norway, we hear of a man who is helped by a troll woman in a competition against a *jutul* (a giant or troll):

> A *jutul* and a man once competed in mowing. The *jutul* was to mow first, and the man was to walk behind him. But the man got something from a troll woman, which he smeared on his scythe so that it would stay sharp. Soon the man caught up with the *jutul*. 'Why don't you whet your scythe?' asked the *jutul*. 'Mow today, whet tomorrow', said the man. And so, he beat the *jutul*. (Nordmøre)[55]

Other examples of positive interactions between humans and trolls can be found in Swedish-speaking Finland. In one account, a hunter is blocking the path of a supernatural wedding procession and refuses to leave his spot when the troll asks him to move aside. The interaction leads to angry threats before the hunter finally moves to the side. He then realizes that the troll had saved his life, because he would have been trampled to death if he had stayed![56] When the trolls offer money for human services, it can be a hefty sum. The sudden acquisition of wealth was then, as it is now, a prominent feature in many stories. One example of this originates from Sweden (Hälsingland):

> A farm maiden helped the trolls to dry their clothes for their babies. The trolls rewarded her by placing a silver chain on her dung hill spade, and after that she always had luck with the cattle.[57]

Another legend describing a different kind of reward comes from Halland in Sweden:

> At one time, a farmer's wife found a small child lying and screaming on the ground when she was out in the wild. She took pity on the small child, picked it up and breastfed it. Soon a troll woman appeared and said that it was her child. The troll woman was grateful for the act of kindness and as a way of showing her appreciation, she promised the farmer's wife that her future children would be stronger than other humans.[58]

This legend was probably meant to explain why a certain family featured many strong individuals.

There are some stories about generous trolls from Västergötland in Sweden. A couple of stories say that the people of Ramberg got along well with the trolls living in Ramberget. They even borrowed money from them. One informant, born in 1848, recounted the following:

> My grandfather had travelled far and was destitute and lived in poverty. And then he looked for employment at Ramberg. Trolls lived in those mountains. And he borrowed money from them, but they said that he did not have to pay them back because they were about to leave the mountain. So, I do not think these trolls were wicked. The trolls moved to Halle- and Hunne Mountain.[59]

Generous trolls that helped the poor are also known from Tämta parish nearby. Poor people there used to spin flax and hemp yarn during the winter, and place it in a woodshed in the evening for rich trolls in the mountains. The morning after, there was their wage, and new working material: the yarn they had placed there was gone.[60]

But even if there are examples of friendly or neutral trolls, many humans still fear them and therefore the exchange of assistance or rewards does not always go smoothly. In many cases the rewards given are not fully understood until it is too late. For example, the reward given could be something that at first looked like useless leaves or wood carvings. The person believes it to be worthless and throws it away. They realize too late that it was actually silver or gold.[61]

## Conclusion

It might seem like a hopeless task to show that trolls were not all bad. After all, today 'troll' is a slang word on the internet used for someone who is purposely seeking conflict. When we do find supernatural trolls, it is usually in popular culture where they are portrayed as angry and witless monsters: for example in *Dungeons and Dragons*, or movies based on books such as *Harry Potter* or *The Hobbit*. However, there is, as I have shown above, more to trolls than that.[62] When I started writing this chapter, I wanted to describe as much of the interaction between trolls and humans as possible. That, I quickly realized, would have required at least a book-length study, if not several volumes. Earlier studies on trolls have focused on their more negative connotations and only mention the neutral, and friendly, aspects in passing. This is natural, as most sources do, indeed, describe trolls as negative and disruptive beings. However, there are also examples of the opposite, when trolls are neighbours, for good and for bad. For this reason, the title of my chapter is a nod towards Hayao Miyazaki's famous anime film *My Neighbour Totoro*, where his *Totoro* is a Japanese play on the word 'troll'. Totoro is a good-hearted nature spirit that occupies the imagination of the young protagonists.

But are trolls really good neighbours? Not in most cases. But this could also be said of human neighbours. Trolls embody this contrast, the different social tensions, conflicts and interactions that take place between humans and the uncertainty in meeting and interacting with unfamiliar people with different agendas. Trolls are liminal beings and they can be said to represent a topsy-turvy worldview. They symbolize and represent danger. They threaten human society at different levels. Trolls are therefore, in most cases, to be feared. This danger intrudes on the established order, momentarily snatching control away from humans. Trolls inhabit a counter-world, with physical and psychological anxieties around untamed and unfamiliar spaces. But the trolls' world is, in the folk imagination, a space for controlling, projecting and thereby reinforcing norms and taboos. They function as symbolic keepers of boundaries and limits. In many folklore legends and beliefs, the trolls take steps to correct errant behaviour. In other cases they enforce norms and can threaten or force humans to act. It is therefore safe to say that troll stories help encourage proper conduct. What is most distinctive about trolls in the folklore accounts, compared to humans? Trolls live and are normally encountered outside or on the borders of the human community, at night or at certain times of the year.

In his book on medieval Icelandic trolls, Ármann Jakobsson argues that trolls are categorically alien, and that they are 'seen as an essential part of us: residing within us, like a menacing double or an uncanny ancestral core'.[63] John Lindow, on the other hand, writes that Scandinavian legends about trolls are as 'ambivalent about the ultimate religious status of trolls as they are about their dealing with the human community (sometimes helpful, sometimes threatening)', and that the trolls to some degree 'are like nature, or like life itself'.[64] Trolls seem to blur categories. They can be sociable and exist in 'friendly coexistence' with man. But most disrupt order and are dangerous or unpleasant. They are as wild and unpredictable as nature itself. If trolls remind us of humans, they also embody the wilderness, the unknown and otherness. In a way, they are what we are not, and still they are what we are, or what we do not want to be—and paradoxically, as we have seen here, some are what we want to be too.

## Notes

1. Google search 25 Jul 2022 11:10.
2. G.W. Knutsen and A.I. Riisøy, 'Trolls and Witches', *Arv* 63 (2007), 1–69 at 34.
3. Most material used here reflects rural life in the mid and later parts of the nineteenth century. Scandinavia during the mid-nineteenth century had roughly 7.5 million inhabitants. Of these, 3.5 million lived in Sweden, 1.5 million in Denmark, the same number in Norway, and around 1 million in the Swedish-speaking provinces of Finland. In addition, around 60,000 lived in Iceland and 20,000 on the Faeroe Islands. See R. Kvideland and H.K. Sehmsdorf, *Scandinavian Folk Belief and Legend* (Minneapolis–London: University of Minnesota Press, 1988), 3.
4. At this time Finland was a part of Sweden, Iceland was a part of Denmark, and Norway was in a union with Denmark with Denmark as the dominant power.
5. See T. Kuusela, 'The Giants and the Critics: A Brief History of Old Norse "Giantology"', *Folklore and Old Norse Mythology*, eds Frog and J. Ahola (Helsinki: The Kalevala Society, 2021), 471–98.
6. See A. Vídalin, 'The Man Who Seemed Like a Troll: Racism in Old Norse Literature', *Margins, Monsters, Deviants: Alterities in Old Norse Literature and Culture*, eds R. Merkelbach et al. (Turnhout: Brepols, 2020), 215–38.
7. For trolls in the Old Norse material, see for example K. Schulz, *Riesen: von Wissenshütern und Wildnisbewohnern in Edda und Saga* (Heidelberg: Winter, 2004), or Á. Jakobsson, *The Troll Inside You: Paranormal Activity in the Medieval North* (Reykjavík:

Punctum, 2017). There are similarly some books on trolls written by scholars for the general public, i.e. J.-Ö. Swahn and B. Lundwall, *Trollen, deras liv, land och legender* (Stockholm: Bonnier, 1984); E. Schön, *Troll och människa: gammal svensk folktro* (Stockholm: Natur & kultur, 1999); O. Bø, *Trollmakter og godvette: overnaturlege vesen i norsk folketru* (Oslo: Det Norske Samlaget, 1987); B. Henriksson, *Trollen och vi: folkliga föreställningar i Svenskfinland* (Vasa: Scriptum, 2012).

8. E. Hartmann, *Die Trollvorstellungen in den Sagen und Märchen der skandinavischen Völker* (Berlin: Tübinger germanistische, 1936). There is an unpublished English adaptation of Hartmann by Ronald M. James, which draws on her work complemented by the folklorist Sven Liljeblad's comments, and includes initial and concluding sections on how the troll diffused to England and North America: R.M. James, *Trolls: From Scandinavia to Dam Dolls, Tolkien, and Harry Potter*, unpublished manuscript (2014).

9. Hartmann, *Die Trollvorstellungen*, 77, 134; 143. In this, she was clearly inspired by her mentor, the Swedish folklorist Carl Wilhelm von Sydow.

10. V. Amilien, *Le troll et autres créatures surnaturelles dans le contes populaires norvégiens* (Paris: Berg International, 1996).

11. C. Asplund Ingemark, *The Genre of Trolls: The Case of a Finland-Swedish Folk Belief Tradition* (Åbo: Åbo Akademi University Press, 2004).

12. J. Lindow, *Trolls: An Unnatural History* (London: Reaktion Books, 2014). There is also Rudolf Simek, *Trolle: ihre Geschichte von der nordischen Mythologie bis zum internet* (Köln: Böhlau, 2018). Unfortunately, I was not able to consult his work while writing this article.

13. Compare, for example, with *trow* in modern dialect.

14. R. Cleasby and G. Vigfusson, *An Icelandic–English Dictionary* (Oxford: Clarendon, 1957), 641.

15. Martin Arnold questions this phrase and wonders whether it means that the authors suggested the troll was semantically distinct from other supernatural beings. I agree that this can hardly be justified by the textual sources—though there are some more hostile branches of families of different supernatural beings, for example giants; see M. Arnold, '*Hvat er tröll nema þat*? The Cultural History of the Troll', *The Shadow-Walkers: Jacob Grimm's Mythology of the Monstrous*, ed. T. Shippey (Tempe: Arizona University, Brepols, 2005), 111–55 at 114.

16. Here the six volumes of Danish folk legends by Evald Tang Kristensen, the most proficient folklore collector in Denmark in the nineteenth century, prove interesting. Trolls are only mentioned a few times, compared to other supernatural beings that are mentioned time and time again. But the word *bjærgfolk*, literally mountain folks, has a whole section. These can, of course, be interpreted as trolls, but are made up of several types of supernatural beings: Evald Tang Kristensen, *Danske sagn som de har lydt i folkemunde: udelukkende efter utrykte kilder* (Aarhus: Jydsk Forlags-Forretning, 1892–1901).

17. Many of the sagas certainly go back to oral traditions; see for example G. Sigurðsson, *The Medieval Icelandic Saga and Oral Tradition: A Discourse on Method*, translated by N. Jones, Milman Parry Collection of Oral Literature (Cambridge, MA: Harvard University Press, 2004).

18. See for example the dictionary by L. Peterson, *Nordiskt runnamnslexikon* (Uppsala: Språk- och folkminnesinstitutet, 2002).

19. Inscription N B257 in Samnordisk runtextdatabas 2020, Institutionen för Nordiska språk, Uppsala universitet. http://kulturarvsdata.se/uu/srdb/c0162b72-0be1-4841-be92-f2a618300db9.
20. T.H. Wilbur, 'Troll, an Etymological Note', *Scandinavian Studies* 30, 3 (1958), 137–39; Lindow, *Trolls*, 11; Tommy Kuusela, *'Hallen var lyst i helig frid': Krig och fred mellan gudar och jättar i en fornnordisk hallmiljö*, PhD thesis (Stockholm: Stockholms universitet, 2017), 27–28.
21. For a study in English that gives a good overview of how the word troll is used for *trolldómr*, Scandinavian witchcraft and other magical practices, see C. Raudvere, 'Trolldómr in Early Medieval Scandinavia', *Witchcraft in Europe III: The Middle Ages*, eds K. Jolly et al. (London: Athlone, 2002), 73–169.
22. R. Keyser and P.A. Munch, *Norges gamle love indtil 1387* (Christiania, 1846–48), vol. 1, 19, 351, 362, 372, vol. 2, 323; Á. Jakobsson, 'The Trollish Acts of Þorgrímr the Witch: The Meanings of Troll and Ergi in Medieval Iceland', *Saga Book* 32 (2008), 39–68; Knutsen and Riisøy, 'Trolls'.
23. Arnold, *'Hvat er tröll'*, 123.
24. Ibid., 129.
25. Schulz, *Riesen*; Á. Jakobsson, 'Vad är ett troll? Betydelsen av ett isländskt medeltidsbegrepp', *Saga och sed* (2008), 101–17.
26. Lindow, *Trolls*, 44.
27. See the contributions in D. Bula and S. Laime, eds, *Mapping the History of Folklore Studies: Centres, Borderlands and Shared Spaces* (Newcastle-upon-Tyne: Cambridge Scholars Publishing, 2017).
28. I have met individuals who claim to have seen trolls. The description of these trolls seems to be inspired by how trolls are portrayed in popular culture rather than older folk traditions.
29. Hartmann, *Die Trollvorstellungen*, 52.
30. B. af Klintberg, ed., *The Types of the Swedish Folk Legend* (Helsinki: Suomalainen Tiedeakatemia, 2010), 169.
31. S. Solheim, *Norsk sætertradisjon* (Oslo: Aschehoug, 1952).
32. See H.F. Feilberg, *Bjærgtagen: studie over en gruppe træk fra nordisk alfetro* (København: Schønberg, 1910). For *bergtagning*, see motif F375 'Mortals as captives in fairyland'; in Klintberg, ed., *The Types*, it is catalogued as legend-type K111–30. The motif of abduction into an otherworldly realm is also known for other supernatural beings; see Tommy Kuusela, 'Spirited Away by the Female Forest Spirit in Swedish Folk Belief', *Folklore* 131 (2020), 159–79.
33. It is this image of the trolls that inspired the trolls of many late nineteenth- and early twentieth-century artists, such as the Norwegians Erik Werenskiold and Theodor Kittelsen or the Swedes John Bauer and Elsa Beskow.
34. K. Olofsson, *Folkliv och folkminne i Ås, Vedens och Gäsene härader* i Västergötland (Göteborg: Elanders, 1931), 54–55.
35. Götaland and Svealand are made up of the following territories: Småland, Blekinge, Östergötland, Västergötland, Västmanland, Närke, Södermanland, Uppland, Gästrikland.
36. Klintberg, ed., *The Types*.
37. D. Arill, 'Folksägner från norra Bohuslän', *Folksägen och folkdiktning i västra Sverige*, eds D. Arill et al. (Göteborg: Wald. Sachrissons boktryckeri, 1923), 13–30 at 16.

38. Motif F321.1 'Changeling'. Trolls can be replaced with other hidden folk in this context, usually depending on region.
39. Kvideland and Sehmsdorf, *Scandinavian Folk Belief*, 11. Each transition worked as a rite of passage and before each change, the person was vulnerable as a target for supernatural beings.
40. Asplund Ingemark, *The Genre of Trolls*, 86.
41. J. Lindow and T.R. Tangherlini, 'Nordic Legends and the Question of Identity', *Scandinavian Studies* 67 (1995), 1–7 at 2.
42. C.-M. Bergstrand, *Värmlandssägner* (Göteborg: Gumpert, 1948).
43. The greatest number of troll stories (131 of 270) in this collection refers to ATU 113A 'Pan Is Dead' (previously known as AaTh 113A 'King of the Cats Is Dead'). The 'cat' in these stories is a troll.
44. Archival: ULMA (Dialect and Folklore archives in Uppsala), 111:492.
45. ULMA 1452:5.
46. ULMA 3068:1.
47. Archival: The Nordic Museum 26793.
48. ULMA 4097.
49. ULMA 5385.
50. ULMA 1838:6.
51. ULMA 1811:2.
52. ULMA 1836:1.
53. ULMA 2671: 1.
54. J. Göransson, *Skånes landsbygd: historisk och arkeologisk beskrifning* (Malmö: Emil Jansson, 1904), 91. Editors' note: for British examples, see Chapter 4 of the current volume.
55. Kvideland and Sehmsdorf, *Scandinavian Folk Belief*, 306. Originally in E. Langset, *Segner, gåter, folketru frå Nordmør* (Oslo: Norsk folkeminnelag, 1948), 47–48.
56. Example from Asplund Ingemark, *The Genre of Trolls*, 107. The story can be found in the folklore archive of The Swedish Literature Society in Finland; archival: SLS 220, 240–42.
57. A. Hjelmström, 'Från Delsbo: seder och bruk, folktro och sägner, person- och tidsbilder upptecknade', *Bidrag till kännedom om de svenska landsmålen ock svenskt folkliv* 11, 4 (1896), 37.
58. J. Kalén, 'Folksägner från norra Halland', *Folksägen och folkdiktning i västra Sverige*, eds D. Arill et al. (Göteborg: Wald. Sachrissons, 1923), 61–88 at 68.
59. H. Olsson, *Folkliv och folkdikt i Vättle härad under 1800-talet* (Uppsala: Almqvist & Wiksell, 1945), 79.
60. Olofsson, *Folkliv och folkminne*, 53.
61. See Klintberg, ed., *The Types*, legend-type K191–193: V11–14: 'Treasure is transformed'.
62. One famous literary motif is that trolls live under bridges, something that can also be found in some folktales. But there is little of this in folk belief, even though a bridge serves as a border and liminal space.
63. Jakobsson, *The Troll Inside You*, 49.
64. Lindow, *Trolls*, 68.

CHAPTER SEVEN

# The Netherlands: *Witte Wieven* and Other White Apparitions

Yseult de Blécourt (Meertens Instituut)

> Memories of the Norns [...]; the Valkyres [...]; Frau Holle the goddess of Death and the holy women of the Germanic people, of whom Tacitus writes that they predicted the future are strangely mixed with histories of castle damsels who could not find rest after their death.[1]

Are there any equivalents to fairies in Dutch folklore? Several candidates present themselves—for instance, the *kaboutermannetjes* (dwarfs or gnomes), immortalized by the artist Rien Poortvliet (1932–1995), with their pointy hats.[2] In folklore texts they are nearly always male—little helpers active at night who must not be observed, otherwise they stop working or even blind the observer in one eye. These tiny men are sometimes confused with gypsies, because they are said to leave after their king has died. An occasional story from the Catholic province of Noord-Brabant describes their wives, as 'neatly' dressed in white and dancing in a circle.[3] Folklore is supposed to occur in multiple variations, but early folklorists were more interested in unique stories than systematically interviewing people in the countryside. Nor did they record the names of the people they spoke to, and thus firm conclusions are difficult. In the provinces of Noord-Brabant or Limburg one can reasonably assume that the interlocutors were Catholics, but even that will have to remain a supposition.

Here I will be concentrating on the 'white women'. Yet the nineteenth- and early twentieth-century folklore is about so-called *witte wijven*, *wijven* being dialect for women. As the texts are highly divergent the figures are, too. This divergence is partly due to the narrators, but also to the folklorists who collected, ordered and theorized the stories. Gnome motifs make their appearance more often, for instance. There will also have been some genuine local differences. The entries in the 1943 Sinninghe catalogue, although taking stock of the narratives of the previous period, cannot serve as a reliable indication let alone a description of these figures. This is because the white women appear in two guises, once as *Erddämonen* ('demons of the earth') and once as *Luftdämonen* ('demons of the air'). In the first section they appear as *Witte Wieven (Weisse Weiber)* and in the second as *Weisse Frau*; these are just headings.[4] The catalogue is still in use today but needs to be thoroughly revised.

Another pre-war undertaking was the sending out of questionnaires to local dignitaries by the folklore committee of the Royal Academy of Sciences in Amsterdam. In the 1937 questionnaire the respondents were asked about Vrouw Holle, the queen of the elves (*elfen*), and whether 'people' believed in 'fairies, white women [...] and similar ghosts',[5] a question not without some prejudice. It was in all likelihood formulated by Jos. Schrijnen (1869–1938), at that time chair of the committee.[6] Holle, also named Holda, was not really Dutch, certainly not in the early twentieth century.[7] The 1953 survey adapted its question about the *witte wieven*. Now they were joined with the *varende vrouw*, which indicates that the question was worded in Flanders, possibly by Maurits de Meyer (1895–1970), the Flemish editor of the folklore atlas. The approach had become more naturalistic as well. In twentieth-century Flanders the *varende* or the *barende vrouw* was the name for the whirlwind.[8] It turned the white woman into a scud of mist.

Making sense of the white woman (or white women) depends very much on where you start. I have chosen to commence my contribution in Ede, a town in the province of Gelderland, some 10 kilometres north of the Rhine, and then to move north- and slightly eastwards to Hoog-Soeren, a hamlet west of Apeldoorn in the same province. Next, I will discuss Buurse in the province of Overijssel. These places serve as a point of departure for an examination of the relevant legend motifs. They also present fragments of Dutch folklore history which are underlined by the culminating theories of the folklorists. I will leave homogenous Catholic Flanders out here. The catalogue gives an imperfect overview of the literature and the patchy questionnaires give only some sense of its reception. Throughout this chapter I will weigh the different theories about the white women and discuss the differences between local folklore and invented or imported traditions. This approach is inspired by a critical appraisal of the work of Tjaard W.R. de Haan (1919–1983), during the post-war decades the only Dutch folklorist with a PhD on a subject related to folk narratives.[9]

The folklore texts derive from a mixture of oral and written traditions; they often reflect romantic notions and confuse local identity and tourist interests. They probably first appeared in the nineteenth century; they mention older, mostly Latin reports about the *wijven*, some with different content but again with some gnome motifs—those cannot be pursued here. In what follows I will start with present-day traditions and then move back towards earlier sources.

## The Castle of Kernhem

> It is a long time ago, but people talked about it. In Ede, at the road to Lunteren stood the old castle Kenhem [*sic*] and in the evening a white lady often crossed the road. The place was haunted and no one dared to pass there in the evening. But the white lady is true.[10]

This text was taken down in 1966 by Engelbert Heupers (1906–1978), one of the most diligent Dutch fieldworkers of the 1960s. The informant was a Protestant farmer. The white lady (*witte dame*) should be translated as 'white wight', yet this is untypical in several respects—apart from the fact that the castle of Kernhem was several times destroyed and rebuilt and ended up as a stately home. Although Heupers did not interview many people in this area, as it lay on the edge of his range of action, another informant of his in the neighbourhood who was born in Ede but raised in Barneveld mentioned *witte wieven*.[11] Heupers did not cross the Veluwe, a mostly uninhabited and uncultivated heath area. Only one other of his informants remembered that her mother had told her about the *witte wieven* walking (the verb she used) on the heath, which was rather a superficial and not overly informative account.[12] Yet in an answer to the 1937 folklore survey, mention is made of the Protestant minister at Ede who had to pass by the *witte wieven* (plural) at Kernhem. He *did* meet the white lady (*juffer*).[13] The last text is ambiguous, possibly because of the wording of the question. A reply from neighbouring Veenendaal hardly brings us clarity. It concerns a witch story about a suitor who is suspicious of his girlfriend.[14] He sees a white figure on a white horse and when the girl appears, she tells him it was not her.[15]

In 1966 when a farmer mentioned Kernhem to Heupers, the ghost of Kernhem had been widely publicized and discussed. It is unlikely that the Protestant farmer had read the Sunday Catholic journal *Katholieke Illustratie* in 1949 with its retouched black-and-white photos that suggested vague pale figures.[16] Ede was predominantly Protestant and the members of different denominations hardly mingled at that time. I have only found one other mention of a ghost at Kernhem in the newspaper *De Tijd*, but that also was Catholic and did not feature the lady.[17] A related story about the knight Udo which appeared at the end of the 1940s, also in the *Illustratie*, referred to a narrative from the early fifteenth century. The unique item of the 'bloodstone' has been part of this story since the late twentieth century; as was pointed out in 2019, this is not very old either.[18] Both these references and that to the god Woden were incorporated into a popular cartoon which first appeared in 1990.[19] All these sources were produced in a Catholic setting. Jac. Gazenbeek (1894–1975), a local journalist who was raised as a Protestant, only mentioned Udo in his 1940 book, as the knight had actually once lived in the castle. His most historical story was an explanation of the local dialect name *Keer-um* (literally, 'turn around') and concerned Spanish soldiers who fled when someone played the Wilhelmus, the Dutch national anthem, on a horn.[20]

This kind of fake etymology was popular in those years and linked Kernhem folklore to the Dutch Golden Age. But for Gazenbeek the etymology pointed to a deeper meaning. In the rest of the chapter he featured a number of his local contemporaries, who all agreed that there was something uncanny about Kernhem, something invisible. When different people agreed in principle then there should have been a sort of reality behind their observations. Gazenbeek looked for it in the archaeology of knowledge. The phenomenon, he wrote, was related to the religion and the rites of 'our distant ancestors'. Speculating on the local name, he thought Kèèr was probably connected to the goddess of death (Kali?), who had been worshipped within a circle of stones, a *cairn* (as in Kern). In this ancient cult the white women were the priestesses who provided the link between 'the holy deity and the common people'. The word *witte* (white) reminded one of *weten* (to know) and of *verwittigen* (to notify).[21] This way of thinking betrayed theosophical influences. Since Gazenbeek had no compunction publishing in journals like *Hamer* and *Volk en Bodem* during the Nazi occupation, he may well have been influenced by Nazi ideology.[22] After the war Gazenbeek slightly adapted his theory to suggest that there had been human sacrifices there (hence the bloodstone), but any relation with the goddess of death was 'too speculative'.[23]

## Castle Ghosts

The white lady at Kernhem can also be seen in conjunction with castles and their ghost stories along the southern and eastern edge of the Veluwe. An initial inventory yields narratives about Kwadenoord in Renkum, Castle Doorwerth, Biljoen in Velp and the Nevelhorst at Didam. The story of Scheele Guurte located east of the Veluwe also contains traces, as it was situated near

Castle Wildenborch in Lochum.[24] In the early nineteenth century a ghost story seems to have given castles extra cachet; when there was no ghost story, it could always be invented. The most telling examples in this respect are Kwadenoord and Biljoen.

Tjaard de Haan notes how Mark Prager Lindo (1819–1877) wrote the story of Mooi-Ann of Biljoen (a castle in Velp, just east of Arnhem) in honour of his fiancée Johanna Nijhoff, one of the daughters of the Arnhem publisher and editor Is[aac] An[ne] Nijhoff.[25] His story first appeared in the *Arnhemsche Courant* and it revolved around a mysterious young lady, an 'alabaster' beauty whom the writer met at a dance. As a ghost she lured young men to their death, but her latest target was spared and she disappeared in the local pond, never to be seen again.[26] Lindo's story lacks credibility. He hailed from the United Kingdom, and had not learned to speak Dutch before he was nineteen. He had also read his Walter Scott. Nineteenth-century Dutch folklorists, on the other hand, identified the beautiful (*mooi*) Ann as the ancient goddess of death, or Urdr ('well').[27]

The story of Mooi-Ann was anthologized in Dutch folktale compilations, but it could at least be unpicked. This was not the case with the story about Kwadenoord (or Quadenoord).[28] A haughty countess would only walk to church when the ground was suitably covered; when she died, the earth did not want to accept her and rejected her coffin. Her burial was repeated until she found a reluctant resting place in the stream of Quadenoord where she continued acting as a bogey-person of sorts. Her story derived from abroad (De Haan called it a transplanted tradition). It was authored and published by Jacques Clemens Perk (1818–1868) and based on a poem by the German writer Johann Peter Hebel (1769–1826), *Die Häfner-Jungfrau*. Nevertheless, the responses to the 1937 survey claimed that *witte wijven* danced in the moonlight at Kwadenoord.[29]

A third instance can be found in a story about Nevelhorst Castle at Didam.[30] In the 1970s the local folktale researcher Arnold Tinneveld found a 'bombastic' tale about a wife who promised her husband, before he departed on a crusade to the Holy Land, that she would never remarry were he to die. De Haan recognized it as a borrowing (he called it a 'dropping') from Bürger's *Lenore*.[31]

The habit of using English or German narratives and especially poetic material to enhance the reputation of castles along the Veluwe can probably be found in other cases, too, although I have not looked beyond this area.[32] Female castle-ghosts thus become suspect, and this is certainly true of Kernhem and the white lady who did not manifest herself before the 1920s. As I will show in the following paragraphs, the cross-pollination with what I consider as the more genuine *witte wieven* tradition (in contrast to the presumed one at Renkum or the imposed one at Ede) also extended beyond castles. To bring this out clearly, another element needs to be scrutinized: the influence of religious history as it came to the fore in the early nineteenth century, when nationalism was closely allied to Romanticism. I will do this via the early twentieth-century work on Hoog Soeren.

## The Damsel Tree

Hoog Soeren (west of Apeldoorn) had its own white damsels. It is hard to know whether there were more in this place, since Heupers (see above) did not venture further than the hamlet of Garderen, about 15 kilometres to the west. His informant, a farmer living even further away, had only heard that there were *witte wieven* there and that they were dangerous.[33] The same was true of the respondent to the 1937 questionnaire: he lived too far away, too.[34] As the white damsels were associated with a big, hollow tree, local reports were crucial. We will thus have to rely on the publications of Gustaaf van de Wall Perné, an artist born in Apeldoorn (1877–1911). In the early twentieth century he lived in Amsterdam where he also died, but during the summer he stayed in a cabin he had built in Hoog Soeren.

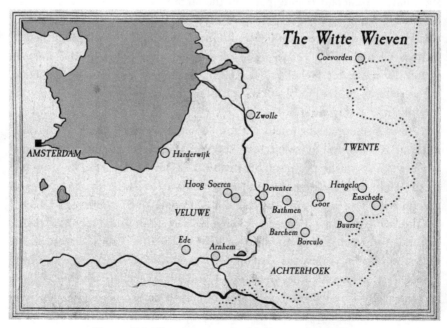

**Figure 7.1:** The *witte wieven* in the nineteenth century.

Perné wrote in the 1909 preface to his collection *Veluwsche sagen* (originally 1910) that he had adopted material from the *Edda* to introduce the legends he had found among the locals. In a note he explained that the *witte wieven* were wise women, the spirits of the female priestesses who guarded the barrows.[35] He actually situated the *Edda* in the Veluwe. In 1911 a Dutch *Edda* translation appeared with his drawings; he named his cabin *Mjölnir*, after the hammer of Thor. It is not always clear where his enthusiasm for the Icelandic sagas ended and where his rendering of the opinions of the Soeren locals began. He was a *romanticus* rather than a *mysticus*, as one of his necrologists wrote.[36]

Perné's text predated Gazenbeek by some thirty years. He was possibly a better artist than writer. The following mimics Perné's style with all its non sequiturs and staccato rhythm. The artist considered Hoog Soeren one of the oldest settlements on the Veluwe. He mused that some people could remember the location of a very old beech tree, which had been there since time immemorial; around this spot were Germanic (= archaic) burial mounds. The white damsel would already have been there 'a long, long time ago'. Old people could still tell stories that she was spinning in this old hollow tree. She probably was one of the Norns and may have been called Urth, as a certain *Urthensula* ('pillar of Urth') was mentioned in 855. Would that have been at the place of the damsel tree? Who could tell? 'Generations of oaks had grown up around the burial mounds and have fallen down', he continued, 'storms ruled [...] when the old god of thunder reigned.' During the night Woden himself went through the forest.[37]

Several inhabitants of Soeren told him that the tree was so hollow that a man could stand in it upright. At night one could see a little light and hear the damsel spin. A labourer in the pub bragged about the damsel and had received a thrashing on his way back home. A little girl had put her head into the tree to see whether the damsel was still there, and she became stuck because the damsel was holding her by the hair. The most elaborate story, over six pages long, was about digging for a treasure.[38] In the early twentieth century this was told in several places in the Netherlands and the figure of the woman was not always white.[39] What remained were three fairly short narratives about a hollow tree containing light and a spinning damsel who could be heard rather than seen. They were not all pure fantasy. Certainly the spinning was associated with the *wieven* (see the skewer stories below).

Perné's ideas about the Norns predated him. Urdt already figured in 1844. On the other side of the IJssel, in the region of Achterhoek, Hendrik Willem Heuvel (1864–1926), the headteacher of a school in Borculo (some 50 kilometres to the east of Soeren), had a similar opinion. After mentioning sightings of floating, flying or standing-still *wieven*, he explained them as the three Norns of Germanic mythology. He proceeded to cite mostly German examples and introduced the Valkyries before turning his attention to the 'belief' in *witte wijven*.[40]

## The Skewer in the Door

The map drawn up in 1956, using the folklore surveys, did not survive the test phase. But, since it incorporated the earlier Dutch results, it still proves interesting.[41] Oddly it combined white and black women and identified them both with ghost symbols or scuds of mist.[42] The different symbols appearing on the map need to be unpacked. Omens of death (a horizontal line, which occurs only three times) may have indicated black women. Horses being ridden to exhaustion at night is a nightmare motif; nightly labour rewarded (a circle crossed by a vertical line) belongs more to the dwarfs.

The most frequent symbols on the map are open circles, denoting (white or black) women harming people, and diagonal lines, indicating women floating or dancing. The last two occur all over the map except in the provinces of North and South Holland which have practically none. Given the number of respondents all over the Netherlands, this gap implies that the concept of the *witte wieven* was unknown in these areas.

These women were deemed harmless, above all in the province of Groningen. In the province of Overijssel and the adjacent eastern quarter of Gelderland (called Achterhoek), fifteen respondents reported that the women chased people (read men) who challenged them, and hurled a skewer at them. This motif is typical for that region and it was not mentioned anywhere else, although research in neighbouring Germany may yield other instances. It can also be followed in the literature. A (slightly inaccurate) description of the motif can be found in Sinnighe's catalogue, where the skewer is replaced by an axe.[43]

Of the five texts currently in the folktale bank, four refer to the skewer, even when an axe is mentioned. The other implement is a cudgel. A valid argument can thus be made for the skewer as an intrinsic part of the story, and there are more sources to validate this. In her 1938 compilation of *witte wieven* tales Cato Elderink (1871–1941), a retired nurse, calls the skewer the most frequent motif. She cites the example of an old peasant in Buurse (south of Enschede). He told her about *brulfteneugers*, two men who invited wedding guests. To tease them the groom said that they had not invited his closest neighbours, the *witte wieven*. One of the *neugers* responded to the challenge and brought the *witte wieven* a dead cat on a skewer, saying if they wanted more, they should visit the groom. The moment the *neuger* had thrown the skewer with the cat, he ran away. He had just reached the groom's home when the skewer, which had been thrown after him, hit the door. One could hear the little *wiefken* behind him: 'had I put on my shoes and tied my laces, then you would have been roasted', she said.[44]

In this tale the skewer is thrown and thrown back. In other tales the young man throws the skewer but is chased by a *wieve* with an axe, which still speaks to the prominence of the skewer. This is the more so because the reference was already familiar in the late nineteenth century, when an inhabitant of Goor (west of Enschede) related two versions.[45] The postman of Bathmen (to the west) in 1892 wrote the story up for the collector Gerrit Jacob Boekenoogen (1868–1930) and constructed it around a wager. A *knecht* ('servant' or 'farm-hand'; Dutch uses the word for both) boasted that he would throw a skewer into the hole of the *wieven*. There follows a brief exchange in rhyme, in which he tells the *wieven* that he brought the skewer, whereupon one of them replies that if he gave her time to tie her shoes, he would be roasted. The man gallops home and his horse is so quick that he is not hit by the skewer that ends up in the door.[46] This story was also told in Barchem about 25 kilometres to the south-east, in the province of Gelderland.[47] Barchem was an hour on foot from Borculo, where headmaster Heuvel (see above) found that the skewer story was 'generally known'.[48] The area in these reports is the same as that shown on the later map, yet the particular details (such as the Deventer beer below) as well as the rhyme raise the question of whether there was independent generation or mere copying.

Cato Elderink had qualified as a nurse at a hospital in Amsterdam. It is not known whether she met Perné there (she was his senior by about five years). Around 1910 she returned to her place of birth in Enschede where she was employed by the Society to Combat Tuberculosis. Her family was well-off; she was unmarried and had taught herself a kind of dialect to communicate with locals in the countryside. From the early 1920s, she dedicated her time to writing, mostly poetry. She was familiar with the pervading theories, but she stuck to reporting elderly people's stories, though sometimes she also doubted them. She was aware that her interlocutors occasionally made fun of her and were 'telling her tales' (lies, inventions, jokes) that 'had nothing to do with legends'.[49] Perhaps her women interlocutors were more honest, but here too, class difference probably proved more important. A woman who related the motif of flames that did not cause a fire was telling Elderink something that elsewhere was told about dwarfs. Another tale, told by a farmer's wife, concerned a *wiefken* that had been threatened by a man, whereupon the *wiefken* covered all the silverware in excrement. This sounds like a joke.[50] Since Elderink talked more to men than to women and all the other mentions of *wieven* occurred among men, a comparison between women's and men's reports is not possible.

Elderink herself remarked on the similarity of the skewer tale to the behaviour of lads when young girls gathered to spin. Once girls had finished spinning and wanted to enjoy a pancake, the young men threw a skewer with a dead cat or something similarly unsavoury in the girls' room. At that point the girls chased the boys.[51] This may also have mirrored the story about the wedding invitation mentioned above. In that context white women were spinners and this could have been one of the reasons that the story was told.

Nearly a century earlier, the then burgomaster of Hengelo, the baron B.W.A.E. Sloet tot Oldhuis (1808–1884), had recorded the skewer tales in the same area Elderink had encountered them.[52] In his first version, however, a farmer who had sampled too much Deventer beer [!] challenged three *wiven*, telling them that he did not have a skewer but that his words should suffice. One of them replied that he just had to wait until she tied her shoes. When he raced away, they almost succeeded in jumping on his horse. The second tale is about a wager. A farmhand threw a pointed iron wedge at one of the hills, was chased, and just managed to avoid a little axe. These examples show the existence of these particular versions, but they do not preclude other ones. The skewer story was either well known, or later reporters took the easy way out and simply copied different versions, or both.

## Invention, Transplantation and 'Folk'-Tale

Joost Hiddes Halbertsma (1789–1869), who was minister of Deventer from 1822, wrote an essay at the end of 1836, which turned out to be hugely influential.[53] Deventer is a town on the IJssel and borders *witte wieven* country. As far as can be seen, Halbertsma did not hear about them from his parishioners;[54] at the time the *wieven* were unknown in his native Frisia and the examples he quoted at the end of his essay were taken from his friend 'Sloet' (see above). More important than any empirical material was Halbertsma's status as scholar and his criticism of the preceding expert, the minister of Coevorden, Johan Picardt, who wrote a century and a half before him. Picardt, as Halbertsma said, was 'no friend at all' of the *wieven*. As a minister Picardt was also rather conservative.

Halbertsma identified the *wieven* as heathen—their habitats were always to be found at pre-Christian burial sites and, as Tacitus had written, among the

Germanic people the women outclassed the men; they stood much closer to the spirit world. As he was 'wandering in the realm of uncertainties', Halbertsma guessed that the *wieven* had once been *Walkuren* (Valkyries).[55]

In contrast to Picardt, Halbertsma did not believe in white women; he merely believed in the existence of *witte mutsen* (white caps)—that is to say, contemporary maidens.[56] The intellectual engagement was distinct from day-to-day experiences and the latter could be conveyed in poetry, at least during the second quarter of the nineteenth century. In the 1920s Elderink still followed this convention, but at least, having desisted from speculation, she made astute observations about the contemporary customs remembered in some of the remote villages of Twente.

In 1838 Sloet became a judge at the court of Zwolle and turned the *witte wieven* into a poem. It was thus no contradiction that he neglected his earlier local findings and took a clue from another conjecture of Halbertsma. In his poem a young girl named Elske was trapped in a hill by the king of the elves, Elfrik, the Dutch version of Alberich.[57] The poem has two strands. The first is about Elske spending too much time out of doors in the evening; she meets a friendly *wief* who rewards Elske for all the milk she has left for her. The second is about another group of *witten* who take her to their king; he desires her as his bride, but she is protected by the ring the first *wief* gave to her. In the meantime her human lover realizes what has happened to her and manages to track her down. Since he had chosen a female victim, Sloet could only succeed in this composition by juxtaposing her with a male antagonist, something alien to local lore. The whole poem therefore took on a British flavour, even though the idea of an interrupted love affair may have been a theme in the area.

There was an ambiguous attitude to local legends. They were berated intellectually but also used to create art. This is true of the work of A.C.W. Staring, who may well have initiated this trend. Anthony Staring (1767–1840) was a Protestant squire who had studied law at the University of Harderwijk and botany in Göttingen. He championed local education. He was also one of the few Romantic Dutch poets.[58] His Castle Wildenborch was situated south of Lochem and due west of Barchem, thus in *witte wieven* country. He published a volume titled *Kleine verhalen* ('Small Stories'), a prose narrative but with poetic content which included an episode of some *wieven*, a girl and the boys competing for her. The successful boy had to throw a skewer into the *wieven* pit. Staring had turned this into a contest between two boys and he played with the homonymy between the skewer and the mowing implement (the *haarpit*); he could only succeed if the components of his story were already familiar. The response by the *wief* about her shoelaces was omitted and the thrown-back skewer was turned into gold, to emphasize the love between the couple. The other boy failed this test badly. Staring explained a few years earlier that the *wieven* in their underground dwelling were literally sitting on gold. He did not call them by name, but instead referred to Walter Scott's *uriskin*.[59] The subsequent story in *Kleine verhalen* featured the Wilhelmus account of Kernhem we saw earlier, now situated at Hoekelum, on the other side of Ede.[60] It, too, has been transplanted.

Staring's rational attitude is apparent in his biography, but it is also evident if we focus on the white wives. In a note to his poem 'De zwarte vrouw' ('The Black Woman') about his own Castle Wildenborch, he remarked that in his youth 'sharper eyes than his own' had seen a black damsel there. She was confused with the *Witte Juffer* ('White Damsel') who lived in the nearby *Wittewijvenkuil* ('White Women Pit') in the nearby Lochemschen *berg* ('hill') and sometimes a holly shrub, lit up in the moonlight, was taken to be her.[61]

## Conclusion

By writing this history chronologically in reverse, I found it easier to contextualize the different fragments. This also helped in examining today's white women outside their core area of Twente and the Achterhoek. My comments have touched not just on today's popular texts but focused on the scholarly practice of Dutch folklore since the 1930s. In both his books on Gelderland's legends, as well as in his *Katalog*, Sinninghe thought the folklore surveys were beyond criticism and wholly supported the literature. He did not consider that respondents had sometimes reworked the literature in their replies. Nor did he take the power of the questions into account. If he mentioned any theory, it was mainly to separate it from 'folklore'. After the war, professional folklorists,—that is to say those working for the Royal Academy of Sciences in Amsterdam—were not trained academically in folklore. De Haan, who was employed as a schoolteacher, worked from a completely different angle. Even though he recognized poetic influences, he did not pay any attention to religion, let alone 'heathen' religion. The way nineteenth-century intellectuals interlinked *witte wieven* with both this religion and poetics thus remained largely unexamined. Moreover, de Haan only discussed relatively minor figures such as Sloet or Lindo. He ignored Staring. The *witte wieven*, plural in form and yet unsocial compared to many of the other beings recorded in this volume, are a rich and engaging topic. They deserve to be explored further both in the modern and the early modern period, something I intend to do on another occasion.[62]

## Notes

1. J.R.W. Sinninghe, *Overijselsch sagenboek* (Zutphen: Thieme, 1936), 40. My translation.
2. W. Huygen and R. Poortvliet, *Gnomes* (London [etc.]: Harry N. Abrams, 1979).
3. W. de Blécourt, *Volksverhalen uit Noord-Brabant* (Utrecht: Spectrum, 1980), 17–18. The original text is from 1883. See also the poem *Die Heinzelmännchen zu Köln* by August Kopisch, in his *Gedichte* of 1836.
4. J.R.W. Sinninghe, *Katalog der niederländischen Märchen-, Ursprungssagen-, Sagen- und Legendenvarianten* (Helsinki: Suomalainen Tiedeakatemia, 1943), 62–63 (nr. 161–64); 68–71 (nr. 301–11).
5. *De Volkskundevragenlijsten van het P.J. Meertens-Instituut* (Amsterdam: P.J. Meertens-Instituut voor Dialectologie, Volkskunde en Naamkunde, 1989), 32.
6. J. Schrijnen, *Nederlandsche volkskunde* (Zutphen: W.J. Thieme & Cie, 1914), 66–67.
7. See the article in the Dutch *Volksverhalenbank* by Liesbet Altena: www.verhalenbank.nl/items/show/51220. Holde was an evasive goddess, probably a misreading of the adjective *holden*. See especially W. Schild, 'Holda zwischen und jenseits von Göttin und Hexengestalt: eine christliche Geschichte', *Frau Holle: Mythos, Märchen und Brauch in Thüringen*, ed. A. Jakob (Meiningen: Meininger Museen, 2010), 49–69.
8. H. Brok, 'De varende vrouw en de barende vrouw', *Taal en tongval*, 25 (1973), 106–21.
9. Tj.W.R. de Haan, *Volk en dichterschap* (Assen: Van Gorcum, 1950).
10. E. Heupers, *Volksverhalen uit Gooi- en Eemland en van de westelijke Veluwe*, vol. 3 (Amsterdam: Instituut voor Dialectologie, Volkskunde en Naamkunde, 1984), 120, n. 3147. The 'r' of Kernhem was lost in translation.
11. Ibid., n. 2552.
12. Ibid., n. 1861.
13. *Volkskundevragenlijst* 2 (1937), formulier F.193, archief Meertens Instituut. Consulted from the Dutch folktale repository *Volksverhalenbank*, www.verhalenbank.nl/items/show/13627 (LYST283).
14. See W. de Blécourt, 'Het verhaal van de verkeerde vriendin: heksensagen herzien', *Volkskunde* 118 (2017), 319–41.
15. Volksverhalenbank, LYST282.
16. www.delpher.nl/nl/tijdschriften/view?identifier=MMKDC09_017359001_00019 to 00021.
17. *De tijd: dagblad voor Nederland* (9 May 1947).
18. www.edestad.nl/lokaal/mensen/258283/het-ware-verhaal-van-de-bloedsteen-625029.
19. https://nl.wikipedia.org/wiki/Het_witte_wief. The writer of this story consulted the owner of the local occult bookshop.
20. J. Gazenbeek, *Fluisteringen van het verleden: veluwsche sagen* (Putten: Terwee, 1940), 112; 120.
21. Ibid., 121.
22. *Provinciale Drentsche en Asser Courant* (15 Jan 1948).
23. J. Gazenbeek, *Sagen en legenden van de Veluwe* (Wageningen: Zomer & Keuning, 1971), 25–33.
24. For the last, see H. Krosenbrink, 'Werkelijkheid en fantasie in Gallée's verhaal van Schaele Guurte', *Neerlands volksleven* 33 (1983), 20–31, esp. 25.

25. Tj.W.R. de Haan, 'Mooi-Ann van Biljoen en de oude heer Smits', *Volkskunde* 49 (1948), 55–56; De Haan, *Volk en dichterschap* (Assen: Van Gorcum, 1950), 66–68; *Nederlandse volksverhalen: herkomst en geschiedenis* (Den Haag: Kruseman, 1976), 159–66.
26. *Arnhemsche Courant* 162 (Sunday 16 Aug 1840), Mengelwerk. On Nijhoff, see A.E.M. Janssen in *Biografisch woordenboek Gelderland* 2 (2000), 78–81.
27. D. Buddingh, *Verhandeling over het Westland* (Leiden: Arnz, 1844), 125–26.
28. J.R.W. Sinninghe, *Geldersch sagenboek* (Zutphen: W.J. Thieme, 1943), 31–33, after the text by Perk in the *Geldersche volksalmanak*. In the 1975 edition, *Gelders sagenboek* (Zutphen: W.J. Thieme), 29, Sinninghe shortened the text and added the footnote: 'the story is too good to be true'.
29. Sinninghe, *Geldersch sagenboek*, 33; *Gelders sagenboek*, 29, with a reference to the *volkskundelijsten*. See also De Haan, *Nederlandse volksverhalen*, 173, 175: 'ideal for *witte wijven*, or scuds of mist'.
30. J. van der Veur, *Geldersche volksalmanak* 1838 (1837), 100–05; reprinted in: A. Tinneveld, *Vertellers uit de Liemers* (Wassenaar: Neerlands Volksleven, 1976), 248–50.
31. G.J.H. Krosenbrink, *Volksverhalen uit Gelderland* (Utrecht–Antwerpen: Het Spectrum, 1979), 185. De Haan was the editor of the volume and should in this particular instance be considered as the author. Bürger refers to the German poet Gottfried August Bürger (1747–1794).
32. See Sinninghe, *Geldersch sagenboek*, 33–34.
33. Heupers, *Volksverhalen*, n. 1086.
34. Volksverhalenbank, LYST223 [Putten].
35. Gustaaf van de Wall Perné, *Veluwsche sagen* (Amsterdam: Scheltens & Giltay, 1911), 129. This is the second printing; the first one appeared in 1910—see *Het vaderland* (6 August 1910).
36. J.D.C. van Dokkum, 'Gust. van de Wall Perné: in memoriam', *Den gulden winckel* 11 (1912), 1–3. See in general the contribution by A. Kalb-Huisman, *Biografisch woordenboek Gelderland*, vol. 5 (Hilversum: Verloren, 2006), 141–43.
37. Van de Wall Perné, *Veluwsche sagen*, 36–38.
38. Ibid., 38; 42–43; 43–49.
39. SINSAG 0401; T. Meder and C. Hendriks, *Vertelcultuur in Nederland: volksverhalen uit de Collectie Boekenoogen (ca. 1900)* (Amsterdam: Aksant, 2005), 697–700.
40. H.W. Heuvel, *Volksgeloof en volksleven* (Zutphen: Thieme, 1909), 31–34.
41. P.J. Meertens and Maurits De Meyer, *Volkskunde-Atlas voor Nederland en Vlaams-België. Commentaar. Aflevering I.* (Antwerpen - Amsterdam: Standaard Boekhandel, 1959), 57–69, esp. 64–65.
42. The combination of white and black women was probably taken from Sinninghe, *Overijselsch sagenboek*, 38. The *witte wieven* are also categorized in this book as ghosts of the air and ghosts of the earth (5–17, 38–40). It is understandable that a feature from Sinninghe's 1936 book turned up in his catalogue; there is no reason why it should be part of the title of the test map. By the time the map was drawn up, Sinninghe had not worked for the Bureau for about ten years; he was never involved in the atlas project.
43. Sinninghe, *Katalog*, 62, n. 161. See also Sinninghe, *Overijselsch sagenboek*, 6–8, primarily skewer, edited out of the *Katalog*.

44. C. Elderink, 'Twentsche verhalen over witte wieven', *Volkskunde* 42 (1938), 33–37, esp. 36. Elderink first published this story in rhyme on her *Oet et laand van aleer* (Enschede: Van der Loeff, 1924), 64–66.
45. J.N. v[an] Hesteren, 'De witte wieven', *Vragen van den dag* 10 (1899), 113–16. This article was actually copied after Halbertsma (see n. 56).
46. *Vertelcultuur in Nederland*, 375, n. 405 plus note 358. Note 357 on the same page is questionable as the rhyme in the text refers to a roast and not to mowing. Unlike some of the other texts Boekenoogen collected, the Bathmen one was not published at the time.
47. A.C.W. Staring, *Kleine verhalen* (Arnhem: Nijhoff, 1837), 73–93.
48. Heuvel, *Volksgeloof*, 33. He meant a much wider area than just Borculo; he gave the story Sloet had given to Halbertsma as an example (see n. 55).
49. C. Elderink, *Twenter Laand en Leu en Lèven* (Enschede: Van der Loeff, 1937), 160.
50. Elderink, 'Twentsche verhalen', 34, 36–37.
51. Elderink, *Twenter Laand en Leu en Lèven*, 48–49.
52. As reported to J.H. Halbertsma; see his 'De Witte Wiven', *Overijsselsche Almanak voor oudheid en letteren* 2 (1836), 217–52, esp. 241–43.
53. The *Almanak* ('Almanac') appeared at the end of 1836; it has 1837 on the cover page. Halbertsma was born in Frisian Grouw but relocated to Deventer in Overijssel, where he eventually died. On its influence, see for example L.Ph.C. van den Bergh, *Nederlandsche volksoverleveringen en godenleer* (Utrecht: Altheer, 1836); *Proeve van een kritisch woordenboek der Nederlandsche mythologie* (Utrecht: Bosch, 1846). See also nn. 48 and 51.
54. Halbertsma's manuscript at the Fryske Akademy does not contain any references. On Halbertsma: A. de Jong, *Joost Halbertsma 1789–1869: Triomfen en tragedies van een uitmiddelpuntig man: een biografie* (Grou: Louise, 2018).
55. Halbertsma, 'De Witte Wiven', 235–36.
56. Ibid., 249–50.
57. Tj.W.R. de Haan, 'Sagepoezie van B.W.A.E. Sloet tot Oldhuis', *Neerlands volksleven* 13 (1963), 342–77, esp. 355–57.
58. M. Evers, 'Antoni Christiaan Wynand Staring', *Biografisch Woordenboek Gelderland* 1 (Hilversum: Verloren, 1998), 88–90.
59. 'Een paar woorden over enkele sporen van voorouderlijk heidensch bijgeloof, in het Zutphensche overgebleven', *Mnemosyne* 1 (1830), 317–20.
60. A.C.W. Staring, 'Het Wilhelmus te Eede, eene geschiedkundige anecdote van het jaar 1624', *Kleine verhalen* (Arnhem: Nijhoff, 1837), 94–104.
61. Staring, *Gedichten* (Zutphen: Thieme, 1861), 371. This is the popular edition, with an introduction by Nicolaas Beets.
62. Editors' note: on 3 November 2023 our author presented a paper titled 'The Translation of *Witte Wieven*' at the Legends! conference in Groningen.

CHAPTER EIGHT

# Iberia: Moors, *Gentiles* and *Encantadas*

José Manuel Pedrosa (University of Alcalá)

## Iberia: Almost an Island, Almost a World

Drawing up a brief but representative sketch of any aspect of 'Iberian popular mythology' is an extremely difficult challenge.[1] There are multiple chronologies, geographies, languages and traditions to factor in: pre-Roman and Roman; early medieval Latin; medieval Arabic and Hebrew; modern Morisco; late medieval Romance languages and dialects (Castilian, Portuguese, Galician, Catalan, Aragonese, Leonese, Asturian, etc.); and their modern and contemporary equivalents, along with, of course, Basque. A useful way to look at 'Iberian popular mythology' is through the solitary versus social breakdown.[2] Only the Iberian social supernatural will be treated here.[3] Limitations on space mean that we will not cover pre-Roman and Semitic traditions in this study, or the wider Hispanic influence in the Americas, Asia, Africa and elsewhere in Europe.[4] Nor will we investigate the Sephardic Jews, expelled to other parts of Europe and the Mediterranean. This is regrettable, for the social supernatural in Semitic traditions seems to be more given to supernatural monarchies and hierarchies.

The *moros* (and their female counterpart the *moras*) may share a name with the Muslims of medieval Al-Andalus. But these are chthonic or telluric beings, living in subterranean communities, and associated with the depths of the earth, water and hidden treasures.[5] There are also the *encantadas* ('the enchanted women') and, as we shall see, the male *gentiles*. These different communities, we are often told, have been wiped out by the march of civilization. But representatives continue to appear to some humans, particularly at certain moments in the year like the day of San Juan.[6] There are then, too, the caves, mountains or ruins in which they sheltered or were confined; and sometimes these societies left marks on the landscape itself.

---

José Manuel Pedrosa, "Iberia: Moors, *Gentiles* and *Encantadas*" in: *The Exeter Companion to Fairies, Nereids, Trolls and Other Social Supernatural Beings: European Traditions.* University of Exeter Press (2024). © José Manuel Pedrosa. DOI: 10.47788/HUME1621

The sources bring with them two important complications:

- the meagre and inadequate nature (when compared to oral traditions) of the texts that have come down to us. Stories are almost always transcribed imperfectly, with little by way of ethnographic explanation and distorted by the obsessions of the literate elites (often clerics). The beliefs and narratives being recorded were, all too frequently, ridiculed by those who wrote about them;
- the adulteration of folklore, especially since the nineteenth century: when many writers published tales of magic that they claimed were folkloric. There is, then, a pseudo-popular folk repertoire of legends, which amounts to nothing less than the 'invention of tradition'. Take, for instance, the encyclopaedias (often illustrated) of fairies, gnomes and elves that owe more to global mass culture than to local beliefs.[7]

Traditional Iberian supernatural beings stand out, when we can recover them, within European folklore for their richness and variety. There are several reasons for this, including geography: the Pyrenees isolate Iberia from Europe and abundant mountain ranges break up the peninsula. Then there is linguistic and cultural fragmentation, and the relatively late arrival of modernity: industries, technologies and other globalizing impulses.

Until recently many foreign visitors considered a trip to the south of the Pyrenees as a journey into a land of barbaric and atavistic peoples, legends and rituals. Jan Potocki's *Manuscrit trouvé à Saragosse* (1810) or Washington Irving's *The Alhambra* (1832), among many others, fed such stereotypes. Spaniards (especially Andalusians) were much written about, and associated with the *moros* and devils living in their secret underground communities.

## Geography and Supernatural Taxonomies

Let us turn now to the taxonomies of Iberian supernatural beings. The thematic classification (with separate chapters for witches, goblins, lycanthropes, etc.), which has been the one commonly used by Iberian and international scholarship, is frankly problematic. Take, for instance, the story about the supernatural being that transports large rocks or megaliths. This tale is told about witches, mermaids and other supernatural women, goblins, child stealers, *moros*, giants and *gentiles*. Such supernatural beings have no unique attributes or functions. There is overlap and crossover, and so precise thematic classification proves difficult or impossible.

An attempt to establish a taxonomy was proposed, with satisfactory results, by María Fernanda Martínez Reyes and the present author, for a heterogeneous corpus of 461 stories about supernatural beings. These had been recorded at the beginning of the twenty-first century in Honduras. The resulting topographical arrangement is perfectly applicable to Iberian and international legends: indeed, I will refer to it below. It is not thematic but, rather, it is based on disposition in space. There are three main concentric circles (and many subsidiary ones) in which contacts between human and supernatural beings occur:

- the human world: the centre of that circle and of all the other circles is the bed in which dreams and nightmares come; there is the bedroom, in which other apparitions are perceived (souls in pain, for example); the bathroom, in whose mirror 'Veronica' and other Iberian avatars of Bloody Mary appear; the house and its outbuildings (stables are, in lore, magnets for witches and goblins); the street (where it is said that the *sacamantecas* lurk or the processions of the dead wander); the neighbourhood, the town or the city (where there are haunted houses and other cursed places);
- the intermediate, liminal or frontier world, where there are still marks of human civilizing actions. Supernatural beings appear, there, in cemeteries, hermitages, roads, highways, bridges, houses and farms, the ruins of buildings or uninhabited villages, spaces with archaeological remains or megalithic constructions;
- the uncivilized: mountains, caves, deserts, wastelands, forests, rivers, lakes, seas. Here the wildest supernatural beings have been located.[8]

Iberian tradition had, prior to decisive and relatively recent invasions from the global supernatural, abundant and valuable reports about supernatural beings linked to local territories and to these three circles: settlement, frontier and the wilds.

## Nymphs, Fairies and Other Imports

Records, from antiquity to the present, of Iberian supernatural beings resemble a shipwreck. The only texts that can be excluded are some ancient epigraphical works and some ancient written sources that mention contemporary deities and *genii* to whom the more or less Romanized natives dedicated offerings and cults.

Christianization brought changes. Those who, until the modern age, communicated their beliefs and stories risked being condemned as pagans, idolaters, and so on. The admonitions of Bishop Martin of Braga (sixth century) in his letter 'On the Instruction of the Rustics' are very expressive in this respect: 'to light candles near stones and trees and fountains and at crossroads, what else is this but devil worship? To observe divination and omens, as well as the days of idols, what else is it but devil worship?'[9]

Condemnatory ecclesiastical literature, a crucial source of information about the cults that it sought to eradicate, flourished in the following centuries. It experienced a boom in the Renaissance and passed to the Americas, where furious treatises and ordinances against idolatries and the 'demons' of the Amerindians' respectable religions were circulated.

Archaeological research shows that pre-Roman and Roman Iberia were abundant in cults to sometimes local and sometimes more widely known deities. Indeed, much emphasis has been placed on the fact that a more or less systematic Celtic religion operated for centuries across much of Western Europe (including north-western Iberia), and that many of the supernatural beings documented (sometimes Latinized and Christianized) proved to be manifestations or residues of the same.[10]

As almost all surviving ancient documentation is from Roman times, it is not easy to distinguish indigenous and Roman ingredients. A well-studied example, which could go back to the pre-Roman period, is that of the divinity of the wells whose name, 'Airo(nis)', is known because it was inscribed in the first century AD in the Fuente Redonda de Uclés (Cuenca). More than a hundred 'Airon wells' have been attested across Iberia.[11] Even twentieth-century oral tradition details romances and legends around human sacrifices perpetrated in these gloomy wells.[12] Here perhaps we have a millennia-old, though constantly changing, numinous tradition.

Another case is the 'nymphs' associated in epigraphy with fountains and thermal waters, in the Roman West, including North Africa.[13] There can be little doubt that the generic Latin 'nymph' must have replaced various indigenous theonyms. It hardly follows, then, that the 'nymphs' were a coherent community of supernatural beings with a systematic cult in the Roman West. It is more reasonable to think in terms of generic labels, and religious, cultural and political imperialism.

There are many more considerations that could be made about Iberian 'nymphs'. I will limit myself here to highlighting how, incredibly, as late as the seventeenth century in Spain, 'nymph' continued to occasionally assume a neutralizing function similar to the one it had many centuries before.[14] The humanist Sebastián de Covarrubias, in his *Tesoro de la lengua castellana o española* (*Treasure of the Castilian or Spanish Language*, 1611), pointed out that 'the old women, when they entertain the children by telling them some hoaxes, usually say that a certain nymph, with a golden wand in her hand, works wonders and transmutations, alluding to the wand of Circe, the enchantress, and they use this term: "Wand, wand, by the virtue that God gave you, may you do this or that"'.[15] It is striking that Covarrubias avoided labelling as 'fairies' (*fadas*) the supernatural women who carried magic wands. But he also wrote that 'the fabulous writers of books of chivalry call nymphs or enchanted women *fadas* or *hadas*, who claim they cannot die'.[16] *Fadas* or *hadas* were not, therefore, part of the vernacular. Rather they belonged to the elite literate lexicon and that is why Covarrubias did not employ them here.

Maxime Chevalier, after a meticulous survey of magic wands in the Spanish literature of the sixteenth and seventeenth centuries,[17] writes the following:

> the insistent repetition of these allusions suggests that the wand of virtues would be a common magical object in the oral stories of the seventeenth century, and the fairy a key character in them. Indeed, around 1600–1650, the fairy and her wand can hardly have come from written sources: none of the Spanish medieval texts that mention fairies refer to the fairy/wand association, and the date when Perrault's tales were printed is still far off.[18]

There were, then, tales of enchantment featuring supernatural women in the oral tradition of the early modern Iberian Age. But why did Covarrubias prefer to use the word 'nymph', which was a cultism, and in his time was also a derogatory word for a prostitute? 'Nymph' was obviously alien to the oral and popular world. Why use 'nymph' instead of the words preferred by the majority of the population? Probably because 'the people' preferred words that a seventeenth-century lexicographer would find unattractive or uninteresting: above all *vieja* ('old woman'), but also *señora* ('mistress') or *dama* ('lady').

That these names have survived is corroborated by the canonical 280 Spanish tales published by Aurelio M. Espinosa in 1946–47. There the word 'fairy' never appears in the vernacular. It does appear, however, up to thirty-five times, in Espinosa's learned commentary.[19] The peasants interviewed opted for the customary *viejas*, *señoras*, *damas* and even *monjas* ('nuns'). I cannot fail to quote, here, an old goatherd from Herrera del Duque (Badajoz), Tomás Zárate. Tomás told me in 1989, with masterful verbal art, a story of 'when the old man and the old woman were walking around the world'.[20] The 'old man' did not appear in the story, but 'the old woman' did make three appearances with the familiar protocols of magical donations. Figures like these are conventionally associated with those who outside the Hispanic world are called 'fairies'.

The relevance of the *vieja* in the Iberian popular supernatural is confirmed by a varied and profuse flow of legends. These associate, just as in the rest of Europe, the *vieja* with the rainbow, or with nightmares, or with wild mountain dwellers.[21] There are also foundation stories with one or several *viejas* who survive a disaster in their village and who then go on to found new villages, or who challenge other *viejas* to a race, so that each one can found a village in the place she reaches.[22] The *vieja* protagonists and the *viejas* who all too often transmit the stories mean different things. But, of course, the *cuentos de viejas* ('old woman's tales') in Spanish and other Iberian languages are deeply rooted in popular culture.

Although less frequently used than the word *vieja*, the word *dama* ('lady') has also appeared regularly in Iberian folklore. Thus, in a Spanish tale from Zamora, taken down in the early twentieth century by Espinosa: 'And the dogs guarded and the men saw that they were always coming with food and gave it to a beautiful *dama* who was suspended from the tree. And the *dama* was so beautiful that the king's son is said to have taken her down from the tree'.[23] *Dama* as a synonym of *hada* has never come under the notice of specialists, but it was clearly an old and traditional label which conveyed both respect and fear (as a noa-name).[24] I will limit myself here to noting its appearance in the Zamora tale; in medieval Basque, where the supernatural mother of the first lord of Vizcaya was called the Dama do Pé de Cabra; in modern Basque, where the Dama de Amboto is usually called the goddess Mari; and in Catalan-Balearic, where *Sa dama de sa cova murada* and *Sa cova de sa dama* are the protagonists of two Minorcan legends.[25]

In Iberia, it is worth adding that *fada* or *hada* were associated with medieval literary productions (chronicles, allegories, etc.) and, at the end of that period, with the deities of destiny, traced from Greco-Latin literature. In the early modern period, 'fairies' were identified with the magicians and enchantresses of the often Italian-inspired books of chivalry (as Covarrubias emphasized). Then, from the eighteenth century, the *fées* arrived in books from France (reinforced in the twentieth century by anglophone fairies). These *fées* became the supernatural females of marvel tales filtered or produced by elites. In short: there were no 'fairies' (except for some that may have crept in late from imported or foreign-inspired books) in traditional Iberian tales and legends. That is why we use the name 'supernatural women' for the *moras* and *encantadas* (in Spanish), *mouras* (in Galician), *encantades*, *dones d'aigua*, *donas* and *señoras* (in Catalan), *lamias* or *lamiñak* (in Basque), *xanas* (in Asturian), *anjanas* (in Cantabrian speech), *serranas* ('women of the mountains'), *hilanderas* ('spinning women'), *viejas*, *señoras*, *damas*, etc.

*Ogro*, another Gallicism (from *ogre*) followed a similar path. The word was imported at the end of the eighteenth century (and reinforced in the twentieth century by English 'ogre'). But it could not compete, in Iberian folklore, with the ancestral and consolidated 'giant' or its equivalents *diablo*, *ojanco*, *ojáncano* and *olharapo* (these last three for a one-eyed giant).[26]

## Supernatural Women: Between Loneliness and Sociability

Although rare, there are some *fadas* ('fairies') attested in Iberian folklore. A spell written down in 1455 in High Aragonese dialect began as follows: *Por la manyana de Sanct Johan, tres buenas fadas* ('For the morning of Saint John, three good fairies').[27] It is a sister formula to other Iberian and international examples that invoke three women magically associated with healing rites and often with spinning.[28] They are presumably relatives of *moiras*, *parcas* and other magical triads, controllers of the threads of human destiny; of the protagonists of the international tale-type ATU 501 'The Three Old Spinning Women', of which there are Iberian versions; and of the three magical women (mothers, many times, of the winds) that in countless Iberian tales and, indeed, tales from around the world guide the hero or heroine on their zigzagging journey through the universe. That the traditional Iberian supernatural had, since the fifteenth century and probably since antiquity, beliefs and formulas that followed this scheme is significant. After all, three (sometimes four, when there is a mother and three daughters) can be considered a community, albeit a small one.

There is also the solitary female captured in the wilderness by a human male. She goes on to beget children who will become heads of prosperous noble houses. Worth remembering here is the Dama do Pé de Cabra ('Lady with a goat's foot') evoked in the Portuguese *Livro de Linhagens* (1340–44) by the Count of Barcelos: a beautiful woman that the hunter Don Diego López found on a rock. Years later, when Don Diego broke his promise and mentioned a sacred person, she escaped to the mountains with her daughter. The son who stayed with Don Diego would be the founder of the House of Haro, holder until the fourteenth century of the lordship of Vizcaya.[29] Dona Marinha was, according to the same book, captured in the sea by Don Froiam. From their union several children were born, among them the legendary founder of the Mariños or Marihnos lineages of Galicia and Portugal. The marriage was happily formalized when Don Froiam managed to cure Marinha's inability to speak.[30]

There are similar Basque legends. The goddess Mari escapes surrounded in flames when a man with whom she has had seven children ties her up to take her to church.[31] There are, too, the Catalan legends of *La dona d'aigua de Casa Blanch* and *La dona d'aigua de Valldarrós* who disappeared, abandoning their children, when they heard forbidden words from their husbands.[32] The Portuguese legend of O Zé-da-moura, about a Moor and a hunter who founded the family of the Mouras, also belongs to this category.[33] Some scholars consider these stories to be Melusinian in inspiration. But the truth is that they are outshoots from the larger tradition, documented since antiquity, of 'The marriage of fairy and mortal'. These women are separated first (when alone and vulnerable) from their worlds and families, and then become founders of fertile human lineages. They move from the wild to the civilized, and finally they return to the wild.

A different solution is proposed by the ballads of *La infantina* ('The Little Princess') and *El caballero burlado* ('The Mocked Knight'). There a supernatural woman, enchanted for several years up among the branches of a tree, avoids the sexual assaults of the knight who brings her to a city. She manages to remain there, for a time, without male company. There are also the sullen protagonists of the ballads of *La serrana de la Vera* ('The Woman of the Mountains of la Vera') and *La gallarda matadora* ('The Killer "Gallarda"'). These female supernatural beings kidnap and seduce male travellers. Some versions suggest that the *serrana* came from a lineage of horses, and researchers have linked her to ancestral numinous females.[34]

The Elpha in verses 2604–05 of the *Cantar de mio Cid* (early thirteenth century) also appears to be solitary in habit: *A siniestro dexan a Griza, que Álamos pobló / (allí son caños do a Elpha encerró)* ('To the left they leave Griza, that Alamos populated / (there are the pipes [of a fountain] in which he enclosed Elpha)').[35] Maybe that mysterious female (whose name suggests links with the Elphic legends from the North of the Pyrenees), enclosed in some *caños* (that is, in a fountain) by a founding hero no less enigmatic than she, Alamos, is a relative of the many Iberian supernatural women who are said to have been confined in fountains because the human entrusted with their liberation made some mistake.[36] The human who botched the job also lost, it should be noted, the chance of obtaining a great treasure, since such supernatural females are considered guardians of subterranean gold.

There is no lack of stories, of course, of humans who steal or attempt to steal the often golden combs, goblets, chalices, towels or sheets of a single woman or of a community of supernatural women. Some of these humans become rich themselves, while precipitating the decline of the magical community;[37] others are severely punished; many see the stolen gold become coal or ashes, as soon as they return home. Stories of this type were also assigned to *duendes* (goblins), in such a way that the expression *tesoro de duende* ('goblin treasure') became very common in Spain. Indeed, Sebastián de Covarrubias dedicated an entry to just this in his lexicographical compilation of 1611.[38]

It should be noted here that some supernatural women show themselves to humans for brief moments (especially on the feast of San Juan) at fountains, wells, bridges (there is a close association with water), caves and ruins. They typically appear alone. There are also the sometimes gigantic *hilanderas* ('spinners'), who carry big rocks (or megaliths) on their heads, rocks that they deposit in the wilds in prominent places: these stones are sometimes unsteady and can be rocked by visitors. In Basque-Navarre tradition there are male giants who move or throw great rocks from one place to another.

Other supernatural women include the rulers of hosts of humans, wolves and other beasts. Among these is the Galician Queen Lupa or Loba (who was also associated with snakes and Moorish treasures).[39] One Ana María la Lobera from Asturias was prosecuted in the mid-seventeenth century by the Inquisition for allegedly leading a party of seven diabolical wolves.[40]

Reports on the sociability of Iberian supernatural women tend to be imprecise, voluble and even contradictory. Basque *lamias* and Catalan *dones d'aigua* ('women of water') or *encantades*, for example, are described in most, but not all, accounts as being social. A large number of Catalan tales speak of humans who go into some wild place and who are led by a magical woman to an underground city full of enchanted people. There are also Catalan tales about the men who steal or try to steal the golden sheets that such women, almost always in the plural, lay out to dry on the mountain slopes. The Iberian versions of the tale of the Midwife to the Fairies (ATU 476** 'Midwife in the Underworld') narrate how a human midwife is called to assist 'a *gentil* woman' or a *lamia* (in several Basque versions), or a *moura* (in some Portuguese versions). The folktale implies that the new mother is supported by a family network, since there is no lack of relatives to carry, bring and pay the human midwife.[41]

There is a Cantabrian legend about *anganas* or *anjanas*: their names have, incidentally, very interesting connections with those of other more or less analogous European creatures.[42] There we learn of a cave in which 'these tiny women, called *anganas*, lived. They had long breasts, carried children on their backs and sometimes went out to steal the *borona* [hot corn bread]'.[43] This points to some elementary family unit. Other data on supernatural females (*gigantas*, *moras*, *ojáncanas*) with enormous and hanging breasts suggests that they survived their male giant cousins.[44] The legends about supernatural beings stealing the *borona* are attributed, in the north of Spain, to the *trasgos* or *trasgus* (usually goblins). The theft of milk is considered, of course, to be typical of witches.

The mythological *moras* seem to have been more unsociable than their male counterparts the *moros*. Let us consider the evidence of toponymy. The 2018 compilation of Salamancan legends by José Puerto does not report any toponyms alluding to *moras*, females, in the plural.[45] But there are a few relating to solitary *moras*: *La peña la mora* ('The Mora's Stone'), *La cueva de la mora* ('The Mora's Cave'), *La casa de la mora* ('The Mora's House'). With the *moros* there are, instead, only a handful of toponyms that speak of males in the singular: *La fuente del moro* ('The Moro's Spring'), *El caño del moro* ('The Moro's Pipe'), *La peña del moro* ('The Moro's Stone'). There are many, many more toponyms that point to the *moros* in the plural: *La sala de los moros* ('The Moros' Room'), *El pozo de los moros* ('The Moros' Well'), amongst others.

Over a large part of Iberia there exists folklore about *la encantada* ('the enchanted woman') or *las encantadas* ('the enchanted women'), but not of the masculine *los encantados*.[46] This, then, serves as additional proof of the general importance of the feminine in the social supernatural.

## *Gentiles:* The Male Social Supernatural?

Perhaps the supernatural guild that in Iberia seems to refer to cultural strata of more archaic resonance is that of the *gentiles*. These were a 'race' or lineage of prehistoric giants who were said to live in caves and desolate rocks, governed by elders. The elders prophesized to their people that the hour of their extinction was coming. This was usually because the appearance of a star or some other natural event announced the birth of Christ or the imminent invasion of their lands by Christians.

The *gentiles*' bones, 'tombs' and colossal footprints were, tradition tells us, to be found in wild landscapes and at desolate ruins. The *gentiles* must have had common roots across Iberia in past centuries, though in the last generations they have been increasingly limited to the Basque-Navarre region.[47] A Spanish ballad of the sixteenth century ran together the story of the ruin of the *gentiles* with that of the Moors expelled from the kingdom of Granada, at the other end of the country.[48] In Asturias in the eighteenth century, 'tombs of *gentiles*' in old prehistoric *castros* (ruins of villages or forts) were still pointed out to visitors.[49] It is significant that more or less analogous beliefs and narratives about *gentiles* have been well documented in various traditions in both North and South America.[50] There are similar gigantomachies elsewhere in Europe and, indeed, throughout the world. Particularly interesting are the stories, documented in points as distant as Minorca and the Canary Islands,[51] about giants that killed each other before the time of the humans.

There are some Basque-Navarre folklore stories that speak of giants with gregarious habits. One of them narrates that giants (in the plural) used to come to spend evenings at the house of a couple in the town of Ataun—though this friendship between humans and giants ended when the couple stole the giants' golden sheet.[52] The *Baxajaunes* are said to have been another prehistoric race, whose memory is also associated with the Basque-Navarre area. They lost the monopoly on cereal sowing when Saint Martin or Saint Martinico, a kind of trickster more Promethean than Christian, hid and stole grain by putting it in his boot: 'They say that at a certain time the Baxajaunes lived in the cave of Muskia. Cultivating the lands of the nearby mountain peaks, they gathered a great quantity of wheat.'[53]

We might also consider here an account from the *Diálogos familiares de la agricultura cristiana* (*Christian Agriculture Family Dialogues*, 1589) by Juan de Pineda, about a piper who was taken by the Devil to an underwater palace where many no doubt diabolical hunchbacked goblins danced to the sound of his instrument. The piper was so frightened that when he returned to his village he gave up his trade and sold his pipes.[54] This is a very rare type of narrative, though in the oral tradition of the province of Cádiz there is a story about a goatherd who, after entering a cave in search of a lost goat, is led by a mysterious individual to a valley of happy people. When he left, so many years had passed that almost all his contemporaries had died, and he was recognized only by his now aged daughter.[55] In remotest Peru a tale has been recorded that follows the same narrative and whose hero is called Doroteo the harpist.[56] In spite of the scarcity of known parallels, the tale dated to 1589 has this annotation: 'I have often heard of various pipers or drummers who have been taken to hell to play'. Here is a reminder (were we to need it) that the oral stories that have been written up are a small sample in comparison with those that circulate or that once circulated orally. Here too we find proof that magical subterranean communities, a mirror held up to humanity, have played their part in the Iberian supernatural.[57]

## Notes

1. The term 'popular mythology', although debatable (because 'myth' primarily refers to times of origins and religious, mystical or heroic records), has an interesting scholarly tradition in Iberia and, indeed, Europe. See J.M. Pedrosa, '¿Literatura oral? ¿Tradicional? ¿Popular? ¿Mitología popular?', *Literatura popular: simposio sobre literatura popular. Definición y propuesta de bibliografía básica* (Urueña: Fundación Joaquín Díaz, 2010), 31–38. Relevant works that have used the term 'myth' or 'mythology' include: Z. Consiglieri Pedroso, *Contribuições para uma mythologia popular portugueza* (Porto: Imprensa Commercial, 1880); A. de Llano Roza de Ampudia, *Del folklore asturiano: mitos, supersticiones, costumbres* (Madrid: Talleres de Voluntad, 1922); C. Cabal, 'Mitología ibérica', *Folklore y costumbres de España*, vol. 1, ed. F. Carreras y Candi (Barcelona: Editorial Alberto Martín, 1931–34), 165–288; J. Caro Baroja, *Algunos mitos españoles: ensayos de mitología popular* (Madrid: Editora Nacional-Sociedad

Española de Antropología, Etnografía y Prehistoria-Rústica editorial, 1941); *Ritos y mitos equívocos* (Madrid: Istmo, 1989); J. Camarena Laucirica, 'Mitología del lobo en la Península Ibérica', *La légende: anthropologie, histoire, littérature* (Madrid: Casa de Velázquez, 1989), 267–89; and J.M. Pedrosa et al., *Gilgamesh, Prometeo, Ulises y San Martín: mitología vasca y mitología comparada* (Ataun, Guipúzcoa: Fundación José Miguel de Barandiarán, 2009).

2. Editors' note: see further Chapter 1 of the current volume.
3. We will thus ignore solitary storm genies (e.g. the *nubero* or 'cloud devils'), vampires (the *sacamantecas* or 'grease stealers'), bogeymen, lycanthropes, ghosts and *ánimas en pena* or 'the damned', fish men (e.g. the fish Nicolás, the fish man of Liérganes), hens with their golden chicks, monstrous reptiles (the lizard of Jaén, the *cuélebres*, 'dracs' or dragons), infernal dogs and many other of the traditional fauna of magical Iberia.
4. Ideally, we need not just an 'Iberian popular mythology', as I have partially attempted here, but a 'pan-Hispanic popular mythology', charting Spain and Portugal's wider influence on the supernatural.
5. The bibliography on this subject is extensive. See F.X. d'Athaide Oliveira, *As mouras encantadas e os encantamentos no Algarve* (Tavira: Typographia Burocratica, 1898); M. Llinares García, *Os mouros no imaxinario popular galego* (Santiago de Compostela: Universidade, 1990); F. Alonso Romero, 'Las mouras constructoras de megalitos: estudio comparativo del folklore gallego con el de otras comunidades europeas', *Anuario Brigantino* 21 (1998), 11–28; J. Suárez López, *Tesoros, ayalgas y chalgueiros: la fiebre del oro en Asturias* (Gijón: Muséu del Pueblu d'Asturies-Ayuntamiento, 2001); A. Parafita, *A mitologia dos mouros: lendas, mitos, serpentes, tesouros* (Vila Nova de Gaia: Gailivro, 2006); *Os mouros e as mouras: máxicos enigmáticos da mitoloxía popular: actas das V Xornadas de literatura de tradición oral* (A Coruña: Asociación de Escritores en Lingua Galega, 2012); M.J. Lacarra, 'La imagen del Otro: moros y moras en el folclore aragonés', *Le forme e la storia* 8 (2015), 455–67; J.J. Dias Marques, 'Os Mouros e Mouras Encantados: sua patrimonialização em Portugal e na Galiza e teorias sobre a origem do seu nome', *Galiza e(m) Nós: estudos para a comprensão do relacionamento cultural galego-português*, eds C. Pazos-Justo et al. (Lisboa: Edições Húmus-CEHUM, 2021), 229–69.
6. J.M. Pedrosa, 'Las brujas de Nochebuena y los diablos de San Juan: calendario pagano, calendario cristiano y ritos de paso', *Espejo de brujas: mujeres transgresoras a través de la historia*, eds M.J. Zamora Calvo and A. Ortiz (Madrid–Zacatecas: Abada Editores-Universidad Autónoma de Zacatecas, 2012), 265–96.
7. P. Vega Rodríguez, ed., *Descubre leyendas: legendario literario hispánico del siglo XIX* (Alicante: Biblioteca Virtual Miguel de Cervantes, 2018).
8. M.F. Martínez Reyes, *La narrativa oral en Honduras: nuevas exploraciones en los inicios del siglo XXI*, PhD thesis (Alcalá de Henares: Universidad, 2016), 101–02. Editors' note: for other similar reflections, see page 202 of the current volume.
9. M. de Braga, *Obras completas*, ed. Ursicino Domínguez del Val (Madrid: Fundación Universitaria Española, 1990), 145–53, 150–51.
10. The bibliography on this subject is enormous. Nearly all of it has been cited in the monumental treatise by P.R. Moya-Maleno, *Paleoetnología de la Hispania céltica: etnoarqueología, etnohistoria y folklore*, 2 vols (Oxford: Bar Publishing, 2020), above all in vol. 2. Fundamental studies on the continuity of the cults of sacred stones

and associated objects, from antiquity to contemporary folklore, include: M. Almagro-Gorbea et al., *Berrocales sagrados de Extremadura: orígenes de la religión popular de la Hispania Céltica* (Badajoz: Fondo de Educación y Promoción de Caja Rural de Extremadura, 2021); M. Almagro-Gorbea and F. Alonso Romero, *Peñas sacras de Galicia* (Betanzos, A Coruña: Fundación L. Monteagudo, 2022).

11. Moya-Maleno, 'Airo(nis)', *Paleoetnología*, vol. 2, 433–34.
12. See J.M. Pedrosa, '*El pozo airón*: dos romances y dos leyendas', *Medioevo Romanzo* 18 (1993), 261–75.
13. F. Díez de Velasco, *Termalismo y religión: la sacralización del agua termal en la Península Ibérica y el norte de África en el mundo antiguo* (Madrid: Universidad Complutense, 1998).
14. For Greco-Roman nymphs, see J. Larson, *Greek Nymphs: Myth, Cult, Lore* (Oxford: Oxford University Press, 2001).
15. S. de Covarrubias Horozco, *Tesoro de la lengua castellana o española*, eds I. Arellano and R. Zafra (Madrid–Frankfurt am Main: Iberoamericana-Vervuert, 2006), s.v. '*vara*'.
16. Covarrubias Horozco, *Tesoro*, s.v. '*fada*'.
17. Maxime Chevalier, 'Fórmulas de cuentos tradicionales en textos del Siglo de Oro', *Cuento tradicional, cultura, literatura (siglos XVI–XIX)* (Salamanca: Universidad, 1999), 29–37 at 37.
18. Ibid., 30.
19. A.M. Espinosa, *Cuentos populares recogidos de la tradición de España*, eds L. Díaz Viana and S. Asensio Llamas (Madrid: Consejo Superior de Investigaciones Científicas, 2009).
20. The tale was published in J.M. Pedrosa, '*Del caballero que hacía hablar a los coños*: un *fabliau* francés del siglo XIII y sus paralelos orales hispánicos (ATU 1391)', *Artifara* 21 (2021), 225–48 at 237.
21. For the international context, see G.L. Beccaria, *I nomi del mondo: santi, demoni, folletti e le parole perdute* (Torino: Einaudi, 1995).
22. G. Rohlfs, 'El problema de la *vetula*', *Estudios sobre el léxico románico*, trans. M. Alvar López (Madrid: Gredos, 1979), 79–103; M.P. Benito, 'Las abuelas: mito, leyenda y rito', *Temas de Antropología Aragonesa* 3 (1987), 46–66; L. Mariño, 'Arco da Vella, vaite de aí… Relatos míticos que explican porque esconxuramos ó Arco', *O medo é libre: os mecanismos do medo na literatura de tradición oral. Actas da XIV Xornada de Literatura de Tradición Oral* (A Coruña: Asociación de Escritoras e Escritores en Lingua Galega, 2021), 35–60; 'Anna Perenna, la diosa nutricia anciana: del pan de los vivos a la leche de los muertos', *Liburna* 19 (2022), 109–62.
23. Espinosa, *Cuentos populares*, núm. 99, 'La niña sin brazos', 348.
24. In the *Diccionario de la Real Academia Española*, the word *dama* has no meaning related to the supernatural. Note that 'Lady' is one of the most common names for fairies in Europe: think of *Dame Abundia*, the *dominae nocturnae*, the Sicilian *donni di fori*, etc.
25. F. Camps y Mercadal, *Folklore menorquín (de la pagesía)*, vol. 2 (Mahón: M. Sintes Rotger, 1918), 42–43.
26. J. Camarena Laucirica, M. Chevalier, J.L. Agúndez García, Á. Hernández Fernández and A.J. Sánchez Ferra, *Catálogo tipológico del cuento folklórico hispánico*, vol. 5: *Cuentos del ogro tonto* (Cabanillas del Campo, Guadalajara: Palabras del Candil, 2022): tale-type ATU 1137 'The Blinded Ogre'. For the Italian context in which *orco* has

replaced a range of local terms, see T. Braccini, *Indagine sull'orco: miti e storie del divoratore di bambini* (Bologna: Il Mulino, 2013).

27. M. del Carmen García Herrero, 'Curar con palabras' [together with María Jesús Torreblanca Gaspar], *Del nacer y el vivir: fragmentos para una historia de la vida en la Baja Edad Media*, ed. Á. Muñoz Fernández (Zaragoza: Institución 'Fernando el Católico, 2005), 387–406.

28. J.M. Pedrosa, '*Las tres hilanderas*: memoria oral y raíces míticas de algunos ensalmos hispánicos y paneuropeos', *Entre la magia y la religión: oraciones, conjuros, ensalmos* (Oiartzun: Sendoa, 2000), 172–206; *Des Fata aux fées*, eds M. Hennard Dutheil de la Rochère and V. Dasen, Études de Lettres 3–4 (2011); E. Cianci, *The German Tradition of the Three Good Brothers Charm* (Göppingen: Kümmerle Verlag, 2013).

29. J.R. Prieto Lasa, *Las leyendas de los señores de Vizcaya y la tradición melusiniana* (Madrid: Fundación Ramón Menéndez Pidal, 1995); A. Dacosta, 'De la conciencia del linaje a la defensa estamental: acerca de algunas narrativas nobiliarias vascas', *Medievalista* 8 (2010), 1–51; L. Krus, 'La muerte de las hadas: la leyenda genealógica de la dama de pie cabra', *La conciencia de los antepasados: la construccion de la memoria de la nobleza en la Baja Edad Media*, eds A.F. Dacosta et al. (Madrid: Marcial Pons Historia, 2014), 43–86.

30. F. Delpech, 'La légende de Dona Marinha: mythologie et généalogie', *Cuadernos de Estraudios Gallegos* 55, 121 (2008), 407–26; 'Dona Marinha: avatars auriséculaires', *L'imaginaire des espaces aquatiques en Espagne et au Portugal* (París: Presses de la Sorbonne Nouvelle, 2009), 237–59; M.V. García Quintela, 'Mariña concubina, Mariña Virgen, Boand adúltera: fecundidad extramarital y genealogía de los paisajes', *Folclore y leyendas en la Península Ibérica: en torno a la obra de François Delpech*, eds M. Tausiet and H. Tropé (Madrid: Consejo Superior de Investigaciones Científicas, 2014), 57–80.

31. 'Mari de Muru', [*Eusko-folklore: materiales y cuestionarios*, enero-junio de 1957, 3ª serie, nº 9]; J. Caro Baroja, 'Las lamias vascas y otros mitos', *Algunos mitos españoles: ensayos de mitología popular* (Madrid: Editora Nacional, 1941), 23–69, 48–49.

32. See V. Balaguer, 'La leyenda de la mujer de agua', *Revista contemporánea* 22, 103 (julio–agosto 1896), 16–18; F. Maspons y Labrós, 'La dona d'aigua', *Tradicions del Vallés* (Barcelona: Estampa de la Renaixensa, 1876), 15–25; see also R. Violant i Ribera, *El món màgic de les fades* (Sant Vicenç de Castellet, 2002).

33. A. Parafita, *A mitología dos mouros: lendas, mitos, serpentes, tesouros* (Porto: Gailivro, 2006), n. 83, 259.

34. J. Caro Baroja, 'La Serrana de la Vera, o un pueblo analizado en conceptos y símbolos inactuales', *Ritos y mitos equívocos* (Madrid: Istmo, 1989), 259–338.

35. *Cantar de mio Cid*, ed. A. Montaner (Madrid: Real Academia de la Lengua, 2011), 165.

36. J.M. Pedrosa, 'La contribución de Asturias a la mitología y la leyendística hispánicas: a propósito del cinturón de la xana', *El patrimonio oral de Asturias: Actas del Congreso Internacional*, eds X.C. Busto Cortina, J. Suárez López and J.C. Villaverde Amieva (Oviedo: Ediciones Trabe, 2016), 89–127. One should also remember the beings that certain gods or classical héroes managed to confine: Typhon crushed by Zeus under Etna, or the monster that ends up stuffed inside a wooden post in the novel (inspired by old folklore legends) *Die schwarze Spinne* (*The Black Spider*), 1842, by the Swiss author Jeremias Gotthelf.

37. J.M. Pedrosa, 'El ocaso de las hadas: mitologías del triunfo de lo civilizado sobre lo salvaje y de la religión sobre la magia', *Litterae Vasconicae* 13 (2013), 87–133, 102–10.
38. Covarrubias Horozco, *Tesoro*, s.v. 'duende'.
39. M. del Mar Llinares, *Mouros, ánimas, demonios: el imaginario popular gallego* (Madrid: Akal, 1990), 57–73; M.J. Lacarra, 'Una colección inédita de *Milagros de San Antonio de Padua*: edición y estudio', *Revista de Literatura Medieval* 14 (2002), 9–33, 15–17.
40. J.M. Pedrosa, 'Ana María la Lobera, capitana de lobos, ante la Inquisición (1648): mito, folclore, historia', *Edad de Oro* 27 (2008), 219–51.
41. Ó. Abenójar, 'El cuento tradicional de *La comadrona en el otro mundo* a la luz de nuevas versiones ibéricas y saharianas', *Revista de literaturas populares* 15 (2015), 375–401.
42. *Fate: madri, amanti, streghe*, ed. S.M. Barillari (Alessandria: Edizioni dell'Orso, 2012); see also the review of D. Ermacora, in *Studi e materiali di storia delle religioni* 2 (2013), 678–86.
43. J. Haya Martínez, 'Sobre mitología montañesa (Las *anjanas*)', *Narria* 12 (1978), 27–9 at 29.
44. J. Suárez López, 'La mujer salvaje que voltea sus pechos sobre los hombros: una leyenda asturiana y sus paralelos universales', *Imaxes de muller: representación da feminidade en mitos, contos e lendas*, ed. C. Noia (Vigo: Universidade, 2012), 83–98; Haya Martínez, 'Sobre mitología montañesa', 29. Editors' note: for other examples of pendulous breasts among the supernatural, see pp. 238, 249 and 250–51.
45. J.L. Puerto, *Leyendas de tradición oral en la provincia de Salamanca* (Salamanca: Diputación-Instituto de las Identidades, 2018).
46. See J.F. Jordán Montes, 'Las encantadas de Murcia y su vinculación a las aguas y a la luz de San Juan', *Revista Murciana de antropología* 22 (2015), 13–52.
47. A. Ercoreca, 'Los gentiles (El mito de los gigantes en el País Vasco)', *Cuadernos de etnología y etnografía de Navarra* 23 (1976), 309–65.
48. J.M. Pedrosa, '*La profecía del moro santón de Granada, ca.* 1530: romancero, taumaturgia y milenarismo', *Mirando desde el puente: estudios en homenaje al profesor James S. Amelang*, eds F. Andrés, M. Hernández and S. Martínez (Madrid: Universidad Autónoma de Madrid, 2019), 201–13.
49. V. Álvarez Martínez et al., 'Percepciones míticas y pautas de comportamiento en torno a los espacios megalíticos de montaña. Un caso de estudio: *La Carreiriega de los Gallegos* (Ayande, Asturias)', *Actas de las II Jornadas de Jóvenes en Investigación Arqueológica (Madrid, 6, 7 y 8 de mayo de 2009)* (Madrid: Pórtico-Organización de Jóvenes en Investigación Arqueológica, 2011), 157–65.
50. J.M. Pedrosa, 'Los gentiles de los Pirineos y los gentiles de los Andes: razas prehistóricas, apocalipsis y geomitologías', *Sacra saxa: creencias y ritos en peñas sagradas. Actas del Coloquio Internacional celebrado en Huesca del 25 al 27 de noviembre de 2016*, eds M. Almagro-Gorbea and Á. Gari Lacruz (Huesca: Instituto de Estudios Altoaragoneses, 2017), 200–23.
51. Camps y Mercadal, 'Tradicions dels gegants', *Folklore menorquín*, 59–62; of special interest, too, is the chapter 'Recorts des temps dels Moros', 63–87. M. Trapero, *La flor del Oroval: romances, cuentos y leyendas de San Bartolomé de Tirajana* (Las Palmas de Gran Canaria: Ayuntamiento de San Bartolomé de Tirajana, 1993), 69.
52. R.M. de Azkue, *Euskalerriaren Yakintza: literatura popular del País Vasco*, vol. 2 (Madrid: Euskaltzaindia-Espasa Calpe, 1989), §237.

53. J.M. Pedrosa et al., *Gilgamesh, Prometeo, Ulises y San Martín: mitología vasca y mitología comparada* (Ataun, Guipuzcoa: Fundación José Miguel de Barandiarán, 2009).
54. J. de Pineda, *Diálogos familiares de la agricultura cristiana*, vol. 3, ed. J. Meseguer Fernández (Madrid: Atlas, 1963–64), 290–91.
55. J.I. Pérez and A.M. Martínez, *Leyendas y cuentos de encantamiento recogidos junto al Estrecho de Gibraltar* (Tarifa: Asociación LitOral, 2004).
56. *Tradiciones orales de Huancavelica: relatos del primer concurso de recopilación de tradiciones orales* (Lima: Biblioteca Nacional de Perú, n.d.), 115–19.
57. *The Tower of the Seven Hunchbacks* is the name of a novel by Emilio Carrere (1920) and of a masterful film (1944) by Edgar Neville, set at the end of the nineteenth century, which narrates how an archaeologist discovers a subway city under Madrid that had been a former refuge for many Jews resisting expulsion. The place would later be occupied by a disturbing band of hunchbacks. The novel and the film, while being very valuable examples of sophisticated literate culture, are also examples of the debt that the culture from above owes to the folklore that radiates from below.

CHAPTER NINE

# France: Humanlike Societies and Spaces among the *Fées*

Andrea Maraschi (University of Bari)

## Sources and Essential Terminology

An analysis of the *fées* in medieval France can usefully start with Gervase of Tilbury (*c*.1150–1221), an Anglo-Norman lay intellectual. Gervase was one of the leading exponents of a renewed elite interest in natural wonders, and in phenomena which early medieval culture had not troubled to record, often viewing it as peasant nonsense.[1] Gervase spent a large part of his youth at the court of Henry II Plantagenet, and then went to study canon law at the University of Bologna, where he later taught.[2] He decided to collect numerous *mirabilia* in a volume for his patron, Henry the Young King (r.1170–83), but the project was completed only in 1215, when he published his famous *Otia imperialia* (*Recreation for an Emperor*) for the Holy Roman Emperor Otto IV. The Plantagenet court attracted many clerical intellectuals and was particularly eager to collect popular lore.[3] What is more, Gervase visited many Western cities, and lived in Arles in southern France after being appointed Marshal of the Kingdom of Burgundy.

The *Otia imperialia* were meant to entertain the emperor in his spare time. But they were also intended as a serious compendium of traditional and folklore knowledge, as well as a *speculum principis*.[4] An extremely curious intellectual, Gervase can be considered a folklorist and anthropologist *ante litteram*.[5] His collection of wonders includes demons of various sorts, dragons, sorcery, sirens, werewolves, sybils, mysterious caves, rivers, stones and, of course, *fées*.[6]

The medieval idea of *fées* is rather different from our own. The distinction is the result of an evolution which occurred in the seventeenth century and that turned *fées* into enchantresses and the like.[7] The Modern English noun

Andrea Maraschi, "France: Humanlike Societies and Spaces among the *Fées*" in: *The Exeter Companion to Fairies, Nereids, Trolls and Other Social Supernatural Beings: European Traditions*. University of Exeter Press (2024). © Andrea Maraschi. DOI: 10.47788/WYMP2420 'fairy' comes from the Old French *faerie*, *fae*. *Fae* is, in turn, derived from Latin *fata*, plural of *fatum* ('destiny').[8] The medieval concept of 'fairy' or *fée* was thus linked with ancient mythological figures who controlled human destiny: the Greek Moirai, later called Parcae by the Romans. Isidore of Seville,[9] in the seventh century, noted that the Parcae were also called *fata* or *fatae*.[10]

Gervase drew many of his stories from locals when he was living and working in Arles,[11] and he was sure to record the vernacular word for *fata*: the Provençal *fadas*.[12] The major terminological problem is that *fées* (Modern French, via Middle French *feie*) were rarely, if ever, called as such: *fée* is used as a term of convenience here for the social supernatural in France.[13] Traditions concerning similar social supernatural beings were ancient and widespread, which contributed to creating several versions of the same roles/stories. Besides, most of what we know about French *fées* comes from clerical accounts. Ecclesiastical authors easily distorted folklore traditions and translated local terms with Latin equivalents. This resulted in a powerful filter and historians thus cannot clearly see popular traditions. Several Latin terms describing *fées* were originally employed by the Romans to designate sylvan and rural deities, whereas some medieval sources (e.g. in Britain) used these terms to describe solitary domestic spirits.[14] The medieval *fées*, however, as well as inheriting the divinatory powers of the Parcae, also had erotic features which were more typical of classical nymphs. For this reason, Alfred Maury held that medieval fairies derived from both the Parcae and the nymphs, sometimes called *fatuae*.[15] Laurence Harf-Lancner suggests that the double nature of medieval fairies (*amantes* and *marraines*) stemmed from a conflation of two different mythological entities,[16] one symbolizing fate, and the other eros.[17]

A fundamental resource for central and southern French folklore are the writings of a thirteenth-century Bishop of Paris, William of Auvergne (in post 1228–49). William addressed local traditions in his *De universo* just a few years after Gervase. He noted that *vulgum* (the common people) called some creatures *fatatae*, 'for they have the power to *fatare*' (i.e. to predict the future).[18] Gervase, in turn, drew upon the major authority on the topic, Augustine, especially in the section of the *Otia imperialia* dedicated to nocturnal spirits. In a passage which Jacques Le Goff defined as the 'act de naissance' of the demon *incubi* (and from which also originated the term *cauchemar*, Old French *caucher* meaning 'to trample'),[19] Augustine writes that this was the name that people used to address *Silvanos et Panes* (Faunos), while aerial demons were in Gaul called *dusii*; Gervase writes *dusios*.[20]

Gervase adds a reference to *succubi*, which he addresses as *lamiae* and *larvae*. These were generic terms identifying 'all sorts of evil creatures of the night', though of an ambiguous nature.[21] As we shall see, Gervase put forward ideas that came from both ancient tradition and local folk beliefs. The meaning of *lamia* Gervase draws specifically from Isidore, who had it derive from the verb *lanio*, 'to tear apart'. *Lamiae* were thus female spirits who kidnapped and devoured newborns during the night.[22] The second term, *larva*, was thoroughly discussed by Augustine in his polemic against Apuleius in *De civitate Dei*. In his *De deo Socratis*, Apuleius claimed that such entities were originally human souls called *daemones* ('demons') inhabiting the second sphere—that is, air.[23] Apuleius argued that human souls were, to some extent, *daemones* (i.e. mediators between man and the gods) which had been deprived of their divine nature.[24] Furthermore, the destiny of human souls was morally determined: the souls of good humans became *lares*, otherwise they became *laruae*. *Lares* were guardian household deities, while *laruae* were wandering and frightening ones.[25]

To Augustine, though, Apuleius' taxonomy was unacceptable. Indeed, Augustine argued that such terms merely identified malicious entities. After Augustine, Isidore explained that *larvae* were fearful spirits of the dead, demons which were originally wicked men, and that frightened children at night.[26] The early medieval understanding of such beings was revolutionized first by Burchard of Worms, and then by Gervase himself. In the early eleventh century, Burchard introduced our earliest reference to female supernatural lovers (called *agrestes feminae* in Latin and *sylvaticas* in the local language), which would become a motif in courtly literature.[27] In the same passage Burchard mentions the Parcae as well. This time, however, they are not the typical spinners, but rather beings who are able to turn men into werewolves. It was a clear change in tradition, which took place between the eleventh and the twelfth century. Gervase, for his part, was the first to link this new tradition with *fées*. He states that *larvas*—he reports their Provençal name as well, *fadas*—were feminine beings who became the lovers of men:[28] the term *fées* had now lost its original connection with *fatae*, and thus with the power of prophecy.[29] While Gervase represents a key turning point in the conceptualization of these entities in medieval France, however, he does not offer a definitive taxonomy of *fées*.[30]

The aim of this volume—outlining supernatural societies parallel to humans—is every bit as challenging. Nonetheless, in the following sections I will try to highlight the social and human features of the French social supernatural, so as to verify whether they represented parallels of the society that produced them. I will analyse various social aspects of *fées*: i) beings who shared their living space with humans; ii) groups of *fées* who had similar features to human society; and iii) *fée* societies which actually mirrored human society. The last part of this chapter will consider the development of legends of social *fées* in early modern and modern France.

## Social and Human Features of the *Fées*: Shared Spaces

There were two medieval traditions concerning *fées*: a northern one, featuring the figure of Melusine, *lamiae*, *nutons* and *lutins*, and a southern one, which includes *follets* ('sprites', 'goblins'), *fadas*, *dracs* and dolphins.[31] Not all such beings have humanlike characteristics in terms of social mores, hierarchies, features, and so on. After all, medieval intellectuals tended to collect information which they believed was useful for their own purposes, and all too often ignored important details.

*Follets* (the folk of southern France called them *folettos*) were invisible demons (resembling poltergeists, kobolds, hobgoblins) with human attitudes.[32] They inhabited peasant houses (whether individually or in groups, it is impossible to say), and spoke the same language.[33] Though not dangerous, they pestered humans with God's permission.[34] Unfortunately, Gervase does not add further details since he included them in his now lost *Vita abbreuiata et miraculis beatissimi Antonii*. *Folettos* seem to have corresponded to the northern French *neptunos* (another word which Gervase draws from the vernacular), visible beings who could help with various tasks in the household.[35] These creatures were likely the French *nutons* or *lutins*,[36] and since the author was a careful recorder of local legends, he may have used a Latinized version or simply opted to Latinize them as *neptunos*. It was an interesting terminological choice, since it overlaps with the god Neptune from which the terms *nutons*, *lutins* and other variants in turn derive.[37] However, it seems clear from the text that *neptunos* were not sea deities, which suggests that Gervase may have used a Latin word to report a folk legend 'due to a similarity in the sound of their names'.[38] *Neptunos* shared the hearth as well with human beings. There these undersized *fées* used to warm themselves and to cook their own food.

If their look, clothes and habits were those of their hosts, their diet was peculiar. According to Gervase, these beings used to eat roasted *ranunculas* ('little frogs'). Frogs and toads enjoyed an ambiguous reputation in medieval Christendom. Toads were associated with the Devil, lust and greed,[39] while frogs recall biblical plagues (Exodus 8) and impure demonic spirits (Revelation 16:13). Nonetheless, the Church allowed frogs on meatless days and thus placed them in a similar category to fish. A recipe for frogs is included in the famous guidebook for women entitled *Le ménagier de Paris* (c.1393), and frogs' legs became a delicacy in French gastronomy.[40] Were *neptunos*' food habits a positive or a negative? The answer may be that it was a liminal diet for liminal figures. But note the very human act of *roasting* the frogs.[41]

As for *lamiae* and *laruae*—Gervase notes that the French called them *mascae* or *striae*—they sneak into houses for different purposes.[42] Gervase offers both a theological and a scientific explanation for the creatures. They could be demonic beings of either sex or nocturnal hallucinations caused by *grossitie humorum* ('thickening of the humours'). They disturbed sleepers by causing heaviness, an idea which clearly recalls Augustine's *incubi*.[43] Gervase also notes that it was believed they could fly through the skies at night. The same belief had already been attested in the early tenth-century *Canon Episcopi* and in Burchard's *Corrector*, and recalls the Wild Hunt tradition.[44] The female leader of the flying cortège, sometimes named Abundia, sometimes Satia, Diana, Herodias or Perchta, seems to have been some kind of queen of the fairies.[45] These beings engaged in some horrible practices, such as eating human meat, drinking human blood, and dismembering human bodies then later putting them back together in an incorrect fashion.[46]

Eating human meat (or drinking human blood) was an attribute of otherness—one which ancient and Christian intellectuals had long associated with uncivilized peoples, the most dreadful among the pagans, and finally with witches.[47] Yet Gervase states that such creatures could also perform harmless actions typical of household spirits, such as emptying (and then refilling) barrels of wine, or moving cradles from place to place (again, only because God allowed them to do so).[48] Gervase shares Apuleius' idea of *daemones* as experiencing the same emotions as humans, liking the same things (such as gifts, honours, etc.), and being experts in divination and *miracula magorum*—activities which were hardly Christian.[49] They thus represented a very close, though beastly, replica of humans, which may explain why humans were sometimes believed to become such beings.

## Social and Human Features of the *Fées*: Shared Features

Gervase was particularly familiar with the folklore of southern France, and he is most reliable when writing about local traditions there. In the province of Aix, in the Kingdom of Arles, he recorded the presence of *domine due uel plures* (which Jacques Le Goff identified as *fées*[50]) who used to appear to travellers on the vertical face of a crag. The cliff had several little cavities which looked just like windows and women leant out of these. To people observing them, it looked as if these women were chatting and joking like next-door neighbours, which reassured travellers since they were both beautiful and lovable. Gervase holds that this was a mere *fabula*, an illusion, because when one came closer to the crag, the ladies would disappear.

Though it is not easy to infer what the meaning of such a vision may have been, it suggests that humans could have *fée* counterparts, and Gervase includes dolphins among them. A very popular belief had it that on the bottom of lakes, rivers and seas were the dwellings of supernatural creatures.[51] As is already clear from Marie de France's and other Breton *lais*, water could become an entrance to the world of the *fées*.[52] A long-standing tradition dating back to Pliny had it that any land creature had a marine parallel, or that the motion of waves could create animal hybrids due to the abundance of moisture in the ocean.[53] Pliny anthropomorphized dolphins by stating that they lived in couples like husband and wife, emitted sounds similar to those made by humans in language, were lovers of music and were extremely friendly to humankind.

It should come as no surprise, then, that around AD 1200 people in southern France believed that dolphins were born as knights. Gervase tells the story of a dolphin which was struck by a spear thrown by a man on a vessel.[54] A storm arose soon after, and then, as the crew were facing death in the tempest, a knight appeared in the sea riding a horse. He took the sailor who had thrown the spear in exchange for calming the weather, and rode off with his hostage to a distant land.[55] Once there, the prisoner found out that the dolphin he had wounded was in fact a knight, but the human was fortunately able to heal him and so was released. This territory was then the abode of human–dolphin hybrids who could warn of imminent danger from storms.[56]

Regarding human-looking *fées*, Gervase was the first to write about the legend of Melusine to a learned audience. Much has been written about this famous story,[57] and here it will suffice to highlight the specific aspects of the legend which are relevant. The *Otia imperialia* feature the earliest form of the tale, which came from Provence and would later serve as the main source for Jean d'Arras's *Roman de Mélusine* (1392).[58] The story conforms to the motif of the *fées amantes*: the human protagonist, Raymond, lord of Rousset, falls in love with the astoundingly attractive Melusine (such beings were typically beautiful).[59] The lady has rich clothes and ornaments, and rides a splendid, caparisoned horse. Carnal union follows a mutual promise of marriage, which also has, though, a condition: the groom-to-be will enjoy great prosperity as long as he does not see his bride-to-be naked. The man later spies on his naked wife, something he will regret. Despite the supernatural characteristics of this *fée* (a human–serpent hybrid), there is no hint that these are inherited by her offspring in Gervase's text. For that detail we have to wait for Jean d'Arras and Coudrette.[60] On the evidence of Melusine, the *fée* appreciated human food. The night when the prohibition was broken, Raymond had been out hunting, and brought home wild game which he cooked for his wife.[61] This is a strong sign of affinity between *fées* and humans for, as suggested above, food was often a critical element in stories involving liminal entities. In fact, one finds several examples of how mortal food could be inedible to supernatural beings and vice versa, or could cause undesirable transformations/effects.[62] The ability to eat human food was likely another condition which allowed *fées* to become lovers of men and to live with them.

## Social and Human Features of the *Fées*: Mirrored Spaces

Not only could *fées* share habits and spaces with humans, but they could also look like humans, and their homes could resemble human abodes. If Melusine was unnaturally beautiful, other beings were simply indistinguishable from humans. This was the case with the *draci* (*dracs*).[63] These went to local markets in human form and knew human nature well enough to be able to lure people into their lairs. *Draci* lived in the depths of rivers and could take on the form of golden rings or cups. They would then float, in this golden form, in the waters where people were bathing or washing their clothes, encouraging them to stretch their hands to grab the shiny object.[64] *Dracs* especially employed this strategy to seize nursing-mothers and drag them down to their abodes.[65] They needed help in nursing their *drac* babies. Aristotle held that children absorbed qualities of their mothers' souls through milk, and this idea remained popular in medieval Europe.[66] Was this practice meant to forge a link with the surface world, and was it the reason they were able to morph into humans?

Gervase claims to have himself witnessed a woman being dragged down into the river Rhône. Women would be released by the *dracs* after seven years. They could then return to the surface. Those who made it back said that they were led to 'spacious palaces' under the water and were given some kind of remuneration there. As inhabitants of an upside-down world, *dracs* ate human flesh, but fed their human nursing-mothers appropriate food for humans.[67] This food could have supernatural powers. For instance, a woman in Beaucaire received an eel pasty and, after smearing her face with its fat, she gained underwater vision and was able to recognize *dracs* that walked the markets in human form: powers which were exclusive to such creatures.[68] This story (ML 5070 'Midwife to the Fairies') suggests that communication between these two worlds was meant to remain secret.

Women who were allegedly seized by such creatures described *drac* society as being similar to human society, both in terms of living spaces and social structures: they mentioned the presence of *drac* wives, for example. This *drac* realm could also be glimpsed from the banks of rivers: Gervase notes that along the river Rhône, to the north of Arles, a large submarine precipice was visible, inside which were said to be mansions and their *drac* inhabitants. Huge palaces with gates recall the *demones* in Mont Canigou, located in the French Pyrenees. Subterranean buildings often reflected human architecture but could be built with precious materials. In one Provençal legend, a human visitor follows a green-haired *fée* under the waters and enters her crystal palace.[69]

Humans could enter the realm of the *demones* if they were literally told to go to the Devil. According to Gervase, a father did just this to his little girl in La Junquera due to her constant crying. A demon seized her and carried her into the mountain, and she was only freed seven years later.[70] Her father found her like a ghost, with rolling eyes. She was incapable of communicating with other people. The same demons were also using humans as 'vehicles' (*uehiculo utebantur*). This may mean that they possessed human bodies for their own ends. A man who had been possessed described a subterranean cave filled with darkness, where the creatures would gather and greet each other after travelling through the whole world. Their society was hierarchical, for there were *maiores* ('superiors') to whom the creatures were supposed to report their accomplishments.[71]

The hierarchical structure of *fée* societies was no novelty. In Marie de France's *Lai de Lanval*, the two female *fées* appear to the knight to introduce him to their *dameisele*, who is waiting for him in a richly furnished pavilion fit for a queen. She is later presented to Arthur as the equivalent of a royal figure.[72] A very similar scene is described by Jean d'Arras in Raymond's encounter with Melusine. Melusine was the leading *faée* in the Colombiers forest in Poitou, a region crowded with *luytons, faées* and *bonnes dames*. These entered human houses nocturnally to play their pranks.[73]

The legend concerning Mont Canigou still surfaces in the *Cronaca de Cataluña* (1609),[74] and similar *fées* were believed to inhabit Mont Saint-Barthélemy as well. One finds numerous examples in French folklore of the demonic connotations of mountains and megalithic stones. These likely became the abodes of *fées* due to their traditional association with nature spirits (e.g. Mont Saint-Michel).[75]

## Gervase's Heritage

The medieval French *fée* were sometimes benign and sometimes evil, part supernatural helpers and part devilish deceivers. Their acts depended on the source, the author, the witness, the perspective, and so on.[76] But the Christian intelligentsia demonized them. These were dangerous pagan survivals, in terms that can be traced back, to a certain extent, to Augustine.[77]

Some thirty years after the publication of the *Roman de Mélusine*, the belief in *fées* in Joan of Arc's native village became one of the key accusations against *la Pucelle*.[78] There emerges the fact, in Jean d'Estivet's indictment, that Joan and the other locals used to visit a majestic beech in the Bois Chesnu of

Domrémy. The locals believed that *faees* gathered there. Such beings were evidently part of the village's syncretic supernatural.[79] They had the power of divination in line with the tradition of the *fatae*.[80] Besides, the sources seem to suggest that the belief in the *fée* was particularly popular among women. According to a seventy-year-old labourer who testified at Joan's rehabilitation process in 1456, women and *fées* used to gather under the tree to dance beneath it.[81] These dances may have been part of an ancestral pagan ritual,[82] and both Joan and her godmother Jeannette Thiesselin claimed, wisely, that they had never been involved in them.[83] The reason may be that dancing on certain days or at certain places was associated with pagan rituality.[84] For instance, a Carolingian capitulary from Vesoul (Haute-Saône) forbade dances near churches on Sundays or holy days, for they were, the capitulary claimed, remnants of pagan customs.[85] In medieval French romances, dance could often mark the arrival of the *fées*.[86] In the early 1600s, meanwhile, the French jurist Henry Boguet would say, about the witches' sabbat, that such dances '*semblables à celles des fees, vrays Diables incroporez qui regnoient il ny'y a pas longtemps*'.[87]

The idea of a hierarchical structure among *fées* returns in the Old French *Évangiles des quenouilles*, written in the 1480s. In a clearly biased work, the male author (a learned cleric) collected an oral database of feminine wisdom from a group of spinners, who were experts in midwifery, magic and divination. Among other things, the spinners believed that *faees* had their helpers steal skeins of thread for them: at least they did if the skeins had not been put on the reeling machine on Saturdays. One notes the *fées*' persistent link with spinning, a gendered job traditionally associated with the Parcae. The spinners are described as being particularly interested in '*de Sebile et des faeez*',[88] and their very names closely recall figures of medieval folklore, for instance Gomberde la Faee, Abonde du Four and Sebile des Mares.[89]

Humanoid *fées* or *fées* with humanlike habits survived in French folklore for centuries.[90] Small beings such as *lutins* continued to pester humans during the night, but also emulated human behaviour: they 'amuse themselves by plaiting the manes of horses to make stirrups or swings', Sébillot observed.[91] The same can be said about Melusinesque creatures, which continued to appear in Franche-Comté, Grenoble and Maine-et-Loire, as well as along the coasts of Gascogne and the banks of the Garonne.[92] Most interestingly, later French folklore suggests that *fées* lived in families and acted very much like humans, as in the case of the Martes of Berry.[93] This peculiar group of male and female *fées*, which was known in the regions of Indre and Haute-Vienne, used stone utensils to prepare their food, and while the males among them set the table on stones, females tried (in vain) to make a fire under the waterfall of Montgarnaud, on which they would put their granite pots. Gendered roles of this type surface in traditions linked with Luchon, in the French Central Pyrenees, where female water spirits, half-angels and half-serpents, were believed to wash and hang up their white laundry on stones along the banks of rivers. Similar creatures, all dressed in white, were said to come from crystal palaces in the Occitan town of Limoux.[94] The medieval idea according to which such structures were located at the bottom of bodies of water would still echo in Émile Souvestre's (1806–1854) Breton tale 'La Groac'h de l'Île'.

*Féeriques* societies could be useful narratological tools to reflect or criticize authors' own societies, as has been argued by modern writers such as Marie-Catherine d'Aulnoy and Charles Perrault.[95] D'Aulnoy in particular shows in her stories interesting continuities with medieval French folklore traditions. One striking example is her tale 'Le Dauphin', where the ugly prince Alidor stumbles upon a '*grand royaume*' in the woods, whose king is the '*Rois des Bois*'.[96] As well as offering a parallel society in the forest which may have been instrumental in discussing the myth of the Bon Sauvage, the tale seems to reprise the motif of anthropomorphized dolphins who inhabit a marvellous world: this recalls the early colonial plans of France across the Atlantic.[97] In the tale, a dolphin (also a symbol of French monarchy) helps Alidor to conquer the beautiful princess Livorette, and makes them king and queen of his own beautiful island.

The search for *fée* societies is challenging, for details are often scant in the early modern and modern ages. For instance, Rabelais's Pantagruel is told that his father has been brought to the land of *fées* by Morgan le Fay.[98] But nothing more is said about how its inhabitants live and organize their world, even though Gervase wanted *Morganda fatata* to be Arthur's sister and to live in the enchanted castle of Avalon.[99] In a roughly contemporary *chanson de geste* she was even married to Julius Caesar.[100] D'Aulnoy's tale 'Le Prince Lutin' by Marie-Catherine d'Aulnoy features the *fée* princess Abricotine, who lives secluded on a peculiar island, called *Ile des Plaisirs tranquilles*, which was inhabited only by women.[101] This island society had been set up by an old *fée* mother who abandoned the world of humans due to an unfortunate love affair. In response, she created 'an imbalance in the social order':[102] a society where men were not allowed, and where women of the Amazon race became '*les gardes et les officiers*'.[103]

These alternative supernatural worlds offered the chance for writers and storytellers to play with fantastic versions of human society, be they desirable or dreadful. They were an opportunity to populate the unknown and unknowable, filling it with soothing as well as with threatening beings. These worlds may have been a way of lessening loneliness, finding comfort, reminding the community that the world created by God was full of *mirabilia*. The *fées* could help humans, but were also liminal and therefore dangerous. Their world (both culturally and materially) was a mirror held up to human societies. Here was a reflection: close by, familiar, but one that was impossibly different.

## Notes

1. Gervase of Tilbury, *Otia imperialia: Recreation for an Emperor*, vol. 3, eds S.E. Banks and J.W. Binns (Oxford: Oxford University Press, 2002), 558. On this, see also L. Daston, 'Marvelous Facts and Miraculous Evidence in Early Modern Europe', *Critical Inquiry* 18 (1991), 93–124.
2. W. Maaz, 'Gervasius von Tilbury', *Enzyklopädie des Märchens*, vol. 5, eds R.W. Brednich et al. (Berlin–New York: De Gruyter, 1987), 1109–22.
3. Gervase of Tilbury, *Otia imperialia*, xxv.
4. F. Latella, 'Come lavorava un intellettuale laico del medioevo: gli Otia imperialia di Gervasio di Tilbury tra inventio e compilatio', *Revista de literatura medieval* 25 (2013), 103–34 at 108. On the immense success of Gervase's work, see Gervasio di Tilbury, *Il libro delle meraviglie*, ed. E. Bartoli (Ospedaletto: Pacini, 2009), 14–16. Gervase's written sources were proper *auctoritates* such as Pliny, Augustine, Gregory the Great, Sulpicius Severus, Isidore of Seville, Peter Comestor and others.
5. J. Le Goff, *Il meraviglioso e il quotidiano nell'Occidente medievale* (Rome–Bari: Laterza, 1983); Gervasio di Tilbury, *Il libro delle meraviglie*, 20.
6. M. Rothmann, '"Ex oculata fide" et "probatione cotidiana": die Aktualisierung und Regionalisierung natürlicher Zeichen und ihrer Ursachen im "Liber de mirabilibus mundi" des Gervasius von Tilbury', *Kloster und Bildung im Mittelalter*, eds N. Kruppa and J. Wilke (Göttingen: Vandenhoeck & Ruprecht, 2006), 355–83.
7. L. Harf-Lancner, *Les fées au Moyen Âge: Morgane et Mélusine. La naissance des fées* (Paris: Champion, 1984), 13.
8. C. Lecouteux, 'Les fées au Moyen Âge. Quelques remarques', *Bulletin de la Société de Mythologie Française* 146 (1987), 26–31; L. Harf-Lancner, *Le monde des fées dans l'Occident medieval* (Paris: Hachette, 2003). Until the fifteenth century, in Middle English, the word 'fairy' referred to a region (the place where the entities which in French were called *fées* lived). The term did not identify a specific type of creature, then, but could either be a place-name or a word for 'wonder', 'magic'. R.F. Green, *Elf Queens and Holy Friars: Fairy Beliefs and the Medieval Church* (Philadelphia: University of Pennsylvania Press, 2016), 208, n. 18. Editors' note: see also Chapter 4 (p. 58) of the current volume.
9. Isidoro di Siviglia, *Etimologie o origini*, ed. A. Valastro Canale (Turin: UTET, 2013), VIII.11.92–93, 715.
10. They could also have powers concerning fertility, childbirth and regeneration. On medieval terminology concerning fairies, see also J. Wade, *Fairies in Medieval Romance* (New York: Macmillan, 2011), 4–5; A. Byrne, *Otherworlds: Fantasy & History in Medieval Literature* (Oxford: Oxford University Press, 2016), 16–17.
11. Gervase of Tilbury, *Otia imperialia*, xxix–xxx.
12. Ibid., 730.
13. Green, *Elf Queens*, 2, 79.

14. C. Lecouteux, *The Tradition of Household Spirits: Ancestral Lore and Practices*, ed. J.E. Graham (Rochester, VT: Inner Traditions, 2013), 118.
15. A. Maury, *Le fées du Moyen-Âge: recherches sur leur origine, leur histoire et leurs attributs* (Paris: Librairie philosophique de Ladrange, 1843), 6ff.
16. On this kind of dichotomy, see Harf-Lancner, *Le monde des fées*; P. Gallais, 'Les fées seraient-elles nées au XIIe siècles? (À propos d'un ouvrage recent)', *Cahiers de civilisation médiévale* 116 (1986), 355–71; C. Ferlampin-Archer, 'Le don des fées à la naissance (Xe–XVe siècles): propositions autour d'un succes litteraire tardif', *Cultura dotta e cultura folclorica nei testi medievali*, ed. M. Lecco (Alessandria: Edizioni dell'Orso, 2019), 21–38.
17. Harf-Lancner, *Les fées au Moyen Âge*, 17–19.
18. William of Paris, *De universo*, in *Opera omnia* (Paris: D. Thierry, 1674), 593–1074, I, 3, XXIV, 791.
19. J. Le Goff, 'Culture cléricale et traditions folkloriques dans la civilisation mérovingienne', *Annales: economies, sociétés, civilisations* 22, 4 (1967), 780–91 at 785, n. 1.
20. Augustine, *De civitate Dei*, CSEL xl, 2, ed. E. Hoffmann (Prague: F. Tempsky, 1900), xv.23, 110.
21. M. van der Lugt, 'The *Incubus* in Scholastic Debate: Medicine, Theology and Popular Belief', *Religion and Medicine in the Middle Ages*, eds P. Biller and J. Ziegler (York: York Medieval Press, 2001), 175–200 at 182.
22. Isidoro di Siviglia, *Etimologie o origini*, VIII.11.102, 717. See Augustine, *De civitate Dei*, xv.23, 110. This tradition was consistent with the original Greek myth, according to which Lamia kidnapped and killed human children to take revenge on Hera, who had previously stolen her own children. H.C. Lea, ed., *Materials toward a History of Witchcraft*, vol. 1 (Pennsylvania: University of Pennsylvania Press, 1939), 109–11. It is worth noting that the meaning of *lamia* was not always the same in early medieval sources, and that the interpretation of nightly spirits depended on the author's background. M. Montesano, *Classical Culture and Witchcraft in Medieval and Renaissance Italy* (New York: Palgrave Macmillan, 2018), 95; B. Filotas, *Pagan Survivals, Superstitions and Popular Cultures in Early Medieval Pastoral Literature* (Toronto: Pontifical Institute of Mediaeval Studies, 2005), 81; S. Gordon, *Supernatural Encounters: Demons and the Restless Dead in Medieval England, c. 1050–1450* (London–New York: Routledge, 2020), 194–95.
23. Middle Platonist philosophers postulated the existence of three spheres: heaven (inhabited by the gods), earth (inhabited by men) and air (inhabited by *daemones*). V. Hunink, '"Apuleius, qui nobis Afris Afer est notior": Augustine's polemic against Apuleius in *De Civitate Dei*', *Scholia: Studies in Classical Antiquity* 12 (2003), 82–95 at 89–91.
24. Following Plato, *Timaeus*, 90d.
25. Apuleius, 'De deo Socratis', *Apulée: opuscules philosophiques et fragments*, ed. J. Beaujeu (Paris: Les Belles Lettres, 1973), xv–xvi, 34–37. If the moral judgement on an individual was uncertain, their soul would become gods known as *manes*.
26. Isidoro di Siviglia, *Etimologie o origini*, VIII.11.101, 717. See also Montesano, *Classical Culture*, 83–84.
27. Burchard of Worms, *Decretorum libri viginti*, *PL* 140, ed. J.P. Migne (Paris: Migne, 1880), 971.

28. Gervase of Tilbury, *Otia imperialia*, 730.
29. Harf-Lancner, *Le monde des fées*, 175–80.
30. S. Young, 'Against Taxonomy: Fairy Families in Cornwall', *Cornish Studies* 21 (2013), 223–37; Green, *Elf Queens*, 2.
31. T. Keightley, *The Fairy Mythology, Illustrative of the Romance and Superstition of Various Countries* (London: H.G. Bohn, 1850), 465ff.
32. Gervase of Tilbury, *Otia imperialia*, 98. The word is of French origin. See 'Follet', in *Le trésor de la langue française informatisé*, ATILF-CNRS and Université de Lorraine: http://atilf.atilf.fr/tlf.htm. The possible southern French origin of *folettos* is suggested by their popularity in the upper Aude Valley, the French Alps and Romandy (Lecouteux, *The Tradition of Household Spirits*, 46, 123, 131, 136, 165). The reference to local language is often a strong indication that the author collected such information first-hand. See R. Künzel, 'Paganisme, syncrétisme et culture religieuse populaire au haut Moyen Âge: réflexions de méthode', *Annales: economies, sociétés, civilisations* 47, 4–5 (1992), 1055–69.
33. F. Liebrecht, *Des Gervasius von Tilbury Otia imperialia, in einer auswahl neu herausgegeben und mit Anmerkungen begleitet* (Hannover: C. Rümpler, 1856), 74–75.
34. This idea dated back to Augustine, *De civitate Dei*, ii.23, 96–97.
35. Gervase of Tilbury, *Otia imperialia*, 674.
36. A much later source casts light on *lutins*' abilities: in 1697, Marie-Catherine d'Aulnoy would write in her *Le Prince Lutin* that they became invisible at will, that they could travel infinite distances at the speed of thought, and that they could go through the ground and the sea without dying, as well as through closed windows and doors. Marie-Catherine d'Aulnoy, *Contes des fées*, 2 vols, ed. P. Hourcade (Paris: Société des Textes Français Modernes, 1997–98), vol. 1, 122. See also D. Ermacora, 'Una nota su Leland, le sopravvivenze etrusche e la continuità dei teonimi del mondo classico nel folklore moderno', *Studi e materiali di storia delle religioni* 1 (2013), 277–86 at 280.
37. M.I. Gerhardt, *Old Men of the Sea: From Neptunus to Old French 'Luiton': Ancestry and Character of a Water-Spirit* (Amsterdam: Polak & Van Gennep, 1967), 36–37.
38. Gervase of Tilbury, *Otia imperialia*, 675, n. 2. See also: É. Dantinne, 'Les mystériuex habitants de nos cavernes: les Nutons de Wallonie et leur origine', *Les chercheurs de la Wallonie* 17 (1958–60), 173–99; C. Lecouteux, *Nos bons voisins les lutins: nains, elfes, lutins, gnomes, kobolds et compagnie* (Paris: José Corti, 2010); *Les nains et les elfes au Moyen Age* (Paris: Imago, 1988), 174–78.
39. N.J. Saunders, *Animali e spiritualità* (Turin: EDT, 2000), 106.
40. M. Weiss Adamson, *Food in Medieval Times* (Westport, CT: Greenwood Press, 2004), 44–45, 126, 198, 228.
41. C. Lévi-Strauss, *Le cru et le cuit* (Paris: Plon, 1964).
42. Gervase of Tilbury, *Otia imperialia*, 722–24. These terms are confusing, as they could mean different things depending on time and place. They date back to the laws of early Germanic peoples: C. Lecouteux, 'Mara, Ephialtes, incubus', *Études germaniques* 42 (1987), 1–24 at 3–4.
43. These were likely symptoms of sleep paralysis. S. Gordon, 'Medical Condition, Demon or Undead Corpse? Sleep Paralysis and the Nightmare in Medieval Europe', *Social History of Medicine* 28, 3 (2015), 425–44 at 433. Gervase's scientific explanation

was derived from Aristotle: Aristotle, *On Sleep and Dreams*, ed. D. Gallop (Warminster: Aris & Phillips, 1996) 3.37, 97–98.

44. Regino of Prüm, *Libri duo de synodalibus causis et disciplinis ecclesiasticis*, ed. F.W.H. Wasscherschleben (Leipzig: Engelmann, 1840; repr. Graz: Akademische Druck, 1964), 2.371, 354–56: *Canon episcopi*, *Corpus iuris canonici*, vol. 1, ed. E. Friedberg (Graz: Akademische Druck, 1955), 1030–31; Burchard of Worms, *Decretorum libri viginti*, 962–64.
45. Keightley, *The Fairy Mythology*, 476. She is also mentioned in the *Roman de la rose*, completed by 1280. G. de Lorris and J. de Meun, *The Romance of the Rose*, ed. C. Dahlberg (Princeton: Princeton University Press, 1995), 305–06.
46. This closely recalls *Edictus Rothari*, MGH LL, 4, *Leges Langobardorum*, ed. G.H. Pertz (Hannover Hahn, 1868), c. 376, 87. On this specific passage, see S. Gasparri, *La cultura tradizionale dei Longobardi: struttura tribale e resistenze pagane* (Spoleto: Cisam, 1983), 96–99.
47. On cannibalism as a negative marker in medieval Europe, see A.A. Montanari, *Il fiero pasto: antropofagie medievali* (Bòlogna: Il Mulino, 2015).
48. Gervase draws upon the authority of Imbert, Archbishop of Arles, who claimed his cradle had been moved outside his house by one of these *fantasmata* when he was a child. The motif of moving cradles or removing babies from them was still circulating in the seventeenth century in Piedmont and Liguria (near the border with France): Montesano, *Classical Culture*, 107–08. On the creatures' role on earth, the source was Augustine, *De civitate Dei*, xv.23, 109–14.
49. Apuleius, *De deo Socratis*, 12–14. On the development of the reputation of magic, see G. Marasco, 'L'accusa di magia e i cristiani nella tarda antichità', *Augustinianum* 51, 2 (2011), 367–421.
50. J. Le Goff, 'Une collecte ethnographique en Dauphiné au début du XIIIe siècle', *Le mond alpin et rhodanien: revue régionale d'ethnologie* 1–4 (1982), 55–65 at 63.
51. E.g. motifs F93.1 'River entrance to lower world'; F153 'Otherworld reached by diving into water (of well or lake)'; F213.3 'Sea-riding horse carries mortals to fairyland'.
52. Maria di Francia, *Lais*, ed. G. Angeli (Rome: Carocci, 2007), 393.
53. Pliny the Elder, *Naturalis historia libri XXXVII*, ed. K.F.T. Mayhoff (Leipzig: Teubner, 1906), ix.2.7–8; ix.4.10–11.
54. Gervase of Tilbury, *Otia imperialia*, 678–80.
55. The characteristics of the voyage (time distortion: the journey is long but takes a very short time; space distortion: the sea is a solid ground for the rider) recall the early medieval Irish tale *Immram Brain*. See *Immram Brain: Bran's Journey to the Land of Women*, ed. Séamus MacMathúna (Tübingen: Niemeyer, 1985).
56. This idea seems to have been quite widespread in European folklore (Gervase of Tilbury, *Otia imperialia*, 678, n. 1; see motif B300 'Helpful animal'), and birds especially had long been given the ability to forewarn of danger. See A.H. Krappe, 'Warning Animals', *Folklore* 59 (1948), 8–15.
57. E.g. Harf-Lancner, *Les fées au Moyen-Âge*; C. Lecouteux, 'Zur Entstehung der Melusinensage', *Zeitschrift für deutsche Philologie* 98 (1979), 73–84; *Mélusine et le chevalier au cygne* (Paris: Payot, 1982); W. Wunderlich, 'Frauen, die sich nicht über Wasser halten: zur kulturgeschichtlichen Genealogie von Nymphen, Nixen, wasserfeen', *Engel, Teufel und Dämonen: Einblicke in die Geisterwelt des Mittelalters*, eds

H. Herkommer and R.C. Schwinges (Basel: Schwabe, 2006), 141–62; E. Le Roy Ladurie and J. Le Goff, 'Mélusine maternelle et défricheuse', *Annales: economies, sociétés, civilisations* 26, 3–4 (1971), 587–622.
58. Gervase of Tilbury, *Otia imperialia*, 88–90. A similar Breton story was told by Marie de France in the *Lai de Lanval* (*Lais*, 170–207). Jean d'Arras calls the *fées* in Poitou *bonnes dames* or *luitons*.
59. The same can be observed in *Lanval*.
60. In later versions, Raymond and Melusine pass down to their Lusignan children both a human and a *fée* nature. D. Kelly, 'The Domestication of the Marvelous in the Melusine Romances', *Melusine of Lusignan: Founding Fiction in Late Medieval France*, eds D. Maddox and S. Sturm-Maddox (Athens, GA: University of Georgia Press, 1996), 32–47; S.L. Hahn, 'Youth and Rebellion in Jean d'Arras' *Roman de Mélusine*', *Melusine's Footprint: Tracing the Legacy of a Medieval Myth*, eds M. Urban et al. (Leiden–Boston: Brill, 2017), 183–207.
61. Gervase reprises a part of this story in an exemplum about the lady of a castle called L'Éparvier, in the Kingdom of Arles (near Valence). Gervase of Tilbury, *Otia imperialia*, 664–68. The lady in question is defined as an angel of Satan who had turned into an angel of light to deceive human beings (a reference to 2Cor 11:14). On this story, see R. Chanaud, 'Le chevalier, la fée et l'héretique: une ancêtre valentinoise de Mélusine, la dame du château de l'Éparvier', *Le mond alpin et rhodanien: revue régionale d'ethnologie* 13 (1985), 31–54. Some eighty years later, this story is echoed in the Middle English romance *Richard Coer de Lyon*. On wild game as a status-symbol food for medieval nobles, see M. Montanari, *La fame e l'abbondanza: storia dell'alimentazione in Europa* (Rome–Bari: Laterza, 2010), 17ff.
62. A. Maraschi, 'Þórgunna's Dinner and Other Medieval Liminal Meals: Food as Mediator between This World and the Hereafter', *Paranormal Encounters in Iceland 1150–1400*, eds Á. Jakobsson and M. Mayburd (Berlin: De Gruyter, 2020), 49–70. Medieval Irish tradition is particularly interesting, in this sense, for food often represents an identity and religious marker. See, for instance, Saint Brigit's intolerance to her druid's milk, *Bethu Brigte*, ed. and trans. D. Ó hAodha (Dublin: Institute for Advanced Studies, 1978), ch. 5, 21. On the motif of the *repas des fées*, see Harf-Lancner, *Le monde des fées*.
63. In Occitania, *dracs* were considered *fées*, and the expression '*fa le drac*' was synonym for '*faire le diable*'. 'Dracus', *Glossarium ad scriptores mediae et infimae Latinitatis*, eds C. Du Cange et al. (Niort: L. Favre, 1883–87). Liebrecht notes that the belief in such beings survived in Languedoc, even though they lost their demonic features (*Des Gervasius von Tilbury*, 135). See also P. Sébillot, *Le folk-lore de France*, 4 vols (Paris: Librairie orientale et américaine, 1904–07), vol. 2, 343. Fundamental dialectological studies on the relationship between *drac/draco* and *follet/lutin* include M. Alinei, 'Geografia semantica: continuatori di *draco* in Italia e in Francia', *Espaces Romans: études de dialectologie et de géolinguistique offertes à Gaston Tuaillon*, vol. 2 (Grenoble: Ellug, 1988–89), 459–87; X. Ravier, 'Sur le lexique des esprits follets et autres lutins en Languedoc et en Gascogne', *Romania sans frontières: homage à Jacques Allières*, vol. 2, eds M. Aurnague and M. Roché (Anglet: Éd. Atlantica, 2002), 539–52. Alinei notes that the transformation (anthropomorphization) from *drac* to *follet* is attested in France and Germany, in particular.

64. Gervase of Tilbury, *Otia imperialia*, 716–20.
65. The motif of submarine worlds inhabited by humanlike *dracs* persisted in French folklore, as is evident in Upper Brittany: Sébillot, *Le folk-lore de France*, vol. 2, 344.
66. J.D. Penniman, *Raised on Christian Milk: Food and the Formation of the Soul in Early Christianity* (New Haven, CT: Yale University Press, 2017), 31–33.
67. Again, the other is identified by consumption of a taboo food.
68. Once again, Gervase is one of the earliest (if not the earliest) source for this widespread motif (Gervase of Tilbury, *Otia imperialia*, 720 n. 5). On food as a means to transfer supernatural qualities to the eater, see A. Maraschi, *Similia similibus curantur: cannibalismo, grafofagia, e 'magia' simpatetica nel medioevo (500–1500)* (Spoleto: Cisam, 2020).
69. Maury, *Le fées du Moyen-Age*, 75. See also Sébillot, *Le folk-lore de France*, II, 196, 200, 343, 345–46. French folklore often featured water spirits dressed all in green.
70. Another parallel with *dracs*.
71. Gervase of Tilbury, *Otia imperialia*, 686–88. As suggested by Sébillot, the story survived for a long time in that area (*Le folk-lore de France*, vol. 2, 410).
72. Maria di Francia, *Lais*, 172–76, 196.
73. Jean d'Arras, *Mélusine ou la noble histoire de Lusignan: Roman du XVIeme siècle*, ed. J.-J. Vincensini (Paris: Librairie Générale française, 2003), ch. VI.
74. Sébillot, *Le folk-lore de France*, II, 410.
75. Ibid., IV, 11.
76. Wunderlich, 'Frauen'; Green, *Elf Queens*, 2, 79; Montesano, *Classical Culture*, 106–07.
77. Harf-Lancner, *Les fées au Moyen Âge*, 23; Le Roy Ladurie and Le Goff, 'Mélusine maternelle', 598–99.
78. J.-C. Mühlethaler, 'Translittérations féeriques ay Moyen Age: de Mélior à Mélusine, entre histoire et fiction', *Études de lettres* 3–4 (2011), 167–90 at 182; A. Maraschi, 'The Tree of the Bourlémonts: Gendered Beliefs in Fairies and Their Transmission from Old to Young Women in Joan of Arc's Domrémy', *Cultural Exchanges: Some Cases in the Domain of Folklore, Magic, and Witchcraft*, ed. M. Montesano (London: Routledge, 2021), 21–32.
79. Harf-Lancner, *Les fées au Moyen Âge*, 7–8; J.-C. Schmitt, 'Le traditions folkloriques dans la culture médiévale', *Archives de sciences sociales des religions* 52, 1 (1981), 5–20 at 7.
80. They were also connected with the nearby healing spring. *La minute française de l'interrogatoire de Jeanne la Pucelle, d'après le requisitoire de Jean d'Estivet et les manuscrits d'Urfé et d'Orléans*, eds P. Doncoeur and Y. Lanhers (Melun: d'Argences, 1952), 197. See also Green, *Elf Queens*, 28–29. The association between fairies and springs continued to be a widespread motif. According to a sixteenth-century proverb: '*nue comme une fée sortant de l'eau*'; see Béroalde de Verville, *Le moyen de parvenir*, vol. 1, ed. C. Royer (Paris: A. Lemerre, 1896), 28. In the late seventeenth century, Charles Perrault has a fairy woman meet Rose at a well in the tale 'Les Fées': Charles Perrault, *The Complete Fairy Tales*, ed. C.J. Betts (Oxford: Oxford University Press, 2009), 127–29.
81. *La réhabilitation de Jeanne la Pucelle: la redaction épiscopale du procès de 1455–1456*, eds P. Dancoeur and Y. Lanhers (Paris: Desclée de Brouwer, 1961), 110.
82. F. Meltzer, 'Reviving the Fairy Tree: Tales of European Sanctity', *Critical Inquiry* 35 (2009), 493–520 at 496.

83. Maraschi, 'The Tree of the Bourlémonts', 23, 26.
84. A. Arcangeli, 'Dance Under Trial: The Moral Debate 1200–1600', *Dance Research* 12 (1994), 127–55.
85. *Capitula Vesulensia*, MGH *Capitula Episcoporum* 3, ed. R. Pokorny (Hannover: Hahn, 1995), 339–53, xxii, 351.
86. C. Morrison and S.B. Rude, 'Prefacing the Marvelous: Dance in Popular Medieval French and English Literature', *The Cursed Carolers in Context*, eds L. Miller Renberg and B. Phillis (London: Routledge, 2021), 39–53; Green, *Elf Queens*, 1–5.
87. Quoted in Green, *Elf Queens*, 197.
88. *The Distaff Gospels: A First Modern English Edition of Les Évangiles des quenouilles*, eds M. Jeay and K. Garay (Peterborough: Broadview Press, 2006), 240; 246.
89. A. Paupert-Bouchiez, '"Sages femmes" ou sorcières? Les vieilles femmes des *Évangiles aux quenouilles*', *Vieillesse et vieillissement au Moyen Âge* (Aix-en-Provence: CUERMA, 1987), 267–82.
90. For a bibliography on French folklore, see A. van Gennep, *Manuel de folklore française contemporain*, 4 vols (Paris: Picard, 1937–38), vol. 3, 119–52, and vol. 4.
91. Sébillot, *Le folk-lore de France*, I, 141. Translation mine.
92. Ibid., II, 340–42.
93. Ibid., II, 346; P. Dubois, *La grande encyclopédie des fées* (Paris: Hoëbeke, 1996), 62–63.
94. Sébillot, *Le Folk-lore de France*, II, 200–01, 351ff.
95. A.E. Duggan, 'Nature and Culture in the Fairy Tale of Marie-Catherine d'Aulnoy', *Marvels & Tales* 15, 2 (2001), 149–67.
96. Marie-Catherine d'Aulnoy, *Contes des fées*, vol. 2, 501.
97. M.-A. Thirard, 'De l'allée du Roi aux sentiers du bon sauvage: un parcours dans les contes de Madame d'Aulnoy', *Féeries* 3 (2006), 59–74, 65; K.J. Lau, 'Imperial Marvels: Race and the Colonial Imagination in the Fairy Tales of Madame d'Aulnoy', *Narrative Culture* 3, 2 (2016), 141–79.
98. François Rabelais, 'The Very Horrific Life of the Great Gargantua, Father of Pantagruel', *The Complete Works of François Rabelais*, ed. R.C. La Charité (Berkeley: University of California Press, 1999), 209.
99. Gervase of Tilbury, *Otia imperialia*, 428. Avalon, according to a Breton tradition which is recorded by Marie de France, was also the destination of Lanval and her *fée* (Maria di Francia, *Lais*, 206). This was a quite popular motif: F302.3.1.3 'Man is carried to fairyland by fairy and marries her'.
100. *Huon de Bourdeaux: chanson de geste*, eds F. Guessard and C. Grandmaison (Paris: F. Vieweg, 1860), lv.
101. Marie-Catherine d'Aulnoy, *Contes des fées*, vol. 1, 133–34.
102. A.-M. Feat, 'Playing the Game of Frivolity: Seventeenth-Century "Conteuses" and the Transformation of Female Identity', *The Journal of the Midwest Modern Language Association* 45 (2012), 217–42, 233.
103. Marie-Catherine d'Aulnoy, *Contes des fées*, vol. 1, 133. On this, see A.E. Duggan, 'Women and Absolutism in French Opera and Fairy Tale', *The French Review* 78 (2004), 302–15, 313.

CHAPTER TEN

# German-Speaking Europe: *Moosweiblein*, *Wichtel* and *Nixen*

Janin Pisarek and Florian Schaefer (independent scholars)

## Introduction

The supernatural beings of German-speaking Europe appear in many different folktales and legends. German folklore is best known for the *Kinder- und Hausmärchen* (1812–15) collected and written up by Jacob Grimm (1785–1863) and Wilhelm Grimm (1786–1859). But this chapter will dig deeper into the rich treasury of legends and local lore from the German-speaking lands. Because folktales do not stop at political borders, this chapter covers not only present-day Germany, but also Austria and German-speaking Switzerland.

Since German folktales are often about the irruption of the numinous into the human world, human–supernatural interactions define most mythological legends. Nevertheless, numerous legends from German-speaking Europe offer clues as to how people imagined the supernatural world. Supernatural beings act as 'correctors' to human misconduct.

This is particularly clear in the context of the three beings that will form the focus of this chapter: the *Moosweiblein* ('little moss women'), *Nixen* ('nixies') and *Wichtel* ('dwarfs'), as they interact with humans and each other.[1] The abundance of different anthropomorphic or zoomorphic supernatural beings show more variety in their names than in their behaviour. So while legendary figures have relatively few basic narratives, these are enriched by local colour, regional variants and contact with other popular beliefs and legendary figures. The interaction of supernatural beings and humans (e.g. midwives, childcarers, housekeepers, kidnapped children) plays a central role in the stories.[2] However, human–supernatural interactions will only be dealt with in passing in this chapter: the focus is, rather, on the social behaviour of *Moosweiblein*, *Wichtel* and *Nixen*.

Janin Pisarek and Florian Schaefer, "German-Speaking Europe: *Moosweiblein, Wichtel* and *Nixen*" in: *The Exeter Companion to Fairies, Nereids, Trolls and Other Social Supernatural Beings: European Traditions.* University of Exeter Press (2024). © Janin Pisarek and Florian Schaefer. DOI: 10.47788/ZCJG8520

## Sources

The sources for researching the German social supernatural lie primarily in rural legends. This can be explained by the rural population's dependence on a sometimes beneficent but often cruel countryside. These folk traditions were collected and written down by different authors, particularly in the period from the 1830s to the early 1900s. Evidence for *Moosweiblein* is found especially in the Upper Palatinate, where ethnologist Franz Xaver Schönwerth (1810–1886) devoted much of his writing to this mythical figure and collected evidence of belief in forest spirits, usually referred to as *Holzfräulein* ('little woman of the woods').[3] Claude Lecouteux documents how the idea of the 'moss folk' developed, more broadly, from the first mentions in medieval glosses: from Old High German *holzmuun* ('wood man'), Middle High German *holzvrowe* ('wood woman') and *vvildaz wip* ('wild woman'), to the nineteenth-century legends of Central Europe.[4]

*Wichtel* legends have been collected from almost all the German-speaking lands. Over time many local names evolved. The most nuanced *Wichtel* descriptions are found in nineteenth- and twentieth-century collections. They are there especially in Schönwerth's writings. Schönwerth examined the customs and legends of the Oberpfalz, including detailed descriptions of the appearance of *Wichtel*, *Heinzelmännchen* and dwarfs in his books. Schönwerth's detailed descriptions, together with a series of other traditions, give us an idea of how *Wichtel* were perceived and also provide insights into their social character.

The social life of *Nixen* was documented particularly by Ludwig Bechstein (1801–1860), Robert Eisel (1826–1917), Christian Ludwig Wucke (1807–1883), Karl Wüstefeld (1857–1937), Moritz Geyer (fl. c.1900) and Paul Rödiger (1859–1938). The Brothers Grimm collected numerous legends and systematized them. Much evidence can be found as well in the *Sagen, Märchen und Gebräuche aus Sachsen und Thüringen* (1846) by Emil Sommer (1819–1846), a student of Wilhelm Grimm.

## The *Moosweiblein*

The *Moosweiblein* are the forest spirits of the low mountain ranges of Central Europe, particularly the few surviving parts of the Hercynian Forest, the low wooded mountain range north of the Danube and east of the Rhine. They have many different names. In the Harz region, the Thuringian Forest and the Thuringian Slate Mountains they are known as *Moosweiblein*, while in the Lausitz region they are called *Lohjungfern*. In Hesse they are referred to as the *wilde Weiber* ('wild woman'), in the Erzgebirge and the Upper Palatinate as

*Holzfräulein*. In the Bohemian Forest they are known as *Waldweiblein* and in the Ore Mountains as *Rüttelweiber*.

The moss folk are usually female. The generic name is, in fact, always feminine. When male moss people turn up, they only appear on the margins of stories. It is almost exclusively the female spirit who comes into contact with humans or who serves as a household spirit. They are small (F441.5.1 'Wood-spirit tiny'). When visiting human houses they help with household chores or farm work. They are particularly valued for their considerable knowledge of medicinal herbs and for their ability to look into the future. Some *Moosweiblein* also seek intimate interactions with humans—they seduce or start a relationship with them, the *gestörte Mahrtenehe* ('dysfunctional marriage with supernatural partners'). This is motif F441.6.3 'Sexual relations with wood-spirit fatal', one which is also present in mermaid and *Nixen* narratives. The supernatural being lives with a mortal until the human breaks a taboo.

## The Social *Moosweiblein*

*Moosweiblein* are often solitary. Sometimes there are groups of women. Many legends, however, describe them as living in families and having children:

> They live together in marriage, in pairs and have children. Married couples live in hollow trees, the young separated according to sex, usually under a shelter on a bed of moss. When they get married, they ask the humans to bake something for them, even if it's just a little ash cake. If one does them a favour, they repay it with gold.[5]

Schönwerth describes them as a 'tribe' whose everyday life is determined by family life and social interaction.[6] They live under simple conditions, in hollow trees,[7] under roots and rocks[8] or in caves. Their connection to the forest and its trees is strong. They die if their tree is damaged.[9] Moss women not only seek contact with humans and their own kind. They also sometimes fight other legendary figures: as good spirits, the *Moosweiblein* live in fear of the *wilde Jäger* or *Holzhetzer* ('wild hunter') and his *wilde Jagd* ('Wild Hunt') (E501.5.2 'The Wild Hunt'; E501.5.3 'Wood-spirits pursued in Wild Hunt') and are sometimes chased down by this evil fraternity.[10] Johannes Praetorius (1630–1680) described the *Moosweiblein* running from the Wild Hunt as early as 1666.[11]

The *Moosweiblein* care for each other when a member of their family dies. Some legends tell of *Moosweiblein* who are called back into the community from their service as house spirits after a family member's death.[12] They mourn their loved ones, further evidence of the close bonds they form with their own kind. There are no direct references in narratives to leadership, let alone a matriarchy among the moss folk. Mountain spirits such as the *Wichtel* are often subordinate to kings and queens, but only the *Buschgroßmutte*r ('bush grandmother') seems to occupy a position of some power among the *Moosweiblein*:

> According to the legend of the country folk, a demonic being called the Buschgroßmutter lives near Leutenberg [Thuringian Slate Mountains] and on the left bank of the river Saale. She has many daughters, and they are called moss maidens, with whom she roams the land at certain times and on holy nights. It is not good to meet her, she has a fixed gaze and tangled hair. She often rides along on a little cart, and an encounter should be avoided as soon as she is sensed.[13]

The *Buschgroßmutter* is a leader of sorts, then. But her companions are kin, more specifically daughters. The legend itself associates the bush grandmother with the *Perchta*, and the wild hunter. This is remarkable as moss women are, as we have seen, hunted down and killed by the Wild Hunt in numerous folk legends.[14]

## The *Wichtel*

The German *Wichtel*, also known as *Zwerge* ('dwarfs') or *Heinzelmännchen*, are mostly small friendly beings living underground, in the mountains or in rock caves; they are also known as *Unterirdische* ('subterraneans') (F451; F451.4.1; F451.4.1.1; F451.4.1.11). They come into closer contact with humans either as household spirits (F450.1 'Helpful underground spirit'), performing tasks, as long as they and their taboos are respected; or while stealing food, objects or even children from humans (F451.5.2.2 'Dwarfs steal from human beings', and related submotifs).[15] Usually they are small creatures. They are often described as 'grey', 'black' or 'red'. If they do not appear completely naked, their coat-like skirts and pointed, broad hats recall local peasant clothing.[16]

*Wichtel* are physical beings,[17] but they are able to walk through rock,[18] and become invisible using magic hoods or cloaks (*Tarnkappen*) (F451.3.3.8). *Wichtel* mostly speak German; only in a few cases do they use their own language.[19] Where *Wichtel* are not understood as mountain and earth spirits, they are regarded as fallen angels or as ancestor figures.[20] Sometimes archaeological specimens, such as Bronze Age weapons or earthenware vessels, are connected to them:

> Much peculiar art is ascribed to the subterraneans. Especially they are said to be the makers of the variously shaped burial pots that stand in dolmens, and of all the fine ornaments and bronze weapons found in the earth and often even in such pots.[21]

These interpretations linking folklore with material culture, which date back to the Brothers Grimm, have been rejected by numerous folklorists since.[22] *Wichtel* are considered skilful in their artisan work. In this they recall the dwarfs of medieval epic, who were talented craftsmen.[23] The *Wichtel* and dwarfs of the German lowlands in particular excel in smithing and are said to produce impressive objects (F451.3.4.2; F451.3.4.1).[24]

## The Social *Wichtel*

In some places the *Wichtel* live among humans. In other regions they must first be invited into a household. Schönwerth reports:

> When you want the [*Wichtel*] to work for you, you go to the Strazel hole and call them: 'Hey, come here! You'll get something to eat, but you'll need to work!' And later on during the night they will come. You put soup and bread on the table, and the little creatures eat everything, no matter how much you provide. [...] They work extremely hard, but no one is permitted to watch them. In the house where the narrator of this tale served, they threshed the wheat: they had often laid the grains on the threshing floor by the time the people arrived. In the house they did the dishes. [...] They always appeared in groups.[25]

Schönwerth not only describes the appearance and actions of the *Wichtel*, but emphasizes how they come in parties (F451.3.14 'Dwarfs are numerous').[26] This behaviour, which is a characteristic of social creatures, distinguishes *Wichtel* from the solitary kobold of lower German mythology.[27] The appearance and behaviour of the *Wichtel* are human-like: they have male and female forms. They drink and eat. They can be injured and die.[28] They enjoy parties and celebrations (F451.6.3 'Dwarfs have festivities', and related submotifs):

> These dwarfs lived merrily in the bosom of the deep rock chambers and feasted on the innkeeper's wine and beer and other supplies.

They also played many tricks or jokes on the inhabitants of the surrounding villages.[29]

Many legends show *Wichtel* as living under a king (F451.4.5.1) or more rarely a queen,[30] with families and children.[31] The *Wichtel* kingdom may correspond to an idealized medieval society. Romantic beliefs, it is worth recalling here, were very influential during the 1800s, when most German folktales were written down.[32]

In contrast to the ragged appearance of the *Wichtel* household helper with their threadbare clothing,[33] the subterranean realm boasts gold, silver and numerous other precious stones[34] (F451.4.1.3 'Dwarfs live in luxurious underground palace'; F451.4.3.4 'Dwarf home has chandelier of crystals and gems').

Bechstein records the folktale 'Das stille Volk zu Plesse', in which a young student from Göttingen follows a *Wichtel* into his kingdom under a castle (F451.4.1.2 'Dwarfs live in underground castle'). Bechstein not only describes Wichtel living together within village structures, but also five generations under one roof.

> Finally, both [human and *Wichtel*] stepped out of the corridor and saw before them a wide landscape through which a rushing brook flowed, with villages made up of nothing but small houses, like Chinese ones, and painted very colourfully, like quail houses. They entered the loveliest of these little houses, and inside was the dear family of the little grey man who was introduced to the theology student from Göttingen. Thereupon those greeted him with a silent bow. Then the little man introduced the student to the dear family, his father, a snow-coloured old man, and likewise his mother. Both were so old that they could only sit on chairs and could no longer stand or walk; then to his grandfather and grandmother, both of whom had no more hair on their heads and only the barest flesh on their bones and could only lie down. Then there was the little man's wife, [...] and their children from thirty to forty years old and the little grandchildren from about fourteen to fifteen years...[35] They obey willingly (the king) and his family. The country had no estates, and he also had no ministers, which are as expensive as they are useless. In this quiet realm there is only peace, contentment and benevolence. Everyone does his duty unbidden. There are no quarrels, no wars, no so-called politics.[36]

In certain folktales the death of a family member is greeted with dismay by *Wichtel*.[37] However, *Wichtel* are sometimes malicious towards other mythical creatures. On the island of Sylt, *Wichtel* went to war against a merman and some giants.[38] Then there is sometimes murder reported among *Wichtel*.[39] German folklorist Leander Petzoldt, meanwhile, reports on an act of senicide when an elderly *Wichtel* woman was buried alive:

> Dwarfs lived in the vicinity of Unterbäch. They came up here [to a farmer] and asked for a shovel. The farmer who lent them the tools followed them to see what they intended to do with them. Then he saw how the dwarfs were digging a big hole and putting an old woman in it, who was wailing terribly: 'Let me walk, I can still talk!' But the dwarfs remained inexorable and put a jug of wine and bread with her and covered the pit again.[40]

Even when *Wichtel* serve as household spirits (F451.5.1.20 'Dwarfs help in performing task'), they keep to themselves and do not form close relationships with humans. This is another way in which they are different from the kobold—especially in southern Germany, Austria and Switzerland. The kobold typically forms a very close relationship with 'his' humans.[41] When *Wichtel* interact with people, it is either in the form of loans and services, or through theft. Often the motif is midwifery: the *Wichtel* leads a human midwife into their realm to help with childbirth (see also below for the *Nixen*).[42]

Just as the *Wichtel* visit humans in groups, they also collectively leave humankind: the German equivalent of the British fairies abandoning the land. This motif, known as the 'migrating dwarfs' (F451.9 'Dwarfs emigrate', and related submotifs), can be found nationwide and often includes ferries.[43] It is not documented for any other legendary figure in German-speaking folklore.[44] The reasons for their migration, however, differ widely: sometimes it lies in the actions of the people, such as bakers adding caraway seeds to the bread (this also concerns the *Nixen*), or after they have been treated disrespectfully. In other cases, the introduction of Christianity or the first sounding of church bells causes the *Wichtel* to flee (F451.5.9.3 'Dwarfs dislike church bells').

In terms of cultural history the *Wichtel* disappeared with the transition to an industrial age. Many legend researchers now assume that such 'end motifs' were an attempt to retain plausibility, by assigning *Wichtel* tales to a time in the distant past. The disappearance of the *Wichtel* was a (more or less) believable reason for their absence in the present.[45]

## *Nixen*

The *Nixen* are the female water spirits of German folklore. The male counterpart is called *Nix* or *Noeck*.[46] These nature demons not only populate the seas, but according to popular belief also dwell in lakes, ponds, rivers and wells. They have different names depending on the body of water. Their legends are particularly widespread in Silesia, the Upper Palatinate and in the central and southern German-speaking lands. The term *Wassergeist* ('water spirit') has only been documented since the seventeenth century, but undines are a universal phenomenon. Water spirits are based on an animism in which the material world is thought of as having a soul.[47]

*Nixen* and *Noeck* have humanoid bodies, sometimes with the colourful scales of fish or snakes (F420.1.4.1 'Water-spirit with extraordinarily long hair'; F420.1.4.2 'Water-spirits have body covered with fish scales'). Sometimes they appear to be completely human (F420.1.2 'Water-spirit as woman'), but they can still be recognized by the perpetually wet hem of their clothes (F420.1.7.1 'Corner of water-spirits' dress is always wet').[48] All these semi-, hybrid and intermediate beings have magical abilities. They cast spells, prophesize and transform themselves. According to popular belief, they possess a dangerous, malicious nature.[49] They represent the perils of the water. These supernatural beings can bring good and bad to people. Here we have the ambivalence of eroticism/unnatural beauty (F420.1.2.1 'Water-maidens are of unusual beauty'), especially in the way they seductively lure passers-by into the water (F420.5.2.1 'Water-spirits lure mortal into water', and related submotifs).[50]

The Saale, like the Mulde, Elbe and Elster (German rivers), also harbours *Nixen*. Above Kahla rises a high cliff by the river, and there at its base, sometimes in summer you can see a *Nixe* with green-gold hair (F420.1.4.7 'Water-spirits with green hair and beard'), who runs a sparkling comb through her tresses. The youths who approach her, lured by her beauty, are drawn down by the waves from the shore to the bottom of the river, and the Saale demands a sacrifice of this kind at least every year.[51]

In 1846 Emil Sommer wrote about the *Noeck*:

> The *Noeck* usually appears as a small, friendly boy in a green or red garment, with bright sparkling eyes and often with long green hair and green teeth [F420.1.4.8 'Water-spirits with green teeth']. But sometimes he resembles a grown man, with an old, treacherous face and claws on his hands. He lives with his wife and children at the bottom of rivers and lakes; some *Nixen* also live in fountains.[52]

We learn, in the legends, about *Nixen* family life. The relationship between humans and demonic beings are always heterosexual with strong erotic tension. The supernatural hybrid likes to show themselves naked (F420.1.6.7

'Water-spirits are nude': a famous representative is the German water spirit Loreley[53]). Nevertheless, long-term partnership with humans proves impossible.[54] The Swiss natural philosopher Paracelsus (1493/94–1541), who posited a category of this being as intermediate between spirits and humans, wrote that nymphs could marry men, and if they did so they would be given souls.[55] Because of their lack of soul they cannot weep and often feel plagued by the burden of eternal life. They seek the love of a human being in order to win a soul[56] and taste, however briefly, the mortal condition.[57]

## Social *Nixen*

Many legends report the everyday life of the *Noeck* and *Nixen*, who are 'smaller and more misshapen than humans and live mostly unseen, dwelling in swamps and subterranean lakes, malicious and mischievous, and especially after the children of the natives'.[58] Tales of these supernatural beings describe them as behaving similarly to humans. They work hard for their families,[59] and enjoy their free time (F420.3.2 'Water-spirits have likings and occupations like human beings', and related submotifs). Underwater they also make meals, as in the legend 'Süße Pfannkuchen' ('Sweet Pancakes') where the *Nixen* prepare fish and baked goods (F420.3.2.4 'Water-spirits bake') for their guests.[60] In addition to a kitchen, they have living rooms in their underwater houses that resemble those of humans: 'a comfortable and spacious apartment'.[61] Most *Nixen* appear in patriarchal family structures (F420.3.1 'Water-spirits have family life under water'). We lack details, but it can be inferred that each family group consists of an old *Noeck* and his daughters. Often the *Noeck* also has a *Nixe* or a human as a wife. Their relationship often comes up in *Noeck* stories where a human midwife is fetched to help.

> Where whole families [of *Nixen*] are together, they do business like people; They buy what they need in the neighbouring villages and towns, and on the Dolau Heath you can often see them collecting wood. When the weather is fine, the *Nixen* dry their laundry on the willows [F420.3.2.3 'Water-women wash and hang up laundry on beach'] that are in various areas on the Saale and Elster: They then sit in the top of the willow, spread out their shirts and skirts on the branches around them, and when everything is dry, they take it off and get back in the water with it.[62]

They sunbathe on the shore,[63] and the females comb their long hair (F420.5.3.1) while sitting among the willow branches. The males tend to their fish traps.[64] In the legends they are together during the day, mostly outside the water. The female *Nixen* go to the town and villages dressed like the common people to buy food (F420.1.6.1 'Water-spirits are dressed like people of surroundings'; F420.3.2.2 'Water-women come to market and store').[65] In this example the *Nixe* is very sociable towards humans and talks to them:

> A *Nixe* lived in Trotha, who bought everything she needed for her household at the market in Halle. She went to and fro with the other market people and talked to them in private; and they had no idea that she was a *Nixe*: only they noticed that her apron was always wet.[66]

A less communicative *Nixe* appears in a legend collected by the Thuringian writer and archivist Ludwig Bechstein:

> She came with a basket and mingled with other peasant women to buy groceries, but she didn't say a word to anyone; she pointed to the goods, heard the price, offered less money by haggling, finally took it and left. She didn't thank anyone who greeted her. Once two people followed the strange little woman, when they saw her putting her basket down by a small stream, and like lightning she and the basket disappeared. Walking behind the mermaid one saw the road wet, for the hems of her robes were wet two hands high.[67]

In the evening the *Nixen* like to go out together with their sisters, dancing with each other and humans or chatting to people in inns. The humans often praise the *Nixen* as 'beautiful, lively dancers'.[68] In these narratives *Nixen* rules emerge, as does the severity of the punishment for breaking said rules. These tales reflect the *Noeck*'s patriarchal role.

In various legends, especially those from central and southern Germany, it becomes clear that both the male *Noeck* and female *Nixen* like to dance:

> On the Zörnißberge near Wettin the *Nixen* sometimes dance at night. You can hear lively, cheerful music and see many little men and women climbing out of the Saale, who hold hands and perform their circle dance with dainty little steps and leaps: and from time to time some jump into the water and others come back to their place.[69]

Dancing is not just a rhythmic movement of the body accompanied by music, but also an expression of *joie de vivre* and community. It provides the initial spark of an interpersonal relationship. The fact that the *Nixen* dance and make music together, interacting in a circle dance, singing and making sounds together, speaks to the *Nixen*'s social nature. '*Nixen* who come to the village dance [F420.3.2.1.1.] are happy, sing, dance, love and then suffer, as if the legend wanted to symbolize the happiness of the girls' youthful days everywhere'.[70]

As mentioned previously, unforgiving *Nixen* rules are enforced in that community. In most legends the *Nixen* are given a curfew. Also, they are not normally allowed to bring humans with them underwater. Rule breaking all too often means death (F420.3.4.1). In the legend 'Süße Pfannkuchen' ('Sweet Pancakes') some boys follow the wet tracks of the *Nixen* (F420.1.7 'Water-spirits appearing like human beings are recognized by traces of water'; F420.1.7.3 'Water-spirits leave trace of water when standing or walking') after dancing with them, and then pursue them into their underwater realm (F420.3.5 'Water-spirits visited by mortal'). There they enter the *Nixen* house.

> But then old *Noeck* came and the boys had to hide under the bed. The old man sniffed around and said: 'It smells like Christians, it stinks'. 'Oh father', the daughters reassured him, 'that's because we were dancing with Christians'.[71]

In the same type of legend from the Thuringian Slate Mountains, the *Nixen* hide their dancing companions. The humans hear threatening talk between the *Noeck* and his daughters, in which the strict father insists that he smells Christians and orders them to come home by 10 p.m. or he will kill the daughters. One day the boys make sure that the *Nixen* are late, and then the water where they live is blood-red the next day.[72] Here we see the patriarchal relationship and how the vengeful, assertive father punishes his young. There is also 'Die drei Jungfrauen aus dem See' ('The Three Maidens from the Lake') from the Mummelsee area in Baden-Wuerttemberg, which is known for numerous water spirit legends and the idea of a court under the water.[73] In this tale the *Noeck* also takes revenge on the boy for causing his daughters to be late. The *Nixen* come back late because the boy who saw them spinning (F420.3.2.6 'Water-maidens spin') changes their clock:

> [humans] heard a strange whimpering and groaning from the depths, and three large slicks of blood were floating on the surface. Young Erlfried was seriously ill that same night and a corpse in three days. But the three sisters were never seen again in the valley.[74]

There is a similar legend from Hesse, near Kirchhain, where a boy had fallen in love with a *Nixe*.[75] The cruel character of the male *Noeck* is also shown in legends about his need for midwifery services from humans (F420.5.3.2 'Water-spirit calls human midwife'). Besides the legends about the *Noeck* looking for a human woman for a relationship, the tales tell of how he temporarily gets a handmaid from among the humans to take care of his household until his supernatural wife is healthy.[76] Alternatively he looks for a midwife to help with the birth of his child (ATU 476\*\* 'Midwife in the Underworld').[77]

> At the Kelle, a small lake, not far from Werne [Werna] in Hohenstein, *Nixen* used to live. Once the *Noeck* fetched the midwife from the village [...] who performed her office. [...] before she went away, the mother of the newborn lamented secretly with a stream of tears that the *Noeck* would soon choke the newborn child. And indeed, a few minutes later, the midwife saw a blood-red colour on the surface of the water. The child had been murdered.[78]

Not every variant of this story-type ends with the murder of the newborn *Nixe*, but in most cases the *Noeck* is rude and threatening. The female *Nixe* always plays a helping role. When the *Noeck* leaves the room, she warns the midwife, as in this legend from Giebichenstein: 'If my husband comes back now and offers you great treasures [F420.4.8 'Water-spirits have treasures under water'], do not take more than you usually get from people; otherwise it could make you ill'. When the *Noeck* comes back and the woman acts on the warning, he tells her: 'if you had taken more, I would have wrung your neck'.[79] In the Grimms' *Deutsche Sagen* another variant is described. There the human woman is spared as she has apotropaic herbs with her. *Nixen* are wary of the medicinal plants Diptam-Dost (Dittany of Crete) and Andorn Dorant (common horehound),[80] and are driven away by caraway seeds.[81]

Another legend called 'Der Wassermann bei Unterpreilipp' ('The *Noeck* from Unterpreilipp') collected in Thuringia near Rudolstadt can usefully be quoted here. The *Nixe* giving birth has a secret to share with the human midwife: 'I am a Christian, baptized like you, but the greyish *Noeck* [F420.1.1.3 'Water-spirit as small gray man'] exchanged me when I was still a six-week-child, he eats all my children on the third day'.[82] There are other legends which detail kidnapped humans among the *Nixen* (F420.5.2.4 'Water-spirits steal children and leave changeling'). It is said the changelings that the *Noeck* leave are 'very ugly, often hairy all over and learn to speak and walk very late or not at all'.[83]

The *Noeck* takes care to find a good midwife to help during the birth of his child and then kill the newborn. In the last example from Bechstein, for instance, the *Noeck* devours the child. So why does the *Noeck* kill his children after bringing help for the birth? Perhaps the *Noeck* only kills male offspring, to secure his position as head of the family: he has daughters, after all.[84]

Marriages between *Nixen* and *Noeck* are mostly unhappy. These male *Noeck* are of an advanced age. The female water spirits long for young lovers (F420.6.1 'Marriage or liaison of mortals and water-spirits', and related submotifs), because their beauty can last for centuries and they survive numerous pregnancies. Once the *Nixe* lusts for a mortal man the water woman will prove insistent. Sometimes the mortal asks to go back to the village to see his family for a short time. If he does not come back or if he stays there longer than he is allowed to, the *Nixe* will murder him when he comes near any water, even if it is just a puddle.[85] There are cases where an angry *Nixe* drowns a lover who has wronged her (F420.5.2.6 'Water-spirits take revenge on mortals', and related submotifs).[86] What all the figures of the different fairy love affairs (*gestörte Mahrtenehe*) have in common is that relationships with humans are rarely permanent.[87] If a *Noeck* marries a human woman, that relationship lasts only so long as the human partner keeps to the conditions. Another motif involves the *Nixen* threatening mortal partners that they will have to 'share' their child by cutting it in half.[88]

The violence of *Nixen* social interaction becomes clear in narrations of *Noeck* infighting. A man who was going to Halle once met a *Noeck* on the road. The *Noeck* told him that he had lent his wife for some days to the *Noeck* of Giebichenstein, whose wife was sick. But the *Noeck* tells the man that his wife should have come back two days ago. 'That's why he set out to fetch her home and to show the Giebichensteiner what it must be like for those who don't keep their word'.[89] He added that the man should keep an eye out on the bank to see if blood would not soon appear on the water, as that should be a sign that one of them, he or the Giebichensteiner, had fallen in battle. After he vanished, bright blood welled up to the surface of the water. But the man never learned who was killed.[90] Another legend reports a *Noeck* offering his help to a fisherman in return for meat (F420.5.1.4 'Water-spirits work as servants for mortal for small compensation'; F420.5.1.7.5 'Water-spirit gives mortal fish'). He tells the man that he has argued with his *Noeck* brother and wants to become strong to fight against him. 'Thinking he was strong enough, he went back into the water and said to the fisherman: If the water turns green, he should flee, for then his brother would have been victorious, but if it turned brown, he himself would have won'.[91]

A fairly intact social structure becomes visible among the *Nixen*. In their community they take care of each other, and work is carried out and divided up for the benefit of the community. Within this patriarchal structure, while the women take care of the laundry, errands and the preparation of meals, the men guide their families and catch fish. As long as the rules are observed, there is hierarchical cooperation. But it also becomes clear that the communities have fun together by making music and dancing, even if the young *Nixen* are often drawn towards humans. When special events like weddings take place, many other *Nixen* take part in the ritual. On the other hand, bad character traits also crystallize very clearly in the legends, which correspond to the ambivalent character of the *Nixen* as a whole. It turns out that they not only have a thirst for revenge against 'Christians'. They also long for revenge against each other. In these interactions, the male *Noeck* seems to be particularly vindictive, while the females limit their acts of revenge to humans.

## Conclusion

We have here documented the rich tradition of the social supernatural in German-speaking countries. Descriptions of social behaviour are usually found only as marginal notes in narratives, but they provide valuable information on how people, especially in the early modern period, imagined these beings and what social narratives they ascribed to them. It is striking that there is little evidence of the social structure among the *Moosweiblein*, while the legends paint a fairly detailed picture of the homes and social conditions of the *Wichtel* and *Nixen*. Different forms of society are described, from family groups to kingdoms, so that none of the beings examined can be clearly assigned to only one form. We find motifs such as individual beings being recalled after the death of a family member among both the *Wichtel* and *Moosweiblein*. Legends in German-speaking countries have a lot in common when it comes to the description of supernatural figures, which, however, still vary greatly from region to region: for instance the senicide among dwarfs, which is only documented from Switzerland; or the war of the *Wichtel* against giants and *Nixen*, which is only found on the island of Sylt. In contrast, the legends of *Nixen* are more homogeneous within German-speaking Europe. The *Moosweiblein*, *Wichtel* and *Nixen* all, in their different ways, lead an almost human social life. They offer a mirror held up to human desires and fears.

## Notes

1. L. Petzoldt, *Dämonenfurcht und Gottvertrauen: zur Geschichte und Erforschung unserer Volkssagen* (Darmstadt: Wissenschaftliche Buchgesellschaft, 1989), 37f., 144; J. Pisarek, 'Mehr als nur die Liebe zum Wassergeist: das Motiv der „gestörten Mahrtenehe" in europäischen Volkserzählungen', *Märchenspiegel: Zeitschrift für*

*internationale Märchenforschung und Märchenpflege* 27 (2016), 3–8 at 3. Editors' note: supernatural beings are given capitals in accordance with German orthography.
2. L. Lindig: 'Hausgeister', *Enzyklopädie des Märchens*, vol. 6, eds R.W. Brednich et al. (Berlin–New York: De Gruyter, 1990), 610–17 at 610f.
3. R. Röhrich, *Franz Xaver Schönwerth: sein Leben und sein Werk* (Kallmünz: Verlag Michael Lassleben, 1975), 150.
4. C. Lecouteux, 'Lamia—holzmuuowa—holzfrowe—Lamîch', *Euphorion: Zeitschrift für Literaturgeschichte* 75 (1981), 360–65.
5. F. Schönwerth, *Aus der Oberpfalz: Sitten und Sagen*, vol. 2 (Augsburg: Rieger, 1857–59), 358–59.
6. Schönwerth, *Oberpfalz*, 361–62.
7. L. Bechstein, *Thüringer Sagenbuch*, vol. 2 (Coburg: Georg Sendelbach, 1858; repr. Bad Langensalza: Verlag Rockstuhl, 2014), 50.
8. W. Mannhardt, *Wald und Feldkulte* (Berlin, Borntraeger, 1875), 76.
9. Schönwerth, *Oberpfalz*, 145, 152; J. Grimm, *Deutsche Mythologie* (Wiesbaden: Verlagshaus Römerweg, 2014 [1835]), 375.
10. E. Sommer, *Sagen, Märchen und Gebräuche aus Sachsen und Thüringen* (Halle: Eduard Anton, 1846), 6–7. Note that the Wild Hunt is to be found in various Northern European cultures and typically involves a hunt led by a mythological figure escorted by a supernatural group of hunters or dogs (motif E501.4.1 'Dogs in Wild Hunt', and related submotifs). In German folklore the hunt leader is often a figure associated with Odin or Wotan or the ancestral spirit of a hunter.
11. J. Praetorius, *Anthropodemus plutonicus: das ist eine neue Weltbeschreibung von allerley Wunderbarlicher Menschen*, vol. 1 (Magdeburg: Johann Lüderwald, 1666), 298–355.
12. Röhrich, *Schönwerth*, 70.
13. L. Bechstein, *Deutsches Sagenbuch* (Merseburg, Leipzig: F.W. Hendel Verlag, 1930), 379–80.
14. J. Grimm and W. Grimm, *Deutsche Sagen* (München: Winkler-Verlag, 1965), 70–71.
15. K. Bartsch, *Sagen, Märchen und Gebräuche aus Meklenburg 1–2*, vol. 1 (Wien: Braumüller, 1879–80), 62.
16. F. Schäfer et al., *Hausgeister! Fast vergessene Gestalten der deutschsprachigen Märchen- und Sagenwelt* (Köln: Böhlau Verlag, 2020), 69–79.
17. Grimm and Grimm, *Sagen* (1965), 55–56.
18. P. Zaunert, *Hessen-Nassauische Sagen* (Jena: Eugen Diederichs, 1929), 21.
19. J.G.T. Grässe, *Sagenbuch des Preußischen Staates*, vol. 2 (Glogau: Flemming, 1868–71), 1012.
20. Bechstein, *Deutsches Sagenbuch* (1930), 199.
21. Ibid., 141–42.
22. F. Ranke, *Die deutschen Volkssagen* (München: C.H. Becksche Verlagsbuchhandlung, 1924), 133.
23. I. Habicht, *Der Zwerg als Träger metafiktionaler Diskurse in deutschen und französischen Texten des Mittelalters* (Heidelberg: Universitätsverlag Winter GmbH, 2010), 25; B. Harms, 'Kleine Helden: höfische Zwerge und unhöfische Ritter in der Walberan-Version des „Laurin"', *Ruhm und Unsterblichkeit: Heldenepik im Kulturvergleich*, ed. K. Meisig (Wiesbaden: Harrassowitz, 2010), 93–110.
24. L. Strackerjan, *Aberglaube und Sagen aus dem Herzogtum Oldenburg*, vol. 1 (Oldenburg: Druck & Verlag Gerhard Stalling, 1909), 488.

25. Schönwerth, *Oberpfalz*, 298.
26. Ibid., 35.
27. Strackerjan, *Aberglaube*, vol. 1, 488; E. Lindig, *Hausgeister: die Vorstellungen übernatürlicher Schützer und Helfer in der deutschen Sagenüberlieferung* (Frankfurt am Main: Peter Lang, 1987), 163.
28. D. Linhart, *Hausgeister in Franken* (Dettelbach: Röll, 1995), 376–77.
29. Bechstein, *Deutsches Sagenbuch*, 355–56.
30. Strackerjan, *Aberglaube*, vol. 1, 492.
31. Grimm, *Mythologie*, 374; Schönwerth, *Oberpfalz*, 291; Ranke, *Volkssagen*, 133.
32. For German fairy tales and the medieval aspects thereof (kingship, castles, knights, etc.), see A. Classen, 'The Fairy Tales by the Brothers Grimm and their Medieval Background', *German Quarterly* 94 (2021), 165–75. Fairy tales are set 'a long time ago' in an undefined place. Folktales, instead, have local colour and adapt more easily to people's living conditions.
33. Schäfer et al., *Hausgeister*, 79.
34. Ranke, *Volkssagen*, 133; Grimm and Grimm, *Sagen*, 55–56.
35. Bechstein, *Deutsches Sagenbuch*, 267.
36. Bechstein, *Deutsches Sagenbuch*, 267.
37. Strackerjan, *Aberglaube*, vol. 1, 492.
38. Grässe, *Sagenbuch*, 1012–16.
39. H. Pröhle, *Unterharzische Sagen* (Aschersleben: Fokke, 1856), 112.
40. L. Petzoldt, *Deutsche Volkssagen* (München: C.H. Beck, 1978), 230; for similar tales, see J. Jegerlehner, *Sagen und Märchen aus dem Oberwallis, aus dem volksmunde* (Basel: Gesellschaft für Volkskunde, 1913), 248; H. Fehr, *Das Recht in den Sagen der Schweiz* (Frauenfeld: Verlag Huber & Co AG, 1955), 79.
41. Lindig, *Hausgeister*, 163.
42. Strackerjan, *Aberglaube*, 494.
43. K. Müllenhoff, *Sagen, Märchen und Lieder der Herzogthümer Schleswig, Holstein und Lauenburg* (Kiel: Schwersche Buchhandlung, 1845), 299–300; E.K. Wenig, *Thüringer Sagen* (Rudolstadt: Greifenverlag, 1992), 112–13; Grimm and Grimm, *Sagen* (1965), 181–82; Bartsch, *Sagen*, 52–57.
44. Schäfer et al., *Hausgeister*, 88–98.
45. L. Röhrich, *Sage: Sammlung Metzler* (Stuttgart. J.B. Metzler, 1966), 28–34.
46. For convenience, in the following *Nixe* is used for the female gender of the water spirit, while the term *Noeck* is used for the male.
47. L. Röhrich, 'Elementargeister', *Enzyklopädie des Märchens*, vol. 3, ed. K. Ranke et al. (Berlin and New York: De Gruyter, 1981), 1316–26 at 1316ff.
48. H. Moog, *Die Wasserfrau: von geheimen Kräften, Sehnsüchten und Ungeheuern mit Namen Hans* (Köln: Diederichs, 1990), 174.
49. L. Petzoldt, *Kleines Lexikon der Dämonen und Elementargeister* (München: C.H. Beck, 1995), 136.
50. A. Kuhn and W. Schwartz, *Norddeutsche Sagen, Märchen und Gebräuche aus Meklenburg, Pommern, der Mark, Sachsen, Thüringen, Braunschweig, Hannover, Oldenburg und Westfalen* (Leipzig: Brockhaus, 1848), 426; Bechstein, *Sagenbuch* (1930), 410.
51. J.G.T. Grässe, *Der Sagenschatz des Königreichs Sachsen*, vol. 2 (Dresden: G. S'hönfeld's Verlagsbuchhandlung, 1874), 389–90.

52. Sommer, *Sagen* (1846), 38f.
53. Loreley is a *Nixe* living in the Rhine. She sits on the 132-metre slate rock 'Loreley' near St Goarshausen, where she combs her long, golden hair and enchants passing boatmen with her beautiful songs. The boatmen become distracted in the dangerous rapids there and crash against the rocks.
54. L. Röhrich, 'Erotik, Sexualität', *Enzyklopädie des Märchens*, vol. 4, ed. K. Ranke et al. (Berlin–New York: De Gruyter, 1984), 234–78 at 255ff.
55. J. Goodare, 'Between Humans and Angels: Scientific Uses for Fairies in Early Modern Scotland', *Fairies, Demons and Nature Spirits: 'Small Gods' at the Margins of Christendom*, ed. M. Ostling (London: Palgrave Macmillan, 2017), 169–90 at 175–77.
56. L. Röhrich, 'Mahrtenehe: Die gestörte Mahrtenehe', *Enzyklopädie des Märchens*, vol. 9, ed. R.W. Brednich et al. (Berlin and New York: De Gruyter, 1999), 44–53 at 50.
57. Petzoldt, *Kleines Lexikon*, 10.
58. J.K.C. Nachtigal, *Volcks-Sagen* (Bremen: Wilmans, 1800), 338.
59. Sommer, *Sagen*, 92ff.
60. Moog, *Wasserfrau*, 174.
61. L. Bechstein, *Der Sagenschatz und die Sagenkreise des Thüringerlandes* (Hildburghausen: Kesselring, 1935), 475.
62. Sommer, *Sagen*, 38f.
63. Grimm and Grimm, *Sagen*, 77; Moog, Wasserfrau, 175.
64. Pröhle, *Sagen*, 7; H. Pröhle, *Harzsagen, zum Teil in der Mundart der Gebirgsbewohner* (Leipzig: H. Mendelssohn, 1886), 7.
65. L. Ehrhardt and G. Fischer, *Das Ledermännchen: Sagen und merkwürdige Begebenheiten aus Jena und dem mittleren Saaletal* (Pößneck: Stadtmuseum Jena, 1976), 138. Editors' note: for other examples of supernatural shopping, see pages 45, 53, 73 and 144 of the current volume.
66. Sommer, *Sagen*, 40f.
67. Bechstein, *Deutsches Sagenbuch*, 410.
68. Moog, *Wasserfrau*, 174.
69. Sommer, *Sagen*, 40.
70. Bechstein, *Deutsches Sagenbuch*, 531.
71. Moog, *Wasserfrau*, 174. Note how the *Noeck* talks about 'Christian' instead of 'human'. In Germany this religious variant of the motif 'to smell human flesh' is quite common: see G84 '*Fee-fi-fo-fum*. Cannibal returning home smells human flesh and makes exclamation'; G532 'Hero hidden and ogre deceived by his wife (daughter) when he says that he smells human blood'. It shows the man-eating character of the supernatural adversary and the classic formula of the Brothers Grimm's *Ich rieche, rieche Menschenfleisch* ('I smell, smell human flesh'), on which see C. Shojaei Kawan, 'Menschenfleisch riechen', *Enzyklopädie des Märchens*, vol. 9, ed. R.W. Brednich et al. (Berlin–New York: De Gruyter, 1999), 572–76 at 574.
72. Bechstein, *Sagenschatz*, 475.
73. *Pierer's Universal-Lexikon* 11 (Altenburg: Verlagsbuchhandlung Pierer, 1860), 524.
74. A.W. Schreiber, *Badisches Sagen-Buch II* (Karlsruhe: Creuzbauer & Kasper, 1856), 77–78.
75. Moog, *Wasserfrau*, 175.

76. T. Vernaleken, *Mythen und Bräuche des Volkes in Österreich* (Wien: Braumüller, 1859), 203ff.
77. K. Ranke, *Schleswig-Holsteinische Volksmärchen (AaTh 403–665)* (Kiel: Ferdinand Hirt, 1958), 98f. The narrative is also common in ML 5070 'Midwife to the Fairies'; see C. MacCarthaigh, *Midwife to the Fairies: A Migratory Legend*, MA thesis (Dublin: University College Dublin, 1988).
78. J. Grimm and W. Grimm, *Deutsche Sagen* (Berlin: Nicolaische Buchhandlung, 1816), 392–93.
79. Sommer, *Sagen*, 41f.
80. Grimm and Grimm, *Deutsche Sagen*, 84–86.
81. Ehrhardt and Fischer, *Das Ledermännchen*, 138ff.
82. Bechstein, *Thüringer Sagenbuch*, vol. 2, 208–09.
83. Sommer, *Sagen*, 39 (for a return exchange 42ff).
84. Petzoldt, *Kleines Lexikon*, 168f. There is not much evidence about *Nixen* caring for their children or about their gender, but in a legend from Wilhelmsdorf in Thuringia, a man is forced by a *Nixe* to cuddle her little *Nixe* girl in the cradle, so the female offspring survives. Another narrative from this area reports a *Nixe* who mourns the loss of her child. See L. Bechstein, *Aus dem Sagenschatz der Thüringer* (Husum: Husum Druck- und Verlagsgesellschaft, 1986), 145f.
85. Sommer, *Sagen*, 43f; 40f.
86. A. Schulz, 'Spaltungsphantasmen: erzählen von der "gestörten Mahrtenehe"', *Wolframstudien XVIII: Erzähltechnik und Erzählstrategien in der deutschen Literatur des Mittelalters*, ed. W. Haubrichs (Berlin: Erich Schmidt Verlag GmbH & Co KG, 2004), 233–62 at 234.
87. Röhrich, *Schönwerth*, 48f.
88. Sommer, *Sagen*, 177–79; 45f.
89. Ibid.
90. Pröhle, *Sagen*, 7.
91. Sommer, *Sagen*, 92ff.

CHAPTER ELEVEN

# The Hungarians: Heavenly and Earthly Fairy Societies

Éva Pócs (University of Pécs)

This chapter explores Hungarian beliefs and associated ritual practices. My central questions concern the problematics of fairy societies and methods of communication between humans and fairies. In these communications the 'dual being' of fairies plays an important part. I use the term 'dual being' to refer to belief figures who appear in two forms, one human and one spirit, and who can metamorphose between the fairy and the human world. As humans, they can temporarily turn into spirits, and as spirit beings they can temporarily turn into humans. They can also act as mediators between the human and the supernatural.[1]

My research material comprises data on Hungarian folk beliefs and narratives.[2] I start with sixteenth-century sources and range all the way to twentieth- and twenty-first-century oral traditions. I personally collected accounts during extended fieldwork between 1996 and 2016, in the Ghimeș and Ciuc regions on the boundary both between Romanian- and Hungarian-speaking populations, and between the Orthodox/Greek Catholic and Roman Catholic denominational areas.[3]

This chapter will focus on the thematic points indicated above, and only very briefly summarize other traits. Likewise I only provide detailed analyses of belief narratives that are somehow related to local belief. I will not extend my investigations here to fairy tales, historical legends, aetiological legends, and so on. These do not reflect local beliefs or do so only partially.[4] This narrow generic definition of fairy narratives may lead to flaws which will only be eradicated by more extensive future exploration that covers all relevant genres.

As I pointed out back in 1989, the best-documented variant of the Hungarian fairy figure, most commonly referred to as *szépasszony*, is closely related to

Éva Pócs, "Hungarians: Heavenly and Earthly Fairy Societies" in: *The Exeter Companion to Fairies, Nereids, Trolls and Other Social Supernatural Beings: European Traditions.* University of Exeter Press (2024). © Éva Pócs. DOI: 10.47788/JVJT2813 the fairy world of the Balkans.⁵ Here I do not generally intend to focus on parallels with the Balkans. But in certain cases, I will do so. I will not explore questions of origin, as these are far too complex to be reduced to a mere question of lending and borrowing between two neighbouring peoples. All of this is further complicated by the question of the relationship between shared pan-Slavic, pan-East-Central European not to mention general pan-European beliefs and 'genuine' Hungarian beliefs. There is also the issue of whether we are talking about beliefs or narratives borrowed from Serbs and Romanians, or whether, indeed, we are dealing with international fairy motifs. Regrettably, there are rarely definite answers to these questions.

## Terms

The Hungarian word *tündér* (literally, 'ephemeral', 'vanishing')⁶ is a collective term for several fairy-like beings. The term presumably referred originally to a distinctive Hungarian supernatural figure. Even in the modern era we can clearly discern a belief set connected to *tündér*, as well as to some fairy legend-types known mostly in Transylvania and the northern part of the Hungarian-speaking lands.⁷ There is also the *szépasszony* ('fair lady'), the *szépek* ('fair ones') and the *szépleányok* ('fair maidens'). The two types of terminology partially refer to diverging figures (in ways that differ from region to region). Human–fairy societies are mostly associated with the term *szépasszony*, but a few historical sources connect them with *tündér*. The term *szépasszony* and beliefs and narratives related to them were present among central and south-western Hungarians, as well as among the most eastern Hungarian-speaking groups: in Szekler Land (Romania), in the Ghimeș area (in Hargitha and Băcau counties, Romania) and in the Hungarian-speaking Tchango communities in Moldavia (Romania). Witchcraft trial documentation from the seventeenth and eighteenth centuries shows a broader distribution both in terms of terminology and beliefs. Figures referred to in northern Hungary as *menyecske* ('young married woman') and *kisasszony* ('maiden') are in some respects similar: beautiful, seductive dancing women who carry away people.⁸ I will not cover these beings in the present chapter as they have no relevance for my main theme.

*Szépasszony* is likely to have been a euphemistic expression originally, a circumlocution to avoid naming the being in question.⁹ However, there are no such notions in connection with the term in modern data. The term may, though, be replaced by further euphemistic terms: when people simply refer to 'they', 'those' or 'that kind', 'that sort' or 'others', or use impersonal verb forms without including a noun, for example 'there are'.¹⁰

*Szépasszony* can be considered 'dual beings'. This figure is rather diffuse. It is only in etic, scholarly systems that *szépasszony* may be sharply delineated from demons who, like the *szépasszony*, assault people (and who, with the exception of the Devil, may also be defined as 'dual beings'). *Szépasszony* resemble *lidérc* (a *mora/mara/mare*-type demon). Both carry out night-time attacks, in which they carry away human victims, call away people while they sleep or cause a pressing sensation on the sleeper. In other respects the *szépasszony* are similar to the dead or to the Christian Devil. Then there are witch-like traits: the bewitchment of cows and humans; the act of turning humans into horses, bridling them and riding them; and accounts of nocturnal meetings.[11] This may partly be the consequence of waning szépasszony beliefs and the consequent fading of knowledge. But it may be something much older: emic systems may always have been characterized by diffuse categories with fuzzy boundaries. The 'original' social supernatural beliefs of the Balkans are also part of what Otilia Hedeşan called a 'diffuse mythology'.[12]

There are also distinctive *szépasszony* traits: these include the supernatural being appearing as a beautiful, seductive woman whose main attributes are music and dance. There is also the dual nature of humans who come into contact with *szépasszony*, communicate with them or, as the eastern Hungarian term has it, 'go with the *szépasszony*', 'go about with the fair ones'. These humans will temporarily turn into *szépasszony*, or become human–demon beings. The *szépasszony* have been versatile and ambivalent mythical beings in narratives since the seventeenth century. They usually appear at water springs, in groves, along riverbanks, under trees or on the tops of trees, alone or in singing and dancing groups of three, seven or nine. They also turn up as female figures flying in the wind or whirlwind. They can take the shape of birds. Their most important attributes are music and dance. Some Transylvanian sources claim that they are the inventors of songs. New or pretty songs are said to originate among the *szépasszony*, but it is prohibited to sing these songs in their presence and anyone who does so will be punished. In many accounts *szépasszony* are harmless, merely an attractive spectacle. But particularly in the eastern Hungarian areas, they are also seen as deadly demons who punish or possess humans or who dance them to death.

Most *szépasszony* accounts speak about encounters with the *szépasszony* world and about communication with the same: today these accounts are mostly to be found among Hungarians in Szekler Land, Ghimeş and Moldavia. But they are there, sporadically, also across all the Hungarian-speaking lands. Similar but fragmentary accounts appear, too, in witchcraft trial records. Seeing and communicating with fairies takes place in a distinctive dual space-time structure, which is also characteristic of communication between humans and the dead. The universe, according to this logic, is structured into the human and the *szépasszony* world: any particular section of space and of time belongs either to humans or to the *szépasszony*. The *szépasszony* take possession of their own terrain during special times that belong to them: night, midnight or noon.[13] This distinctive structure provides the framework for human–*szépasszony* communication: *szépasszony* appear at specific times and places; encounters are subject to rules; seeing or hearing them is prohibited except under certain circumstances. Prohibitions on entering *szépasszony* dancing spots, or crossing their paths, are known in both the southern and the eastern Hungarian-speaking areas; south Hungarian data speak of prohibitions against stepping onto the 'plate' or 'lunch' of the *szépasszony*. It is also said to be dangerous to lie down on the ground at night, at midnight, at noon or in the period before Saint George's Day, because one may encounter *szépasszony* at those times. Yearly cycles play a role too, in the curing of *szépasszony* diseases: healing may be carried out effectively after one, seven or nine years, on the same calendar date at the same location.

## Carried Away: Dreams and Visions of the *Szépasszony*

Ordinary humans can access the *szépasszony* world and temporarily become spirits through their dreams, through visions or by being 'carried away'. In other words, certain humans become subjects of communication between the two worlds. In Ghimeş, Szekler Land and Moldavia *szépasszony* beliefs were common until very recently. Despite frequent expressions of doubt and distancing, the interpretation of certain illnesses and natural phenomena as fairy attacks stubbornly persists along with traditional knowledge regarding *szépasszony* and texts concerning them. Some of the *szépasszony* stories told here are personal accounts based upon personal experiences of *szépasszony* attacks. Based on night-time apparitions which provoke both delight and terror (unusual noises or lights, bad dreams, bouts of ill health coupled with a pressing sensation) or on experiences of windstorms or whirlwinds, these narratives are founded in deep-rooted personal beliefs. Texts collected from southern Hungarians in the first half of the twentieth century tend to show familiarity with and transmission of a body of knowledge and texts about the *szépasszony*. Only very rarely, though, can we discern any palpable signs of lived experience. My informants from Szekler Land and Ghimeş, by contrast, often gave me vivid personal accounts of meeting beautiful women hovering in the air, flying in the wind, rushing along with the whirlwind, or singing, making music and dancing together. All this provoked both delight with and dread of the numinous.

> They were up there, hovering and floating and dancing and whiling away the time in joy.[14]
>
> We heard them too. We couldn't see them, it was night-time [...] They passed along making music and we were so scared, because they were making their music, making music up there, up in the air.[15]

Some other accounts concern unknown figures, or international fairy legends, and are set in the past—though they are given local coordinates. There are also *szépasszony* versions of some witch legends. Here is the beginning of a narrative from Ghimeş in which the informant did not use the word *szépasszony* and avoided naming them:

> They said that it happened that they, those who knew about these [*szépasszony* matters], they went far away [...] And then a great many of them gathered together in some basement, and they made merry and drank, and the women made merry [...] They made merry even until three o'clock.[16]

In witness accounts of witchcraft trials from practically the whole of the Hungarian-speaking lands we find numerous *szépasszony* apparitions 'seen' in a dream or while falling asleep. Just as in the Western Balkans, notions of a devilish witch sabbath became part of the social imagination through witch persecution. Then, as I suggested in my 1989 work, the fairy world was also 'witchified'.[17] These days I would be a little more cautious. The witches' sabbath did, indeed, arrive in Hungary by way of the persecution of witches. But we cannot know the pre-persecution situation with regard to witch beliefs. In trial testimonies fairy and witch concepts merge effortlessly. Most accounts speak of nocturnal demons who attack people in their homes and who torment them in their sleep. Straightforward fairy visions are very uncommon. For instance, a witness at a trial held in Bihar County related how in the night she had heard the sound of bagpipes and drums, then suddenly the drummer climbed in through her window and all at once there were three young women dancing in the house.[18] Even rarer is the appearance of 'good', healing fairies (or 'witches') in these night visions. A rare example appears in the transcript of a 1742 trial relating to a Mrs András Hegedűs of Barbac (Sopron County, western Hungary). A group of women playing the bagpipes appear at the bed of a person who is ill and

> in her dream she heard music in her room, and she was healed, and it was said, 'Thank the bagpiper for this', and [she] never complained of any malady ever again.[19]

The question is whether the relatively high proportion of 'witchified' accounts is due to the fact that this was recorded before a judge, or whether 'witchified' elements had always been part of the narrative: see the 'diffuse mythology' discussed above. Witnesses do not usually name as fairies or witches the beings who are seen dancing and making music, or who torture them. Their accounts relate to the culpability of the accused. They are not a description of the etic categories of fairy or witch. 'Witchified' versions of fairies' dreams are there even in recent collections. There, too, the beings are only rarely named as 'witches' or 'fairies'. Thus, for example, one account from Bács County speaks of a person who was visited night after night by 'women in red cashmere scarves and lacy underskirts', who 'pulled his mouth over to his ears and made a mess of him. They were making music and he had to dance all night [...] and he couldn't get up they had danced him so hard'.[20]

In the most recently collected material, *szépasszony* attack humans who trespass on their dancing circles, 'their places' or their paths, afflicting them with typical fairy diseases: headaches, muteness, blindness, paralysis, and diseases of the limbs (particularly the lower limbs). Eastern Hungarian accounts speak of 'being snatched away' or 'being carried away'—which usually means a loss of consciousness or bad dreams. Innumerable variants of such accounts describe how people who had caught sight of the dance of the *szépasszony* or heard their songs or who had stepped or lain down in their places at taboo points in time were 'snatched' (lifted in the air and carried away). In other cases people will be called away from their sleep, then brought back and thrown down on the ground sick. In these stories the human subjects are dual beings: for a time they become, as it were, *szépasszony* and gain access to their Otherworld. In the case of personal accounts, people described how upon waking from their sleep they found themselves crushed, paralysed, struck dumb, or feeling lost or in a strange place: She stepped out at such an hour that they caught her.[21]

> I was carried about so hard that they took me to every hilltop and carried me all over the place. I found myself breaking the tips of tall trees, but when they let me down, well, it almost killed me.[22]

> [Their dancing ground] is all the walk of the *szépasszony* [...] If you or I or anybody found their way there, they would pick you up and carry you away. God forbid!²³

One characteristic group of narratives involves men snatched away by dancing and music-making *szépasszony* troupes. They are usually abducted to serve as bagpipe or pipe players, or else they are included in the *szépasszony* ring dance and are danced there into unconsciousness. They are treated to sexual delights, but also driven to sickness, until the *szépasszony* finally discard these worn-out captives on the ground. One of the longest, most vivid accounts speak of a young lad who had heard the singing of the *szépasszony*, stopped to delight in it and even had the audacity to sing along:

> There came a rushing wind and three fair maidens [...] They were fair as the rays of the Sun [...] Oh, you happy world! And so they began to dance him and dance him and dance him endlessly [...] Until the lad collapsed. He collapsed there and then. But then he could speak no more [...] He became sick, so sick, all he could do was breathe, he couldn't do anything else. He was past good sense [...] His sense was all gone.²⁴

Participation in the *szépasszony* dance is often the expression of male desire. Accounts about men who were carried away to dance with the *szépasszony* frequently describe an alternative world of beauty and sexual pleasure. In older sources, motifs related to being snatched by the *szépasszony* are less common, or they appear in connection with the witches' sabbath. These accounts are time and again given by an individual who had been snatched away by fairies, and this textual motif can create the impression that it refers to something that had happened in a dream.²⁵ Similar legends of the merry-making of witches appear in twentieth-century collections from all across the Hungarian-speaking lands. In Ghimeş and Moldavia these are usually told as *szépasszony* legends. Both the seventeenth-century and the current narratives regularly contain international witch-legend motifs.²⁶ Many of these, however, such as the motif of 'spying', also fit well into memorates. They could be an expression of living belief. The 'false feast' legend is known across Europe: a 'heavenly' fairy feast, food and drink, dancing or musical instruments suddenly assume a hellish character or vanish altogether.²⁷ This appears in personal accounts of being carried away in Ghimeş and in Bacău County. In publications, collectors sometimes place narratives of these undefined and unnamed beings in among witches and sometimes *szépasszony*. This is based on knowledge of stereotypical witch or *szépasszony* motifs, or at their individual discretion.

Occasionally, our data also reveal the bodily and psychological circumstances of accessing 'the other world'. Narratives sometimes clearly indicate experiences acquired in a dream or hypnagogic state before falling asleep. But an unconscious (trance?) state or 'soul journey' is also often mentioned, as we have seen in the account above of 'being danced into unconsciousness'. During a conversation at Lunca de Jos, for instance, it became clear that it was ill-advised to sleep outside in the period before Saint George's Day and to lie down on the *szépasszony*'s path:

> or else the evil ones will take your sense away ['snatch your soul']. People like that turn feeble [...] Their strength is all gone [...] (*What is the evil thing that takes their strength away?*) Well, these *szépasszony*, like, yes, the *szépasszony*.[28]

Other narratives clearly speak of being snatched in a physical sense:

> They came to get him one night [...] they took him just as he was sleeping in his bed, in his underpants and long shirt; they picked him up nicely, along with his pipe, took him to a big rose bush [...] they put him down there and he played his pipe until morning, and those witches, those women, they danced around the rose bush [...] Then in the morning when he woke up [...] he couldn't see anyone in the world, and he had to walk home barefoot and in just his shirt.[29]

We have several narratives by people who had been 'carried away', and which are corroborated by external observers. Those 'carried away' speak of their adventure as either a genuine experience of flying or a dream: external witnesses find them lying in their bed or returning home tired in the morning. The young lad described above, who had been snatched by three *szépasszony*, lost consciousness after dancing too long, while the external witness commented: 'Károly, hey! Have you gone crazy [...] what's the matter with you, you are spinning like a whirlwind?' The next day, being questioned on what had happened, the lad reported that

> he had gone out in the morning, around nine o'clock, he began to sing the song of the *szépasszony*, because it was so pretty [...] He started to test his new boots, to see how they spin around, being new [...] And then came a wind, and in the wind came three women,

and they made him dance until István Bucsi finally reached him at around four o'clock in the afternoon. The soles of his new boots were all torn by then, so that his feet were bleeding.[30]

## People Who Walk with the *Szépasszony*

Fairy magicians are also dual beings who temporarily become *szépasszony*. They are initiated into *szépasszony* knowledge, which usually means understanding the use of medicinal herbs, the remedies for demonic attacks or *szépasszony* diseases. There is little Hungarian material on this question. I have employed South Slavic and Romanian (as well as Greek and Albanian) notions and rites to give context. According to material from the Balkans, fairy magicians are usually initiated in a 'fairy heaven' replete with pleasures. Thereafter they communicate with the fairies in a dream or trance; they heal diseases caused by the fairies and, invoking the fairies, perform sacrifices to them which are in many ways similar to the sacrifices offered to the dead.[31] Such practices were recorded among the eastern Serbian Vlachs and in south-west Romania even in the 2010s. On certain festive days (which belong to the fairies, and concurrently to the dead) such as Whitsun, Easter, Maundy Thursday and Sînziene (Midsummer's Day), initiates supported by the fairies will communicate with the dead as mediums or inform anyone who seeks them out on the situation and needs of their dead in the Otherworld. They also tell fortunes.[32]

This rich tradition has few traces in *szépasszony* beliefs or possible rites, but it may be assumed that there were fairy magicians among Hungarians, too. Indeed, I attempted, in 2008, an analysis of the rather fragmented witchcraft trial material with fairy magicians in mind.[33] Consider this revealing point from the 1720 trial of one Zsófia (Mrs Mihály Antal) in Eger. According to witness accounts,

> after lying dead for nine days she was snatched up to the other world to God. There was great rejoicing there and a great feast and she was well treated; but she came back because God had sent her to heal and help people and even gave her knowledge in a letter which was found under her neck, over her shoulders when she rose from the dead after nine days.[34]

From historical and contemporary Hungarian data, we know of at least two different variants of distinctive earthly fairy societies that bring together these half-fairy, half-human dual beings. Gustav Henningsen's research on the Sicilian *donni di fora* between 1588 and 1600 memorably called attention to such societies in both the Mediterranean and South-Central Europe.[35]

## Anti-Witch Societies

The existence of anti-witch societies in western Hungary is documented in the records of the eighteenth-century witchcraft trials. In one such trial held at Csorna (Sopron County) in 1745, Erzsébet Rácz, a witness, quotes the accused as 'saying that witches are not whom people believe them to be, but they "believe they are from the Society of St. Ilona" and are horrified even to mention witches'.[36] There was no monastic order named after Saint Ilona, but the name recalls the figure of Tündér Ilona who plays an important part in Balkan fairy beliefs. Similar notions of 'fairy societies' and hostility between fairies and witches are indicated by the records of the Dubrovnik witchcraft trials of the 1680s published by Zoran Čiča. There we learn of a fairy society of nine members who can identify witches. They distinguish themselves sharply from witches for they heal rather than bewitch.[37]

Even if the Hungarian data is sparse, parallels with the data from Dubrovnik are suggestive. Very possibly the Croats who migrated to Sopron County in the sixteenth and seventeenth centuries may have brought with them beliefs that influenced their Hungarian neighbours. The hypothetical existence of Hungarian 'fairy guilds' is further supported by another document from Sopron County. This refers to a fairy society named Saint Elena (after the Croatian Saint Helen) in the bilingual German–Hungarian documents of the witchcraft trial of a Hungarian named Mátyás Forintos, held at Kőszeg in 1554.[38] The trial records contain an uncommonly detailed description of the anti-witch efforts of the society. This includes their night-time 'soul battles' against witches.

According to the indictment, the accused, a German by the name of Michael Wacker, sent frost to the vineyards of Kőszeg in 1552. He was assisted in this by Forintos. After interrogation by torture, it was revealed that the accused and his accomplices held their gatherings as members of a devilish society of witches at a derelict church on the Hill of Saint Vid. Their ring dances at Whitsun caused snowfall and frost which destroyed the harvest: that the grass on the hilltop had been visibly trampled was taken to be proof of their dancing. One member of the society, Katherine Herter, had a son referred to as Janus who also made a statement. He revealed that he was a member not of the witches' society but of that of their opponents, Sanct Elena Zech ('Saint Elena's Guild') headed by one Michael Schwarz. They were able to access cellars at night through the smallest of holes in order to get food and drink.

Once, the two troupes came upon each other near the church on the Hill of Saint Vid, and Michael Schwarz caught Forintos trying to use bad weather to cause floods and destroy the fruit and the grain harvest. He was prevented from doing so by members of Saint Elena's Guild. Members of the two societies clashed and during the fighting Michael Schwarz wounded Forintos on the leg so badly that he limped for a long time afterwards. Once they had danced, the witch troupe lit candles and a vulture-like bird appeared bringing lightning and a hailstorm. According to one witness account, Wacker fought the vulture in order to stop the hailstorm (then lay sick for days). At the end of the battle Schwarz and other members of the guild drove Forintos as far as the bottom of the hill at Kőszeg. On another occasion they clashed under Pronnendorf.

The battle described in the trial held at Kőszeg is similar to the soul battles that *zduhač* magician troupes engaged in to ensure fertility. This is another case where we may have Croat cultural influence: the Croats settled among Hungarian and German speakers. A very common accusation in the witchcraft trials in the Alps was that of witch covens operating to create a hailstorm; this idea also found its way into western Hungary.[39] Notions of battles that appear here combine fairy beliefs (possibly Croatian and perhaps partly also Slovenian in origin) with the hailstorm accusations of anti-witchcraft demonology. The tribunal documentation suggests that there are real fairy societies working in the background. In the absence of data, we cannot tell whether the battles against hailmakers were occasional exploits of human fairies, or whether this phenomenon had deeper roots and a broader distribution in time and space.

## People 'Walking with the Fair Ones'

A different type of narrative about earthly *szépasszony* societies speaks not about anti-witch activity but regular participation in *szépasszony* dances, as well as their role in protecting certain communities. Sporadic data on these from the late twentieth century come mostly from the larger, eastern part of the Hungarian-speaking area, from Szekler Land, from Ghimeș and from Moldavia.

These *szépasszony* societies were made up of humans who turned into *szépasszony* temporarily. According to tradition, regularly, or every Wednesday or Tuesday and Friday, in their dreams they 'walk with the *szép/szépasszony*', joining them in their merrymaking and dancing, half-turning into *szépasszony* themselves in order to participate at their feasts. Our data from Szekler Land and Ghimeș only vaguely indicate the existence of this phenomenon. Traditions from the older Tchango population in Moldavia who still speak Hungarian are more elaborate. According to these, there are nine or twelve people involved in a village; these can include men as well as women. Men tend to go along with the women as pipers and they are sometimes referred to as *szépemberek* ('fair men'):

> There are still *szépasszony* going about. I heard that they are still about. They are really beautiful. The way they are, they are made

up of these earthly women. Out of real living people. Those that are alive [...] some people go along with them to play their pipe. Others go with bagpipes, they go and sing along with them when they dance at night.[40]

The next story is related by a man who found himself in Budapest in 1919 during the Romanian occupation of that city as a Romanian soldier, who used to visit his home in Moldavia at night to meet the 'fairy men' of his village:

> There was my brother [...] He was there in Budapest in '19 [together with another man from Cleja]. My brother asked [the man] why he was looking so poorly. 'Well, I visit home every night', he said. 'How do you go home from Budapest?' 'I visit home every night'. And he told him that he walked with these *szép*. He was of *that sort* himself [...] and he said that there are seven people from your village; there are others from our village; there are people from every village [...] We dance out on the hills at night and drink wine in the cellars.[41]
>
> People were not very keen to make bagpipes [...] Because they said that if you make a bagpipe, you'll be snatched by the *szépasszony* to play for them in the fields [...] There are *szépasszony* around [...] women who go about at night. They prepare themselves, so that, for instance, she'll be just an ordinary woman during the day, you might be talking to her, but at night she'll prepare herself in different clothing and so they go away and play the bagpipe, or they pipe and they dance outside in the fields somewhere on the edge of the villages.[42]

Most accounts speak of merrymaking as an end in itself. There are, however, also some faint indications that these women fulfil a protective role for the community. According to these, each village has nine or twelve *szépasszony*; 'they guard the village from disease' and 'they are the guardians of the village'.[43] According to one recollection from Cleja:

> When a disease comes into the village, God has given them this that they gather together and drive it away. And if they don't drive it away, it will come in, or a great big disaster may come.[44]

Data on people who go about with the *szép* bring into sharp relief how the two worlds communicate—the transformations of dual beings and the way they switch between two different modes of being. These accounts contain a highly characteristic metaphor for the switch: dressing up in festive (ornate, bright or white) clothes.⁴⁵ A change of clothes plays a part in several accounts based on personal experiences. Thus, for instance, another section of the account from Cleja quoted above states:

> [she could see that] there were those *other ones*, all prepared [...] in silk skirts and pretty *katrinca* [a kind of woollen skirt], all decked out with lots of beads [...] in their best clothes and they were on their way out to the fields to dance.⁴⁶

In Moldavia and Szekler Land, it seems that a popular narrative type was concerned with identifying locals who walk with the *szép*. Identifying witches, note, is a recurring legend-type in Central and Eastern Europe.⁴⁷ It is associated with the motif of a prohibition on telling, and threats against those who had recognized them:

> People at our place also often tell [...] to find out who those *szépasszony* are [...] who they are [...] when you go to the church on Easter day, on Holy Saturday when they dye the eggs red [...] the spoon you use to dye the red egg, well, put that spoon in your belt [...] and bend the back of the spoon this way [toward the body] and with the crooked part forward and then you'll see [...] those women, who they are. And they see you, they have two *colours*, so you see their eyes in their back, and when you have the dyeing spoon, you see that those who have their back towards the altar in the church, is their *person* with whom they walk at night, they are the ones who are towards the back, with their backs to the altar. And they will spot whoever has spotted them.⁴⁸

A point of special interest is the mention of two 'colours' or 'persons', and 'their person with whom they walk at night' (in other words, they have a human and a *szépasszony* side). This sentence connects the switch between two modes of being with beliefs in dual beings (having a double).⁴⁹ This naturally entails the simultaneous presence of the 'real' body and the spiritual body 'travelling' while asleep.

Societies of people who walk with the *szép* are reminiscent of the *donni di fora* of Sicily in that they travel to night-time gatherings on certain days of the week. There, charmingly dressed and accompanied by music provided by their male counterparts, they dance. Here too we are dealing with expressions of women's desire to overcome the hardships of their mundane lives as poor, hard-working women. However, the motif of healing 'earthly' patients (characteristic of *donni di fora*) is unknown here. By contrast, the notion of fairies who guard the village and protect the community from contagious diseases serves as a distinctive, 'witch-free' parallel to the idea of the human *szépasszony* whose activity and anti-witch battles have been documented among western Hungarians. We do not know, of course, to what extent community protection was an active part of the notions of human–*szépasszony* interaction at the end of the last century. The question of whether those walking with *szépasszony* in Moldavia and Szekler Land had any 'genuine' *szépasszony* experiences remains an open one. At least for me, the data seem to indicate only a narrative tradition with perhaps collective recurring dreams about some kind of world of desires.

The historical data indicate that fairy societies protected the entire community from hailstorms and from the harmful activities of witches—perhaps partly due to the influence of witchcraft persecution which was more common in western Hungary. In the present, though, there are hardly any communal missions. The priesthood and cunning men/women have taken on the role of identifying witches and averting bewitchment. Anti-witch activities among those who 'go about with the *szép*' are hardly necessary now (if, indeed, they ever were).[50]

If the activity of *szépasszony* societies expressed an earthly world of desires, in profoundly religious communities some desires were satisfied by the benedictions and sacraments of the Church. Poor people rose, though, above the harsh realities of everyday life by feasting, with music, dance and sexual pleasures. Indeed, an important folklore motif is the desire for sexual liberties forbidden in earthly life. In *szépasszony* narratives there are not only 'foreign' men making music for and dancing with beautiful fairy women. There are also women who trick their husbands and run away from them at night; these were neatly matched by motifs such as broomsticks in beds or people spying on meetings. Dreams involving *szépasszony* can also express unique individual desires. Thus, for example, longing for family left behind is expressed in the above quoted story of the man from Cleja who visited home every night from Budapest.

## Conclusions: Different Forms of Communication

Considering all our sources together, there is no shared Hungarian system of human–fairy societies. Our sources do, however, shed light on the broad distribution of beliefs in dual beings that form the basis of these notions. These systems may be documented in many different locations in a wide range of variants, but their 'historical' connections are, at best, contingent.

Based on my data, the most general form of communication with the fairies turned out to be the sighting and experiencing of apparitions, visions and dreams. This goes hand in hand with beliefs about transfiguration, the notion of dual beings, and the experience of a (heavenly or earthly) Otherworld. This concerns individuals, groups of ordinary people and magical/religious specialists alike. As for motifs of night-time gatherings, some form of (psychologically explicable) common dreams may be behind them. This squares with Gustav Henningsen's notion of the 'dream cult' which emerged in connection with the *donni di fora*. In my opinion, however, the 'dream' category ought to be extended to cover various altered states of consciousness, trance and ecstasy. Furthermore, daydreaming and imaginings can play a very similar role: think of 'seeing spirits' as defined by Lauri Honko's *kasuale Begegnung*.[51]

There are several parallel communication channels. These overlap, but their differences are not significant within the emic categories of switching between modes of being. What is important is that the body adapts to the spirit world. It is transformed into a spirit form and takes on a 'spiritual body'. At least in the case of *szépasszony*, this is associated with the idea of rising above ground, something related to notions of a spirit world being 'above': this may also be expressed by being carried away, being snatched, rising, 'disappearing', being carried about, and so on. The co-occurrence of the bodily and out of body 'journey' of the soul can mean an intertwining of beliefs in doubles (such as we saw in the example of the 'two colours/persons' of the *szépasszony*), or the ineffability of the numinous experience. The soul's journey to heaven while leaving the body behind is an etic category or textual motif of medieval and early modern vision literature. The people of Ghimeș and Moldavia could have learned this, of course, from their religious reading.

The distribution over time and space of the various types of dual beings and this switching between two modes of being is very broad, even without the above-mentioned East-Central European demonic attacking beings (*mora/mare*, werewolf, vampire, 'living' and 'dead' witch) and the 'windy' magicians of the Balkans.[52] Recall, too, figures such as the Swiss-Austrian-South German *Seligen*, *Frau Selga*, *Selige Frauen*, *Gute Leute*, and so on,[53] or eighteenth-century records of the 'seely wights' from Scotland,[54] who have a great deal in common with the *donni di fora*. Likewise, we might think of mortals joining troops of the dead, and a goddess moving about at night with bands of women, known since the Middle Ages.[55] There are also the medieval-modern societies of the dead, Waldensian communities, and 'societies of angels' who bring news from Purgatory and carry 'alms' to souls there.[56] Then there are the seers of the dead who visit Purgatory.[57] All of these concepts combine people who are capable of becoming a spiritual being with beliefs about doubles.

Fairies have one characteristic communication trait which pertains only to them, at least in the twentieth and twenty-first century. The ritual trance or ecstasy (that is to say, the state of being 'carried away') is attained through music and dance (various etic classifications refer to this as divine possession or *enthusiasm*).[58] This is usually an element of the collective possession cults of the Balkans,[59] and stems from the divine aspect of these ritual trances. Hungarian practices include no such rituals. Indeed, altered states of consciousness induced by music and dance are present only in the narrative tradition, which often also reflects the erotic aspect that is generally characteristic of universal forms of being carried away in ecstasy.[60]

Let us, finally, say a few words about the etic categories of the communication of dual beings. Several researchers have proposed interpreting fairy–human communication as a form of 'shamanism' (by extending the category of classical Eurasian shamanism).[61] Others hold that using such an overly general category is not useful. European fairy phenomena lack any of the public performances that we see in shamanism (with the exception of Old Norse and Sami shamanism).[62] I myself have proposed that we use the category of possession rather than shamanism. This, however, cannot be used to cover all aspects of communications between the worlds. Possession is likewise an overly broad category bringing together very heterogenous phenomena.[63] This widespread group of phenomena should, I suggest, constitute an independent category—communication with the spirit world through the transfiguration of dual beings. This could usefully be considered an independent class, distinct from the established categories of supernatural communication (shamanism, possession, mediumship, mystic union, etc.).[64] Thus, it would be possible to study the most important common features of dual beings as parts of a single category. This would lead us to many new and important research questions.

This chapter was supported in the frame of the project NRDI 132535 *Folk belief, vernacular religion, mentality 16th–21st centuries: digital databases, encyclopedic summaries*.

## Notes

1. I introduced this concept (for werewolves) in a 2002 Hungarian-language paper. For a revised and expanded English version of that paper, see: É. Pócs, 'Nature and Culture—"the Raw and the Cooked": Shape-Shifting and Double Beings in Central and Eastern European Folklore', *Tierverwandlungen: Codierungen und Diskurse*, eds W. de Blécourt and C.A. Tuczay (Wien: Francke Verlag, 2011), 99–134. In some of its traits the concept corresponds to the notion of beings possessing a 'double'

or an 'alter ego', or of belief figures with both living and dead formal variants (e.g. Romanian *strigoi*, South Slavic *mara*, werewolf, vampire): see, for example, W.-E. Peuckert, *Verborgenes Niedersachsen: Untersuchungen zur niedersächsischen Volkssage und zum Volksbrauch* (Göttingen: O. Schwartz, 1960), 11–35 ('Das Zweite Leib'); C. Lecouteux, *Fées, sorcières et loup-garous au Moyen Age: histoire du double* (Paris: Éditions Imago, 1992). For 'two-souled' beings in Eastern European research, e.g. the Russian witch, see L.N. Vinogradova, *Narodnaja demonologija I mifo-ritualnaja tradicija slavjan* (Moskva: Indrik, 2000), 289–90.

2. In my 1989 work I offered an overview of the Hungarian *szépasszony* (expanding on the outlines offered by Tünde Zentai in 1976 and Tekla Dömötör in 1982 which, though provisional, covered the most important points): É. Pócs, *Fairies and Witches at the Boundary of South-Eastern and Central Europe* (Helsinki: Academia Scientiarum Fennica, 1989); see T. Zentai, 'The Figure of the "Szépasszony" in the Hungarian Folk Belief', *Acta Ethnographica Hungarica* 25 (1976), 251–74; T. Dömötör, *Hungarian Folk Beliefs* (Bloomington: Indiana University Press, 1982). I wrote there of the 'witchification' which took place with the persecution of witches. In 2008 I discussed traces of Hungarian *szépasszony* magicians in the early modern period: É. Pócs, 'Tündéres and the Order of St Ilona or, Did the Hungarians Have Fairy Magicians?', *Folk Religion and Folk Belief in Central-Eastern Europe* (Budapest: Akadémiai Kiadó, 2008), 379–96. In my 2014 and 2017 papers I analysed questions of human–fairy communication and the Christianization of the fairy world: É. Pócs, 'Kommunikáció a tündérekkel Délkelet-Európában [Communication with Fairies in Southeastern Europe]', *A spirituális közvetítő*, eds M. Vassányi, E. Sepsi and V. Voigt (Budapest: Károli Gáspár Református Egyetem, L'Harmattan, 2014), 143–63; 'Fairies: Small Gods, Small Demons: Remnants of an Archaic Fairy Cult in Central and South-Eastern Europe', *Fairies, Demons, and Nature Spirits: Small Gods at the Margins of Christendom*, ed. M. Ostling (Houndmills: Palgrave Macmillan, 2017), 255–76. In 2022 I analysed popular forms of spirit possession in the Ghimeș region and in Szekler Land (Romania), and discussed the question of fairy possession in this framework: É. Pócs, 'Ideas about Spirit Possession and Anti-Devil Practices in the Religious Life of Some Eastern Hungarian Communities', *Spirit Possession: Multidisciplinary Approaches to a Worldwide Phenomenon*, eds É. Pócs and A. Zempléni (Budapest–Vienna–New York: CEU Press, 2022), 111–92.

3. Besides my own material, other collectors have also amassed considerable data from here and from neighbouring villages in Moldavia. The material in question is in the Néphit és Népi Vallás Archívum [Archives of Folk Belief and Folk Religion] (NNVA), Institute of Ethnology, Research Centre for the Humanities, Budapest, http://eastwest.btk.mta.hu/adatbazisok, main group *Tündér*, subgroups *Tündér*, *Szépasszony*, *Kisasszony*, *Menyecske*. There are some 1,500 entries; these are supplemented by some 150 entries from myself and my students during joint fieldwork (I am particularly thankful for the data provided by Barnabás Csörge, Anita Derjanecz, Orsolya Graf, Anita Györgydeák, Ágnes Hesz and Nóra Muzsai). The most important sources for NNVA have been the following collections: A. Salamon, Gyimesi mondák [Legends from Ghimeș]', *Mai népi hiedelmek*, ed. L. Kákosy (Budapest: ELTE, 1975), 65–154; *Gyimesi csángó mondák, ráolvasások, imák* [Legends, Charms, Prayers of the Tchangos in Ghimeș] (Budapest: Helikon, 1987); Zentai, 'The Figure'; A. Seres,

'Erdők, vizek csodás lényei Háromszéken és a környező vidékeken [The Wondrous Beings of Woods and Waters at Háromszék and Its Environs]', *Népismereti Dolgozatok*, eds K. Kós and J. Faragó (Bukarest: Kriterion, 1981), 185–96; S. Bosnyák, 'A moldvai magyarok hitvilága [The Beliefs of the Hungarians of Moldavia]', *Folklór Archívum* 12 (1980), 11–145; 'A gyimesvölgyi magyarok hitvilága [The Beliefs of the Hungarians in Ghimeş-Valley]', *Folklór Archívum* 14 (1982), 68–154; T. Grynaeus, 'Szépasszonyok és tudósok Dávodon [Szépasszony and Wise Men at Dávod]', *Démonikus és szakrális világok határán: mentalitástörténeti tanulmányok Pócs Éva 60. születésnapjára*, eds K. Benedek and E. Csonka-Takács (Budapest: MTA Néprajzi Kutatóintézete, 1999), 189–204; Z. Magyar, *A csángók mondavilága: gyimesi csángó népmondák* [Folk Legends of the Tchangos at Ghimeş] (Budapest: Balassi Kiadó, 2003); *Csinódi népköltészet: az Úz-völgyi csángók folklórhagyománya* [Folk Poetry from Csinód: Folklore of the Tchangos in Úz-Valley] (Budapest: Balassi Kiadó, 2009); G. Takács, *Kantéros, lüdérc, rekegő: hárompataki csángó hiedelemmondák* [Tchango Belief Legends in Hárompatak] (Budapest: Magyar Napló, 2004); J. Gagyi and V. Dyekiss, *Hiedelemszövegek Székelyföldről* [Belief Narratives from Szekler Land] (Budapest: L'Harmattan, PTE Néprajz-Kulturális Antropológia Tanszék, 2015); G. Csoma, *A megkötött idő: varázslások, ráolvasások, rontások, archaikus imák és népmesék Moldvából* [Magic, Charms, Bewitchments, Archaic Prayers and Fairy Tales from Moldavia] (Budapest: Fekete Sas Kiadó, 2016); and unpublished collections of Vilmos Diószegi and György Takács.

4. The situation is rendered simpler by the fact that Hungarian folklore contains practically no fairy epic in verse, even if the associated popular literature does include some such examples.

5. Pócs, *Fairies*. In this book, I wrote in detail about the beliefs surrounding the fairies of the Balkans and their connections to Hungarian fairy beliefs, using what I now consider to be incomplete information. Here I mention but a few items from the literature of Balkan neighbours of Hungarian-speakers, which I also relied on for the present chapter: L. Saineanu, 'Die Jele oder böse Geister im rumänischen Volksglauben', *Donauländer* 1 (1899), 4–34, 97–104, 199–207, 274–86; F. Ivanišević, 'Poljica', *Zbornik za narodni život i običaje južnih slavena* 10 (1905), 254–61; D. Marinov, 'Narodna vjara i religiozni narodni običaji', *Sbornik za narodni umotvorenija i narodopis* 18 (1914); T. Pamfile, *Mitologie românească I" duşmani şi prietenii ai omului* (Bucureşti: Librăriile Socec & comp., 1916), 262–64; V. Ardalić, 'Vile i vještice', *Zbornik za narodni život i običaje južnih slavena* 22 (1917), 301–11 at 301–02; I.-A. Candrea, *Folklorul medical român comparat: privire generală. Medicina magică* (Bucureşti: Casa Şcoaleror, 1944), 147–54; I. Muşlea and O. Bîrlea, *Tipologia folclorului din raspunsurile la chestionarele lui B.P. Hasdeu* (Bucureşti: Minerva, 1970), 206–18; T.R. Đorđević, 'Veštica i vila u našem narodnom verovaniju i predanju: vampir i druga bita u našem narodnom verovaniju i predanju', *Srpski etnografski zbornik* 66 (1953), 5–255; G. Frankovics, 'Vile-történetek a Dráva-menti horvátoktól [*Vile* Stories from the Croatians along the Dráva River]', *Janus Pannonius Múzeum évkönyve* 17–18 (1972–73), 239–52; S. Zečević, *Mitska biča srpskih predanja* (Beograd: 'Vuk Karadžić' Etnografski Muzei, 1981), 31–49; Z. Čiča, *Vilenica i vilenjak: sudbina jednog pretkršćanskog kulta u doba progona vještica* (Zagreb: Institut za etnologiju i folkloristiku, 2002); 'Vilenica and Vilenjak: Bearers of an Extinct Fairy Cult', *Narodna*

*umjetnost* 39 (2002), 31–65; B. Neagota, 'Communication with the Dead and Feminine Ecstatic Experience', *Dying and Death in 18th Century Europe*, vol. 2, eds M. Rotar et al. (Newcastle upon Tyne: Cambridge Scholars, 2014), 6–38; M. Vivod, 'Šojmanka, Women of Eastern Serbia Who Communicate with the Fairies', *Curare* 41 (2018), 191–200; 'Az utolsó látomás: egy tündérlátó Kelet-Szerbiában [The Last Vision: A Fairy-Seer in Eastern Serbia]', *Ethnographia* 132 (2021), 67–80.
6. D. Pais, *A magyar ősvallás nyelvi emlékeiből* (Budapest: Akadémiai Kiadó, 1975), 213–49 ('Tündér [Fairy]').
7. These include: fairies as pre-human giants; fairies building a castle or a church; fairies living in a castle, a cave or an underwater palace, guarding treasure; golden-haired water fairies playing about in lakes, singing by the side of the water and combing their hair; fairies giving humans treasure (which turns into something worthless); the image of fairyland (also known from fairy tales) (as a golden city in heaven or an earthly paradise), *Tündér Ilona* ('Ilona the Fairy') as queen of the fairies, *Tündér Ilona* on top of the Sky High Tree; see K. Benedek, 'Az égig érő fa (összehasonlító elemzés) [The Sky High Tree: Comparative Analysis]', *A mesesszövés változatai: mesemondók, mesegyűjtők és meséik*, ed. P. Bálint (Debrecen: DIDAKT, 2003), 76–100. Some of these motifs are well known from European fairy epics—see for example F. Wolfzettel, 'Fee, Feenland', vol. 4, ed. K. Ranke et al. (Berlin: De Gruyter, 1984), 945–64.
8. For more on these figures, see É. Pócs, *Hiedelemszövegek* [Belief Narratives] (Budapest: Balassi Kiadó, 2012), 156–84.
9. For more on this, see G. Róheim, *Magyar néphit és népszokások* [Hungarian Folk Belief and Folk Customs] (Budapest: Athenaeum, 1925), 115–16. This fits in with the names of fairies in the Balkans with the meanings 'fair ladies', 'the fair ones', 'good women', 'the pious ones', 'the saintly ones', etc.
10. This also has equivalents in the Balkans: 'those outside', 'they', etc.
11. For more on related traits, see É. Pócs, 'Ideas'; '"We, Too, Have Seen a Great Miracle": Conversations and Narratives on the Supernatural among Hungarian-Speaking Catholics in a Romanian Village', *Vernacular Religion in Everyday Life: Expressions of Belief*, eds M. Bowman and Ü. Valk (Sheffield–Bristol, CT: Equinox, 2012), 246–80.
12. O. Hedeşan, *Pentru o mitologie difuză* (Timişoara: Editura Marineasa, 2000).
13. The widely held belief among the Orthodox Balkans that fairies appear among humans on the festivities of the dead, between Easter and Whitsun, is less prevalent among Hungarians.
14. Gyimesközéplok/Lunca de Jos, Harghita County, author's collection, 2003.
15. Kostelek/Coşnea, Bacău County, Takács, 'Kantéros', 147.
16. Lunca de Jos/Gyimesközéplok, Harghita County, author's collection, 2006.
17. See É. Pócs, *Fairies*. This is known to have been a general process which took place with varying intensity in several areas of Europe.
18. Margita, Bihar County, 1714; F. Schram, *Magyarországi boszorkányperek 1529–1768* [Hungarian Witch Trials 1529–1768], 2 vols (Budapest: Akadémiai Kiadó, 1970), vol. 1, 61.
19. Schram, *Magyarországi*, vol. 1, 169.
20. Grynaeus, 'Szépasszonyok', 195–96.

21. Magyarcsügés/Cădăreşti, Bacău County, Takács, 'Kantéros', 161.
22. Gyimesközéplok/Lunca de Jos, Harghita County, author's collection, 2006.
23. Kostelek/Coşnea, Bacău County, Takács, 'Kantéros', 168.
24. Gyimesközéplok/Lunca de Jos, Harghita County, Salamon, 'Gyimesi mondák', 109–10.
25. See on this question É. Pócs, *Between the Living and the Dead: A perspective on Seers and Witches in Early Modern Hungary* (Budapest–NewYork: CEU Press, 1999), 73–106.
26. Being shod like a horse; being turned into a horse; a knife being thrown into the whirlwind; flying around on a broomstick, with a magic spell, with witch's fat or on a barrel to a feast; a magic spell misunderstood or misused; falling down as a result of a secret word; turning into a horse; being carried away in an animal form or on the back of an animal; placing a broom in the bed to deceive the husband. See these as international motifs of witch legends: H. Gerlach, 'Hexe', *Enzyklopädie des Märchens*, vol. 6, ed. R.W. Brednich et al. (Berlin–New York: De Gruyter, 1990), 959–91.
27. Ibid., and H.-J. Uther, 'Gaben des kleinen Volkes', *Enzyklopädie des Märchens*, vol. 5, ed. R.W. Brednich et al. (Berlin–New York: De Gruyter, 1987), 637–42.
28. Gyimesközéplok/Lunca de Jos, Harghita County, author's collection.
29. Collected by Mária Vámos, Egyházaskozár (Baranya County), from settlers from Gajcsána/Găiceana, Bacău County, 1961. NNVA, group *Szépasszony* (see n. 737).
30. Salamon, 'Gyimesi mondák', 109–10.
31. I summarized the data and literature on fairy magicians and fairy sacrifices on the Balkans in Pócs, *Fairies*, 47–53; 'Tündéres'; 'Kommunikáció'. There is, note, more material to add.
32. P. Tomić, 'Vilarke i vilari kod vlaških Cigana u Temniću i Belici', *Zbornik Radova SANU* IV (1950), 237–64; Neagota, 'Communication'; Vivod, 'Šojmanka'; 'Az utolsó látomás'.
33. Pócs, 'Tündéres'.
34. V. Diószegi, *A sámánhit emlékei a magyar népi műveltségben* [Remnants of Shamanism in Hungarian Folk Culture] (Budapest: Akadémiai Kiadó, 1958), 77.
35. G. Henningsen, '"The Ladies from Outside": An Archaic Pattern of the Witches Sabbath', *Early Modern European Witchcraft: Centres and Peripheries*, eds B. Ankarloo and G. Henningsen (Oxford: Clarendon Press, 1990), 191–215. This can be supplemented by other descriptions from Sicily; see C. Gower Chapman, *Milocca: A Sicilian Village* (London: Allen and Unwin, 1971). There is more data in conjunction with various names ('Diana's society'; the 'Good Ladies'; 'Signore Oriente's Society'), most of which came to light during Inquisition interrogations in Milan between 1384 and 1390: G. Bonomo, *Caccia alle streghe: la credenza nelle streghe dal secolo XIII al XIX con particolare riferimento all'Italia* (Palermo: Palumbo, 1959), 74–84.
36. Schram, *Magyarországi*, vol. 2, 236, 240.
37. Čiča, *Vilenica*, 81–93; 'Vilenica and Vilenjak'.
38. Records of this trial were first explored and published by István Bariska: 'Egy 16. századi kőszegi boszorkányper és tanulságai [A 16th Century Witch Trial from Kőszeg and Its Lessons]', *Vasi Szemle* 42 (1988), 247–58 (Vas County Archives, Sub-Archives at Kőszeg; Documents of the Citizens of the Town of Kőszeg, Acta Miscellanea July 4th, 1561). For a new publication of all the documentation in German, see Pócs, 'Tündéres'.

39. Éva Pócs, 'Weather Magic in the Early Modern Period as Reflected in the Minutes of Witchcraft Trials', *The Role of Magic in the Past. Learned and Popular Magic, Popular Beliefs and Diversity of Attitudes,* ed. Blanka Szeghyová (Bratislava: Pro Historia Society, 2005), 86–100 at 89–90. There is also contemporary data on weather magicians among ethnic Croatians along the Drava River in Hungary: Frankovics, 'Vile-történetek', 247–48; Tekla Dömötör, 'A vilák ajándéka [The gift of the vile]', *Filológiai Közlöny* 14 (1968), 339–46.
40. Klézse/Cleja, Bacău County; F. Pozsony, *Szeret vize martján: Moldvai csángómagyar népköltészet* [Tchango-Hungarian Folk Poetry from Moldavia] (Kolozsvár: Kriza János Néprajzi Társaság, 1994), 223.
41. Bosnyák, 'A moldvai magyarok', 112. My emphasis.
42. Klézse/Cleja, Bacău County; I. Pávai, 'Zenés-táncos hiedelmek a moldvai magyaroknál [Beliefs Concerning Music and Dancing among the Tchangos in Moldavia]', *Néprajzi Látóhatár* 3 (1994), 171–87 at 184.
43. Klézse/Cleja, Külsőrekecsin/Fundu Răcăciuni, Somoska/Somuşca, Bacău County; Csoma, *A megkötött idő*, 287, 288.
44. Bosnyák, 'A moldvai magyarok', 110.
45. This is characteristic of a category of dual beings which goes beyond fairy-like figures and which spreads, in both time and space, way beyond that of fairy beliefs. For example, the notion of the werewolf turning into a human by putting on its clothes is a widely known idea; or we can think of the transfiguration of Jesus: 'His face shone like the sun, and his clothes became as white as the light' (Matthew 17:2). Shining clothes are used expressly as the metaphor of the spiritual body being elevated to the heavens in early Christian and Jewish pseudepigrapha and apocrypha: A. Conway Jones, '"Whether in the body or out of the body I do not know": Corporeality and Heavenly Ascent', *PaRDeS: Zeitschrift der Vereinigung für jüdische Studien* 18 (2012), 79–90.
46. Pávai, 'Zenés-táncos', 184. My emphasis.
47. See for legend-types: Z. Kovács, 'Das Erkennen der Hexen in der westeuropäischen und der russischen Tradition', *Acta Ethnographica Hungarica* 26 (1977), 241–84.
48. Pávai, 'Zenés-táncos', 184–85. My emphases.
49. This may be a key characteristic of different dual beings in different areas of Europe—e.g. the *Mahr* or *Alp* of Lower Saxony (see n. 2).
50. On this question, see É. Pócs, 'Ideas', 157–69; 'Curse, Maleficium, Divination: Witchcraft on the Borderline of Religion and Magic', *Witchcraft Continued: Popular Magic in Modern Europe*, eds W. de Blécourt and O. Davies (Manchester: Manchester University Press, 2005), 174–90.
51. Honko described '*kasuale Begegnungen*' as spontaneous spiritual experiences, when the circumstances of the experience (an unexpected frightening phenomenon, e.g. the appearance of a suspicious animal at night) and traditional knowledge as a frame of reference jointly induce the experiencing of spiritual beings. See L. Honko, *Geisterglaube in Ingermanland* (Helsinki: Academia Scientiarum Fennica, 1962), 88–110.
52. On the *zduhač* as a dual being, see É.Pócs, 'Stoikheion, Stuha, Zduhač: Guardian Spirits, Weather Magicians, and Talismanic Magic in the Balkans', *Magic, Ritual, and Witchcraft* 15 (2021), 386–410 at 401–07.

53. E.g. R. Brandstetter, *Renward Cysat 1545–1614: der Begründer der Schweizerischen Volkskunde* (Luzern: Haag, 1909), 41.
54. E. Wilby, *The Visions of Isobel Gowdie: Magic, Witchcraft and Dark Shamanism in Seventeenth Century Scotland* (Brighton: Sussex Academic Press), 2010, 239–375; J. Goodare, 'The Cult of the Seely Wights in Scotland', *Folklore* 123 (2012), 198–219.
55. From the voluminous literature, a short overview: K. Beitl, 'Die Sagen vom Nachtvolk: Untersuchung eines alpinen Sagentypus (Mit 1 Verbreitungskarte)', *Laografia* 22 (1965), 14–21; C. Ginzburg, *The Night Battles: Witchcraft and Agrarian Cults in the Sixteenth and Seventeenth Centuries* (Baltimore, MD: The Johns Hopkins University Press, 1983), 33–68; W. Behringer, *Chonrad Stoeckhlin und die Nachtschar: eine Geschichte aus der frühen Neuzeit* (München: Piper, 1994), 32–40; Wilby, *The Visions*, 302–04.
56. E.g. F. Byloff, *Hexenglaube und Hexenverfolgung in den österreichischen Alpenländern* (Berlin und Leipzig: Walter de Gruyter, 1934), 137–38; L. Rushton, 'The Angels: A Women's Religious Organisation in Northern Greece', *Cultural Dominance in the Mediterranean Area*, eds A. Blok and H. Driessen (Nijmegen: Catholic University of Nijmegen, 1984), 55–81; W. Behringer, 'How Waldensians Became Witches: Heretics and Their Journey to the Other World', *Communicating with the Spirits*, vol. 1: *Demons, Spirits, Witches*, eds É. Pócs and G. Klaniczay (Budapest–New York: CEU Press, 2005), 155–92.
57. Such seers were also active in Hungarian communities at the end of the 20th century: see, for example, Éva Pócs, 'Jánó Ilona és az újkori magyar látomások [Ilona Jánó and modern Hungarian visions]', Kóka Rozália, *Bételjesítem Isten akaratját... A lészpedi szent leány vallomásai* (Budapest: L'Harmattan—PTE Néprajz—Kulturális Antropológia Tanszék, 2006), 230–51.
58. For more detail on this, see Pócs, 'Ideas', 170.
59. Members of Serbian, Bulgarian, Romanian and Macedonian *rusalia*, *rusalje* and *călușarii* kept in contact with the world of fairies through rituals involving music and dancing. I have briefly explored these cults in the framework of human–fairy communication: Pócs, 'Kommunikáció'; 'Fairies: Small Gods'. For the most complete summary of Balkan possession cults, see D. Antonijević, *Ritualni trans* (Beograd: Srpska Akademija Nauka u Umetnosti Balkanološki Institut, 1990), 7–57.
60. See, for example, various forms of Dionysian ecstasy which could be traced in Thrace to late antiquity: M.P. Nilsson, *The Dionysiac Mysteries of the Hellenistic and Roman Age* (Lund: C.W.K. Gleerup, 1957).
61. Some authors use 'European shamanism': A. Closs, 'Der Schamanismus bei den Indoeuropäern', *Innsbrucker Beiträge zur Kulturwissenschaft* XIV (1968), 289–302; S. Zečević, 'Neki primeri šamanske prakse u istočnoj Srbiji', *Etnološki pregled* 15 (1978), 37–43; Behringer, *Chonrad Stoeckhlin*; Wilby, *The Visions*, 278–82 (about 'popular fairy-related shamanism'). I earlier wrote on the 'European shamanistic substrate', following C. Ginzburg, *Storia notturna: una decifrazione del Sabba* (Torino: Einaudi, 1989), 186–295. I have come to consider this unhelpful.
62. E.g. R. Hutton, *Shamans: Siberian Spirituality and the Western Imagination* (London–New York: Hambledon, 2001), 145–46; O. Davies, *Cunning Folk: Popular Magic in English History* (London–New York: Humbledon, 2003), 182–83; Antonijević, *Ritualni trans*, 7–57.

63. C. Ginzburg et al., 'Round-Table Discussion', *Witchcraft Mythologies and Persecutions*, vol. 2: *Demons, Spirits, Witches*, eds G. Klaniczay and É. Pócs (Budapest–New York: CEU Press, 2008), 35–49; and most recently: Pócs, 'Ideas'. For more on the drawbacks of using a loose and heterogenous category of possession, see now A. Zempléni, 'Discerning Spirit Possessions: An Introduction', *Spirit Possession: Multidisciplinary Approaches to a Worldwide Phenomenon*, eds É. Pócs and A. Zempléni (Budapest–Vienna–New York: CEU Press, 2022), 1–50.
64. I have already proposed the use of this category in a slightly different formulation, to distinguish this category from possession and shamanism: É. Pócs, 'Possession Phenomena, Possession-Systems: Some East-Central European Examples', *Communicating with the Spirits*, vol. 1, eds Pócs and Klaniczay, 84–154.

CHAPTER TWELVE

# Western Balkans: 'A *Vila* Like a *Vila*'

Dorian Jurić (Indiana University)

## Introduction

Of the numerous supernatural beings that haunt the Western Balkans, none are so well known or so prevalent across a range of folklore as the *vila* (nom. pl. *vile*, which I will use throughout). In the nations more commonly known to the West as the former Yugoslavia, the *vile* factor in every form of oral tradition (ballads, lyric and epic song, all subgenres of oral narrative, riddles, expressions, incantations, jokes, and more) as well as a number of ritual traditions, some practised into the present day. The *vile* are imagined at the most basic level as svelte, tall, ghostly young maidens[1] wrapped in translucent white vestments and with long, golden (more rarely swarthy) hair let down along their backs. They are often said to be winged, though the exact form of the appendage is never explicit—given their regular ornithomorphic transformations and deployment in swan maiden motifs, these were surely conceived of as bird wings for most of the *vila*'s history rather than the modern Western-influenced conception of insect wings. *Vile* are also often said to have the bestial legs and hooved feet of a goat, cow, horse or ass from the knees or hips down, which they hide in shame. Beyond their normal corporeal forms, they transform into various animals, but particularly egg-laying faunae, primarily birds, snakes, and frogs. They remain eternally young and unscathed by the passage of time but can be warded off, harmed and even killed by great heroes, the violence of other *vile*, or by the use of certain apotropaics—most commonly garlic, wormwood, and iron.[2]

The *vile* live in natural zones that are most distant from human settlements—in caves on the peaks of high mountains or in cliff faces, in dense forests, in karstic chasms, pits and caves, on top of clouds, in or around all sources of freshwater, and in the sea where they often take the form of mermaids with fish tails below their waists.[3] Gregarious by nature, the *vile* are fond of gathering in small groups to dance roundels (*kolo*) and are regularly depicted as living together. Their society parallels and overlaps with that of our own and, like many of their cognate figures in Europe, often requires them to live symbiotically (sometimes mutualistically, sometimes parasitically) with human society. The *vile* represent a beneficent but also dangerous invisible or hidden folk who are both revered as givers of bounty and knowledge, and feared as a source of illness, deformity, and malady. Their morals are difficult to gauge.[4] They can be cruel or kind, often apparently at random, and are regularly jealous and vindictive, repaying even unintentional and incognizant slights in unequal measure. Like most of their counterparts across the continent, they are hemmed in by taboos—they hate to be spied upon, to be cheated or ill-treated, to be disturbed when dancing or feasting, to have their congress with humans revealed, to have their gifts disrespected, or to have their imperfections noticed or commented upon. In this and many other ways, the *vile* can be said to parallel the fairies and elves of north-western Europe, though some caution is required with that designation. There are a series of important distinctions that lend a localized character to their depiction and that have a direct influence on the nature of the society in which they live.

## Etymologies

*Vila* is the most common name for this being in the Balkans, ranging in geographic distribution from Slovenia to Serbia and south to Montenegro. Bulgarians prefer the compound *samovila* ('true-*vila*') and the similar *samodiva*, while the name *juda* and the compound *samojuda* are found in Bulgaria and Macedonia. The East Slavic name *rusalka* is encountered in Serbia, connected to a particular calendrical rite, and was most often imagined as a figure separate from the *vila* despite their histories being clearly linked.[5] Aromanians in the region have mostly adopted Slavic names, but one also finds among them the titles *dzune* and *džoe*.[6] There is also a unique name (or perhaps cognate figure), the *andre*, found in one Serbian village,[7] the history of which has not yet been fully explored. A range of similar beings are also encountered in neighbouring countries. The Albanian *zâna/zonjë/zëra/zina* and *ôra* are perhaps the closest cognate(s) to the *vila*, followed by the Romanian *irodia/irodita/irodiada*, *zîna* or *iele* and the Greek nymphs/nereids.[8]

*Vila* appears to be the oldest extant Slavic name for female social supernatural figures and is also found among the Western Slavs (Czechs, Slovaks, Poles, etc.). It is attested as early as the eleventh century in Russian confessional books, but was replaced in the east by the similarly ancient *rusalka* in the course of the sixteenth century. In the Balkans, *vila* first appears in the thirteenth century in an Old Bulgarian manuscript associated with Emperor Konstantin Asen,[9] as well as in an oft-copied Glagolitic church reader from Dalmatia.[10] The etymology of the name *vila* has been fiercely contested since the late nineteenth century, with a plethora of explanations proposed. Among the most convincing are derivation from: i) the verb *viti* ('to twist, flutter, or weave'); ii) a Proto-Slavic term for wind *\*vějati* ('to blow, to winnow'); iii) an earlier *\*vidla* as a term for or about magical entities; and iv), Indo-European *\*wilā* ('little holy/ghostly woman').[11] The Bulgarian compounds *samovila* and *samodiva* are first attested in sixteenth-century Serbian codices. The terms combine *vila* and *diva* (linked to IE *\*dyēus* in the feminine, 'goddess') with the word *samo* ('just/only', or possibly 'true/real').[12] The term *juda*, predominantly found in Macedonia, is thought to have started as a multivalent adjective for *vila* and *diva* which became concatenated into a stock onomastic compound, before later being decoupled and reinterpreted as its own noun and figure.[13] Finally, following Miklosich,[14] most have connected the name *rusalka* to the Latin Rosalia festival (Grk. *roisalia*),[15] but Barber and Colarusso have argued for a native Slavic origin in the root *rus-/ros-* found in various hydronyms.[16]

Like other examples of the social supernatural, the *vile* are often dangerous to invoke and the title *vila* might very well be an ancient euphemism for a name or names now lost. The *vila* is a strong *tradition dominant* in South Slavic culture,[17] and her name is widely considered to have subsumed a number of disparate supernatural beings as well as various tropes and traditions.[18] By the nineteenth century, though, when the most comprehensive collection of *vila* lore began, the name was understood as a proper noun and a wealth of other terms were regularly employed to avoid invocations or incitement to wrath. *Vile* were commonly referred to as the *gospođe/gospoje/gospače* ('mistresses'), *dame* ('ladies') and *tete* ('aunts'). Many referred to them in positive obfuscation as the *dobre/dobrice* ('good ones'), *lepe* ('beauties'), *čestitice* ('clean ones') or, with a title aimed at reflecting their true age, *babe* which can act as an honorific ('grandmothers'/'old women'), but can also be a pejorative ('hags'). Others were bolder, apparently feeling safe enough in their use of euphemism to bring up dangerous aspects by calling them *nedobrice* ('no-goodnicks') or *nesretnice* ('unlucky ones').[19]

## Is the *Vila* a Social Supernatural Being?

In her 2013 study on Eastern European *vila* cognates, *The Dancing Goddesses*, Elizabeth Barber posits a firm divide between what she calls the Eastern Willies (the *vila* and her kin) and Western Fairy Folk. This distinction holds crucial implications for the *vila*'s social nature. Noting the root of the name 'fairy' in the Roman *fata*, Barber elides a diverse range of traditions in Western Europe into a streamlined depiction as divine mothers and ancestresses, suggesting that the true parallel of the *vile* in the West is the Wild Hunt.[20] In fact, there are many strong equivalences between the *vile* and the social supernatural in Western, Northern, and Central Europe. The role of *vile* as patrons and adoptive mothers to heroes is mirrored in the *fée* in Western European medieval romances concerning heroes like Lancelot and, particularly, Maugis D'Aigremont. Even the Moîrai/*fatae* complex finds a home in *vila* lore through the South Slavic cognates, the *suđenice*, *orisnice*, or *rođenice*, who assign destinies to newborns and who are often understood to be *vile*.[21] Furthermore, the parallels between Balkan and British and Irish hidden people are legion.[22] Given the terminal geographical position of British and Irish fairies, their familiarity to an English-reading audience, and the many ways they parallel a number of continental Northern and Western European elves and fairies, it seems apropos to use them as an exemplar of the Western European social supernatural in some of the comparisons I explore in this chapter.

The ambiguous origins of the fairies as wind spirits, nature spirits, biblical outcasts, or the dead[23] is mirrored in the polygenetic *vila*,[24] as is their departure from our world.[25] They often voice a desire to lead Christian (or Muslim) lives while being viewed as unholy beings.[26] They fire arrows at humans, causing strokes and other ailments,[27] and steal horses at night, returning them exhausted in the morning with their hair tightly braided.[28] Some major and minor motifs appear in both traditions such as *vile* and fairies giving money purses which never empty,[29] a shared distaste for loud noises and human industry or expansion,[30] and the brewery of eggshells motif which occurs in changeling (*podmetak*, *podmeče*) stories throughout Europe.[31] There is even the idea that fairies and *vile* are more dangerous in certain periods: May Day and Hallowe'en in fairylore,[32] whereas, among the *vile*, it is a slightly shifted calendar of Pentecost and Christmas.[33]

My own research has led me to see the world of European hidden folk split into three zones: elves and fairies in the north-western zone, outlined well by Briggs[34] and Christiansen,[35] dwell in mounds, party in human homes, and are noted for living in a realm that distorts time. An Eastern European zone running from Russia to Greece is described convincingly by Barber.[36] These are dancing, dangerous aquatic maidens like the *rusalka* who bring fertility to crops. Finally, the Mediterranean zone produces predominantly nature spirits built in mosaic and bricolage from the fragmentary tesserae of the classical world—nymphs, satyrs, harpies, sirens, the goddess Diana, and other figures whose depictions have been blended, mixed and matched over the centuries. It is unclear whether these three zones reveal divergent but homologous and monophyletic figures, functional but coincidental homoplasies in polyphyletic figures, or convergent polyphyletic forms as the result of the migration of peoples and stories. In this matrix, the *vila* is, in any case, a transitional figure, situated at the meeting place or crossroads of the three zones and borrowing from all of them.

Thus, there is much that distinguishes the *vile* from fairies. There is no *vila* rade and no *vila* markets.[37] Time spent with the *vile* is never multi-temporal[38] magical time that runs faster or slower than that of humans,[39] but only a mundane shared time.[40] So too abduction by *vile* is less often seen as a kind of death—taken away to an invisible realm with few options to return—and more as a simple kidnapping to a distant but earthly location such as deep caverns, high cliffs, or cloud-top kingdoms. There are also no wooden 'stock' dummies left in place of the kidnapped.[41] *Vila* lovers often return home after a span of time but, if they once more return to the *vila* or choose to remain with her indefinitely, it is conveyed as a tragic but cognizant decision, albeit perhaps with some hint of the influence of glamour.[42] These elements ground the *vile* in the corporeal realm of humans, perhaps placing them in a society that even more closely mirrors our own than that of some of their British and Irish peers. *Vile* were also seldom depicted as small until the late twentieth century when Western pop-culture Tinker Bells replaced traditional representations in popular media. I know of only two instances of nineteenth-century depictions of *vile* as being diminutive, and even these are quite ambiguous.[43] The *vile* also have a very strong martial character that is less common among fairy figures, with myriad motifs connecting them to birds, fallen heroes, lightning, and more suggesting linkages to other female warrior figures in wider Indo-European traditions such as the Norse *valkyrjur/dís*, or Vedic *apsarāses*.[44]

Most importantly, the *vila* and her Eastern kin have no male counterparts as the fairies and elves of north-western Europe do. Since the late twentieth century, a related traditional figure, the *vilenjak* (pl. *vilenjaci*, also regionally *vilovnjak*, *vilenik*, *vilovnak*, etc.) has often been slotted into this position under Western influence—Djed/Deda Mraz (Santa Claus) in modern cartoons now has *vilenjaci* that work in his workshop. But this is not traditional; originally the *vilenjak* figure was only a mortal man. While the name *vilenjak* was occasionally applied to the heroes and the beautiful men that *vile* help and support, the term was mostly given to men who were abducted by or invited into the congress of *vile*. They became marginal to human society but still remained human, forever marked as *sa vilovske strane* (literally, 'from the *vila*'s side').[45] Often taught healing magic and other secrets in what Henningsen would call the *vile*'s White Sabbath[46]—that is, a native peasant conception of gatherings of humans with the social supernatural that mirrored but contrasted with (and possibly predated and influenced) Church conceptions of the Black Sabbath—*vilenjaci* regularly became local folk-healers.[47] However, they were also depicted as itinerant hermits or madmen whose minds had been swept away (*smesti mu pamet*) by the *vile* and who inevitably weakened and deteriorated from the contact or, in Christian terms,[48] 'lost their eternal souls'.[49]

There are various other supernatural beings in the region who resemble male fairy-elves in the West: small, dwarven men with red caps, diminutive horsemen, and others.[50] But they are never connected to the *vile*. Some rare supernatural male consorts are given to the *vile* in isolated examples, but they are always vaguely described and bear traces of borrowings or blendings, or suggest the breakdown of traditional depictions. In the Imotska Krajina region of Croatia, a small supernatural partner, the *vilac*,[51] is described, but his attestation is late (1930s) and there is absolutely no lore provided for him. In the Croatian town of Samobor, the name *vilovnak* was given both to men dear to the *vile* and to a mythic 'lord' of the *vile* who was also referred to as the *kosmati čovik* ('hairy man'), signalling conflation with male water spirits.[52] *Vile* are prone to enticing human shepherds to play pipes for their roundels. However, sometimes a mysterious male piper of unknown origin and character accompanies them.[53] So too the *vilenjak* was occasionally employed in oral traditions in ways that hint at a male *vila*,[54] particularly in regions where the division between *vile* and witches had broken down.[55] Many tradition bearers connected *vile* and dragons (*zmajevi*) in abstract mythological terms, but no lore ever brought them together. All of these represent rare aberrations in a larger matrix of oral tradition that is explicit in having the society of *vile* be strictly female.

## The Social Nature of the *Vila*

The fact that *vile* are all female leaves them a very small window of social interaction independent of humans. This has a direct effect on traditional depictions of their society, since they lack a necessary counterpart and must depend upon humans for their social life to mimic ours. While the Danish *huldra* will dance and mate with human men, she still has her elfin husband.[56] Though British fairies of either sex may mate with humans, they also mate endogamously, producing pure-blood offspring for which only a human midwife is required.[57] This option does not exist for the *vila*, for whom the midwife trope (ML 5070 'Midwife to the Fairies') is rare.[58]

What is perhaps surprising, then, is that the *vila*'s society is in fact less interconnected with that of humans than the Western elf-fairy, and she less often exhibits parasitic behaviour. While fairy society often requires humans to suckle and nourish its young, to provide victuals for its folk,[59] or human habitation to shelter it,[60] the *vile* are able to do most of this on their own. They herd and milk their own wild game, such as roe deer, hinds, and chamois,[61] harvest grain and vegetables themselves (though often from human farms),[62] and are able to make their own wine, bread, halva and other food, though they often require the use of human mills to grind their flour.[63] In some areas, *vile* do live off human crumbs,[64] or else on 'denials' (*nika, nijekovi*), the food or money that humans ignore, throw away, lie about not having, or complain about;[65] but these are localized tropes. It is occasionally understood that *vila* food cannot sustain humans, but it is always adequate for *vile*.[66] While Irish fairies need humans to help them win their hurling matches and faction fights, the opposite is true of the *vila*. In the battles depicted in epic songs and historical legends, where the *vila* sheds her domestic function for a martial nature,[67] she is often the ace up the sleeve of her human *pobratim* ('oath-brother'), unless his enemy also has a *vila* to contend with her.[68] Most importantly, while *vile* do produce offspring with humans, there are also numerous competing accounts of their origins—their numbers are replenished by the souls of dead maidens, women and unbaptized babies; human maidens are adopted into their ranks and become *vile*; or they are born naturally and asexually from morning dew or rain gathered on field plants or tree blossoms.[69] Indeed, their symbiosis is regularly facultative. Beyond an occasional need for food, clothing and sex, *vile* live independently of human society, and numerous accounts provide them the means to autonomously fulfil even these necessities.

Unlike the fairies, who are often found in raths and forts near human settlements, *vila* society occurs predominantly in the other fairy zone, the *uasal* or 'noble places'.[70] *Vile* are always to be found outside of human settlements in the South Slavic tradition, in the wild, overgrown, abandoned, lofty, and dangerous places where humans generally do not go. Their incursions into human territory are always temporary and spatially liminal. They dance, feast, and gather at crossroads, around notable trees in or on the outskirts of villages, and sometimes invade individual human farms or homes to carouse in their basements, reap crops, or steal clothing. Their domiciles, though, are always set far apart.

In a 1991 study, Peter Narváez posits a tripartite realm in Western folk imagination. Fairies exist in a liminal zone between the human realm and an oddly unelaborated 'other' realm, presumably of loftier deities.[71] This conception perhaps works in a mythological framework, but it is unsuitable for lived practice. In the traditional Western Balkan worldview, *vile* and other supernatural beings are seldom aligned in relation to deities but exist on earth as a mirror opposite to human society with its noise and bustle, culture, village-life, and diurnal proceedings. *Vila* society is in the 'other realm' of dense nature, high mountain peaks, deep chasms, clouds, and forests. It is a realm of quiet, nocturnal and dark foreboding.[72]

As Kaarina Koski has astutely noted, the physical distance in this division is subservient to the normative distance.[73] *Vile* live in the places that humans cannot get to, but also places where humans are not supposed to be.[74] There are liminal zones in this worldview, but they are not the *vila*'s realm as Narváez suggests. Rather, they are the places between nature and culture—the mills, crossroads, meadows, fields, and ruins where humans most often encounter *vile* and, indeed, the supernatural more generally. One may escape unscathed from encounters with *vile* in village fields or at local mills, but enter their caves and only the most cunning will survive and escape. So, too, daytime is seen as human time, the night for dark spirits, but dusk as a transitional period when many encounters occur. If humans enter *vila* abodes, particularly at night, the intent is deemed to be ill and intrusive. By day, they may be tolerated but warned not to linger, speak of what they have seen or been given, or to be greedy with the *vila*'s bounty.[75] Unlike fairies, if *vile* enter human houses in the day, they generally seek amicable exchanges. At night, their intent is generally malicious.[76] Here too, the relationship is not fully reciprocal; only the most naïve or foolhardy humans seek *vila* abodes, while the *vile* largely avoid but still intrude into human domiciles. The liminal spaces are shared in split-shift: human by day, *vila* by night. Thus, in legends about encounters with *vile*, it is most commonly in the *gluvo/gluho doba noći* (literally, 'the deaf time of night'—that is, the dark/middle of the night or witching hour) that *vile* appear in or just outside the community. They take horses from stables and ride and braid them, dance in fields and meadows close to human settlements rather than in the deep forests or mountains, bathe in village rivers, use local mills and cavort about them, frequent human middens and ash heaps, and gather around notable trees, crossroads or abandoned ruins.

## The Social Life of the *Vila*

Given that the *vile* are all female, their social life is hyper-feminized and mirrors the roles, practices, and work of women in traditional Balkan societies, albeit with some supernatural additions. In epic songs and historical legends *vile* often appear individually or in triads, while rarer groupings (commonly of seven or nine) will gather before individuals in their ranks are sent out into the action of the plot. In oral narratives they are more often collective, with smaller groupings variously encountered (generally twos and threes) and coming together in immense gatherings for more important revels. These groupings are always depicted as hierarchical. They invariably include an elder *vila* (often theorized as a remnant of Balkan Diana/Artemis/Bendis cults) and a younger *vila* who most often serves as the actant in lore.

## Public life

The activity most commonly ascribed to *vile* is dance. They dance roundels (*kolo*) on mountain peaks, and in woods, glens, farmers' fields, and wherever else they gather. Like much of the European social supernatural, they leave remnants of the act in rings which may appear as circles of grass trodden down or denuded, verdant and voluminous, or filled with mushrooms.[77] Their dances are a common site of engagement with the human world. In epic songs and oral narratives, *vile* engaged in dance deliver secret knowledge to protagonists or are espied and captured as brides. Shepherds are often enticed to play pipes in a competition against the dancing *vile*, where rewards are provided if the songs outlast the dancers but penalties generally demand the removal of the shepherd's eyes.[78] That trope speaks to a large body of supernatural legends that treat the *vile*'s dances as something to be avoided at all costs. Those who enter their dances do not enter another realm as in the Western model, but instead are danced to exhaustion, and often to illness in the human world. The grass circles that the *vile* leave behind—generally *vilinsko kolo* ('*vila*'s roundel') but also *vilinsko igralište* ('*vila*'s playground/dance floor') or *vilinsko gumno* ('*vila*'s threshing floor')[79]—remain dangerous long after the dances are concluded. Stepping upon them unknowingly causes strokes, illness, and often wasting. The peasant Šimun Antolak from the village of Virje in Croatia described one such experience:

> I was cutting grass in the meadow when I came upon a *vila* roundel, where the *vile* had danced. There were twelve small rings, about as big as a sieve, in the shape of one large ring. I wanted to leave that spot un-mowed, but it was a shame to me to leave that grass that was in the middle of those rings. I mowed in those rings too but, in a terrible moment, some kind of wind blew me and immediately I became completely terrified; a chill came over me, my head hurt and I barely made it home. Six weeks I was laid up in bed. Not a single doctor could help me until I gave myself over to some old women and those crones rubbed me with some kind of ointments. But they told me that I would never be healthy and, you see, something is always weeping from my neck, and there's no way [...] to heal it.[80]

The role of dance in fertility ritual is also critical here. *Vile* are spirits of fertility, which they generally bequeath to nature, crops, and livestock, but which also connects them to human unions and marriage rituals.[81] Dance served a critical role in mate selection in rural human societies,[82] but that role is profaned in the image of the *vila*. Dance as a proxy for sexual activity was tolerated in a traditional Christian milieu only when it led to union and propagation. As an unpredictable social unit of supernatural females, the *vile* dancing carries implications of Sapphic venery. When humans of the opposite sex are introduced into the dance, the act does not serve to portend fruitful union in contribution to the collective but an obscene act of control, violation and defilement. The control aspect works both ways: heroes or shepherds may abduct an unwitting *vila* in swan maiden motifs by stealing her doffed bird garment, hiding it, and forcing her into union in an effort to produce heroic male issue; conversely the *vile* regularly abduct men into carnal revelries that leave the victims dissipated and abused.[83]

The *vile* also love to sing. Their singing sometimes has a siren effect in drawing males towards them, particularly those who have escaped their abduction and enchantment before.[84] Generally, the singing is a beautiful but ominous sound encountered at night. Many accounts relate that their melodies are arrestingly beautiful but that humans cannot understand the words, while a trope in Dalmatia relates how their singing sounds like the buzzing of bees.[85]

Other common public activities include washing or bleaching their linens in rivers and hanging them in trees to dry, bathing in open water, and combing their hair in the boughs of trees or on riverbanks.[86] These social, feminine activities also link them to their Eastern cousins (*rusalki* or *mavki*) and the mythic fertility complex that plays a large role in their lore.[87] Moreover, the riverbank is the most common location where, having doffed her vestments or wings (commonly *krila i okrilja/e*[88]), the *vila* is captured and drawn into a swan maiden story pattern.[89] By night, the river becomes a dangerous zone of encounter where one might startle a bathing *vila* and suffer dire consequences.[90] Combing their hair after bathing is both a practical and metaphoric act. It links the beautiful and vain *vile* to the young maidens they resemble while also offering a mundane symbolic vehicle for them to transfer water from rivers to the soil. Their hair is often said to hold their life-force and power,[91] a trope evidenced in a common motif where *vile* grant wishes to humans who free their hair from a bramble.[92]

*Vile* have a special connection with horses and love to take them from humans and ride them at night.[93] They may also steal cattle and goats in pasture, but often return them having milked them for their own use and then refilled their teats to brimming, or else having fertilized them with powerful offspring.[94] Unlike their British and Irish peers, they do not have their own dogs, cattle or other stock.[95] Instead, they domesticate wild stock of roe deer, hinds, and chamois, sometimes with bobcats for sheepdogs,[96] and cultivate deer as mounts using reins of living snakes.[97] Beyond husbandry, the *vile* also engage in traditional food-gathering practices. They protect wild beehives, presumably for honey cultivation, use grapes for wine making, and, as notable healers, collect wild herbs to make balms and poultices.[98] Cultivated crops are also an important source of their food, but for these they must rely on human settlements. *Vile* are said to harvest human crops of various kinds, but their thefts produce fertility rather than scarcity. Those who relinquish the goods of their garden are repaid in bounty. Those unwilling to share find their gardens blighted.[99]

The *vile* are also known to build and topple structures. In lyric songs where *vile* are often employed in a poetic fashion, these are mostly mystical castles, built by individual *vile* in the clouds.[100] In legends, they communally build stone structures. Many notable ancient ruins, including the Roman colosseum in Pula, Croatia, are said to have been built by *vile*. Monoliths, standing stones, erratics, or prominent rubble nearby are described as abandoned materials left when cock's crow aborted the night's proceedings.[101] In epics and ballads, *vile* often topple bridges, mosques, or fortresses built by humans,[102] but never because these have been built on their homes as with the north-western European social supernatural.[103] Most often they seem to be agents of nature, punishing human hubris for building great structures or expanding into nature for economic exploitation.[104] Elsewhere, the epics ascribe odd habits of using the bones and skulls of heroes and their horses as building materials.[105]

Finally, *vile* regularly gather in small, outdoor revels in open fields around notable trees, outside mills, or in other liminal zones, to dance and feast (most commonly, *vilina večera*, '*vila*'s dinner' or *vilina sopra*, '*vila*'s table'). In Bosnia-Herzegovina, they are often said to surreptitiously steal women's dresses from trunks and armoires in order to have new clothing for their festivities.[106] These public congresses reach their apex in the White Sabbaths, when *vile* from distant regions gather on (sometimes multiple) mountain tops to meet, dance and sing, and engage in orgies. Individual *vile* will often bring human males they favour to these events and the meetings are occasionally used to teach newly initiated *vilenjaci* and *vilenice*—respectively, male and female human folk-healers—the *vile*'s arcane crafts, magic spells and knowledge of healing herbs.[107] At the conclusion of these affairs, smaller groups often bring their 'after parties' to the wine cellars of noted humans, where they drink their fill and replace the missing brew with their own urine, spoiling the barrels.[108] They never, though, leave their unwitting human companions behind as in the West.[109]

## Private life

The *vile* also have an active, albeit quieter domestic life. They are predominantly cave-dwelling creatures,[110] and their homes are filled with gilt furniture and various finery that become mundane speleothems when the inhabitants are absent or the caves abandoned. Polished stones in such caves are often later identified as *vila* furniture—tables, chairs, candelabra—based on their size and shape.[111] Their home lives are often tenebrous, chthonic, and silent until humans are introduced, when glamour transforms the environment.[112] When encountered in their homes, *vile* are most often found spinning wool or silk yarn, or even running looms.[113] These practices are reflected in ancient Balkan belief regarding the pastimes of nymphs (Homer, *Od.* 12 ll. 349) or the primary role of the Moîrai who spin and measure the threads of human life.[114] Spinning is a pervasive symbol in *vila* lore: lost spindles bring humans into their caves and *vile* can give limitless hanks of yarn as gifts.[115] More enigmatic stories involve folk-healers learning their craft from *vile* while eating yarn, and the anthropophagy of uniquely demonic *vile* averted by feeding them yarn.[116]

Food figures regularly in the mundane home and social lives of the *vile*. Their food is often said to be green-[117] or gold-coloured[118] and is commonly harvested from human crops, though prepared by the *vile*. In their caves and at their revels, *vile* bake bread or *halva* (a simple Bosnian pastry made from butter, sugar and flour, not the Middle Eastern dish of ground sesame seeds), brew coffee, and serve wine.[119] These episodes litter many oral traditions without figuring in their plots in any significant manner. When the motif is central to supernatural legends, it often carries an olfactory element. In fact, these stories are imbued with an odd blend of comforting familiarity and creeping terror. The priest and folklore collector Frano Ivanišević related one such memorate from Dalmatia:

> Mate Proso from Gata also told me that in Prosik [canyon] above [the neighbouring village of] Zakučac in the morning you can smell the scent of coffee, and in the afternoon the aroma of hot bread, as though you just took it out of the oven [...] 'But Mate, did you ever really smell that?' I asked him. 'By God's sign, the holy cross,' he says to me, crossing himself.[120]

These accounts reminded listeners that mundane village life was charmed with magic but also fraught with supernatural danger. The *vile* live so close to human settlements that one can smell their delicious food, but one should never be foolish enough to wish for a taste.[121]

The most common domestic practice of the *vile* is tending to their children. This occurs in a variety of lore and always serves as a vehicle for interaction with humans. Because of this, the depiction is often quite flat and vague; there are regularly hints at a deeper imaginative realm, but the representations are too rife with contradictions to reveal any consensus. Some accounts suggest that *vile* have a female-only brood,[122] while others give them both male and female children without ever elaborating on the fate of the males. When the children derive from union with humans, it is assumed that the boys will grow to be heroic men—in one song, a *vila* fleeing in the conclusion of a swan maiden story vows to take the female children with her, but to leave the males with her husband.[123] However, the deformed and ugly changelings that *vile* swap with human children are always male.[124] It is clear that depictions of *vile* children, as much else in folklore, serve functional narrative and social needs rather than cohesive logic.[125]

In legendry, human children abducted by the *vile* and brought to their caves are often fed and then given the task of rocking *vila* babies in golden cradles.[126] Humans who thoughtlessly cast objects into caves and chasms are sometimes punished for striking those same sleeping infants. Elsewhere, the tireless work of putting these babes to sleep keeps *vile* from aiding their oath-brothers in battles in epic songs. *Vile* are also said to bathe or baptize their children in open bodies of sweet water.[127] Their unclean nature leaves the water poisoned, though the harm is ascribed variously to only their male or only their female offspring. Despite their doting, *vile* are often negligent mothers. In a common story tradition, a youthful protagonist comes upon a *vila*'s infants left exposed in the summer heat.[128] The protagonist cuts some branches to make shade for them and is later rewarded for this kindness by their mother with various gifts, or special powers. Most commonly, a male protagonist is given three draughts from the *vila*'s breast, with her magic milk imbuing supernatural strength, and a social connection through milk-motherhood (as *pomajka* or *ebejka*).[129] Elsewhere, the *vile*'s invisible children are found strewn about fields and fairy rings, or in mud puddles where humans may unknowingly crush and trample them.[130] The strokes and other maladies brought on by these common, inadvertent slights generally required fairy-healers' interventions.[131]

## Conclusion

It is much easier to talk about the *vile* as hidden people than as fairies. While their status as cognate figures with the fairies of Britain and Ireland has been noted since the nineteenth century, there are important distinctions, in both their motifs and intrinsic features. As outlined above, the critical aspect of

Eastern European 'willy' society[132] that differs from the fairy-elf societies of north-western Europe is the notable absence of supernatural male companions. This crucially means that *vile* can only be a mirror to one half of human society. That said, their solid grounding in the terrestrial sphere, their accentuated character as nature spirits, and their highly independent behaviour provides a very strong, supernatural reflection of human female society. The reflection takes on the frightening distortion of a carnival mirror as one draws close enough to reveal the *vile*'s bestial legs, their fevered dancing, their predatory relationships with humans, and their pathological nature. This bipolar depiction is one of the many provocative aspects of the *vila*'s character that have led to her proliferation in Western Balkan folklore. Even as Western models increasingly encroach upon traditional depictions, active *vila* legendry can still be found in rural regions of the Western Balkans,[133] holding up a fantastic, distorted, but revelatory mirror to human society.

## Appendix: Sources for Further Reading

The *vile* factored heavily in Western Balkan literature as early as the Renaissance, and in church missals, prayer books, and treatises. However, these depictions did not generally represent local folklore but, respectively, literary tropes borrowed from classical Greek and Italian depictions of nymphs, and flat, categorical demonization for didactic religious purposes.[134] True oral narrative lore only emerges in publications in the nineteenth century as Romantic nationalism, predominantly in the German model, provided a guide for academic folklore collection. The Serbian language reformer and ethnographer Vuk Stefanović Karadžić was the first to take an empirical approach to describing the *vila*, but this largely in footnotes to his folklore collections and briefly in various entries in his Serbian dictionaries.[135] The *vila* is found throughout early folk song and oral narrative collections produced by scholars like Stefanović Karadžić, Kosta Hörmann, Matija Kračmanov Valjevec, Veselin Čajkanović, and the team at the publishing house Matica Hrvatska.[136] Folk songs were subjected to less drastic editing than were oral narratives in these earliest collections.[137] Starting towards the end of the nineteenth century and continuing through the twentieth, various academic and lay folklore collecting projects including *vile* were carried out, guided by and later published within local ethnological and folkloristic journals like the *Glasnik zemaljskog muzeja (Herald of the National Museum)*, the *Srpski etnografski zbornik (Serbian Ethnographic Review)* and the *Zbornik za narodni život i običaje južnih Slavena (Review on Folk Life and Customs of the South Slavs)*.

The first academic treatise on the *vila* was published by the Croatian historian and politician Ivan Kukuljević Sakcinski, soon followed by the first comparative mythological analysis by Natko Nodilo, and the first book-length survey study, completed in the interwar period, by the Serbian ethnologist Tihomir R. Đorđević (1953).[138] The last work provided a synthesis of the wealth of data published in various academic texts to that point. Since that time, many scholars have provided more academically robust oral narrative data—the key players in the socialist Yugoslav-era being Maja Bošković-Stulli and Nada Milošević-Đorđević, whose works are numerous; a renewed wave of folklore collection has been going on since the late 1990s.[139] Some important contemporary discussions of the *vila* include those by Dejan Ajdačić, Stipe Botica, and Suzana Marjanić.[140] A handful of scholars have also attempted to return to questions of the origin of the *vila* based on modern data.[141] In 2019, my doctoral dissertation aimed at furnishing an updated and refined survey study on the *vila*. This work is based on a detailed and ongoing systematization and mapping of extant lore. This has led to a series of publications discussing particular historical-ethnographic and folkloristic questions using data drawn from an accompanying database.[142]

Finally, there are also a range of works focused on historical and contemporary fairy-healers (*vilenice/vilarka* and *vilenjaci*) in the Western Balkans. Early data provided by Friedrich Salomon Krauss[143] was reviewed starting in the 1960s by Carlo Ginzburg in his studies on the Friulian Benandanti.[144] Ginzburg's work prompted Croatian scholar Zoran Čiča to search for these figures in seventeenth-century church trials, ethnographic and folklore research, and even Renaissance literature.[145] Serbian ethnographic data on contemporary Aromanian fairy-healers who fall into trances in ritual dance has been documented since the 1950s.[146] This has prompted further comparative perspectives,[147] research into *vile* in neighbouring areas,[148] and explorations of contemporary neopagan practices.[149]

## Notes

1. *Vile* are often said to resemble a girl of between twelve and sixteen years of age; D. Jurić, *Singing the Vila: Supernatural Beings in the Context of their Traditions*, PhD thesis (Hamilton: McMaster University, 2019), 68.
2. V. Ardalić, 'Vile i vještice (Bukovica u Dalmaciji)', *Zbornik za narodni život i običaje južnih Slavena* 22 (1917), 302–11 at 304; E.J. Barber, *The Dancing Goddesses: Folklore, Archaeology, and the Origins of European Dance* (New York: Norton, 2013), 92; V. Vrčević, 'Narodno sujevjerije, ili vračanje, slutanja i bajanje: skupio i opisao Vuk Vrčević. Dio deveti. Nečisti duhovi', *Srbadija: ilustrovan list za zabavu i pouku* 2, 6 (1876), 87–91 at 89.
3. D. Jurić, 'Where Does the *Vila* Live? Returning to a Simple Question', *Folklore* 134 (2023), 59–64.

4. Abstract questions regarding contradictory aspects of *vila* nature are often met with a tautological folk idiom, '*vila k'o vila*' ('A *vila* [behaves, is, etc.] like a *vila*').
5. Jurić, 'Where', 57–58, 51 n. 5; S. Zečević, *Mitska bića srpskih predanja* (Belgrade: Vuk Karadžić and Etnografski muzej, 1981), 30–39.
6. D. Antonijević, *Ritualni trans* (Belgrade: SANU, 1990), 197.
7. M. Filipović and P. Tomić, 'Gornja Pčinja', *Srpski etnografski zbornik* 68 (1955), 105.
8. Editors' note: for discussion of nereids, see pages 217–32 in the current volume.
9. Jurić, 'Where', 57 n. 13.
10. R. Strohal, *Cvêt vsake mudrosti: najstarije hrvatsko umjetno sačuvano književno djelo iz 14. vijeka* (Zagreb: Tisak C. Albrechta, 1916), 6, 29.
11. Jurić, 'Where', 51 n. 5, 57 n. 13.
12. Jurić, *Singing*, 8 n. 5.
13. G.A. Il'inskii, 'Iuda: Stranichka iz slavianskoi mifologii', *Sbornik' vŭ chest' na Prof. L. Miletich' za sedemdesetgodišninata ot' rozhdenieto mu (1863–1933)* (Sofia: izdanie na makedonskiia nauchen' institut', 1933), 467–74 at 472–73.
14. F. Miklosich, *Die Rusalien, ein beitrag zur Slavischen mythologie* (Vienna: Kaiserlich-königliche Hof- und Staatsdruckerei, 1864).
15. É. Pócs, *Fairies andWitches at the Boundary of South-Eastern and Central Europe* (Helsinki: Academia Scientiarum Fennica, 1989), 17 n. 46; Zečević, *Mitska*, 35.
16. Barber, *Dancing*, 98; Jurić, 'Where', 57 n. 13.
17. A. Eskeröd, *Årets äring* (Stockholm: Nordisk Museet, 1947), 81.
18. Jurić, 'Where'.
19. Jurić, *Singing*, 258–59.
20. Barber, *Dancing*, 262–64.
21. Jurić, *Singing*, 85; Zečević, *Mitska*, 77–84.
22. É. Pócs, 'Small Gods, Small Demons: Remnants of an Archaic Fairy Cult in Central and South-Eastern Europe', *Fairies, Demons, and Nature Spirits:'Small Gods' at the Margins of Christendom*, ed. M. Ostling (London: Palgrave Macmillan, 2018), 255–76 at 256.
23. K.M. Briggs, *The Fairies in Tradition and Literature* (London and NewYork: Routledge, 1978), 37–38, 169–79.
24. Jurić, 'Where', 57–59.
25. Briggs, *Vanishing*, 50–51; Jurić, *Singing*, 297–98.
26. Briggs, *Vanishing*, 72; T. Keightley, *The Fairy Mythology, Illustrative of the Romance and Superstition of Various Countries* (London: H.G. Bohn, 1968 [1850]), 158; Jurić, *Singing*, 99.
27. Jurić, *Singing*, 116–19, 186–87, 215; A. Hall, 'Getting Shot of Elves: Healing, Witchcraft and Fairies in the Scottish Witchcraft Trials', *Folklore* 116 (2005), 19–36.
28. Jurić, *Singing*, 303–04; J. Harte, 'Fairy Barrows and Cunning Folk: Dorset', *Magical Folk: British & Irish Fairies 500 AD to the Present*, eds S. Young and C. Houlbrook (London: Gibson Square, 2018), 65–78 at 75–76.
29. Briggs, *Vanishing*, 179; Jurić, *Singing*, 268.
30. Jurić, *Singing*, 74, 222–23, 298; Harte, 'Fairy', 70–71; S. Young, 'Fairy Holes and Fairy Butter: Cumbria', *Magical Folk*, eds Young and Houlbrook, 79–94 at 82.
31. ML 5085 'The Changeling'. See Jurić, *Singing*, 337; R. Wildhaber, *Der Altersvers des Wechselbalges und die Übrigen Altersverse* (Helsinki: Academia Scientiarum Fennica, 1985), 12–27.

32. Briggs, *Vanishing*, 125, 163–65; but see A. Bruford, 'Caught in the Fairy Dance: Rip van Winkle's Scottish Grandmother and Her Relations', *Béaloideas* 62–63 (1994–95), 1–28 at 4.
33. Barber, *Dancing*, 34–35, 69–90.
34. K.M. Briggs, *The Fairies in Tradition and Literature* (London and New York: Routledge, 1967); Briggs, *Vanishing*.
35. R.Th. Christiansen, ed., *The Migratory Legends: A Proposed List of Types with a Systematic Catalogue of the Norwegian Variants* (Helsinki: Academia Scientiarum Fennica, 1958).
36. Barber, *Dancing*, 13–109, 183–200, 267–90.
37. Briggs, *Vanishing*, 39–49.
38. C. Asplund Ingemark, 'The Chronotope of Enchantment', *Journal of Folklore Research* 43 (2006), 1–30 at 12–13.
39. Briggs, *Fairies*, 123–26; Bruford, 'Caught'; D. Jurić, 'Supernatural Legends in the Western Balkans', *The Oxford Handbook of Slavic and East European Folklore*, ed. M. Beissinger (New York: Oxford University Press, 2023) https://doi.org/10.1093/oxfordhb/9780190080778.001.0001.
40. This trope seems more commonly ascribed to human spirits/ghosts in the Western Balkans. See M. Mencej, 'Spaces of Passage into Supernatural Time', *Tautosakos darbai* 44 (2012), 30–48.
41. Briggs, *Vanishing*, 104–13; 104.
42. Jurić, *Singing*, 286–89.
43. Ibid., 92 n. 3.
44. N. Nodilo, *Stara vjera Srba i Hrvata* (Belgrade: MVTC, 2003), 266–74; D. Jurić, *A Treatise on the South Slavic Vila*, MA thesis (Hamilton: McMaster University, 2010), 58–70; Jurić, *Singing*, 96 n. 14; Pócs, *Fairies*, 32, who sees *vile* protecting heroes in battle as an outgrowth of older Balkan guardian spirits, an explanation I find unconvincing.
45. Ardalić, 'Vile', 303.
46. G. Henningsen, '"The Ladies from Outside": An Archaic Pattern of the Witches' Sabbath', *Early Modern European Witchcraft: Centres and Peripheries*, eds B. Ankarloo and G. Henningsen (Oxford: Clarendon, 1990), 191–215 at 207.
47. He also has a female counterpart in the *vilenica/vilarka*, though she does not figure in songs or tales. See Z. Čiča, *Vilenica i vilenjak: sudbina jednog pretkršćanskog kulta u doba progona vještica* (Zagreb: Biblioteka Nova Etnografija, 2002); 'Vilenica and Vilenjak: Bearers of an Extinct Fairy Cult', *Narodna Umjetnost* 39, 31–63; M. Vivod, 'The Fairy Seers of Eastern Serbia: Seeing Fairies—Speaking through Trance', *Oral Tradition* 32 (2018), 53–70. See also Jurić, *Singing*, 330–32, and I. Kukuljević Sakcinski, 'Bajoslovlje i crkva', *Arkiv za pověstnicu jugoslavensku* 1 (1851), 86–104 at 89–90, 99, for oral traditional depictions of the training of fairy-healers.
48. M. Mencej, *Styrian Witches in European Perspective: Ethnographic Fieldwork* (London: Palgrave Macmillan, 2017), 59–75; Ü. Valk, 'Discursive Shifts in Legends from Demonization to Fictionalization', *Narrative Culture* 2 (2015), 141–65 at 143–50.
49. Jurić, *Singing*, 77–80, 338–39.
50. Z. Lovrenčević, 'Mitološke predaje Bilo-Gore', *Narodna umjetnost* 7 (1970), 71–100 at 80–84; I. Lozica, 'Dva demona: Orko i Macić', *Narodna umjetnost* 32 (1995), 11–63 at 20–58.

51. F.S. Kutleša, *Život i običaji u Imockoj Krajini* (Imotski: Matica Hrvatska Ogranak Imotski and Hrvatska akademija znanosti i umjetnosti, 1993), 396.
52. M. Lang, 'Samobor: narodni život i običaji', *Zbornik za narodni život i običaje južnih Slavena* 19 (1914), 39–152 at 137, 139; see Zečević, *Mitska*, 22–30.
53. I. Filakovac, 'Vjerovaña (Retkovci u Slavoniji)', *Zbornik za narodni život i običaje južnih Slavena* 10 (1905), 144–49 at 144; Filipović and Tomić, 'Gornja', 105; J. Lovretić, 'Otok: narodni život i običaji', *Zbornik za narodni život i običaje južnih Slavena* 7 (1902) 57–206 at 122; see Henningsen, 'Ladies', 196.
54. Jurić, *Singing*, 259; S. Marjanić, 'Telurni simbolizam konavoskih vila: zapisi vilinskih pripovijedaka Katine Casilari u Bogišićevoj cavtatskoj rukopisnoj zbirci usmenih pripovijedaka', *Spomenica Valtazara Bogišića o stogodišnjici njegove smrti 24. apr. 2008. godine knj. 2*, ed. L. Breneselović (Belgrade: Institut za uporedno pravo, Pravni fakultet Univerziteta u Nišu, 2011), 559–82 at 562.
55. Čiča, *Vilenica*; Lovretić, 'Otok'; Pócs, *Fairies*.
56. Briggs, *Vanishing*, 168.
57. Ibid., 94–97; C. Mac Cárthaigh, 'Midwife to the Fairies (ML 5070): The Irish Variants in Their Scottish and Scandinavian Perspective', *Béaloideas* 59 (1991), 133–43.
58. However, see M. Bošković-Stulli, *Narodne pripovijetke* (Zagreb: Zora and Matica hrvatska, 1963), 272–73, 334; Kutleša, *Život*, 395.
59. Since the *vile* rarely steal human livestock, it is unsurprising that their 'elf-shot' is exclusively reserved for human victims and not cattle as in Britain and Ireland; R.P. Jenkins, 'Witches and Fairies: Supernatural Aggression and Deviance among the Irish Peasantry', *The Good People: New Fairylore Essays*, ed. P. Narváez (Lexington, KT: University Press of Kentucky, 1991), 302–35 at 317–18.
60. Jenkins, 'Witches', 314.
61. Jurić, *Singing*, 298–99; Ljubomir Pećo, 'Običaji i verovanja iz Bosne', *Srpski etnografski zbornik* 32 (1925), 363–86 at 378.
62. Jurić, *Singing*, 75, 281, 299.
63. Jurić, *Singing*, 263, 295, 299–300, 304–06, 311; Pećo, 'Običaji', 377–78, offers a notable exception where *vile* have their own mills and waterwheels.
64. Lovretić, 'Otok', 122.
65. Jurić, *Singing*, 73; F. Ivanišević, 'Poļica: narodni život i običaji', *Zbornik za narodni život i običaje južnih Slavena* 10 (1905), 181–307 at 254–55; V. Vuletić-Vukasović, 'Prizrijevanje', *Srpski etnografski sbornik* 50 (1934), 155–95 at 157.
66. Jurić, *Singing*, 287–88; compare Briggs, *Fairies*, 142; *Vanishing*, 136–39.
67. See D. Jurić, 'A Call for Functional Differentiation of the South Slavic *Vila*', *Journal of Indo-European Studies* 38 (2010), 172–202, reframed in Jurić, *Singing*, 356–61.
68. Jurić, *Singing*, 100.
69. Jurić, 'Where', 55 n. 9.
70. Jenkins, 'Witches', 314.
71. P. Narváez, 'Newfoundland Berry Pickers "In the Fairies": Maintaining Spatial, Temporal, and Moral Boundaries Through Legendry', *The Good People: New Fairylore Essays* (Lexington, KT: University Press of Kentucky, 1991), 336–68.
72. *Vile* are one of the few supernatural beings in the Western Balkans that are encountered both diurnally and nocturnally; however, nocturnal encounters are more common and generally more dangerous since they expect not to be interrupted by humans.

73. K. Koski, 'Narrative Time-Space in Belief Legends', *Space and Time in Europe: East andWest, Past and Present*, ed. M. Mencej (Ljubljana: Oddelek za etnologijo in kulturno antropologijo, Filozofska fakulteta, Ljubljana, 2008), 337–53 at 340–42.
74. Bratić, *Gluvo*, 193–213.
75. Jurić, *Singing*, 339–40, 278–79; Kutleša, *Život*, 388–96.
76. Jurić, *Singing*, 280, 319; Kutleša, *Život*, 351.
77. Jurić, *Singing*, 296–97.
78. Ibid., 138–39, 315–17.
79. Threshing floors often doubled as dance floors in traditional societies.
80. J. Tomec, *Virje 1897.–1904., Zbornik za narodni život i običaje* 62 (Zagreb: Hrvatska akademija znanosti i umjetnosti, 2021), 365.
81. V. Čajkanović, *Studije iz srpske religije i folklore 1925.-1942.: sabrana dela iz srpske religije i mitologije*, vol. 2, ed. V. Đurić (Belgrade: Srpska književna zadruga, Prosveta, and Partenon, 1994), 332–38; Jurić, *Singing*, 216–18, 219–22, 229.
82. Barber, *Dancing*, 176–81.
83. Jurić, *Singing*, 288–89.
84. Ibid., 72, 82, 301.
85. Jurić, *Singing*, 301–02; Vuletić-Vukasović, 'Prizrijevanje', 156.
86. Jurić, *Singing*, 299, 142–43, 312.
87. Barber, *Dancing*, 13–27, 37–60.
88. 'Wings and o-wings'. A poetic reduplication, the exact concept described by the 'o-wings' has been a topic of much debate: S. Marjanić, 'Životinjsko u vilinskom', *Između roda i naroda: etnološke i folklorističke studije*, eds R. Jambrešić Kirin and T. Škokić (Zagreb: Institut za etnologiju i folkloristiku, 2004), 231–56 at 249; Zečević, *Mitska*, 47.
89. Jurić, *Singing*, 149–55, 302.
90. T. Dragičević, 'Narodne praznovjerice', *Glasnik Zemaljskog muzeja u Bosni i Hercegovini* 20 (1908), 449–66 at 450.
91. Kukuljević, 'Bajoslovlje', 87
92. Jurić, *Singing*, 306–07. Some tales in Dalmatia include frightening, cave-dwelling *vile* with stinking hair full of lice; see A.I. Carić, 'Narodno vjerovanje u Dalmaciji', *Glasnik Zemaljskog muzeja u Bosni i Hercegovini* 9 (1897), 703–17 at 708; Marjanić, 'Telurni', 568–69; Jurić, *Singing*, 316–18.
93. Jurić, *Singing*, 303–04.
94. Ibid., 183–86. Compare with R.M. James, 'Piskies and Knockers: Cornwall', *Magical Folk*, eds Young and Houlbrook, 181–92 at 181–83.
95. Briggs, *Fairies*, 84–97.
96. Jurić, *Singing*, 298–99; Pećo, 'Običaji', 378. See Keightley, *Fairy*, 271–72.
97. Jurić, *Singing*, 104–06.
98. Ibid., 278, 166–71, 321.
99. Lang, 'Samobor', 137.
100. Jurić, *Singing*, 222–23.
101. Ibid., 89.
102. Jurić, *Singing*, 171–75; 'Back in the Foundation: Chauvinistic Scholarship and the Building Sacrifice Story-Pattern', *Oral Tradition* 34 (2020), 3–44.
103. Christiansen, *Migratory*, 108–09.

104. D. Bratić, *Gluvo doba: predstave o noći u narodnoj religiji Srba* (Belgrade: Biblioteka XX vek, 2013), 89.
105. Jurić, *Singing*, 133, 216.
106. Ibid., 304–06.
107. Ibid., 330–32.
108. Kutleša, 'Život', 351; see C. Ginzburg, *The Night Battles:Witchcraft and Agrarian Cults in the Sixteenth and Seventeenth Centuries* (Baltimore, MA: John Hopkins University Press, 1983), 3, 5; *Ecstasies: Deciphering the Witches' Sabbath* (New York: Penguin, 1992), 89, 101.
109. Briggs, *Vanishing*, 139. Pócs, *Fairies*, 19, 26, suggests this *vila* behaviour represents contamination from another spirit. The Western parallels draw that conclusion into question.
110. Jurić, 'Where'.
111. Jurić, *Singing*, 87–88, 291.
112. Bratić, *Gluvo*, 57–58; Marjanić, 'Telurni', 565–68.
113. Jurić, *Singing*, 288; Pećo, 'Običaji', 377.
114. On connections between Greek nymphs and *vile*, see T.R. Đorđević, 'Veštica i vila u našem narodnom verovanju i predanju', *Srpski etnografski zbornik* 66, ed. V.S. Radovanović (Beograd: SANU, 1953); Jurić, 'Where', 52–57, 58–64; A. Sánchez i Bernet, 'Circe y la vila Ravijojla como oponentes y aliadas del héroe: dos episodios análogos en la épica griega y serbia', *Anali filološkog fakulteta* 34 (2022), 255–75.
115. Marjanić, 'Telurni', 565–68; Jurić, *Singing*, 267.
116. Kukuljević, 'Bajoslovlje', 89–90; Jurić, *Singing*, 319.
117. Dragičević, 'Narodne', 451; Jurić, *Singing*, 295; I. Zovko, 'Mańi prinosi Vjerovańa iz Herceg-Bosne', *Zbornik za narodni život i običaje južnih Slavena* 6 (1901), 115–60 at 145.
118. Vuletić-Vukasović, 'Prizrijevanje', 156.
119. Jurić, *Singing*, 191.
120. Ivanišević, 'Poļica', 258 n. 1.
121. Ibid., 261.
122. Jurić, *Singing*, 73.
123. Ibid., 126, 152.
124. Ibid., 336–38. Compare with J. Harte, *Explore Fairy Traditions* (Loughborough: Heart of Albion Press, 2004), 108–22. *Vila* changelings prove particularly contradictory. Western changeling lore is tied to the idea that fairy women are unable either to bear healthy children or to feed them, hence they need to abduct wet-nurses from the human world: Jenkins, 'Witches', 315. Not only are *vile* able to bring healthy children to term and raise them, but their milk is even used to feed human children and endow them with supernatural power: Jurić, *Singing*, 183–86, 218–19, 266–68. More research on Balkan changelings is needed. See Greek parallels in J.C. Lawson, *Modern Greek Folklore and Ancient Greek Religion: A Study of Survivals* (Cambridge: Cambridge University Press, 1910), 141.
125. Jurić, 'Where', 64.
126. Vuletić-Vukasović, 'Prizrijevanje', 155–57.
127. Jurić, *Singing*, 279 (sleeping infants); 99 (putting babes to sleep); 73, 83, 201–02, 312, 333 (bathing or baptizing).

128. Ibid., 183–86, 266–68.
129. Ibid., 218–19.
130. Filipović and Tomić, 'Gornja', 105 (fields and fairy rings); Kukuljević, 'Bajoslovlje', 103 (mud puddles).
131. For some Serbian and Aromanian rituals to lift these maladies, see Antonijević, *Ritualni*, 147–88; Jurić, 'Where', 56–57, 63; Vivod, 'Fairy Seers'.
132. Barber, *Dancing*, 17.
133. See for example M. Dragić, 'Vile u tradicijskim pričama šibenskoga i splitskoga zaleđa', *Godišnjak Titius* 10 (2017), 219–40; L. Šešo, *Živjeti s nadnaravnim bićima: vukodlaci, vile i vještice hrvatskih tradicijskih vjerovanja* (Zagreb: Jesenski i Turk, 2016).
134. Jurić, 'Where', 52–54; Strohal, *Cvêt*.
135. Jurić, 'Where', 49.
136. V. Stefanović Karadžić, *Srpske narodne pjesme*, 4 vols (Vienna: Štamparija Jermenskoga manastira, 1841–62); *Srpske narodne pripovijetke: skupio ih i na svijet izdao Vuk Stef. Karadžić* (Vienna: Štamparija Jermenskoga manastira, 1870); K. Hörmann, *Narodne pjesne Muhamedovaca u Bosni i Hercegovini*, 2 vols (Sarajevo: Zemaljska Štamparija, 1888–89); M. Kračmanov Valjevec, *Narodne pripovijedke skupio u i oko Varaždina* (Varaždin: Josip pl. Platzer, 1858); V. Čajkanović, *Srpske narodne pripovetke*, vol. 1 (Beograd–Zemun: Grafički zavod 'Makarije', 1927); *Hrvatske narodne pjesme*, 10 vols, ed. N. Andrić (vols 5–10), S. Bosanac (vol. 2), I. Broz and S. Bosanac (vol. 1), L. Marjanović (vols 3–4) (Zagreb: Matica Hrvatska, 1896–1942).
137. Jurić, 'Supernatural'.
138. Sakcinski, 'Bajoslovlje'. Nodilo's analysis of the *vila* was published in 1888 as one of a series of articles (1885–90) in the periodical *Rad JAZU*. They are collected in book form in Nodilo, *Stara*, 266–74. Đorđević, 'Veštica'.
139. Jurić, 'Supernatural'.
140. D. Ajdačić, 'O vilama u narodnim baladama', *Studia Mythologica Slavica* 4 (2001), 207–24; S. Botica, 'Vile u hrvatskoj mitologiji', *Radovi zavoda za slavensku mitologiju* 25 (1990), 29–40; Marjanić, 'Životinjsko'; 'Telurni'.
141. Barber, *Dancing*; Pócs, *Fairies*, 12–38; Jurić, 'Where'.
142. 'Back'; 'Where'; 'Supernatural'.
143. *Volksglaube und religiöser Brauch der Südslaven* (Münster–Vienna: Aschendorffschen Buchhandlung, 1890), 97–108, 110–28.
144. *Night Battles*, 142–43; *Ecstasies*, 153–81.
145. *Vilenica*, with the most important findings in 'Vilenica and Vilenjak'.
146. Antonijević, *Ritualni*; P. Tomić, 'Vilarke i vilari kod vlaških Cigana u Temniću i Belici', *Zbornik Radova, SANU* 4 (1950), 237–62; Vivod, 'Fairy Seers'.
147. Pócs, 'Small Gods'; L. Šešo, 'Problem istraživanja nadnaravnih bića u hrvatskoj etnologiji i folkloristici', *Mitski zbornik*, eds S. Marjanić and I. Prica (Zagreb: Institut za etnologiju i folkloristiku, Hrvatsko etnološko društvo, Scarabeus-naklada, 2010), 115–25 at 120–21.
148. V. Petreska, 'The Secret Knowledge of Folk Healers in Macedonian Traditional Culture', *Folklorica* 13 (2008), 25–50.
149. M. Tkalčić, 'Faeries and Faery Pedagogy in Neopagan Spiritualities in Croatia', *Studia ethnologica Croatica* 27 (2015), 189–246.

CHAPTER THIRTEEN

# Greece (and Italy): The Nereids, 'Those from Outside'

Tommaso Braccini (University of Siena)

## Introduction

In the post-Byzantine and contemporary Greek world, the term *exotika* (or *xotika*) was frequently used to refer to a wide range of monsters and apparitions. This word clearly derives from *exo*, 'outside'; it is attested only from the seventeenth century onwards, but the concept can be traced back as early as the fifteenth.[1] The *exotika* would thus be the 'things outside', referring to the otherness, spatial and substantial, of supernatural creatures in relation to human society. Nymphs and devils inhabit wooded and desolate places, far from human communities; at the same time they, along with witches, female demons (such as the infanticidal Gello),[2] *kallikantzaroi* and vampires, besiege houses from the outside and try to break in to kill their inhabitants. These *exotika* are 'aliens', in the sense that they have nothing to do with the human condition: they are demonic entities, whose actions are often unpredictable and incomprehensible. This way of looking at the world presupposes an everlasting 'siege mentality', a perpetual fear of an external enemy always lurking and ready to breach the 'walls' that surround the family, the village and society.

In the macrocategory of the *exotika* are also to be found the entities that, within modern Greek folklore, seem to occupy the 'ecological niche' of the fairies of Britain, the nereids (νεράϊδες),[3] characterized by a marked social life. They share this aspect with the nymphs of antiquity, from whom they derive and with whom they have much in common.[4]

## Loved, Abducted and Made Sacred by the Nymphs

This is, of course, not the place to deal in detail with classical nymphs.[5] Suffice to say that they were extremely long-lived (but not immortal) supernatural figures.[6] The nymphs of antiquity were linked above all to the natural elements, such as streams, pools of water and trees, with whose existence they were intimately connected. We have a tendency to liken them to the harmless and fragile literary fairies of Victorian England. But in antiquity they were portrayed as far more fearsome. Various myths, in fact, depict them as vengeful, jealous and, above all, given to kidnapping (often young) men and women with whom they had fallen in love. The best-known case is surely that of Hylas, a handsome young man, who having strayed from his friend Heracles to draw water during the Argonauts' expedition, was snatched by the nymphs who haunted a pond.[7] There is no shortage of other such cases in myth, and this theme also emerges in funerary epigrams.[8] In Callimachus and elsewhere, boys or girls who died prematurely, often drowned, are said to have been 'abducted' or 'snatched from life' by the nymphs, who made them 'sacred'.[9]

It is likely that, in linking the disappearance of these young people to the nymphs, the authors of the epitaphs resorted to a euphemistic and consolatory motif analogous to the phrase 'he is now among the angels' that we use when faced with infant or otherwise premature deaths. For many, yesterday and today, these are 'just words', without concrete meaning; for many others, however, perhaps yesterday more than today, there is also a real belief here. A series of offerings and graffiti found in sacred caves, such as the one near Pharsalus, in Thessaly, suggests that sanctuaries dedicated to nymphs were much frequented in antiquity, right up to Roman times.[10] Many people at the time evidently believed in their reality, and therefore probably also in stories about their interactions with humans, including abductions.

Various events treated by poets and men of letters in a mythical key may also have been refined reworkings of the 'picturesque' beliefs that circulated among the *apaideutoi* (literally, the 'uninstructed') as folklore.[11] One might think, for instance, of a story such as that of Dryope, which had apparently been treated in the Hellenistic era by the sophisticated poet Nicander in his *Alterations*, a now-lost poem dedicated to metamorphoses that inspired Ovid. We are left with a bare summary of the story, from which we learn that the protagonist, an only daughter, had gone to graze her father's flocks. She had ended up becoming a playmate of the nymphs, who had taught her how to dance. A series of complicated events took her far away. When Dryope finally found herself passing again through the places of her childhood, the nymphs abducted her and 'made her disappear into the forest'. This, however, was not a hostile act, but rather a gesture of benevolence, for eventually 'Dryope was transformed and from a mortal woman became a nymph'.[12]

## Nymphs in a Christian Context

Tales of this kind continued to circulate as folklore, probably without interruption, long after the end of antiquity. Indeed, in modern Greece similar occurrences are attested with the nereids as protagonists. Beliefs, however, do not travel from one era to the next as unalterable monoliths. What in ancient times might have been seen, all things considered, as a blessing, in a Christian context provoked quite different reactions. A Byzantine scholar, John Kanaboutzes (first half of the fifteenth century), in a note entitled *On nymphs, who they are and what their species are, and that they are species of demons, which common people ungrammatically call 'nereids'*, described them as 'demons that have taken the form of women'. They are termed by common folk 'those from outside' (*hai ap'oxo*), since they lived in the wilderness, on mountains and hills.[13]

These same ideas are evident in a famous episode reported by a German traveller, Ludwig Ross, who in 1833 found himself passing through Chalandri, a village in Attica. Seeing the local priest's wife in mourning, he asked her what had happened to her and heard this story, a source of anguish and distress for the woman and her family:

> I had a daughter, a twelve- to thirteen year-old girl, with a very peculiar character. Although we all treated her kindly, she was always in a sad mood and would run away from the village to the wooded slopes of the mountain (the Vrilessos) whenever she could. There she would wander lonely for days, early in the morning as late at night; sometimes she would take off her dress and remain in her petticoat to be less hindered in running and jumping. We did not dare oppose her, for we realised that the nereids had bewitched her, but we were deeply saddened. In vain my husband often took her to church and read prayers over her; the Panagia [the Virgin] could no longer help her. After this went on for a while, she fell into a deep melancholy and finally died a short while ago. At the time of the funeral, the neighbours told us: 'Do not be surprised at her death, for the nereids wanted her, and already two days ago we saw her dancing with them'.[14]

This is by no means an isolated testimony. Indeed, it is a reliable 'snapshot' of what the perception of the nereids might have been among nineteenth-century Greeks. Even at the beginning of the last century, fear of the diabolical nereids could give rise to reactions that were, to say the least, uncontrolled. The personal experience of John Cuthbert Lawson, a famous English scholar of Hellenic folklore, is illustrative in this regard, as well as amusing. He once gave a lecture on the nereids at the English School in Athens, which was also attended by members of the local high society. He had barely finished speaking when an Athenian gentleman, who had Western manners and was counted among the city's cultural elite, stood up visibly upset, made the sign of the cross and fled without a word. Lawson later claimed that during one of his trips to Greece, he saw at dusk a mysterious and imposing female figure, dressed in white, who was moving among the twisted trunks of a distant olive grove. He would have liked to investigate, but was prevented from doing so by his guide, who, making the sign of the cross and repeatedly invoking the Virgin, hastily dragged him away from the place.[15]

In short, even when many of the traditional deities remained only in the memory of the literati, the nymphs continued to be feared among the *apaideutoi* ('the common folk'), for whom the name nereids was generalized, perhaps also to avoid any lexical confusion, since νύμφη also meant 'young girl' and 'bride'. 'Nereid' was originally reserved in Ancient Greek for those nymphs who populated the sea (as is evident from their name: they were in fact the daughters of the sea god Nereus).[16] The evolution is attested in the spoken language already in the Late Middle Ages (at least from the beginning of the fourteenth century). We see this in some glosses to classical texts in which the term Νηρηΐδες (*nereids*) is used to explain precisely the archaic and now ambiguous *nymphai*.[17] The wide range of forms assumed by the demotic Greek names (including *naragides*, *anarades* and *narades*) is further evidence that this term belonged to the spoken language.[18]

## The 'Nice Ladies' of Midday

We are fortunate to have an extensive account from the early modern age which deals with the 'new' nereids: terrestrial spirits no longer bound to the marine element. It is provided by the erudite Leone Allacci (1586–1669), who was born in Chios but who moved to Rome at an early age. The references comes in his *De Graecorum hodie quorundam opinationibus*, the first treatise on Byzantine and Neo-Greek folklore, published in 1645.[19] Allacci draws not only on his direct knowledge, but also on a short text by the Byzantine philosopher Michael Psellos (eleventh century), who was famously interested in folklore (he has been called 'the first folklorist of the Middle Ages').[20] We will follow now the testimonies offered by Allacci and Psellos,[21] supplementing them with more recent evidence.

Common people, as Allacci says, euphemistically called the nereids *kales archontisses* ('the nice ladies'),[22] and Psellus attests to a variant of this in the singular, called *kale ton oreon* ('the nice one of the mountains').[23] These enchanting maidens did indeed sometimes also appear in urban areas, but more often they frequented the fields, the thickest woods, the remotest valleys, especially if they were crossed by streams and brooks. There they amused themselves playing and fooling around. Social life and communal activities were characteristic of these entities. Some people swore they saw them dancing,[24] or chatting in the shade of the trees, especially when the hot midday sun was shining,[25] perhaps their favourite hour.

This, too, is a trait that is found in antiquity in reference to the nymphs:[26] midday is, in fact, not a random time. It is an ominous, dangerous hour, in which—especially in the heat of summer—men and animals are immersed in sleep, while spirits roam freely. Some people in Calabria (an Italian region heavily influenced by Greek culture, and the home of peculiar nereid traditions that will be discussed below) called it *controra* ('counter-hour'), as the English writer Norman Douglas recalled over a hundred years ago remembering a torrid day at Capo Colonna:[27] it is, in short, a moment when *exotika* can freely break into the dimension of men.[28]

Similarly, when whirlwinds (*anemostroviloi*) were seen in the countryside, whirling up dust, leaves and twigs, it was said that these were the nereids moving about.[29] In some places, it was claimed that the nymphs responsible for the windstorms were much uglier than the others, dark-skinned, with large wings like those of a partridge: they were also malevolent and often tried to strike men and animals by hurling objects in gusts of wind. In this case, in all probability, under the label 'nereids' the Greeks had come to include malevolent spirits of the air.[30]

## Dangerous Nymphs, with a Penchant for Human Flesh

The attitude of nereids towards human beings was ambivalent. They were powerful creatures, capable of hurting people, especially if they felt they were being disrespected. However, if they wanted to, they were also able to bring great benefits. It might happen, says Allacci, that someone, while walking in the countryside, especially towards the middle of the day (see above), would fall to the ground seized by sudden convulsions. These seizures usually had unfortunate consequences: the victim could find himself lame, crippled, with a contracted face, even hunchbacked. In such cases, everyone believed that the sufferer had been a victim of the nereids. There were many reasons why these creatures were offended, but according to Allacci one of the most frequent, as extravagant as this may seem, was the custom of the commoners of relieving themselves in the middle of the fields. The gesture was very risky: there could be some nymphs nearby, who would be enraged by this slight. So, when someone was compelled by such an inescapable necessity, he would always take the precaution of spitting three times on the ground: this apotropaic gesture would protect him from the wrath of the nereids.[31]

According to Allacci, people avoided calling them by name: when someone was struck by their vengeance, people would say generically that they had 'suffered from outside' (*ap'exo echei*).[32] It is interesting to note this further use of 'outside', *exo*, which we have already found in the writings of the Byzantine scholar John Kanaboutzes, and which refers to the above-mentioned fear of the *exotika*, 'things from outside', a category to which nereids belong.[33] Monstrosities, as we have already stated, lurked just outside the village boundaries. The fear of the nereids was also widespread in exactly these terms in the Greek communities of Calabria. The *anarades* (*nadare*, *narade*) were often anthropophagous and had donkey legs.[34] Until a few decades ago they were thought to roam in the valleys that surrounded Greek-speaking villages, such as Bova, Precacore and Roghudi. In Roghudi, even at the beginning of the last century, it was customary to close one of the village gates at night against the nereids: the gate faced an area believed to be haunted by the *narades*, female mule-footed creatures. The texts collected by Taibbi and Caracausi[35] and the precious notes by Vito Teti[36] bear witness to this, and the living voice of a few elderly people, natives of these villages, can still confirm it, as Elsa Guggino recalls:

> 20/6/2003 Antonino Pangallo is the only inhabitant of Upper Rogudi, at the end of what used to be a street with houses,[37] where voices came from windows, and where households faced each other in very narrow alleys [...] he celebrates us by addressing me in Grecanico [the local Greek dialect] [...] 'The *naradi*? They were *animali sarbaggi* ['wild animals'], *fimmini, omini, ma lu pedi di lu cavaddu* ['women, men, but with horse feet']. *Stavanu ni sti pagghiara* ['They stayed in these stone huts'], in the caves, which were, however, very low. But that was at the time of the Bourbons, then it ended. They ate men, they stole. They came at night. At night the gates were locked. There were two gates in the village. Then the *naradi* were no longer seen: there were the monarchs, the governments, they came and threw them out. Before the war *li naradi* were no more; in my time there were none.[38]

## The Immortal 'Queens of the Nereids'

According to Antonino Pangallo these creepy beings have, in the course of time, become extinct. This should not come as too much of a surprise. Although the nereids were often likened to demons or spirits, they were not necessarily immortal—something also true of the nymphs of antiquity (see above). According to a saying common in Arcadia a century ago, 'A raven lives twice as long as a man, a tortoise twice as long as a raven, and a nereid twice as long as a tortoise.'[39] Sometimes it was said that only the 'queens' of nymphs, who identified themselves as the sisters of Alexander the Great, were immortal. The story told, according to a testimony quoted by Nikolaos Politis, was roughly this: Alexander, during his travels, had found the source of immortality. He had filled two jars with its precious water and sent them sealed to his home in Greece, in order to use it when he returned. The messenger who brought them, however, could not keep the secret and revealed it to the king's sisters, who chose to exploit the situation. They opened the jars, drank the liquid and even bathed in it, pouring the dirty water into the street. Unwittingly, in this way they ended up wetting a hen and an evergreen bush, which have never since aged. The sisters themselves became immortal spirits and, year after year, began to subjugate young maidens,[40] with some deformity or physical defect, who were in turn transformed into nereids, albeit 'second-class' (mortal?) ones. It was precisely these 'second-class' nereids who were very numerous and who constituted a danger to men, especially those who, unaware, passed the nereid-plagued places at noon or midnight. The unfortunate man, however, had one chance at salvation: he had to shout loudly, 'King Alexander lives, lives and reigns!' Then the king's sisters, the queens of the nereids, would immediately rush in and free him.[41]

## A Passion for Young People and Children

As we said, however, the nereids, the 'beautiful ladies', were also capable of doing good, or at least of doing no harm to men. It often happened that they fell in love with handsome young men, and abducted them in a whirlwind, taking them to their secret abodes: if these handsome young men cooperated, the nereids gave them riches and good luck (but at other times it was said that having an affair with a nereid was very exhausting and wore out the body). Nereids were often jealous lovers; sometimes children were even born from these unions.[42] Moreover, they had a real passion for children of both sexes. In some cases, they would kidnap them, exchanging the human children for their own, of weak and unhealthy constitution. Often, when the mothers saw that their child, healthy until the day before, suddenly became sickly and suffering, they began to suspect that a terrible exchange had taken place (this is the well-known changeling motif F321.1). They understood, then, that they were raising the child of some nereid.[43]

In other cases, nereids did not take possession of the children forever, but contented themselves with pampering them for a while, and then returned them to their parents, who saw them come back much more beautiful than before, perhaps bearing in their hands some precious gifts from the 'ladies'. Allacci recounts an episode that was told to him by acquaintances, 'absolutely trustworthy people' he declared. Some time before, to escape the unbearable heat of the Chios summer, a family had gone to the countryside to get some fresh air. One day, while everyone was outdoors, an extremely pretty little girl had wandered away from the others and casually approached a well. Intrigued, she had leaned over to mirror herself in the water below. Under the horrified eyes of her parents, the little girl had fallen into the well, as if some invisible force had plunged her in. The family rushed to her aid, but as soon as they looked down, they saw an astonishing scene: the little girl was sitting on the surface of the water and seemed to be playing with someone. The father, unable to understand what was happening, tried to lower himself to the bottom of the well, but was seized by the same mysterious force and found himself on the water, next to his daughter. In the meantime, other people also arrived. They lowered ladders down, calling to the man. He, in turn, grabbed the girl with one arm and climbed out of the well. They both emerged without a scratch, to their great surprise, with their clothes and bodies completely dry. The only explanation for this portentous event was that the father and daughter had been abducted by the nereids, who were in fact, someone remembered, said to live there.[44] And at that point the little girl confirmed the fact, saying that when she had looked, she had seen some women joking and playing on the surface of the water, and they had invited her to join them.[45]

## The Dangerous Gifts of the Nereids

The nereids, if they wanted, could bestow many gifts: wealth, beauty, health, even artistic skills. All too often, however, they were malignant and whimsical and one had to act with cunning and skill in order to obtain something from them.

Two particularly interesting examples of this are to be found in the material collected by Nikolaos Politis. It was said that in a cave on Mount Bourinos, in Macedonia, a miraculous water oozed out, coming ultimately from the breasts of the nereids, and capable of curing all illnesses. It was called 'silent water', and in fact those who wanted to draw from it had to do so in absolute silence. This, however, was not enough: a green lamp was needed to enter the cave, and the water container also had to be green. When the jug was full, one had to leave a shred of one's clothes there and run away, without being frightened by the voices and the noise that would erupt, and above all without looking back. If you did look back, then you would lose your wits, and the water would no longer have any power.[46]

According to what was said in Crete, those who wanted to learn to play the *lyra* well (it was a stringed instrument, named after its ancient ancestor) could also exploit the nereids. The would-be musician would leave home at midnight and go to a deserted crossroads. There, he would draw a circle on the ground with a black-handled knife, sit inside the circle and wait, strumming the instrument. After a while, nereids would appear everywhere, surrounding the man with a menacing manner. Since they could not cross the circle, they tried in every way to induce the man to come out, trying to bewitch him with songs, dances and enticements of all kinds. The would-be musician had to remain impassive and continue strumming his *lyra*. After a while the nereids, annoyed by his music, would exclaim: 'If you come out, we will teach you to play it in such a way that you will make even stones dance.' But, once again, the man had to turn a deaf ear. Then the nymphs would ask whether they might not examine his instrument. The man could hold it out, but being very careful not to let his hand, not even a finger, come out of the protection of the circle, for otherwise it would immediately be cut off. After playing the *lyra* for a while, the nereids would give it back to him, exhorting him to trust them and leave the circle, but the player, once again, had to refuse. The nereids would ask him several more times to play his *lyra*, always hoping that he would inadvertently put his hand outside the invisible barrier. Finally, at the first cockcrow, they would offer him one last deal before fleeing, so as not to be surprised by daylight: they would teach him to play in exchange for any part of his body. At that point, the would-be musician would put the tip of his little finger outside the circle, which would be cut off instantly; but from that instant, the man would be able to play the *lyra* divinely. That is why it was said of a good player that he 'learned at the crossroads'.[47] According to other accounts, those who learned to play the *lyra* from the nereids did not grow old but died a bad death while still young.[48]

A certain gloomy Christian imagery is evident, with the presence of the crossroads (D1786 'Magic power at cross-roads'), a magic circle and one's own flesh in payment (albeit the smallest amount possible!). The gift of music from supernatural creatures is known elsewhere in Europe and is classified as motif F262.2 'Fairies teach bagpipe-playing' and ML 4090 'Watersprite Teaches Someone to Play', with attestations from Norway, with spirits asking for pieces of meat, at crossroads and elsewhere, for music lessons. The story, incidentally, may have an early attestation in the traditions associated with the ancient poet Archilochus, who was said to have obtained his poetic skill as a gift from the Muses in a night-time encounter along a road, in exchange for a cow he was taking to market.[49] Night was also the time when people were taught the guitar by the Devil. This is a tradition widespread in the southern United States and associated in particular with a 'cursed' musician, with a short life and an apparently inexplicable talent. We refer here to the bluesman Robert Johnson, from Mississippi, who died in 1938 at the age of 27. Since at least the 1960s, the story has spread (first in print, then in the movies and finally on the internet) that Johnson obtained his incredible musical talents by selling his soul to the Devil at the crossroads.[50]

## From Allomotifs of the Devil to Tinker Bell Clones

What is important, however, is that even when they dispense gifts, the nereids prove dangerous. As the typological parallel with Robert Johnson's story shows, they can feature as the Devil's 'allomotifs'—that is, his symbolic equivalents: Kanaboutzes, it will be remembered, wrote that they are 'demons that have taken the form of women'. There we see once again that like other similar figures of antiquity they have passed through a pervasive Christian reinterpretation.[51] Ancient nymphs could be hazardous to deal with, since they were jealous, touchy and vindictive. Medieval and modern nereids, however, could be much worse. Apoplectic strokes and paralysis are widely attributed to them, and it has also been seen how the nereids in Calabria are even described as anthropophagous, sharing this trait, it must be remembered, with the Italian *fate*.[52] Moreover, in the aforementioned tale about Alexander's sisters (a veritable 'foundation myth'), the origin of their queens, who in turn ended up creating the 'race' of the nereids, occurs through betrayal and deception. These disturbing features place the traditional Greek nereids in glaring contrast to the contemporary use of the term 'nereids', especially in Greek media intended particularly for girls. There, the word indicates elegant, Disney-like winged 'fairies'.[53] In Greece too, in short, a 'globalization of folklore' is taking place, a phenomenon through which every peculiarity of the 'old' Greek nereids, the disturbing *exotika* 'from outside', is flattened and sweetened. A similar phenomenon occurred with the *vrykolakas*, the Hellenic folkloric vampire now turned into a series of Hollywood clichés.[54] And there is no doubt that many Greek children today would be astonished to learn that their grandparents, if not their parents, were frightened by the nereids—the cute, harmless and friendly creatures that in the contemporary imagination are evoked by the term 'fairy' and its correspondents in various languages.

As to the social nature of nereids, traditions vary dramatically. In Calabrian sources, nereids are animal-like supernatural beings that prey on humans and that often act alone.[55] In Greece, we find stories about 'nereid queens' of ancient lineage, who enlist new female followers into their ranks. Here we have a kind of 'inner aristocracy' and a hierarchy (see Chapter 1, p. 6). In most tales, the nereids act in a choral manner: they eat, play and dance together. It is, as so often in the social supernatural, dance that is particularly important, not least in linking the modern nymphs to their classical counterparts.[56] Since dance has been highlighted as 'a quintessential liturgical action of village life' in modern Greece, it too emphasizes the social nature of these beings and the sense that they belong to a community.[57]

I would like to thank Davide Ermacora for many friendly and valuable suggestions, and Simon Young for his helpful suggestions and for valiantly helping me to improve my English.

## Notes

1. See E. Kriaras, *Λεξικὸ τῆς μεσαιωνικῆς Ἑλληνικῆς δημώδους γραμματείας*, 21 vols (Thessaloniki: Hypourgeio Paideias kai Threskeumaton, Kentro Hellenikes Glossas, 1968–2019), vol. 6 (1978), 165, s.v. 'εξωτικός'; the concept is, however, already implicit in John Kanaboutzes (see *infra* 219). For a detailed and thoughtful discussion of the *xotika*, coteries of 'demons, fairies and spirits' of a malevolent kind that 'cluster around the marginal areas of the physical environment—the mountains, springs and caves that lie beyond the safe confines of the village', and at the same time constitute 'a set of figures that allows individuals to map and understand the traumas and ambiguities of life', offering 'a means of navigating within a morally structured cosmos', see C. Stewart, *Demons and the Devil: Moral Imagination in Modern Greek Culture* (Princeton: Princeton University Press, 1991), xvff.
2. On which see T. Braccini, 'Revisiting the "Exorcism of Gello": A New Text from a Vatican Manuscript, with a Typological Analysis of the Known Variants', *Medioevo greco* 21 (2021), 149–70.
3. For an introduction to the folklore nereids of modern and contemporary Greece, in addition to the indispensable mass of testimonies collected in N.G. Politis, *Μελέται περὶ τοῦ βίου καὶ τῆς γλώσσης τοῦ Ἑλληνικοῦ λαοῦ: Παραδόσεις*, vol. 1 (Athens: Sakellariou 1904), 285–362, and to the century-old but still useful J.C. Lawson, *Modern Greek Folklore and Ancient Greek Religion* (Cambridge: Cambridge University Press, 1910), 130–73, see, too, T. Braccini, *La fata dai piedi di mula: licantropi, streghe e vampiri nell'Oriente greco* (Milano: Encyclomedia, 2012), 51–57, 121; *Folklore* (Roma: Inschibboleth, 2021), 122–27.

4. It is well known how the use of the concept of 'continuity' between antiquity and the present can be problematic, and often biased, for the Greek world: see M. Herzfeld, *Ours Once More: Folklore, Ideology, and the Making of Modern Greece* (New York: Berghahn, 2020). In the case of the nereids, however, we find all the desiderata postulated by L.M. Danforth, 'The Ideological Context of the Search for Continuities in Greek Culture', *Journal of Modern Greek Studies* 2 (1984), 53–85, here 58–59, i.e. 'relevant evidence from the periods of late antiquity, the Byzantine Empire and the Turkish occupation'.
5. For the nymphs of antiquity, reference can be made to J. Larson, *Greek Nymphs: Myth, Cult and Lore* (Oxford: Oxford University Press, 2001).
6. See Hesiod, fr. 304 M.-W., and Larson, *Greek Nymphs*, 29–30: 'A chattering crow lives out nine generations of mature men, but a stag's life is four times a crow's, and a raven's life makes three stags old, while the phoenix outlives nine ravens. But we, the rich-haired nymphs, daughters of aigis-bearing Zeus, outlive ten phoenixes' (Larson's translation).
7. For Hylas see Theocritus, 13; Apollonius Rhodius, *Argonautics* 1.1207–39; for the similar case of Bormos see Athenaeus, *The Deipnosophists*, 14.619f–20a.
8. See D. Fabiano, '*Raptus a nymphis*: emozioni e *gender* nelle epigrafi funerarie di bambini', *La presenza dei bambini nelle religioni del Mediterraneo antico: la vita, la morte, i rituali e i culti tra archeologia, antropologia e storia delle religioni*, ed. C. Terranova (Roma: Aracne, 2014), 111–40.
9. See Callimachus, *Epigrams* 22 Pfeiffer and the metrical epitaphs 952 and 1595 Peek.
10. See R.S. Wagman, *The Cave of the Nymphs at Pharsalus: Studies on a Thessalian Country Shrine* (Leiden–Boston: Brill, 2016).
11. For the problems posed by the recovery of folklore material from antiquity through the filter of the 'high' literary tradition, and the identification of the so-called *apaideutoi* as bearers of folklore culture, see, *inter alia*, Braccini, *Folklore*.
12. The story of Dryope appears in Antoninus Liberalis, *Metamorphoses* 32; see *The Metamorphoses of Antoninus Liberalis: A Translation with a Commentary*, ed. F. Celoria (London–New York: Routledge, 1992), 91, 197–99; see also the commentary in Antonino Liberale, *Le metamorfosi*, eds T. Braccini and S. Macrì (Milano: Adelphi, 2018), 325–30.
13. See *Ioannis Canabutzae magistri ad principem Aeni et Samothraces in Dionysium Halicarnasensem Commentarius*, ed. M. Lehnerdt (Leipzig: Teubner, 1890), 42.
14. See L. Ross, *Reisen auf den griechischen Inseln des Ägäischen Meeres*, 3 vols (Stuttgart–Tübingen: J.B. Cotta, 1840–45), vol. 3 (1845), 181–82.
15. See Lawson, *Modern Greek Folklore*, 131–32.
16. The first attestation is already in Homer, *Iliad*, 18.38. On classical nereids, see J.M. Barringer, *Divine Escorts: Nereids in Archaic and Classical Greek Art* (Ann Arbor: The University of Michigan Press, 1995).
17. See T. Braccini, 'Leggere i bucolici minori a Tessalonica: un sondaggio sulle glosse tricliniane del *Parisinus gr.* 2832', *Erytheia* 49 (2021), 79–115 at 104–07.
18. See Lawson, *Modern Greek Folklore*, 130.
19. On which see K. Hartnup, *On the Beliefs of the Greeks: Leo Allatios and Popular Orthodoxy* (Leiden–Boston: Brill, 2004).
20. See at least G.A. Megas, 'Ὁ Μιχαὴλ Ψελλὸς ὡς λαογράφος', *Laographia* 25 (1967), 57–66 (57 for the quotation); P. Schreiner, '*À la recherche d'un folklore byzantin*',

*Analele Universității 'Dunărea de Jos' Galați—Istorie* 4 (2005), 81–89 at 89; *Mothers and Sons, Fathers and Daughters: The Byzantine Family of Michael Psellos*, ed. A. Kaldellis (Notre Dame: University of Notre Dame Press, 2006), 45–47.

21. See L. Allatius [Allacci], *De templis Graecorum recentioribus... de narthece ecclesiae veteris... nec non de Graecorum hodie quorundam opinationibus* (Coloniae Agrippinae: apud Iodocum Kalcouium & socios, 1645), 158–60, followed by Psellus' pamphlet on 160–61.
    Publication of this short Psellian text (n. 1000, Gra/Rhe. 8, in Moore's *Iter Psellianum*) in the *Tractatus grammatici et rhetorici* edited by A.R. Littlewood is long overdue; *faute de mieux*, it should be consulted in Allacci's edition (see previous footnote).

22. For a little-known and very interesting account illustrating beliefs from the island of Cos in the early twentieth century, see T. Braccini, 'Credenze popolari di Cos e Lero dalle carte inedite di Iakovos Zarraftis', *Erytheia* 40 (2019), 307–36, esp. 311: '[there are also] the *Neraides* or *Anerades* (Νεράϊδες, Ἀνεράδες), who are also euphemistically called "nice women" (καλὲς γυναῖκες)'. For other euphemistic denominations, see Lawson, *Modern Greek Folklore*, 132.

23. For an incantation centred on the specific figure of the 'nice ones of the mountains', handed down from the Bologna manuscript BUB 3632 (fifteenth century) and accompanied by an illustration depicting the nereid as a lady with a snake's tail, see A. Delatte, *Anecdota Atheniensia*, 2 vols (Liége–Paris: H. Vaillant-Carmanne, É. Champion, E. Droz, 1927–39), vol. 1 (1927), 600 (for other attestations of the variously declined *kale*, 119, 12; 122, 27; 245, 33–34).

24. The dances of the nereids are mentioned by various later observers of Greek folklore: B. Schmidt, *Das Volksleben der Neugriechen und das hellenische Alterthum*, vol. 1 (Leipzig: B.G. Teubner, 1871), 109–11; Politis, Παραδόσεις, 391 n. 657, 400–01 n. 679, 404 n. 688, 406 n. 692, 434–35 nn. 737–38; Lawson, *Modern Greek Folklore*, 141–42; S. Vios, Χιακαὶ παραδόσεις, *Laographia* 8 (1921), 427–46 at 441–42; R. Blum and E. Blum, *The Dangerous Hour: The Lore and Culture of Crisis and Mystery in Rural Greece* (New York: Chatto & Windus, 1970), 49; 113–16, 118; D. Dialektos, Νεράϊδες—καλλικάντζαροι—βρικόλακες στίς λεσβιακές παραδόσεις (Athina: s.n., 1979), 10–11; Braccini, 'Credenze popolari di Cos e Lero', 311.

25. See also Politis, Παραδόσεις, 401 n. 681, 410 n. 697, 430–32 n. 731–32, 449 n. 760, 471–73 n. 784, for modern parallels.

26. See for example Callimachus, *Hymn to Demeter* 37–38, ἧς δέ τις αἴγειρος, μέγα δένδρεον αἰθέρι κῦρον, / τῷ ἔπι ταὶ νύμφαι ποτὶ τῶνδιον ἐψιόωντο ('There was a poplar, a great tree that skimmed the sky, / by which at noon the nymphs played'). See also the classic R. Caillois, 'Les démons de midi', *Revue de l'histoire des religions* 115 (1937), 142–73 and 116 (1937), 54–83 and 143–86, esp. 68–83 on nymphs and nereids.

27. See N. Douglas, *Old Calabria* (London: Secker, 1915), 321: '*Controra* they now call it—the ominous hour. Man and beast are fettered in sleep, while spirits walk abroad, as at midnight'.

28. See also Braccini, 'Credenze popolari di Cos e Lero', 311: nereids 'are only encountered in the bad hours (κατὰ τὰς κακὰς ὥρας μόνον)'.

29. See Schmidt, *Das Volksleben der Neugriechen*, 123–26; Politis, Παραδόσεις, 406 n. 691, 410 n. 697, 442 n. 750; Vios, Χιακαὶ παραδόσεις, 442; Dialektos, Νεράϊδες, 12.

30. See Politis, *Παραδόσεις*, 391 n. 656, 435 n. 739; Braccini, 'Credenze popolari di Cos e Lero', 311: 'at other times they [Nereids] are invisible and deliver their terrible blows, which are conceived as being inflicted only by an air called *aeriko*; hence it is said, "he was struck by the *aeriko*"'.
31. See Allatius, *De templis Graecorum recentioribus*, 159–60: '*saepe etiam in meridie, animi relaxandi causa, juvenis, vel puerulus, qui indecora facie non est, sua meditans exspatiatur, statimque in terram procidens, vel nervis contractis incurvatur, vel ore deformatur, vel altero pede claudicat, si non utroque; vel in gibbum rotundatur; vel alia corporis noxa afficitur: tunc una omnes convenire, eum similia passum a dictis mulieribus... Quod adeo apud eos certum est, ut, cum alias viderint homines, dum excrementa deponunt, in foedissimas corporis aegritudines prolapsos; si simile quid conentur per campos, non antea id agant, quam ter prius in terram spuerint*'. See also T. Braccini, 'Credenze popolari di Cos e Lero', 311: 'their blows make the recipient maimed, lame, mute (in which case it is said that "the good women took his voice") and blind (in which case it is said that "the good women took his light"), and also crippled, with his neck turned backwards; in which case it is said that, when they called him, he turned towards their sweet voice, and his neck remained turned'. The apoplectic blows inflicted by nereids are also mentioned by Schmidt, *Das Volksleben der Neugriechen*, 119–21; Politis, *Παραδόσεις*, 389 n. 653, 431–32 n. 732, 433 n. 735; Lawson, *Modern Greek Folklore*, 139 and 142–44; K.I. Mantzouranis, Κυνουριακαὶ παραδόσεις, *Laographia* 4 (1912–13), 464–75, here 464; Blum and Blum, *The Dangerous Hour*, 104, 112, 114; Stewart, *Demons and the Devil*, 106, among others. The detail of the wry neck finds a parallel in a tradition from Lesbos, according to which 'ὅποιος γυρίσει τό κεφάλι του νά τίς κοιτάξει, στραβώνει ὁ λαιμός του γιά ὅλη του τή ζωή' ('he who turns his head to look at them, his neck remains crooked all his life'): see Dialektos, *Νεράϊδες*, 13.
32. Allatius, *De templis Graecorum recentioribus*, 159.
33. In Sicily, too, the belief in the so-called *donne di fora* ('women from the outside'), *un po' streghe, un po' fate* ('a little bit witch, a little bit fairy') has been well documented. See G. Pitrè, *Usi e costumi, credenze e pregiudizi del popolo siciliano*, vol. 4 (Palermo: L. Pedone Lauriel, 1889), 153–77 (quotation from 153); G. Henningsen, '"The Ladies from Outside": An Archaic Pattern of the Witches' Sabbath', *Early Modern European Witchcraft: Centres and Peripheries*, eds B. Ankarloo and G. Henningsen (Oxford: Clarendon Press, 1993), 191–215; M.S. Messana, *Inquisitori, negromanti e streghe nella Sicilia moderna (1500–1782)* (Palermo: Sellerio, 2007), 724–56.
34. An element also known to the folklore of Greece proper: see for example Politis, *Παραδόσεις*, 390 n. 654, 401 n. 680, 440–41 n. 748. For an overview of this motif in antiquity and in the Near East, see T. Braccini, 'Luciano e il diavolo nella sala da ballo: una nota a *Storie vere* 2,46', *Quaderni urbinati di cultura classica* 119, 2 (2018), 127–38.
35. See *Testi neogreci di Calabria*, eds G. Rossi Taibbi and G. Caracausi (Palermo: Istituto siciliano di studi bizantini e neoellenici, 1959), 21–22, for a testimony from Roccaforte (end of the nineteenth century), referring among other things to the belief about 'exchanged children', and above all 300–01 for an account from Roghudi, dating from 1900: 'the *anarade* were women with the feet of mules. During the day they lay down, in the evening they went out to eat people. That is why in Roghudi at night they closed the door towards Agriddea and the Plache, and that way the *anarade* could not enter the village'.

36. See V. Teti, *Il senso dei luoghi* (Roma: Donzelli, 2004), 91–92, where, among other things, vernacular explanations are also provided for the disappearance of *narade*, *anarade* and *nadare*: 'the elderly people of Roghudi in the early 1980s recalled that they had all plunged down from the depths of Sporicema (a place near Roghudi) where they had hidden themselves after the pope's excommunication […] I have also heard of *nadare* in ancient Samos, in Precacore, along the beautiful gorge that hosts the La Verde torrent. This was a privileged place for their apparition, before Precacore, destroyed by an earthquake in 1908, was also abandoned'.
37. Roghudi, much like the other old Greek-speaking villages in the Calabrian hinterland, has long been abandoned by the population due to hydrogeological instability.
38. See E. Guggino, *Fate, sibille e altre strane donne* (Palermo: Sellerio, 2006), 126–27 (and 123–30 for the *nadare* of the Aspromonte in general).
39. See Lawson, *Modern Greek Folklore*, 156.
40. The maidens 'seduced' by the nereids was a recurring theme, as the above-mentioned case of the daughter of the Orthodox priest of Chalandri shows.
41. See Politis, *Παραδόσεις*, 387–88 n. 651. The prodromes of this tradition can already be found in some versions of the Greek *Alexander Romance* handed down by late medieval manuscripts; see B.L. Cook, 'A Watery Folktale in the *Alexander Romance*: Alexander's Byzantine *Neraïda*', *Syllecta classica* 20 (2009), 105–34.
42. See for instance Politis, *Παραδόσεις*, 389 n. 653, 449 n. 760, 453–56 n. 766–67, 769–71.
43. See Politis, *Παραδόσεις*, 435–43 n. 739, 741–44, 746, 748, 750–51. On changelings, see J.-M. Doulet, *Quand les démons enlevaient les enfants. Les changelins: étude d'une figure mythique* (Paris: Presses de l'Université de Paris-Sorbonne, 2002).
44. Wells were frequently considered to be haunted by nereids; narratives of this kind were probably also spread as *Warnmärchen* to try to keep children away from danger.
45. See Allacci, *De templis Graecorum recentioribus*, 159.
46. See Politis, *Παραδόσεις*, 402 n. 683.
47. See Politis, *Παραδόσεις*, 412–14 n. 702; Braccini, *La fata*, 56–57.
48. See E.K. Frangaki, Συμβολὴ στὰ λαογραφικὰ τῆς Κρήτης (Athens: s.n., 1949), 73.
49. See T. Braccini, *Lupus in fabula: fiabe. Leggende e barzellette in Grecia e a Roma* (Roma: Carocci, 2018), 80–85; for the episode, see also W.F. Hansen, *The Book of Greek and Roman Folktales, Legends and Myths* (Princeton–Oxford: Princeton University Press, 2017), 89–90 n. 5.
50. See G. De Vos, *What Happens Next? Contemporary Urban Legends and Popular Culture* (Santa Barbara–Denver–Oxford: Libraries Unlimited, 2012), 177–225.
51. In Margaret Alexiou's words, 'continuity is less a process of survival than of constant assimilation and integration with other influences'. See M. Alexiou, 'Modern Greek Folklore and Its Relation to the Past: The Evolution of Charos in Greek Tradition', *The 'Past' in Medieval and Modern Greek Culture*, ed. S. Vryonis Jr (Malibu: Undena, 1978), 221–36, esp. 221.
52. Italian *fate* still in the nineteenth century could be described as gluttonous for human flesh: see T. Braccini, *Indagine sull'orco: miti e storie del divoratore di bambini* (Bologna: Il Mulino, 2014), 129–30. For an example of anthropophagous *fate* in nineteenth-century Italian fairy tales, see the story of Prezzemolina collected in Florence by V. Imbriani, *La novellaja fiorentina…* (Livorno: Vigo, 1877), 209–15.

53. On wings, see S. Young, 'When Did Fairies Get Wings?', *The Paranormal and Popular Culture: A Postmodern Religious Landscape*, eds D. Caterine and J.W. Morehead (New York: Routledge, 2019), 253–74. In Greek bookshops and news stands it is easy to come across publications (including colouring books and sticker books): for example, *Barbie Μαριπόζα και η Νεραϊδένια Πριγκίπισσα—Νεράϊδες και πεταλούδες!* and *Νεράϊδες χρωματίζω*; in their illustrations, the nereids in question perfectly comply with Disney's fairies.
54. On which see, for instance, T. Braccini, *Prima di Dracula: archeologia del vampiro* (Bologna: Il Mulino, 2011).
55. See *Testi neogreci di Calabria*, 21, 300.
56. See Larson, *Greek Nymphs*, 62.
57. See J. du Boulay, *Cosmos, Life and Liturgy in a Greek Orthodox Village* (Limni: Denise Harvey, 2009), 416.

CHAPTER FOURTEEN

# The Balts: *Laumės* and *Laimės*

Francis Young (Oxford University) and
Saulė Kubiliūtė (independent scholar)

## Introduction

The Lithuanian word *laumė* (Latvian *lauma*) is often translated in English as 'fairy'; but, as we shall see, the *laumės* of Baltic folklore are not straightforward analogues of British fairies, not least because their identity is entangled with another class of folkloric being, the *laimės*. Both *laumės* and *laimės*, who are imagined as exclusively female, can be described as social supernatural beings, insofar as they are each a class of multiple beings which interact among themselves as well as with humans. Several other classes of Lithuanian folkloric being can be pluralized, such as the *kaukai*, *barstukai*, *žemėpačiai* and even *aitvarai*, but these are all social supernatural beings who might take up residence in the household. The *laumės* are distinctive in their association with nature, with water and with mounds, as well as the abduction of children—all characteristics that bring them closer to the Western European concept of a fairy.

This chapter will consider the extent to which *laumės*/*laumas* and *laimės* can be considered social supernatural beings, belonging to a broader European continuum of social spirits of nature, drawing mainly on Lithuanian ethnographical and folkloric material, with some reference to Latvian folklore. It should be noted, however, that the Lithuanian and Latvian nation states are the last survivors of what were once many Baltic nations and people groups, stretching from the Vistula to what is now the Moscow Oblast of the Russian Federation. These peoples spoke Indo-European languages of a notably archaic character, and some of these extinct Baltic peoples, such as the Prussians and Nadruvians, survived long enough for their folklore and customs to be recorded by early modern ethnographers.[1]

The comparatively late conversion of the Baltic peoples to Christianity, and their resistance to that conversion, provides the historical context for the development of Baltic folklore. While any suggestion that the folklore of the region represents a 'pristine' pagan tradition must be set aside as fanciful, it is nevertheless true that the influence of the Church in rural Lithuania (in particular) was weak for much of the modern period. Visitation records and missionary reports continue to record apparently pagan activity up to the end of the eighteenth century.[2] When folklore collectors such as Eduard Gisevius (1798–1837) began ethnographic surveys of the Lithuanian population from the late 1830s onwards, therefore, pagan or semi-pagan rites were still well within living memory. For this reason, when it comes to Lithuania talk of 'pagan survivals' is rather more than wishful thinking—even if caution must still be exercised when drawing conclusions about a pre-Christian Lithuanian religion only described by Christian commentators.

### Early Accounts of *Laumės* and *Laimės*

Etymological explanations for the word *laumė* vary. C.D. Buck saw a possible connection with the Old Slavic word *loviti*, which meant 'to grab'.[3] Jasiūnaitė presented a more complex explanation, and believed *laumė* could share an etymology with words like *lāmis* ('submissive person'), *lāmė* ('slacker') and *lāmažis* ('lazy person'), which are linked to *laméti* ('to break'), *lamóti* ('to steal, to slurp, eat greedily') or *lómyti* ('to eat greedily, to stuff') and *lamžúoti* ('to break, caress; eat greedily'). She also linked the word *laũmės* to the verb *laumóti* ('to eat greedily'). Furthermore, *laũmas* is what a clumsy, useless person is called. These and many other examples, according to Jasiūnaitė, create the image of *laũmė* as a clumsy, rather ugly creature.[4] Zinkevičius argued for the possibility that Latvian *lauma*—which meant a flying wizard, a witch—could have been the mixture of *laumė* and Laima, the Baltic Goddess of Fate.[5]

Eric Hamp, by contrast, argued that the Lithuanian word *laumė* (Latvian *lauma*) derives from *liaudis* ('the common people'), and is cognate with Venetic *Louderai*, the name given in the Venetic language to the Roman goddess Libera, consort of Liber Pater (a sobriquet of Dionysus). Hamp postulated an original Indo-European verb *leudh-*, to do with growth and increase, as the root of these words.[6] It is difficult to know what to make of these linguistic connections. What is clear is that the superficially similar words *laumė* and *laimė* derive from different Indo-European roots, with *laimė* related to Lithuanian *leisti* ('to allow'), since the *laimės* are fates who permit or determine people's destinies. In the case of the *laumės* it is possible that, as in other Indo-European languages, the name was originally a euphemism derived from *liaudis* ('the people'), like the term 'the good people' in English or *tylwyth teg* in Welsh.[7]

Neither *laumės* nor *laimės* are named in the late medieval and early modern Latin ethnographic literature on Baltic religion.[8] However, it is possible that the poet Nicolaus Hussovianus was alluding to them in his 'Poem on St Hyacinth' (1525), which makes reference to Lithuanian belief in river spirits as well as deities of fortune:

> Not far from us serpents are worshipped, and men offer libations to the tall trees; they throw grain into the rivers and worship the spirit of the river god, whom they see playing in the moving ripples of the water; and lest this should be thought to arise rashly from empty faith, the whole water is disturbed and a horrible voice murmurs. Having averted by choice the gifts of the god of fortune, they believe they influence they have control of the parturition of the herd.[9]

Since the word *dei* can be used in Latin as a gender-neutral term for deities, the *dei fortunae* could be the *laimės*; although if, as in later Lithuanian folklore, the *laimės* are all female, there would no good reason for Hussovianus not to use the feminine form *deae fortunae*. Similarly, although a river god is mentioned, it is actually the *numina* ('spirits') belonging to the river god who are being venerated—perhaps a reference to the *laumės*, always associated with water in the earliest records, who in Latin would be more accurately described as *numina* than as *deae* ('goddesses').

*Laumės* and *laimės* are first unambiguously named in the German writings of the Prussian cleric Matthäus Prätorius (c.1635–1704), who collected popular traditions primarily in Lithuania Minor (the far-western part of Lithuania at that time under German Prussian rule) in the late seventeenth century among the Nadruvian people. Prätorius makes seemingly clear distinction between *laimės* and *laumės*: 'Laimė is a sky goddess, laumė is a water deity'.[10] He goes on to state:

> Those whom the Nadruvians call *laumės* must have been a kind of water nymphs. The same ancient Nadruvians state that such a person is in all things like a woman's person, except that the hands and feet fall somewhat flat, especially the fingers and toes; but they should not appear monstrous.[11]

Prätorius describes the *laumė* as a *Wasser-Nixe* (mermaid), recounting that a farmer near Insterburg had a child with a *laumė*; the child, called by Prätorius a *laumaitis*, lived to a great age and died in 1664.[12] Prätorius's insistence that the *laumė* was not monstrous, and his implication that *laumės* were attractive to human men, stands in contrast to an alternative tradition of the monstrous *laumė* as a kind of non-human witch or hag. In a study of Lithuanian witch trials, Małgorzata Pilaszek noted that Laumė (a singular entity rather than a class of being) was sometimes imagined as a witch- or hag-like figure who was blamed for tiring out horses at night by riding them. A dead magpie was hung in the corner of the stable in order to deter Laumė. The magpie then came to be associated with witchcraft itself, perhaps on account of the link with Laumė, and women were accused of turning themselves into magpies in order to fly to the Witches' Sabbath.[13]

An even earlier but perhaps garbled reference to Laimis as a deity appears in statutes of the Grand Lithuanian Marshal Jan Stanisław Sapieha, issued at some point between 1621 and 1636 for the parishioners of Kretinga. The statutes forbid the worship of 'strange gods' (*alienos Deos*) including Laimis, who appears first in the list.[14] It is unclear, however, whether Laimis represents a misunderstanding of the Lithuanian plural *laimės* as referring to a singular being, or an alternative name for Laima of the *akis*-type of feminine noun. If Laimis is a confusion for *laimės*, this would be the earliest evidence for *laimės* as plural beings. Whereas Prätorius is clear that a *laumė* is a type of spirit, Laimė appears in his account as a singular deity among the Nadruvians, for whom Laimė was a goddess of childbirth.[15]

## One Laima, or Many *Laimės*?

By the nineteenth century Laimė in Lithuania was usually more than one being, a class of beings known as the *laimės* rather than a singular goddess. The most common tale-type involving the *laimės* collected in the nineteenth century depicts them as three women who are overheard talking outside the window just after a child's birth. Between them, the three *laimės* determine the child's destiny.[16] However, Laima the singular goddess is still encountered living in the forest in some tales. As Greimas noted,

> The dwelling of Laima—in the thick of the forest in a lighted cottage—is a widely known stereotype of a degraded mythology: the forest is a non-human, non-cultural world in which one can come upon utopic places and there encounter ancient mythic beings [...] The solitary cottages in the forest are as if the caricatured remnants of an impoverished, ravaged, ancient pantheon.[17]

In Latvia, by contrast, Laima remained a singular goddess presiding over birth and destiny.[18] Jonas Balys has noted that, among eighteenth- and nineteenth-century ethnographers, the figure of Laima as the one who predestines human fate reinforced a stereotype of the Lithuanians as Europe's most fatalistic people.[19]

Since the *laimės* are not clearly attested as a group of beings before the nineteenth century in Lithuania, it is possible that the influence of wider European culture, perhaps through preaching, brought the idea of the three fates—who, in a Lithuanian context, were naturally named *laimės* after the old goddess of destiny. On the other hand, just because Prätorius never encountered tales of three *laimės* among the Nadruvians, that does not mean the belief did not exist elsewhere among the Baltic peoples before it was clearly recorded in the nineteenth century. It is also possible that Lithuanian folklore preserved a deep-rooted Indo-European motif of three goddesses of fate.[20] Yet for Greimas, the *laimės*' triplicity did not make them a class of being or a social entity, because the mythological significance of triplication is to reinforce the singularity of Laimė as one being; three is a number of unity.[21] In nineteenth- and twentieth-century Lithuanian folklore the *laimės* seem to flicker in and out of reality, sometimes presented as real beings and sometimes as mere personifications of or ciphers for destiny or good fortune.

## *Laumės* and *Laimės*: A Tangled Relationship

The relationship between *laumės* and *laimės* is not altogether straightforward. Balys argued that *laumės* and *laimės* are clearly distinguished in Baltic folklore,[22] while Vėlius insisted that *laumės* were merely a subclass of nature spirit in contrast to *laimės*, who are a primary category of supernatural being in their own right. However, Vėlius was also forced to concede that *laimės* and *laumės* were sometimes confused or conflated, with beings called *laumės* performing the typical roles of *laimės* in a minority of tales.[23] Greimas painted a more complex picture, noting that the terms *laumės juosta* ('*laumė*'s sash') and *laimės juosta* ('*laimė*'s sash') are used interchangeably to refer to the rainbow, for example.[24] If even something as clearly celestial (the *laimės*' domain) as a rainbow could be associated instead with the earthbound *laumės*, this suggests more than casual conflation; one possible explanation, mooted by Greimas, is that Laima became a kind of 'good fairy' in folk stories, and thereby conflated with *laumė*.[25]

Greimas argued that *laumės* are 'syncretic figures, the result of a confusion of different goddesses',[26] but this approach is also problematic. It suggests *laumės* may have no distinct identity of their own, which is not supported by the folkloric evidence. *Laimės* and *laumės* have in common that they are supernatural women, associated with what happens to children and with weaving;

in almost every other respect they are different, but the similarities may have been enough to result in conflation. In addition to Prätorius's identification of *laumės* as a type of water spirit or mermaid, the earliest mentions of *laumės* in eighteenth-century dictionaries make them goddesses of birth (surely a confusion for *laimė*), an earth goddess of the pagans, a ghost (*Gespenst*), a goddess of plague and a fury, as well as referencing the belief that they would appear if someone spun thread on a Thursday evening.[27]

*Laumės* and *laimės* are sometimes in conflict, suggesting some sort of fundamental opposition. In one Lithuanian folktale a man comes across *laumė* and *laimė* in combat in a forest clearing, holding on to one another's hair.[28] One reason why *laumė* and *laimė* may be in conflict is because the *laumė*'s realm is that of justice; she rewards those who respect her and punishes those who show disrespect. Laimė's realm, on the other hand, is that of destiny, where justice is notoriously absent. The conflict of *laumė* and *laimė* could thus be interpreted as the eternal conflict between justice and blind fate. Furthermore, *laumės* are known for stealing children, whereas the *laimės* are sometimes imagined as their protectors.

## Who Are the *Laumės*?

Vėlius considered that tales about *laumės* reflected humans' relationship with nature, and identified certain key characteristics of *laumės*: they do women's work for them, give people gifts, kill children (or steal and replace children with changelings), occasionally consort with men, and harm animals. Lithuanian folklore emphasizes the importance of not teasing the *laumės*, and the tale-type 'the *laumės* and the baby' always follows the same basic plot: a poor woman accidentally leaves her baby in the fields and the *laumės* reward the baby with treasure. Then a rich woman, hearing of this, deliberately leaves her baby in the field for the *laumės* and they kill the baby. The *laumės* are often described as *deivės* ('goddesses'), and Vėlius thought this was a more ancient term for them than *laumės*.[29] However, there is little evidence the *laumės* were worshipped,[30] at least at the time when most Lithuanian folklore was recorded, even if there were certain taboos associated with them. Vytautas Ališauskas, on the other hand, broadly rejects the association between goddesses and *laumės*, noting that *laumės* are so named in only 7% of tales; rather, the association between *laumės* and goddesses is a late 'contamination' of Baltic mythology.[31]

The *laumės* are typically encountered as beautiful young women with golden hair, blue eyes and very large breasts. They are renowned for their skill in spinning and weaving, and in many tales they offer to spin and weave for human women; anyone who selfishly takes advantage of their generosity, however, might find that the *laumės* choose to weave with the greedy person's intestines—and the *laumės* are, in fact, cannibalistic in some tales. The *laumės* weave on Thursday evenings, and for this reason it was taboo to weave at this time, when the *laumės* were working. *Laumės* love children, and desire motherhood; but in one strand of Lithuanian tradition, at least, they are unable to give birth (in other stories some *laumės* marry human men and bear them children). This explains why the *laumės* steal children, although there are also evil *laumės* who steal them out of spite.[32] Jonas Balys argued that the evil *laumės*, who are often shape-shifting beings with birds' feet, a kind of non-human witch or hag, were a later creation under the influence of Christian demonology.[33]

Although *laumės* are closely associated with water, often being found near it, they are perhaps not among the true water spirits of Lithuanian folklore (most of which are male), since they do not inhabit the water itself.[34] However, Vėlius traced the *laumės*' ultimate origin to the water;[35] according to this interpretation, by analogy with other European folkloric beings that began life as water spirits, such as the Greek nereids[36] and Irish leprechauns, the *laumės* have made a gradual journey to the land and taken up residence in the forest. The *laumės*' occasional role as re-modellers of the landscape lends them a chthonic dimension, although Vėlius's insistence on linking the *laumės* with thunder seems rather more far-fetched.[37] Overall, Vėlius paints a picture of the *laumės* as syncretic beings who may incorporate the features of several different minor goddesses presiding over different domains, and perhaps also elements of the monstrous and non-human 'fairy-tale witch'.

## Are *Laumės* Fairies?

The English word 'fairy' has been (and continues to be) used to translate Lithuanian *laumė* and Latvian *lauma*. The Lithuanian *laumė* reflects many classic fairy motifs: supernatural weaving and spinning, child-stealing, changelings, the fairy bride, and the execution of brutal moral justice. The *laumės* are even, like British fairies, associated with unusual fossils.[38] However, although the *laumės* are associated with mounds, like the Irish *aos sí* and English fairies, there is no Baltic fairy Otherworld distinct from the human and natural world.[39] Rather, the *laumės* belong to the 'earthly otherworld' of the forest, which in Lithuanian folklore is the realm of the gods.[40] A further difference between the *laumės* and British and Irish fairies is the absence of any discernible hierarchy or social organization among the former; there is no polity of the *laumės*, nor is there a queen. The *laumės* are also exclusively female, unlike British and

Irish fairies; and while British and Irish fairies are sometimes of surpassing beauty, they do not have the exaggerated secondary sexual characteristics of the *laumės*. However, Latvian *laumas* are rather different; they are said to be the souls of brides stolen by the Devil, Persephone-like, and Latvian *laumas* have more overtly witch-like characteristics than Lithuanian *laumės*.[41]

Balys was struck by the similarities between British and Irish fairies and the *laumės*, and went so far as to suggest that at some date Baltic folklore might have come under 'Celtic' influence, perhaps in the Iron Age.[42] More recently, Karolina Gimževskienė also noted similarities between Lithuanian and 'Celtic' folklore,[43] appealing to Klaus Roth's concept of 'distant closeness'—the idea that sporadic yet repeated contact between distant peoples, often lost to the historical record, can produce surprisingly similar expressions of culture and folklore.[44] However, the idea of 'Celtic' influence on Baltic folklore is problematic when we consider there is no agreement among scholars about the origin of British and Irish fairies, with the latest scholarship tending to identify them as a late medieval or early modern synthesis of a number of different folkloric and literary influences.[45] Rather than 'contact hypotheses' unsupported by historical evidence, it is perhaps better to consider the possibility that peoples living in similar circumstances, against a background of similar cultural and religious influences (and perhaps even a shared Indo-European mythological inheritance, if such a thing can be said to exist), may arrive at similar tale-types independently of any contact between people groups. Furthermore, as Vėlius noted, attachment to 'migration' or 'contact' hypotheses can prevent us looking for the *laumės*' distinctive Baltic origin.[46]

## Conclusion

Of all the supernatural beings of the Baltic peoples, the *laumės/laumas* come closest to the concept of the social supernatural we might associate with, say, the fairies of Britain. Whether the *laimės*, who are entangled and sometimes conflated with the *laumės*, can be considered social beings too remains an open question, since the *laimės* can also be interpreted as reduplications of a single goddess or personifications of an abstract concept. The Lithuanian *laumės*, however, are social supernatural spirits of nature who interact with humans yet also seem to have their own society, and fulfil several mythological functions elsewhere assumed by fairies. *Laumės* are (usually) attractive yet morally ambivalent beings, who can probably be assigned to the broader European tradition of beautiful supernatural women associated with forests, lakes and other natural features.

## Notes

1. The Estonians, while known today as a Baltic nation owing to geographical location, are not a nation of Balts but a Finnic people, and for reasons of space the social supernatural beings of Estonian folklore cannot be considered here.
2. For examples from the 1770s onwards see V. Ališauskas, ed., *Baltų religijos ir mitologijos reliktai Lietuvos Didžiojoje Kunigaikštystėje (XIV–XVIII a.): Šaltinių rinkinys* (Vilnius: Lietuvių Katalikų Mokslo Akademija, 2016), 440–593.
3. C.D. Buck, ed., *A Dictionary of Selected Synonyms in the Principal Indo-European Languages* (Chicago: University of Chicago Press, 1949), 1500.
4. B. Jasiūnaitė, 'Iš lietuvių mitologinės leksikos: baubas bei jo padermė', *Baltistika* 35, 2 (2000), 171–91 at 177–78.
5. Z. Zinkevičius, 'Lenkų-jotvingių žodynėlis', *Baltistika* 21, 1 (1985), 61–82.
6. E.P. Hamp, 'Venetic Louderai—Lith. Laumė', *Baltistica* 33, 1 (1998), 58. On the etymology of *laumė*, see also N. Vėlius, *Mitinės lietuvių sakmių būtybės* (Vilnius: Vaga, 1977), 89–93.
7. The idea that *laumė* is cognate with Latin *Lamia*, still sometimes repeated today, is not now accepted by linguists; for an early account of this purported etymology see A.F. Pott, *De borusso-Lithuanicae tam in Slavicis quam Letticis linguis principatu commentatio*, vol. 1 (Halle: Libraria Gebaueria, 1837), 49, who described *laumė* as 'a goddess of the earth, an incubus of female gender'.
8. For translations of this material, see F. Young, ed., *Pagans in the Early Modern Baltic: Sixteenth-Century Ethnographic Accounts of Baltic Paganism* (Leeds: Arc Humanities Press, 2022).
9. N. Hussovianus, 'De divo Hyacintho carmen', *Nicolai Hussoviani carmina*, ed. J. Pelczar (Kraków: Typis Universitatis Jagellonicae, 1894), 86 (ll. 540–47).
10. M. Prätorius, *Deliciae Prussicae*, ed. W. Pierson (Berlin: Duncker's Buch-Verlag, 1871), 17.
11. Ibid., 12.
12. Ibid., 12–13.
13. M. Pilaszek, 'Litewskie procesy czarownic w XVI-XVIII w.', *Odrodzenie i Reformacja w Polsce* 46 (2002), 7–35 at 13.
14. Ališauskas, *Baltų*, 178.
15. Prätorius, *Deliciae*, 94.
16. Vėlius, *Mitinės*, 35; A.J. Greimas, *Of Gods and Men: Studies in Lithuanian Mythology* (Indiana University Press, 1992), 112.
17. Greimas, *Of Gods*, 113.
18. B. Reidzāne and S. Laime, 'Latvian Folklore Studies and Mythology', *Latvia and Latvians, Part 2: Culture in Latvia*, vol. 1 (Riga: Latvian Academy of Sciences, 2018), 90–125 at 118.
19. J. Balys, *Lietuvių tautosakos skaitymai*, vol. 2 (Tübingen: Patria, 1948), 77.
20. Balys, *Lietuvių*, vol. 2, 78. Greimas, *Of Gods*, 114.
21. Greimas, *Of Gods*, 156.
22. Balys, *Lietuvių*, vol. 2, 79.
23. Vėlius, *Mitinės*, 22, 64–65.
24. Greimas, *Of Gods*, 144.
25. Ibid., 145.

26. Ibid., 114.
27. Vėlius, *Mitinės*, 84.
28. Balys, *Lietuvių*, vol. 2, 79.
29. Vėlius, *Mitinės*, 21; 23–24; 41; 21; 79. Vėlius later (121–22) argued that 'the *laumės* and the baby' story might represent a distant memory of the sacrifice of infants to the *laumės*.
30. Balys, *Lietuvių*, vol. 2, 86. Balys suggested the *deivės* denounced by Martynas Mažvydas in the first Lithuanian catechism (1547) could have been the *laumės*.
31. V. Ališauskas, 'Deivių vaizdinio apmatai pagal XVI–XVII a. rašytinius šaltinius', *Sakralieji baltų kultūros aspektai*, ed. E. Usačiovaitė (Vilnius: Lietuvos kultūros tyrimų institutas, 2012), 350–68 at 363.
32. Balys, *Lietuvių*, vol. 2, 80–82.
33. Ibid., 83–84.
34. On Lithuanian water spirits, see L. Būgienė, 'Water in Lithuanian Folklore: Archaic Survivals and Christian Influences', *Studies in Folklore and Popular Religion*, vol. 2, ed. Ü. Valk (Tartu: University of Tartu, 1999), 209–17 at 213–16.
35. Vėlius, *Mitinės*, 115–16.
36. Editors' note: see Chapter 13 of the current volume.
37. Vėlius, *Mitinės*, 122–23.
38. Balys, *Lietuvių*, vol. 2, 85.
39. K. Gimževskienė, 'Lietuvių mitologinių sakmių veikėjos *laumės* ir jų atitikmenys rusų ir anglų kalbose', *Vertimo Studijos* 12 (2019), 6–21 at 15.
40. Vita Grybauskienė has surveyed Lithuanian place-names derived from the *laumės*: 'Lietuvių mitologiniai vietovardžiai: iš leksemos laumė kilę vietų vardai', *Tautosakos Darbai* 28 (2004), 92–103.
41. Vėlius, *Mitinės*, 126.
42. Balys, *Lietuvių*, vol. 2, 86–89.
43. Gimževskienė, 'Lietuvių', 14.
44. K. Roth, 'Crossing Boundaries: The Translation and Cultural Adaptation of Folk Narratives', *Fabula* 39, 3–4 (1998), 243–55 at 247.
45. R. Hutton, 'The Making of the Early Modern British Fairy Tradition', *The Historical Journal* 57, 4 (2014), 1135–56; F. Young, *Twilight of the Godlings: The Shadowy Origins of Britain's Supernatural Beings* (Cambridge: Cambridge University Press, 2023), 250–304.
46. Vėlius, *Mitinės*, 88–89.

CHAPTER FIFTEEN

# Ukraine: Courtship Rituals and Legends of the *Bohyni*

Natalie Kononenko (University of Alberta)

## Introduction: The Ethnographic Work of Volodymyr Hnatiuk

At the end of the nineteenth and the beginning of the twentieth century much scholarship in western Ukraine was inspired by nationalism. In Russian-dominated Left Bank Ukraine, publications in Ukrainian were forbidden by the Ems Ukaz of 1876, an edict issued by Emperor Alexander II of Russia. This was not the case in L'viv, then under Austrian rule. There work on Ukrainian topics was allowed. This was especially true of studies connected to the Ruthenian version of Ukrainian language and culture. The Shevchenko Scientific Society was founded in 1873 and came into its own at the turn of the century. Well-known scholars and politicians such as Mykola Hrushevsky and Ivan Franko were active there and the society expanded its activities and publications.[1]

Among their students was Volodymyr Hnatiuk. Born in 1871 in Velesniv, Buchach region, Halychyna in western Ukraine, Hnatiuk was passionate about his native culture. He became active in the Shevchenko Scientific Society and served as the secretary of its Philological Section, as a member of the editorial board of *Literaturno-naukovyi vistnyk*, as chair of the Ethnographic Commission, and also as its general secretary. Hnatiuk can be credited with some of the most important collections of western Ukrainian culture and lore, and with effectively helping to create Ukrainian folklore studies. He travelled extensively in western Ukraine, working especially among the Hutsuls and collecting folklore there. He wrote about the lore he collected, its linguistic features, and also about material culture. Unfortunately, he contracted tuberculosis in 1903, had to give up his fieldwork, and had to rely on work submitted by other collectors. Hnatiuk assembled and, through the volumes produced

Natalie Kononenko, "Ukraine: Courtship Rituals and Legends of the *Bohyni*" in: *The Exeter Companion to Fairies, Nereids, Trolls and Other Social Supernatural Beings: European Traditions*. University of Exeter Press (2024). © Natalie Kononenko. DOI: 10.47788/UMXX7077 by the Shevchenko Scientific Society, published folklore data, collected by himself and by others.[2]

His many works included a three-volume set of legends about supernatural beings that appeared as *Znadoby do halyts'ko-rus'koii demonolohii* (one volume) and *Znadoby do ukraiins'koii demonolohii* (two volumes).[3] 'Demonology' here does not refer to what Western scholars would understand as demons; it refers, rather, to spirit beings who are not part of the Christian religious pantheon: house spirits, the unquiet dead, water and forest spirits, and so forth. Devils are included, but they are not the primary focus of Ukrainian 'demonology' and their connection to the Christian Devil is questionable.[4] Furthermore, the narratives in Hnatiuk's massive collection speak not only of supernatural beings, but also of witches and warlocks (among others) who draw power from the spirit world. The spirit world, as presented in the volumes compiled by Hnatiuk, is rich and multifaceted. It is close to the human realm and regularly interacts with it.

Perhaps the most social of the beings described in the *demonolohia* volumes are *bohyni*.[5] They are also called *bisitsi* and *rusalki*, but *bohyni* (singular *bohynia*) is the most widely used term in western Ukraine where Hnatiuk did his work. *Bohynia* has the same root as *boh*, the Ukrainian word for God. These are not goddesses, however. They are to be avoided rather than worshipped and one of the ways to protect oneself from them is to make the sign of the cross.

*Bohyni* can appear and function alone. Humans can also encounter groups of *bohyni* living in forests or on the banks of lakes and rivers, where they can be seen dancing and singing together, especially at night. The social groups in which *bohyni* live are non-hierarchical, with no leader and no subordinates. They resemble collectives of young women in Ukrainian society which were organized for match-making purposes. These groups were also non-hierarchical and served to arrange evening and night-time parties where young women and men could meet and interact, forming pairs that would go on to marry, becoming wife and husband and then parents. These real-life collectives were very effective and marriage was practically universal. When I was doing fieldwork in Ukraine in the late 1990s and the 2000s, I asked about fortune-telling and marriage and one of the women I interviewed responded, 'Why bother. We all knew that we would wed.'[6]

While courtship practices effectively accomplished the societal goal of creating families, they also put a great deal of pressure on young people, especially women. As will be described below, the courtship events were highly sexualized, precisely to encourage the formation of couples. Yet women were supposed to avoid sexual intercourse before marriage and 'proof' of virginity was often part of the wedding ceremony. I believe that *bohyni* narratives are closely related to courtship practices. They are folkloric depictions of what happened in real life. As such, they offered artistic, and thus especially powerful, expression of the dilemmas and dangers of being both sexual and chaste. Certainly, young people were warned about the dangers of courtship, but direct expression does not have the power of art. *Bohyni* narratives provided that potent artistic dimension.

To better understand *bohyni* texts, we need to examine Ukrainian courtship practices. These predated Hnatiuk's work and lasted into the 1970s and the Soviet period. They placed women and men in close contact, while expecting them to remain chaste.[7] Legends about *bohyni* warned both sexes, though primarily women, about the potentially disastrous consequences of premarital sex. Women who appeared particularly sexual were, according to *bohynia* narratives, to be avoided. These tales also talked of the dangers that the supernatural world (and adult human relations with the same) posed for infants. In short, they served to acknowledge the temptations placed on young people by customary courtship practices and warned against yielding to those temptations.

## Traditional Courtship Events and Pressures on Young Women and Men

Rituals as well as narratives were documented in Ukraine at the turn of the twentieth century, and we are fortunate to have descriptions of courtship practices. Mytrofan Dykarev (1854–1899) was an important scholar in this regard and contributed his materials to the Shevchenko Scientific Society, where they were published in the *Materialy do ukraiins'koii etnol'ogii*.[8] Dykarev's descriptions help explain the precarious nature of Ukrainian courtship practices. There were two types of rituals: winter rites and summer rites. The winter rites were called *vechornytsi*, *vechirki* ('evening parties') or *dosvitky* ('celebrations until dawn'). The summer events were called *vulytsi* ('streets') because they typically took place outdoors at crossroads, locations that would be suitable for a gathering of the young. A shorter, but very useful, description of courtship practices appeared in Hnatiuk's article 'Pisnia pro pokrytku shcho vtopyla ditynu' ('Song about a Maiden Who Drowned Her Child').[9] It is particularly applicable here because, unlike Dykarev, it concentrates on western Ukraine.

*Vechornytsi* or *vechirki* were complex affairs, as Dykarev, Hnatiuk and my fieldwork in Ukraine from 1998 onwards attest. They faded as the Soviet Union recovered from the destruction of the Second World War and as government authorities promoted alternative evening entertainments in a central public building called the *klub*.¹⁰ Traditional winter evening parties took place in people's houses, and several could take place simultaneously. The location for a *vechornytsia* (sg.) was the home of a poorer villager, typically a widow, who needed some help on her farmstead. Young women in a village would harvest crops or help with repairs and other tasks in exchange for the use of that person's house during the winter season. Once the harvest was complete, young women would gather in the evening at the house they had 'rented', bringing work such as spinning. They would also bring food to share amongst themselves and with their hostess. After working for a while, the girls would admit young men. The men brought musical instruments and snacks like nuts or pumpkin and sunflower seeds. The young women and men would sing and dance and play games to get better acquainted. Examples of games included musical chairs and 'postman', where the stamps on a letter were kisses. Around midnight, those in attendance would spread straw on the floor of the house. The girls would sleep on one side of the room and the boys on the other. If a couple had formed, the young man could ask the young woman if he might bed down next to her. If she agreed, the couple would sleep together. The young people in attendance who had not found someone to pair up with would also sleep on the floor. They could leave if they wished, the young women heading home and the men going out to play pranks on those inside the *vechornytsia* house or on the young elsewhere in the village. The mistress of the house would sleep on the stove. She was supposed to make sure that relations between young couples did not 'go too far' and lead to the loss of virginity and unwanted pregnancy.¹¹

*Vulytsi* (sg. *vulytsia*) were courtship parties held outdoors, usually at crossroads. Young men made the arrangements for the *vulytsia* by placing large logs in a circle or by digging a circular hole. Those in attendance would sit around the circle while they socialized, sang songs and shared snacks. After socializing at a *vulytsia*, couples could leave to spend the night together. They would go to the home of the young woman and sleep in the barn, the root cellar or other outbuildings; they did not go into the house. It was the young man's responsibility to leave early and quietly enough so that the tryst would remain secret. Couples spent the night in each other's company to become better acquainted. The young woman's virginity was not to be compromised.¹²

Of course, accidents did happen and women did lose their virginity, and some became pregnant. There were many ways of handling this. If the young man did not reject the woman with whom he had had sex—and it seems that in most cases he did not—then the solution was simple. The blood that couples needed to produce as proof of virginity could, as I was told during my fieldwork in Ukraine, come from a variety of sources. Such workarounds were so common that during the Soviet period the hoisting of the red Soviet flag outside the family home became the standard way of announcing that the marriage had been consummated.[13]

But not all young men agreed to marry the woman with whom they had had intercourse, and women did become pregnant outside of marriage. If the woman carried the illegitimate child to term—and abortion was not something that was readily available—then she was subjected to shame and scorn. The struggles of such a woman are described in the work of the famous Ukrainian writer Taras Shevchenko, most notably in his poem 'Kateryna'. Mothers of illegitimate children were given the name *pokrytka*, meaning 'the covered one', and were subjected to a ritual that made their shame visible. During a normal marriage rite, the bride, once she enters the home of her groom, undergoes a ceremony where her hair is re-braided and covered with a headdress that designates her as a married woman. When a woman becomes a *pokrytka*, she undergoes a covering ceremony, only it is done in her own home rather than that of her spouse.[14]

Because becoming a *pokrytka* would damage a woman's chances of marriage and a normal life, women hid their pregnancies and even killed their illegitimate children. This is reflected in ballads which state that *vechirki* are responsible for pregnancy and infanticide. Hnatiuk's 'Pisnia pro pokrytku', a study of one such ballad, tells of fishermen who make a horrible discovery: they find the body of a drowned baby in the reeds. The authorities then call an assembly of girls to discover the guilty party. All the girls appear wearing their wreaths except one—the poor girl who is the unmarried mother of the dead baby. To punish her for her sins, the girl is thrown into the river to drown. As she floats down the river, she sings to her mother, urging her not to let her other daughters, the sisters of the drowning girl, attend *vechirki*. It is there, she makes clear, that she lost her virginity and became pregnant.

> All of the girls, the young maidens, drink and make merry,
> And they throw young Marusenka into the Danube River.
> Young Marusenka, as she was drowning,
> She shook her finger at her mother:
> My mother, my elderly one, you have five daughters,
> Don't let them go to *vechirki*; let them sleep at home.
> At the *vechirki* you are at a strange house and you have to sleep on the ground,
> There, something can happen between them [the boy and girl who agree to sleep together].
> Mother, my elderly one, you have seven daughters.[15]

> Don't let them engage in loose behaviour, the way you let me.
> You let me engage in loose behaviour at night-time, as well as during the day,
> Now I, a young one, have to drown in the Danube.[16]

Of course, *vechirki*, *vechornytsi* or the summer courtship parties were not the only places where sexual contact could occur. As the collection of ballads published by Dei, Iasenchuk and Ivanytskyi shows, women could be seduced and they could be taken by force. There are texts that sing about women who are charmed by men, especially Kozaks who promise love and marriage and then abandon the seduced woman. There are men who get women drunk and use them, sometimes offering financial compensation which, of course, cannot make up for loss of virginity. There are songs about men who take women by force such as when the female victim delivers a midday meal to her brothers working in the field.[17] Whatever the circumstances, the woman who has lost her virginity and is known to have done so finds herself in an untenable position: essentially, she is excluded from normal society. If the father of her baby refuses to marry her, she becomes an outcast. As a number of ballads state, she is then neither maiden, nor wife, nor widow.[18] Essentially, she has lost normal social status. Some women chose suicide rather than this life—which is not really a life at all.[19]

## *Bohynia* Narratives

Stories about *bohyni*, I propose, were important in dealing with the pressures produced by traditional courtship practices. These stories were mostly told as legends, meaning stories that were believed to be the experiences of the narrator or someone known to them. They warned men to be wary of women with pronounced sexual traits, presumably women who made their sexual attributes immodestly apparent, thus cautioning them that such women were not suitable marriage material. The stories also served to frighten women and to keep them away from pleasurable experiences proposed by other women, everything from innocent offers to go berry-picking to more *vechornytsia*-like pastimes such as singing and dancing. They counselled caution, saying that offers of pleasure, and not just sexual pleasure, might expose one to supernatural beings with evil intent.[20] As art, the *bohynia* narratives were at once more cryptic and more powerful than direct statements cautioning young women and men against the possible pitfalls that came with traditional courtship practices.

In addition to serving as a warning to courting couples, *bohyni* provided an explanation for things that might go wrong after the wedding. Both women and men wanted children and the virginity test, I believe, had less to do with actual sexual purity than with the readiness of the groom and his family to accept any children birthed by the woman whom the young man was to marry. But babies were prone to diseases or could fail to thrive. Infant deaths could raise questions, not only about sexual purity but also about parental behaviour. Dysa argues that infanticide was considered a particularly heinous crime, the one most likely to lead to charges of malefice and witchcraft.[21] There were stories about *bohyni* substituting their own babies for human ones and these helped explain infant diseases and infant mortality. These narratives took responsibility for problems with babies away from the human parents.

Legends about *bohyni* use widely known archetypes and motifs, such as that of the changeling, a supernatural creature substituted for a human baby. They draw on folklore, such as the text where the heroine must guess the name of a supernatural helper who helps her fulfil an impossible task. Most Westerners know this story under the name of 'Rumpelstiltskin'. In addition to international story patterns, Ukrainian narratives use individual motifs attested in the lore of other cultures. The exaggerated bodily features of *bohyni*, such as breasts so huge that they must be thrown over the creature's shoulders, are a common folklore motif (F232.2 'Fairies have breasts long enough to throw over their shoulders'). They appear in Turkish folklore as a trait of giantesses. In Nordic lore *skogsrå* look beautiful from the front but not the back, and this common motif involving a changeling bride (F322.1) appears in some Ukrainian *bohyni* texts. *Bohyni*, like Western nymphs and fairies, are said to be fond of singing and dancing and to do so to excess, causing the demise of the humans who participate in their revelries. Ukrainian tales and legends also speak of animal or animal-like spouses, another international motif.

These shared motifs are important for present purposes in showing how the narrators in western Ukraine, recorded at the turn of the century, speak of issues in their own social sphere. Jack Zipes, writing in *Happily Ever After*, explains how different authors of Puss-in-Boots tales varied their texts to meet their own interests and concerns while maintaining the basic Puss-in-Boots narrative.[22] I would argue that western Ukrainian *bohynia* stories, in much the same way, deal with issues important to the society in which they were told even as they used international tale-types and motifs.

It is sometimes implied that *bohyni* were believed to be the unquiet spirits of women who died as the result of *vechirki* and *vulytsia* mishaps, much like the drowning Marusenka in the *pokrytka* ballad discussed by Hantiuk. This is not stated directly in the texts published in the *demonolohia* books. However, the title given to the relevant section there is '*Bohyni* and *rusalki*'. *Rusalki* are much more clearly seen as the spirits of drowned maidens, especially maidens who committed suicide in response to being jilted in love after becoming pregnant. *Rusalki* is the name given to female supernatural beings in two of the texts published by Hnatiuk. In one, the word *rusalka* appears in the title, while the rest of the text speaks about *bohyni*. In the other, the man who has a frightening experience with a spirit woman later learns that she was a *rusalka*.

The classic study of *rusalki*, first published by Dmitri Zelenin in 1916 and republished by Indrik in 1995, makes the connection between *rusalki* and maidens who committed suicide explicit. Zelenin argues that folk belief holds that humans are allotted a certain specified time on earth (*srok*). If they die before that time, they then must live out the rest of their *srok* as unquiet spirits. Women who die, especially those who commit suicide because of unrequited love or because they killed their out-of-wedlock babies, become *rusalki*. They form social groups and dance and sing, most often near the bodies of water in which they took their lives, but also in meadows where their dancing makes circles of particularly verdant grass. They are antagonistic to humans and try to kill both women and men who are foolish enough to enter their domain.[23] *Rusalka* stories are more characteristic of eastern Ukraine and Russia than of the region from which Hnatiuk took his material. Nonetheless, Ukrainian stories, including texts from western Ukraine, do figure in Zelenin's work.[24]

Another publication that speaks specifically about *rusalki*, although more briefly, is Stepan Kylymnyk's analysis of the Ukrainian calendar year. He too connects these creatures to drowned maidens and other young women who died unnatural deaths.[25] *Bohyni*, I propose, is the name given in western Ukraine to creatures who are elsewhere called *rusalki*. Even though the connection between *bohyni* and mishaps in the courtship process is not explicitly made by Hnatiuk, it is not too difficult to see *bohyni* as the spirits of women who died, likely by suicide or by being drowned as punishment. They haunt the living because of the nature of their deaths.

## *Bohyni* and Men

Many legends describe *bohyni* as being highly sexualized with enormous breasts, breasts so large that they can toss them over their shoulders. Text 474, entitled 'What do *bohyni* do?' states that a *bohynia* has hair down to her waist and large breasts.[26] In Text 476, entitled 'A girl who was tortured to death by *bohyni*', we see: 'Those *bohyni* have big breasts and they throw them over their shoulders, from the chest all the way to the shoulders.' Sometimes they are portrayed as being almost animalistic. Text 479, entitled 'A *bohynia* who scattered a fire', comments on their animal-like fur: 'She is furry, big-breasted and her breasts swing'. Text 481, 'A *bohynia* on a wagon', mentions animal-like hands and feet as well as big breasts, and states: 'Well, that *bohynia* has hands and feet like hooves and she throws her breasts over her shoulders.'[27] This is a repulsive sexuality. The mention of body hair and hooves underscores the animalistic nature of these creatures and suggests women who give into their bodily desires during courtship gatherings. A different sort of supernatural feature that also implies attractiveness with a substratum of disgust appears in Text 480, 'Bisitia'. Here the *bohynia* looks lovely from the front but, if you look at her from the back, her intestines are exposed and drag behind her.

As it turns out, men can cohabit with *bohyni*, and two texts imply a marital or marriage-like relationship, with one text having 'marriage' in the title. Such unions do not last, however. In this they are like the relationships from *vechornytsi* that involved intimacy but did not lead to permanent union. Text 476 (see the title above) has a second part. A man sneaks up on a *bohynia* from the back and suckles one of her breasts. He says that she must have had a child because he tasted milk. He gets the *bohynia* to live with him, but she is constantly sad, cries, and eats very little. After a week he lets her go. Text 482, 'A *bohynia* gets married', tells how a man pastures horses and builds a fire. A woman twice approaches the fire. The man does not realize that she is a *bohynia*; he assumes she is a girl who has brought him his horses. The man comes to realize that he is dealing with a *bohynia* and goes to a priest for advice. The priest tells him to take the sash that a priest would use during a service and to tie her up with it. When she comes again, the man does just that and takes the woman to church to have her baptized. The couple seem to marry: this is not explicitly stated, as the rite of baptism is mentioned but a wedding is not. The title, however, implies marriage and, if the *bohynia* is the spirit of an adult woman who committed suicide, she would have been baptized already; marriage would be the missing rite. The *bohynia* tells the man: 'I will live with you for seven years and you will have anything that you desire. Just one thing—never call me a viper. If you do, then I will disappear and you will not know where to find me.' So they live together for seven years, and then he makes the mistake of calling her a viper and she disappears on the wind.[28]

Beautiful supernatural women also exist. There is one mention of such a creature in Hnatiuk and this narrative is an outlier in several respects. Text 485, 'Swimming during Holy Week', is told in the first person, in other words as a memorate, unlike most of the Hnatiuk material. It begins with the narrator stating that he made the mistake of going swimming on the eve of Trinity Sunday. As he swam away from shore, he saw a naked woman standing up to her waist in the water. She was strikingly beautiful—and, when she caught sight of the human swimmer/narrator, she laughed. The man looked more closely and realized that she was not one of the girls from his village. Frightened, he swam for shore as the woman came closer and closer. He scrambled onto the land while the woman laughed and clapped her hands. He grabbed his clothes and started to run home. He was so frightened that he ran naked at least half of the way, glancing back, looking to see if the supernatural woman was following him. Seeing no one, he started to put his clothes on little by little so that by the time he got home he was dressed. The terrible fright that he experienced, he confesses, made him ill and he became wary of swimming alone. He also avoided, from then on, swimming in the evening. When he told his parents about what had happened, they said that he had encountered a *rusalka* and warned him to never swim during Pentecost week because that is the time of year when *rusalki* are about.[29] This text is different from the other narratives in Hnatiuk and may be from eastern Ukraine, where courtship practices virtually identical to those of western Ukraine were, as Dykarev shows, to be found. Whatever the origins of this story may be, it does contain messages very similar to those in the material discussed here, namely that overly attractive or overly sexual women are dangerous to men and that ordinary village girls are to be preferred.

There is one text where longing for dead human women or children can expose a man to supernatural attack. Text 480, '*Bisytsi*', describes supernatural women bearing this name. *Bisytsi* (seemingly from the root *bis*, meaning demon) are described as living in the forest where they can be heard singing. If a man yearns for his wife or his child excessively, presumably a wife or child that he has lost, then the *bisytsi* can grab him and drag him into their company. Text 480 says that these creatures can devour him. Whether the devouring is literal or metaphorical is not clear. In this text the supernatural women seem to be jealous of real women and the families of ordinary people. If these supernatural creatures are, indeed, believed to originate with women who committed suicide or who otherwise died young, then resentment of ordinary life might reasonably follow.

## *Bohyni* and Women

The most obvious connection between *bohyni*, *vechornytsi* and gender relations appears in Hnatiuk Text 484, entitled 'How *bohyni* tried to get a (human) baby'. This text underscores the dangers of excessive desire and provides an indisputable link between *bohyni*, babies, sexual attraction and *vechornytsi*. In the tale some young people attend evening parties, and a young woman falls in love with a young man who has eyes for another. She takes the initiative and begs him to forget the woman that he is interested in and wed her instead. He replies that if she can spin twelve spindles of thread by daybreak, he will marry her. She goes home and cries, lamenting that this is an impossible task. A group of *bohyni* show up and offer to do the spinning if she will promise to give them 'that which she does not know that she has'. The girl accepts and the *bohyni*, who are twelve in number, produce the required spindles. The young man keeps his word and the couple marries. Within a year they have a baby. At this point the *bohyni* show up and demand the child, because that is the thing the woman 'did not know that she had' and that she signed away in exchange for the spindles. The woman is frantic and begs to keep her baby. The *bohyni* respond that, if she can guess their names, they will leave her the child. She tries every common woman's name that she can think of, but all prove to be wrong. It so happens that her husband is away at the time and, as he returns home, he overhears the *bohyni* talking and saying that they are all called Fen'ka. He tells his wife. She tells the *bohyni*. They leave and do not return.[30] This is a story with a happy ending based on a folktale plot—N452 'Secret remedy overheard in conversation of animals (witches)'—and one of the few with a positive resolution in the *bohyni* section of Hnatiuk's book. It also provides the clearest connection between human social practices and social supernatural beings.

Other texts about *bohyni* are not as positive, especially when they concern women. *Bohyni* appear jealous of mortal women, luring them into joining events that have a certain resemblance to *vechirka* parties and then maiming them so that they cannot speak and they eventually die. In Text 477 entitled 'How *bohyni* tortured a girl to death', the supernatural creatures trick women into going into the woods by assuming the appearance of their neighbours and inviting them to gather wild strawberries, or periwinkle flowers, or herbs. The victim of this specific narrative accepts the invitation to go outside the village. Once she enters the forest, the *bohynia* who came to her home and invited her to go into the forest leads her to the place where *bohyni* dwell. There, they involve her in their singing and dancing, an experience which is pictured as a kind of torture and which involves the tearing of the victim's hair. The singing and dancing in which the human girl is forced to participate continues for three days and exhausts her completely. At last, the poor woman is able to return home. When she arrives at her house, she is half-dead. Furthermore, she is unable to speak. It turns out that the *bohyni* had stuck her tongue full of pins and needles. The tongue swells to the point that the poor woman is rendered mute. She dies within a week.

Although, according to the text, the victim could not speak, her experiences were, nonetheless, somehow communicated to others. Now that the other villagers know about the dangers of *bohyni* and their ability to impersonate mortals, the women living in that locale, when someone invites them to go to the woods for some innocent-sounding activity, check to make sure that the invitation does not come from a *bohynia* in the guise of a neighbour. Text 476 entitled 'The girl who was tormented by *rusalki*'[31] is similar, though not as long and detailed. In this narrative, a woman goes to gather periwinkles in the autumn. A group of *bohyni* approach her and take her with them to sing and dance. She does not come home until the next day. When she does return, she cannot speak because her tongue, too, has been pierced with pins. She dies soon after the encounter.[32]

While these texts seem to be related to ATU 306 'The Danced-Out Shoes', they have specifically Ukrainian features which reference *vechornytsi*. In the Danced-Out Shoes folktale, the women who go dancing at night do so willingly—they do not need to be tricked—and they suffer no ill effects from their night-time outings. In the *bohynia* texts the girls are tricked into night-time dancing, much as women might be tricked or tempted into participating in only the pleasurable aspect of *vechirka/vechornytsia* events. Furthermore, the punishment these women experience is pins and needles stuck into their tongues, rendering them mute. The pins and needles reference the needlework women were expected to practise in the early part of the *vechornytsia* evening. Spinning or embroidery were so much a part of women's *vechornytsia* experience that a girl's mother could forbid her from attending until she had spun the requisite amount of thread.

These texts can be usefully interpreted as a folk commentary on the *vechornytsi*, where singing and dancing were part of the entertainment. Such activities, when indulged in excessively, can prove fatal, as these legends suggest. The texts also suggest that *bohyni* might originate in women who were forced to move from the human to the spirit realm because of overindulgence in *vechornytsia* activities. Their resentment and jealousy of mortal women, then, might lead them to force humans into those activities through which they themselves were doomed.

Taking away the power of speech is an interesting aspect of the *bohyni* attack on women. The victims in the narratives above are deprived of their ability to explain what happened.[33] Nonetheless, everyone, and certainly the narrator of each of the legends, claims to know what occurred. Women attending *vechornytsi* or *vulytsi* were supposed to be back home the next morning. Were the stories about women not returning for a length of time a way of explaining why good girls were unaccountably absent? Various details, the singing and dancing, the mention of sewing implements, hint at courtship parties. Were legends such as the two texts above a tactful way of explaining why women were inexplicably gone far longer than they should have been? Did the inability of these women to speak for themselves allow society to impose a traditional explanation? The legends claim that the women died after their *bohynia* encounters. Did this allow their families to remove them from social scrutiny while they took care of their unwanted pregnancies?

The fact that the woman who has danced with *bohyni/rusalki* cannot speak is also likely a reference to Ukrainian courtship practices. As stated at the beginning of this chapter, if a woman who was not a virgin was accepted by a young man, the groom-to-be, and his family, it was they who provided proof of legitimacy, not the girl herself. The groom could provide blood from an alternate source if that was the proof required in his village. The female relatives of the groom could declare the woman to be a suitable bride, even if she was not a virgin. In other words, as in the folk narratives, a woman was deprived of the ability to speak up in her own defence.

*Bohyni* haunt the periphery of the inhabited world. They can be encountered by chance if a young woman ventures away from her village. Text 475, 'A *bohynia* wants to ruin a girl', tells of a frightening encounter. A young woman on her way to visit her aunt is walking by the woods when she senses that something is amiss and starts to run. When she stops, the entity pursuing her stops also. The woman reaches a tavern and shelters inside. When she thinks that she is no longer being followed, she heads home. At her house, she sees a naked woman sitting there and looking at something. This is the *bohynia* whom she had encountered in the forest. Fortunately for the mortal woman, there happens to be a cross by the roadside and, when she crosses herself, the naked *bohynia* flees.[34] As she does so, she warns the mortal woman that they will meet again.

## *Bohyni* and Babies: The Tension between Babies and Spirits of the Dead

In the normal course of events, couples who got to know each other at *vechornytsi* or *vulytsi* would marry and produce progeny. Infertility is considered a great misfortune and couples who do not produce babies, or produce only girls, will adopt other people's children to set things right. A family with no male heirs, for example, will adopt the man who marries one of their daughters and pass on their property to this couple. This practice is so common that it has its own term in Ukrainian: the man who marries into a family and inherits its property is called a *pryimak*.[35]

Because of the importance of children, *bohyni* are regularly pictured as being attracted to infants. Whether this is seen as a desire on their part to be like normal women, or a more general attempt to enter into human-like relationships, they are often presented as trying to steal human babies. In many cases, they substitute their own spirit children for human infants.[36] Text 474, 'What do *bohyni* do?', states outright that *bohyni* take the children of women and substitute their own.[37] The stolen human babies, this text states, can grow up to become, depending on their gender, either devils or *bohyni*. Although the text does not make this point, the spirit children with whom *bohyni* replace human babes tend to die quickly. The text states that the mothers of the human children lost to the *bohyni* will bury these changeling infants when they die. The changelings rise from the grave after seven years and ascend upward calling, 'Christ, Christ.' The text adds that if a woman throws a piece of cloth at this ascending entity and gives it a name—Iavdokha, if it is a girl, and Iantyn (Anton) if it is a boy—then the entity will turn into an angel. Presumably, this act is based on baptism with the cloth being the *kryzhma*, the fabric in which the child is held during this rite, and the granting of a name being the culmination of christening.

In Text 483, 'How *bohyni* substituted a child', the supernatural creatures of the title stage a pretend wedding and sing a song. It is noteworthy that the creation of a child, albeit a supernatural one, is preceded by a wedding. It seems that the creation of a baby, even in the supernatural realm, requires marriage, something that the women who became *bohyni* had not been able to attain in real life. Having performed their 'wedding', the *bohyni* start to beat the shelf in front of the stove with sticks and stir up the ashes. They then use these ashes to shape a babe. The text of the song and the description of how the substitute infant is created are given as if the narrator were an eyewitness. The *bohyni* substitute this 'ash infant' for the real child of the mistress of the house, and take her baby. The fake infant cries a lot and at age seven (presumably seven months not years?) it is still very small, but has a huge head and stomach. The people living in the home debate what to do. They tell the child that they are going out into the field for a while. They leave the building, but drill a hole in the side of the house so that they can observe the child. As they watch through the hole, they see the child grow so huge that it can touch the ceiling. Then it goes and eats all the food on the stove and carefully sweeps the ashes, so that no one can tell what it has done. After that, it lies back down in the crib. The human members of the family take rods and twigs and beat the naked child. A *bohynia* becomes aware of what is happening and takes pity on the changeling, claiming that it is hers. Which *bohynia* does this is not clear, since it was stated earlier that this creature was a group creation. The text merely states that the *bohynia* appears before the family and says: here is your child; give me mine back. Then she takes her own child, leaves the woman's baby, and disappears. The people in the house baptize the human baby, but this does not help and the child lives barely three weeks before it dies.

This is a peculiar text because it has the hallmarks of an eyewitness account. If the narrator did not observe the creation of the *bohynia* infant, how could they know how this baby was formed? How could the narrator know the song that was sung in the process of creation? While this does have traces of a first-person account, it is not told in the first person like the narrative about the man who went swimming on the eve of Pentecost and ran into a *rusalka*. The somewhat confused nature of this text about *bohyni* and babies may well reflect the confusion people experience when the process of going from a single to a married state, and to parenthood, does not go as expected.[38] It also likely reflects the bewilderment that people experience when they encounter problems with their infants.

Some babies can have serious health problems. Some infants simply do not survive. This was a problem not only in nineteenth-century Ukraine, but also among Ukrainians in the diaspora.[39] How does one explain the loss of an infant? Among Ukrainians in Canada, the explanation was medical. In turn-of-the-century Ukraine, the explanation in Hnatiuk was that the baby was not human at all, but a changeling, a *bohynia* baby substituted for the human child because the *bohynia*'s longing for children was so strong. Similarly, some children were born with deformities, perhaps like the overly large head and stomach of the child described in the text above. Again, how does one explain such births? At the time that Hnatiuk's texts were recorded, a common explanation was that the child was a changeling.

*Bohynia* babies do not seem to mature.[40] Be they those babies that *bohyni* produce themselves out of ash or the human babies they steal, there are virtually no narratives about what happens to these children after they enter the supernatural realm. Text 474 states simply that the human babies stolen by *bohyni* become devils or *bohyni* themselves. All other texts about babies stop with the theft of the infant. Text 473 in Hnatiuk, '*Nedolitki*' ('Youths'), is unique because it is about neither a baby nor an adult, but a young boy. This child is, like *bohyni*, antagonistic to humans, especially women. He tricks a woman who has gone to tend her potatoes into thinking he is in distress. She, seeing a beautiful crying child, rushes to comfort him and picks him up. At this point he laughs and grabs the woman by the throat. He then tears at her hair the way *bohyni* do with captive women during their singing and dancing in the forest. The victim in this story faints and is found half-dead only towards evening. This is an isolated narrative, because most legends describe encounters with malevolent adults who are linked to marital issues in some way. This text perhaps serves to warn women not to grow too attached to children, especially children who are not their own.

## Conclusion

The transition from single to married life is, in Ukraine as elsewhere, an important event. In Ukraine, there were ritual parties that encouraged young people to form couples that would go on to wed. These parties—*vechornytsi, vechirki, dosvitky* and *vulytsi*—allowed young women and men to pair up with a view to marriage. But things could go wrong and women sometimes became pregnant out of wedlock. If the man married the pregnant woman, then all was well. If he did not, however, it was the woman, not the man, who was disgraced. Village girls were warned against excessive indulgence in village parties that might lead to unwanted pregnancy. Warnings were reinforced by legends about supernatural beings that were at once more cryptic and more powerful than straightforward warnings. They showed that women who were excessively sexual could also prove to be repulsive. They described dancing and singing that could take away the power of speech and even kill. They featured malformed babies that were believed to come from the spirit world. Legends added an aesthetically effective dimension to warnings around courtship, thus making these warnings all the more effective.

## Notes

1. For the Shevchenko Scientific Society, see *Internet Encyclopedia of Ukraine*, http://www.encyclopediaofukraine.com/display.asp?linkpath=pages%5CS%5CH%5CShevchenkoScientificSociety.htm. See also *Publications of the Shevchenko Scientific Society, 1945–1980* (New York: The Society, 1980).
2. http://www.encyclopediaofukraine.com/display.asp?linkpath=pages%5CH%5CN%5CHnatiukVolodymyr.htm. See also M. Mushynka, *Volodymyr Hnatiuk doslidnyk fol'kloru Zakarpattia: ZNTSh* (Paris: n.p., 1975).
3. V. Hnatiuk, *Znadoby do halyts'ko-rus'koii demonolohii: etnografichnyi Zbirnyk*, vol. 15 (L'viv: Naukove Tovarystvo im. Shevchenka, 1904); *Znadoby do ukraiins'koii demonolohii*, vol. 33 (L'viv: Naukove Tovarystvo im. Shevchenka, 1912) and vol. 34 (L'viv: Naukove Tovarystvo im. Shevchenka, 1912).
4. K. Dysa, *Ukrainian Witchcraft Trials: Volhynia, Podolia, and Ruthenia, 17th–18th Centuries* (Budapest: Central European University Press, 2020), 53–60.
5. Text numbers 473–86 of vol. 33.
6. Nina Basans'ka, Iavorivka, Drabiv region, 2003.
7. M. Maerchik, *Ritual i tilo: Strukturno-semantychnyi analiz ukrains'kykh obriadiv rodynnoho tsyklu* (Kyiv: Krytyka, 2011), esp. 15–72. Maerchik argues that there were many ways to experience sexual pleasure that did not involve intercourse.
8. M. Dykarev, 'Zbirky sil's'koi molodizhy na Ukraiini', *Materialy do ukraiins'koii etnol'ogii* 18 (L'viv: Naukove tovarystvo im. Shevchenka, 1918), 170–275.
9. V. Hnatiuk, 'Pisnia pro pokrytku shcho vtopyla dytynu', *Materiialy do Ukraiins'koii etnologii* 19–20 (L'viv: Etnografichna komissiia Naukoho Tovarystva im. Shevchenka u L'vovi, 1919), 249–389.

10. N.M. Zakovych, P.I. Kosukha and V.A. Perynov, *Sotsialisticheskaia obriadnost'* (Kyiv: Vyshcha Shkola, 1986).
11. Hnatiuk, 'Pisnia', 284–93.
12. Ibid., 293–95. See also O. Voropai, *Zvychaii nashoho narodu: etnografichnyi naris* (Kyiv: Oberih, 1993), 330–34.
13. Oksana Fedirivna Kryvorit, DOB 1918, interviewed 3 June 2000 in Velykyi Khutir, Drabivs'kyi raion, Cherkas'ka oblast'. Hnatiuk, 'Pisnia', 303 describes a virginity test conducted in the *komora* (root cellar) by the female members of the groom's household and says that girls who were not virgins but had lost their virginity to the man they were about to marry were considered acceptable and 'passed' the virginity test.
14. *Slovnyk ukraiins'koii movy*, vol. 8, ed. I.K. Bilodid (Kyiv: Institut movoznavstva, Akademiia nauk USSR, 1970–80), 49; Hnatiuk, 'Pisnia', 305–07.
15. The change in the number of daughters is the result of the demands of rhyme. 'Five' (*piat*) rhymes with 'sleep (*spiat*) at home' whereas 'seven' (*sim*) rhymes with 'all' (*usim*).
16. This particular text is an excerpt translated from the song found in Hnatiuk, 'Pisnia', 261.
17. I. Dei et al., *Balady kokhannia ta doshliubni vzaemyny* (Kyiv: Naukova Dumka, 1987), 319–52.
18. Ibid., 326, 346, 347, 350.
19. N. Kononenko, 'Ukrainian Ballads about the Loss of Virginity and Out-of-Wedlock Pregnancy', *35th International Ballad Conference: Papers and Materials*, eds I. Golovakha and L. Vakhnina (Kyiv: International Ballad Commission SIEF, 2009), 61–80.
20. It is noteworthy that, according to Hnatiuk, men were punished for rape but not other transgressions. Women, however, were subjected to trials and punishments ranging from drowning, as in the *pokrytka* ballad, to decapitation, hanging, a variety of types of beatings and whippings, to prison or expulsion from their village. See 'Pisnia', 332–61.
21. Dysa, *Ukrainian Witchcraft*, 207–25, who uses court records rather than folk sources, shows that infanticide was deemed a crime deserving of the most severe punishment.
22. *Happily Ever After: Fairy Tales, Children, and the Culture Industry* (New York: Routledge, 1977), 15–38.
23. D.K. Zelenin, *Izbrannye trudy. Ocherki russkoi mifologii: umershie neestestvennoiu smertiu i rusalki* (Moscow: Indrik, 1995), 141–233.
24. Ibid., 176–80.
25. S. Kylymnyk, *Ukraiinsk'kii rik u narodnykh zvychaiakh v istorychnomu osvitlenni* (Kyiv: Oberehi, 1994), 371–82.
26. '*Volosia mae do poiasa, tsitski velyki*'. Note that all of the texts in the Hnatiuk collection are assigned titles. These, most likely, were supplied by the collector or the publisher. Folk texts seldom have titles.
27. 476: '*Toti bohyni, to kazhut, zhi maiut taki veliki hrudi, zhi zakydaii zvisti (vid hrudi) azh na plechi*'; 479: '*Taka volokhata, tsitsata, tsitskamy tylipae*'; 481: '*A ta bohynii to maii ruki i nohy, iak ratytsi, a tsytsky to na plechi zakydaii*'.
28. ATU 400 'The Animal Bride'. It is noteworthy that the name the *bohynia* bride does not want to be called refers to a snake. In Ukrainian folklore witches and other supernatural beings are associated with snakes. There is a tale of a snake husband

which follows ATU 400 that I recorded during my fieldwork in the village of Ploske in 2000.
29. Voropai, *Zvychaii*, 396–405. See also Zelenin, *Izbrannye trudy*, 234–44. This period of time is called '*rusalka* week' and it is believed to be a time when *rusalki* and other spirits of the dead return to earth. See also ATU 316 'The Nix of the Mill Pond'.
30. ATU 500 'The Name of the Supernatural Helper'. As here, variants include tasks that require an inordinate amount of spinning followed later by name-guessing, plus the incidental overhearing of the name that the supernatural creature(s) demand(s). See also ATU 316 'The Nix of the Mill Pond'.
31. For a discussion of *rusalki* and their relationship to *bohyni*, see above.
32. ATU 306 'The Danced-Out Shoes', where there is magical and excessive dancing.
33. Taking away the power of speech, often by mutilation of the tongue, is associated with preventing a woman from revealing rape. See the story of Philomela for a classical narrative of a woman who was raped by her brother-in-law and was deprived of the power of speech by having her tongue cut out, so that she could not recount what had been done to her.
34. Roadside crosses are a common feature in western Ukraine. Typically located along the road as one enters a village and again as one leaves it, they are called *figury*. They are usually slightly taller than human height and are decorated with ribbons. A person is supposed to cross themselves upon entering the village, as the woman does in the legend discussed here. See also https://lyubeshiv.rayon.in.ua/gallery/508361-pridorozhni-khresti-figuri-volini-ta-polissya-pokhodzhennya-traditsii-ta-ii-zmist.
35. *Slovnyk ykraiins'koii movy v 11 tomakh*, vol. 7, ed. I.K. Bilodid (Kyiv: Institut movoznavstva, Akademiia nauk USSR, 1970–80), 623. *Pryimak* means 'taken in' or adopted.
36. ML 5085 'The Changeling'.
37. '*I pidstavliae dity, svoii bere, dae babi, a iii bere do sebe. I s tykh dityi e bohyni i chort. Kotra taku vo maie dytynu i zakopaie tu dytynu, to dytyna za sim lit vylyty s toii iamy i letyt tak do hory i krychyt'—Khrystu, khrystu! I kotra mudra baba to voz'mi, kavalchyk platka vdre i kyne za nym i kazhe, iak s'i zve, abo Iavdokha, abo Iantyn, i vono sii zrobyt anhelom.*'
38. In a ballad in Dei et al., *Balady*, 351, a jilted girl contemplates suicide, but then cannot go through with it, and in the ballads on 352–61 the mother of an illegitimate child threatens infanticide if the man who is the father does not take responsibility.
39. N. Kononenko, 'Vernacular Religion on the Prairies: Negotiating a Place for the Unquiet Dead', *Canadian Slavonic Papers/Revue canadienne des slavists* 60 (2018), 108–35.
40. For more on changelings as children that do not thrive, see S. Schoon Eberly, 'Fairies and the Folklore of Disability: Changelings, Hybrids and the Solitary Fairy', *Folklore* 99 (1988), 58–77.

# Index

Abcán, 23
abduction, supernatural, 36, 37–9, 60, 62, 88, 89, 95, 96, 105 n.32, 179, 200, 205, 208, 215 n.124, 218–19, 223, 224, 233
    of infants and children, 7, 10, 35, 38, 39–40, 44, 123, 149 n.22, 158, 208, 223–4, 230 n.35, 233, 238–9, 253, 257 see also changelings
Abundia, 142, 146
*Acallam na Senórach*, 24–6
Achterhoek, Netherlands, 113, 114, 118
Adam and Eve, 74
aetiological legends, 123
Æsir, 88
Aesop's *Fables*, 99
agriculture, 9, 14 n.34, 22, 78, , 94, 98, 206
Ágústsdóttir, Sveinsína, 81
Aironis (deity), 125
*aitvarai*, 233
Al-Andalus, 122, 123
*álfabyggð* (elf settlement), 72–3
Allacci, Leone, 220–21, 222, 224
allomotifs, 226
Ailill Ólomm, 30 n.66
Áine, 30 n.66
*álagablettur*, 77–9
Alexander II, tsar, 243
Alexander the Great, 223, 226
Alfrick, England, 56
Alps, 9, 10, 150 n.32, 183

*Altram Tighe Dá Mheadar*, 24, 29 n.50, 30 n.62
Amboto, Dama de, 127
America, United States of, 32, 104 n.8
Americas, 122, 125, 131
Amilien, Virgine, 89
Amsterdam, Netherlands, 108, 112, 115, 118
Ana María la Lobera, 130
ancestors, 110, 158
*anganas*, 130
angels, 34, 56, 64, 74, 147, 152 n.61, 158, 187, 218, 256
animals, 52, 66 n.19, 78, 91, 94, 97, 99, 143, 192 n.26, 193 n.51, 196, 221, 222, 227, 238, 249, 250–51, 253, 259 n.28
animism, 162
*anguine*, 9, 10
anti-witch societies, 182–3, 186
Antolak, Šimun, 204
aos sí (*áes síde*), 8–9, 18–19, 22, 26 n.2, 28 n.24, 239
    kings of, 6, 8, 19–20, 21, 22, 24, 25
apotropaics, 166, 198, 222
Apuleius, 140, 142
Aragonese language, 122, 128
*arc-vuc-sonney* (pig of plenty), 35
Archilochus, 226
Aristotle, 144, 151 n.43
Arles, France, 138, 139, 142, 144, 152 n.61
Arlington, England, 56

armies, supernatural, 20, 38
Árnason, Jón, 74
Arnhem, Netherlands, 111
Aromanians, 197, 210, 216 n.131
Arthur, king, 59, 145, 147
Asturias, Spain, 130, 131
Ataun, Spain, 131
Athens, Greece, 220
Aubrey, John, 55, 58, 60
Augustine of Hippo, 139–40, 142, 145
Austria, 155, 161, 243

Bacău County, Romania, 179
Bács County, Hungary, 178
bagpipes, 7, 177–8, 179, 184, 226
*Baile in Scáil*, 19, 23
Balkans, 2, 6, 9, 174, 175, 177, 181, 187–8, 190 n.5, 191 n.9, 192 n.31, 196–216
ballads, 129, 130, 196, 206, 247–8, 249, 259 n.20, 260 n.38
Ballamooar, Isle of Man, 37
Ballamoddey, Isle of Man, 37
Ballaugh Curraghs, Isle of Man, 40
baptism, 39, 95–6, 166, 208, 251, 256
Barbac, Hungary, 177
Barber, Elizabeth, 198, 199
Barneveld, Netherlands, 109
*barstukai*, 233
Basque language, 122, 127, 128, 130, 131, 132
bathing, 5, 36, 144, 203, 205, 208, 223
Bauer, John, 105 n.33
*Baxajaunes*, 132
Bé Find, 20
Beaucaire, France, 144
beauty, supernatural, 5, 15 n.45, 87, 89, 111, 127, 128, 142, 143, 144, 147, 162, 164, 167, 174, 175, 176, 179, 183, 186, 198, 200, 223, 224, 238, 240, 249, 251, 257
Bechstein, Ludwig, 156, 160, 164, 166
beer, 97, 98, 115, 116, 159

belief, nature of, 52, 59, 80–83, 89, 218, 219
Benandanti, 210
Bennett, Anne, 53
Bergen, Norway, 91
Beskow, Elsa, 105 n.33
Bible, the, 34, 40, 91, 97
Bihar County, Hungary, 177
*bile* (sacred tree), 21
birds, 20, 151 n.56, 175, 183, 196, 200, 205
*bisytsi*, 252
*bjærgfolk*, 91, 93, 104 n.16
Block Eary, Isle of Man, 36
Bóadach the Eternal, 19
Bodb of Síd ar Femin (Bodb Derg), 20, 24, 25, 26, 30 n.61, 30 n.62, 31 n.73
Boguet, Henri, 146
Bohemia, 157
Bohuslän, Sweden, 95
*bohyni*, 6, 8, 9, 10, 243–60
Boekenoogen, Gerrit Jacob, 115
Borculo, Netherlands, 113, 115
Bošković-Stulli, Maja, 210
Bosnia-Herzegovina, 206, 207
Bourinos, Mount, Greece, 224
Bova, Italy, 222
breasts, 130, 136 n.44, 208, 225, 238, 249, 250–51
Brendan, St, 24
Bres, 28 n.27
'Brewery of Egg Shells' (tale type), 84 n.8, 199
bridges, 7, 57, 106 n.62, 124, 130, 206
Briggs, Katharine, 3, 13 n.28, 65 n.11, 69 n.58, 199
Brigit (deity), 152 n.62
Brión, crown of, 21
Brittany, 10, 143, 147, 152 n.58, 153 n.65, 154 n.99
Budapest, Hungary, 184, 186
*buggane*, 34, 35
builders, supernatural, 61, 191 n.7, 206

Bulgaria, 194 n.59, 197, 198
Burchard of Worms, 140, 142
Bürger, Gottfried August, 111, 120 n.31
*Buschgroßmutter*, 158
Buurse, Netherlands, 108, 114

*cabbyl ushtey*, 35
Cádiz, Spain, 132
Čajkanović, Veselin, 209
'Cake in the Furrow' (tale type), 61–2
Calabria, Italy, 221, 222, 226, 227, 231 n.37
Callimachus, 218
Cambridge, England, 61
Canada, 257
Canary Islands, 131
Canigou, mount, 144, 145
cannibalism, 142, 151 n.47, 166–7, 172 n.71, 222, 226, 230 n.35, 231 n.52, 239
*Canon Episcopi*, 142
Capo Colonna, Italy, 221
Cas Corach, 26
Cashen, William, 35
castles, 2, 6, 57, 94, 107, 109–12, 117, 118, 147, 152 n.61, 160, 170 n.32, 191 n.7, 206
Catalonia, 122, 127, 128, 130
*Cath Maige Mucrama*, 19, 20
*Cath Maige Tuired*, 22–3
Catholicism, 89, 98, 107, 108, 109–10, 173
caves, 6, 35, 57, 87, 94, 98, 122, 124, 130, 131, 132, 138, 145, 157, 158, 191 n.7, 196, 200, 203, 207, 208, 214 n.92, 218, 222, 224–5, 227 n.1
Celtic religion, 125
Cenél nEógain, 28 n.32
Chalandri, Greece, 219, 231 n.40
changelings, 15 n.47, 40, 44, 60, 62, 72, 84 n.8, 88, 95, 166, 199, 208, 215 n.124, 224, 238, 239, 249, 256, 257
Chaucer, Geoffrey, 58
Chevalier, Maxime, 126

childbirth, 44, 148 n.10, 161, 236
childcare, 156, 208
children, 14 n.34, 34, 60, 62, 63, 74, 81, 90, 94, 95, 97, 100, 101, 125, 128, 129, 130, 140, 144, 152, 155, 157, 160, 162, 163, 166–7, 172 n.84, 208, 215 n.124, 223–4, 231 n.44, 235, 237, 247, 249, 251, 252, 255–6, 260 n.38
Chios, Greece, 220, 224
chivalry, books of, 126, 127
'choral' actions, 6, 227
Chourne, William, 54, 55, 56
churches, 6, 39, 57, 61, 96, 111, 128, 146, 182, 185, 191 n.7, 219, 251
  bells of, 161
  elf churches (Iceland), 73, 76–7, 80
Čiča, Zoran, 182, 210
Circe, 126
Ciuc region, Hungary/Romania, 173
Clare, John, 62–3
classification, supernatural, 3–4
Cleja, Hungary, 184–5, 186
clergy *see* priests
Clerk, Agnes, 52, 55
Clerk, Marion, 52, 55
climate change, 42
clouds, 133 n.3, 196, 200, 203, 206
Coevorden, Netherlands, 116
Colby, Isle of Man, 36
Colombiers Forest, France, 145
*Compert Con Culainn*, 19
confirmation (rite), 96
Colling, Mary, 56
Conaire, 20
Conan Doyle, Arthur, 72
Conn of the Hundred Battles, 19, 24
Connacht, Ireland, 8, 20, 21, 22, 26
Coo, Jan, 60
Corbett, Richard, 54
Cormac mac Airt, 24
Cos, Greece, 229 n.22
Coudrette, 143

courtship, 243–60
cows, supernatural, 74–5, 76, 80
cozeners, 6, 15 n.39, 52, 56
Cranstal, Isle of Man, 44
Cregeen, Archibald, 34
Cregneash, Isle of Man, 33, 41, 42
Crete, Greece, 225
Croatia, 2, 182–3, 193 n.39, 201, 204, 206, 209, 210
Cronk Mooar, Isle of Man, 34
cross, sign of the, 95, 220, 244
crossroads, 125, 200, 202, 203, 225, 226, 245
Csorna, Hungary, 182
Cú Chulainn, 21–2, 30 n.66
Cuenca, Spain, 125
*cumachta*, 22
Cumming, J.G., 43
cunning folk (service magicians), 15 n.49, 52, 62, 64, 65 n.5, 181, 183, 186, 187, 189 n.2, 192 n.31, 193 n.39
cups, supernatural, 38–9, 70 n.67, 144
Czechs, 197

D'Aulnoy, Marie-Catherine, 6, 147, 150 n.36
Dagda (deity), 19, 20, 24, 25, 27 n.23
Dalmatia, 198, 205, 207
Dama do Pé de Cabra, 127, 128
Danby, England, 56
'Danced-Out Shoes' (tale type), 254, 260 n.32
dancing, 5, 6, 8, 9, 38, 54–5, 57, 59, 64, 97, 107, 111, 114, 132, 146, 164–5, 168, 174, 175, 176–7, 178–9, 180, 181, 182, 183, 184, 185, 186, 188, 194 n.59, 197, 199, 201, 202, 203, 204–205, 206, 209, 210, 218, 219, 221, 225, 227, 229 n.24, 244, 246, 248, 249, 250, 253, 254, 255, 257, 258, 260 n.32
Danube, river, 156, 247–8
*daoine maithe*, 2, 18

Dartmeet, England, 60
De Haan, Tjaard W.R., 108, 111, 118, 120 n.31
dead, social supernatural beings as the, 54, 66 n.23, 89, 175, 176, 181, 187, 199, 202, 260 n.29
dead, unquiet *see* ghosts
death, goddess of, 107, 110, 111
Death (character), 99
demonology, 183, 239, 244, 249
demons, 5, 90, 125, 138, 175, 177, 181, 187, 217, 219, 223, 226, 227 n.1, 252
  social supernatural beings as, 12 n.18, 14 n.34, 14 n.36, 54, 88, 108, 139–40, 141, 142, 144–5, 152 n.63, 158, 161–2, 207
Denmark, 88, 90, 92, 94, 96, 103 n.3, 104 n.16, 201
destiny, human, 127, 128, 139, 140, 236–7, 238
Deventer, Netherlands, 115, 116, 121 n.53
Devil, the, 14 n.33, 61, 89, 96, 125, 132, 141, 145, 175, 226, 240, 244
Devon, England, 60
Diana (deity), 6, 142, 199, 204
Didam, Netherlands, 110, 111
Dionysus (deity), 194 n.60, 234
disability, 60
Disney, 1, 71, 226, 232 n.53
divination *see* fortune-telling
dogs, supernatural, 35, 37, 97, 133 n.3, 169 n.10
Doinney Oie, 34
dolphins, 141, 142–3, 147
Domrémy, France, 145–6
Donà, Carlo, 1
*dones d'aigua*, 127, 128, 130
Donn, son of Midir, 25
*donni di fora*, 10, 181, 185–6, 187
Đorđević, Tihomir R., 210
Dorset, England, 60
doubles, spirit, 64, 103, 185, 187

Douglas, Norman, 221
*dracs*, 144, 152 n.63
dragons, 133 n.3, 138, 201
dreams, 19, 56, 66 n.21, 75–6, 85 n.16, 88, 124, 176–8, 179, 180, 181, 183, 186–7
drowning, 35, 167, 218, 247, 248, 249, 250, 259 n.20
Dryope, 218–19, 228 n.12
dual being, 173, 175, 178, 181, 184, 185, 186–7, 188, 193 n.45
Dubrovnik, Croatia, 182
*duendes*, 129
*dusii*, 139
Dutch Golden Age, 110
Dykarev, Mytrofan, 245, 252
dwarfs, 96, 107, 114, 115, 155, 156, 158, 159, 160, 161, 168, 201

*Eachtra Airt*, 24
*Echtra Nerai*, 20, 21, 22, 25
*Echtrae Chonnlai*, 18–19, 23
ecology, 1
Ede, Netherlands, 108, 109, 112
Edric the Wild, 54
Eger, Hungary, 181
Eisel, Robert, 156
Elbe, river, 162
Elderink, Cato, 114, 115–16, 117
elementals, 1
elf farms, 2, 73, 75–6, 97
elf-shot, 199, 213 n.59
Elfrik (Alberich), 117
*ellefolk*, 91, 92, 93
Elpha, 129
Elster, river, 162, 163
elves, 33, 39, 52, 58–9, 63, 91, 108, 117, 123, 197, 199, 200, 201
    Icelandic (*álfar*), 71–86
Ems Ukaz (edict), 243
*encantadas*, 122, 130, 131
England, 7, 51–70, 104 n.8, 218
Enschede, Netherlands, 114, 115

Eochaid Feidlech, 30 n.67
Eógabul, 19
*Epistle of Othea*, 58
Erzsébet Rácz, 182
Erzgebirge region, Germany, 156
Espinosa, Aurelio M., 126, 127
Estonia, 241 n.1
Étaíne, 19
etymology, 58, 67 n.33, 91, 110, 197–8, 234
euhemerism, 22, 88
euphemism, 44, 60, 174, 198, 218, 221, 229 n.22, 234
*exotika*, 217, 221, 222, 226

*fadas/hadas*, 126, 127, 128, 139, 140, 141
fairy rings, 204
Fann, 30 n.66
Faragher, Edward, 33, 34, 40–43
Faragher, Phillip, 39
*fatae*, 139, 140, 146, 199
*fatuae*, 139
feasts, 6, 7, 8, 19, 38, 159, 179, 181, 183, 186, 192 n.26, 197, 202, 206
*fées*, 6, 127, 138–54, 199
*ferrish*, 34
fertility, 7, 8, 18, 129, 148 n.10, 183, 199, 205, 206
Finland, 4, 88, 89, 91, 95, 100, 103 n.3, 103 n.4, 106 n.56
Finn mac Cumaill, 24
Flanders, 108
Florence, Italy, 231 n.52
'flower fairies', 1–2
*follets*, 141, 152 n.63
Fomoiri, 23, 28 n.24, 29 n.44
food, supernatural, 19, 25, 44, 61, 99, 141, 143–4, 146, 179, 202, 206, 207
forests, 43, 94, 113, 124, 145, 147, 157, 196, 203, 218, 236, 238, 239, 240, 244, 252, 253, 255, 257
fortune-telling, 125, 139, 142, 146, 181, 244
fossils, 239

fosterage, 20, 26, 31 n.76
fountains, 125, 129, 130, 162
France, 2, 6, 14 n.35, 127, 138–54
Franko, Ivan, 243
Frisia, Netherlands, 116, 121 n.53
frogs, 63, 141, 196
Froiam, Don, 128
funerals, 6, 8, 10, 219

Gaels, 22, 24, 25
Galathe, 58
Galicia, 122, 127, 128, 130
Gazenbeek, Jacob, 110, 113
*geisi* (ritual prohibitions), 20 *see also* taboos
Gelderland, Netherlands, 108, 114, 115, 118
Gello, 217
gender, 10, 146, 172 n.84, 252, 256
*genii*, 124
*gentiles*, 10, 122, 123, 131–2
Germany, 2, 6, 9, 10, 114, 152 n.63, 155–72
Gervase of Tilbury, 63, 138–44
Geyer, Moritz, 156
Ghimeş region, Romania, 173, 174, 175, 176, 177, 179, 183, 187, 189 n.2, 190 n.3
ghosts, 5, 10, 35, 42, 56, 79, 90, 92, 108, 109–11, 114, 120 n.42, 124, 133 n.3, 140, 145, 196, 198, 212 n.40, 238, 244
giants, 35, 90, 92, 94, 96, 100, 123, 128, 130, 131, 132, 161, 168, 191 n.7, 249
Giebichenstein, Germany, 166, 167
gigantomachies, 131
Ginzburg, Carlo, 210
Gisevius, Eduard, 234
glamour, 7, 64, 200, 207
*glashtin*, 34
Glenchass, Isle of Man, 42
globalization of folklore, 123, 226
Gloucestershire, England, 52
gnomes, 44, 107, 108, 109, 123

goblins, 51, 58, 90, 123, 124, 129, 130, 132, 141
Götaland, Sweden, 95, 105 n.35
Gothenburg, Sweden, 98
Göttingen, Germany, 117, 160
Granada, Spain, 131
Great Hunger, the, 2
Greece, 1, 7, 69 n.58, 199, 217–32
Grimm, Jacob, 155, 156, 159, 166
Grimm, Wilhelm, 155, 156, 159, 166
Groningen, Netherlands, 114
Guðmundsdóttir, Ingibjörg, 77, 78, 86 n.25
Guðmundsson, Jón 'the Learned', 74
Guggino, Elsa, 222
gypsies, 107

Haavio, Martti, 3
Hacka (troll queen), 6, 100
Halbertsma, Joost Hiddes, 116–17
Halle, Germany, 101, 164, 167
harm, 5, 36, 41, 43, 53, 81, 93, 99, 114, 196, 208, 223, 238
Haro, house of, 128
harpies, 199
Hartmann, Elisabeth, 3, 88, 93
harvest, 7, 36, 40, 63, 70 n.66, 94, 96, 182, 202, 206, 207, 246
Harz region, Germany, 156
Hälsingland, Sweden, 100, 101
healers, 7, 52, 201, 206, 207, 208, 210, 212 n.47
Hegedűs, András 177
Helsinki, Finland, 89
Henry II, king of England, 138
Henry the Young King, 138
Hera (deity), 149 n.22
Herodias, 142
heroes, 23, 24, 29 n.42, 59, 92, 128, 129, 132, 135 n.36, 196, 199, 200, 205, 206, 208, 212 n.44, 249
Herrera del Duque, Spain, 126
Herter, Janus, 182
Herter, Katherine, 182

Hesse, Germany, 156, 166
Heupers, Engelbert, 109, 112
Heuvel, Hendrik Willem, 113, 115
hiddenness, 14 n.34, 57, 74, 75, 81, 82, 83, 197, 199, 208, 231 n.36
hierarchy, 1, 5–6, 8, 9, 20, 22, 97, 122, 141, 145, 146, 158, 168, 204, 227, 239
*hilanderas*, 127, 130
hills, 14 n.34, 18, 19, 57, 59, 72, 74, 79, 94, 97, 116, 184, 219
Hnatiuk, Volodymyr, 243–5, 247, 250, 251, 252, 253, 257
Höfði, Iceland, 74, 75, 76, 78, 79, 80
Holde (deity), 119 n.7
Holland, Netherlands, 114
*Holzfräulein*, 156–7
homes of the supernatural, 6, 7, 59, 144, 168, 206, 207
Honduras, 124
Hoog-Soeren, Netherlands, 108, 112, 113
Hörmann, Kosta, 209
horses, 109, 114, 115, 116, 129, 143, 146, 175, 192 n.26, 196, 199, 201, 203, 205, 206, 236, 251
horseshoes, 69 n.64
household spirits, 16 n.58, 35–6, 140, 141, 142, 157, 158, 159, 160, 161, 233
Howe, Isle of Man, 38
Hrushevsky, Mykola, 243
*huldra*, 201
*huldufólk* (*huldrefolk*), 72, 74, 92, 93
Hungary, 2, 6, 10, 173–95
hunting, 6, 8, 54, 64, 100–101, 128, 129, 143 *see also* Wild Hunt
hurling, 8, 202
Hussovianus, Nicolaus, 235
Hutsuls, 243
Hylas, 218

Iberia, 10, 122–37
Iceland, 1–2, 69 n.58, 71–86
Ilbrecc of Síd Essa Rúaid, 25

Ilkley, England, 55
illness, 37, 52, 75, 176, 197, 204, 225
Imbert, archbishop of Arles, 151 n.48
immortality, 18, 23, 24, 25, 218, 223
*Immram Brain*, 23
Imotska Krajina, Croatia, 201
incubi, 139, 142
infant mortality, 218, 249
infanticide, 61, 217, 247, 249, 259 n.21, 260 n.38
Ingemark, Camilla Asplund, 89, 96
inheritance, 255
Inquisition, 130, 192 n.35
invisibility, 14 n.34, 24, 59, 79, 94, 95, 97, 110, 141, 150 n.36, 158, 197, 200, 208, 224, 230 n.30
Ireland, 2, 4, 8, 10, 11 n.7, 16 n.52, 18–31, 32, 45, 57, 208, 213 n.59
iron, 97, 98, 99, 116
Irving, Washington, 123
Isidore of Seville, 139–40
islands, 23, 147
Italy, 2, 9, 127, 134 n.26, 209, 221, 227, 231 n.52 *see also* Calabria, Italy
Ivanišević, Frano, 207

Jean d'Arras, 143, 145, 152 n.58
Jean d'Estivet, 145
Jenner, Henry, 32
Jews, 122, 137 n.57
Joan of Arc, 145–6
Johnson, Robert, 226
Jónsdóttir, Guðrún, 74, 78
Julius Caesar, 147
Jurby, Isle of Man, 37

*kallikantzaroi*, 217
Kanaboutzes, John, 219, 222, 226, 227 n.1
*kannerezed-noz*, 10
Karadžić, Vuk Stefanović, 209
*kaukai*, 233
*keimagh*, 35
Keightley, Thomas, 61

Kelly, John, 34
Kermode, Josephine, 43
kings, supernatural, 6, 19–20, 21, 22, 24, 25, 51, 52, 97, 107, 117, 147, 158, 160
kingship, 8, 18, 25–6, 30 n.61, 170 n.32
Kirk Andreas, Isle of Man, 33, 38
Kirchhain, Germany, 166
Kittelsen, Theodor, 105 n.33
Kjós, Iceland, 81
knockers, 10
kobolds, 141, 159, 161
Konstantin Asen, emperor, 198
*kosmati čovik* ('hairy man'), 201
Kőszeg, Hungary, 182, 183
Kozaks, 248
Krauss, Friedrich Salomon, 210
Kretinga, Lithuania, 236
Kúvíkur, Iceland, 80
Kvíaklettar, Iceland, 79
Kwadenoord, Netherlands, 110–11

L'viv, Ukraine, 243
La Junquera, Spain, 145
Labraid Lúathlám ar Chlaidiub, 22
Laima (deity), 234, 236–7
*laimės*, 10, 233–42
Lambhagi, Iceland, 80
*lamiae*, 139–40, 141, 149 n.22, 241 n.7
*lamias* (Basque), 127, 130
Lancelot, 199
landscape, 2, 57, 72–3, 79, 80, 86 n.23, 93, 94, 122, 131, 160, 239
language, supernatural 41, 158
*lares*, 140
*larvae*, 139, 140
Latvia, 233, 234, 236, 239, 240
*laumės*, 233–42
Launfal, Sir, 59
Lausitz region, Germany, 156
law codes, 91
Lawson, John Cuthbert, 220
Laȝamon, 59

Lecouteux, Claude, 156
Leek, England, 56
leprechauns, 12 n.14, 239
lesbianism, 205
Lesbos, Greece, 230 n.31
Leutenberg, Germany, 158
*lhiannan-shee*, 34, 35, 42, 44
Liber Pater (deity), 234
Libera (deity), 234
*lidérc*, 175
Lilly, William, 64
Limburg, Netherlands, 107
Limoux, France, 147
Lindo, Mark Prager, 111, 118
Lindow, John, 89–90, 97, 103
Lir of Síd Finnachaid, 25
Lithuania, 233–42
Lithuania Minor, 235
Lochum, Netherlands, 111
Lóeg (charioteer of Cú Chulainn), 21
Lóegaire mac Crimthainn, 22, 23, 30 n.57
López, Don Diego, 128
Loreley, 163, 171 n.53
Lovell, Agnes, 64
lovers, supernatural, 7, 26, 34, 73, 117, 128–9, 140, 144, 157, 167, 200, 223
Lowy, Donagher, 39
Luchon, France, 147
Lucifer, 74
luck, 38, 44, 61–2, 63, 66 n.23, 75, 78, 101, 223, 256
Lug (deity), 19, 21, 23
Lunca de Jos, Romania, 180
Lund, Sweden, 98
Lunda, Sweden, 99
Lupa/Loba, 130
*lutins*, 141, 146, 147, 150 n.36, 152 n.63
lycanthropes *see* werewolves
*lyra* (instrument), 225

McAnally, David Rice, 3
MacDougall, James, 3

Mag Dá Cheó, realm of, 22
Mag Mell, realm of, 21–2
Magher-y-Breck, Isle of Man, 38
magic, 5, 8, 52, 53, 62, 91, 92, 123, 126, 146, 151 n.49, 158, 192 n.26, 200, 206, 207, 208, 225
magicians *see* cunning folk
Magnus, Olaus, 93
magpies, 236
Malekin, 60, 68 n.53
Malew, Isle of Man, 38
Man, Isle of, 2, 32–50
Manannán (deity), 24, 30 n.62
*manes*, 149 n.25
Manchester, England, 33
Manx Gaelic, 32–3
Mari (deity), 127, 128
Marie de France, 68
Marinha, Dona, 128
Marlborough Downs, England, 55
marriage, with otherworld beings, 5, 25–6, 128–9, 143, 157, 167, 251, 256
Martes of Berry, 146
Martin of Braga, 125
Martin, St, 132
matriarchy, 158
Mátyás Forintos, 182
Maughold, Isle of Man, 40
Maugis d'Aigremont, 199
Mažvydas, Martynas, 242 n.30
mediums, 71, 181, 188
megaliths, 123, 124, 130, 145
Melusine, 14 n.36, 141, 143, 144, 145, 146, 152 n.60
memorates, 55, 87, 179, 207, 251
mermaids, 10, 34, 35, 42, 122, 157, 164, 196, 235, 238
mermen, 10, 35, 160
Methodism, 42
Meyer, Maurits de, 108
Michel, 64
midday, 220–21
Midir, sons of, 25

'Midwife to the Fairies' (tale type), 5, 14 n.34, 14 n.36, 53, 62, 130, 144, 161, 163, 166, 201
migration of supernatural community, 45, 161, 200
Mihály Zsófia, 181
Milan, Italy, 192 n.35
Míl, 25
milk, 35, 75, 97, 117, 130, 144, 152 n.62, 202, 205, 208, 215 n.124, 251
mills, 57, 202, 203, 206, 213 n.63
Milošević-Đorđević, Nada, 210
Minehead, England, 60
mines, 10, 17 n.63, 77
Minorca, Spain, 127, 131
mirrors, 124, 209, 224
misdirection, supernatural, 37
Mississippi, USA, 226
Miyazaki, Hayao, 102
*moddey dhoo* (black dog), 35
modernity, 65, 71, 123
Moirai, 128, 139, 199, 207
Moldavia (region of Romania), 174, 175, 176, 179, 184, 185, 186, 187, 189 n.3
monstrosity, 93, 102, 133 n.3, 135 n.36, 217, 222, 235–6, 239
Mont Saint-Michel, France, 145
Montenegro, 197
*mooinjer-veggey*, 34
Moore, A.W., 33
Moore, Thomas, 51
*Moosweiblein* (moss women), 9, 10, 155, 156, 157–8, 168
Morgan le Fay, 247
*moros/moras*, 122, 123, 130–31
Morrison, Sophia, 34, 43
Moscow, Russia, 233
Moston, England, 56
mountains, 6, 14 n.34, 35, 38, 43, 45, 74, 76, 77, 89, 90, 91, 94, 95, 97, 98, 99, 100, 101, 104 n.16, 122, 123, 124, 127, 128, 129, 130, 132, 145,

156–7, 158, 165, 196, 203, 204, 206, 219, 221, 227 n.1, 229
Mulde, river, 162
Mummelsee, Germany, 165
Munster, Ireland, 8, 20, 24
Muses, 226
music, 7, 23, 24, 25, 26, 38, 143, 164–5, 168, 175, 177–8, 179, 185, 186, 188, 194 n.59, 225–6, 246

Nadruvians, 233, 235, 236, 237
Narváez, Peter, 202, 203
nationalism, Romantic, 112, 209, 243
Naustvík, Iceland, 72, 74–80, 81, 82, 83
Nazism, 110
Neikter, Jacob Fredrik, 88
Nemglan, 20
neopaganism, 210
Neptune (deity), 141
nereids, 2, 197, 217–32, 239
   queens of, 223, 227
Netherlands, 2, 10, 17 n.61, 107–21
New Age, 71
Newman, Francis, 64
Nicander, 218
nightmares, 114, 124, 127
*nikessen*, 35
*Nixen*, 6, 155–72
Nodilo, Natko, 210, 216 n.138
*Noeck*, 6, 161–2, 163, 164, 165–7, 168, 170 n.46, 171 n.71
Noord-Brabant, Netherlands, 107
Nordmøre, Norway, 100
Norns, 107, 113, 114
North Macedonia, 197, 198
Norway, 2, 6, 61, 87, 88, 89, 90–91, 93, 94, 96, 100, 103 n.3, 103 n.4, 226
nudity, 143, 158, 162–3, 251, 252, 255, 256

O'Hanlon, John, 3
Oberpfalz, Germany, 156
Ochall Ochne, 20

Óðinn/Odin (deity), 88, 169 n.10
Ogma, 28 n.27
ogres, 34, 91, 128, 171 n.71
Öland, Sweden, 99
omens, 114, 125
Orkney, 90
Östergötland, Sweden, 100
otherworlds, 15 n.44, 19, 21, 22, 23, 24, 25, 27 n.24, 28 n.35, 29 n.48, 30 n.57, 30 n.66, 34–5, 54, 59, 64, 89, 96, 105 n.32, 151 n.51, 178, 181, 187, 239
Otto IV, Holy Roman Emperor, 138
Overijssel, Netherlands, 108, 114
Ovid, 218
Oxford, England, 61

paganism, 22, 124, 142, 145, 146, 234, 238
Pangallo, Antonino, 222, 223
Paracelsus, 163
Parcae, 128, 139, 140, 146
Parish, Mary, 56, 59
Patrick, St, 26
Perchta, 142, 158
Perk, Jacques Clemens, 111
Perné, Gustaaf van de Wall, 112–13, 115
Perrault, Charles, 126, 147, 153 n.80
Persephone, 240
personalities, distinct, 6, 7, 8, 9
Peru, 132
Perwick, Isle of Man, 41
Petzoldt, Leander, 161
Pharsalus, Greece, 218
Phillips, Judith, 52, 65
*phynnodderee*, 34
Picardt, Johan, 116–17
Pineda, Juan de, 132
pits, 57, 118, 161, 196
pixies, 60, 63
place-names, 32, 57, 64, 67 n.28, 78, 91, 131, 148 n.8, 242 n.40
*plant Annwfn*, 59
plants, 1, 52, 166, 202

Pliny, 143, 148 n.4
*Poetic Edda*, 92, 113
Poles, 197
Politis, Nikolaos, 223, 224
Poortvliet, Rien, 107
Port Erin, Isle of Man, 42
Portugal, 128, 133 n.4 *see also* Iberia
*portuni*, 63
possession, 188, 189 n.2, 194 n.59, 195 n.63
Potocki, Jan, 123
Prätorius, Matthäus, 235, 236, 237, 238
Praetorius, Johannes, 157
Precacore, Italy, 222, 231 n.36
prehistory, 131, 132
Prezzemolina, 231 n.52
priests, 95, 186, 207, 219, 231 n.40, 251
*Prose Edda*, 92, 113
Protestantism, 73, 81, 109, 110, 117
Prussians, 233, 235
Psellos, Michael, 220–21
pucks, 58, 60
Pula, Croatia, 206
Purkiss, Diane, 61
'Puss in Boots', 249
Puttenham, England, 56
Pyrenees, 123, 129, 144, 147

queens, supernatural, 6, 7, 15 n.39, 51–2, 56, 58, 64, 100, 108, 130, 142, 158, 160, 191 n.7, 223, 226, 227, 239

Rabelais, François, 147
rainbows, 127, 237
rape, 30 n.66, 259 n.20, 260 n.33
*raths*, 6, 8, 57, 202
Reykjarfjörður, Iceland, 74, 76, 81
Reykjavík, Iceland, 71–2
Rhine, river, 108, 156, 171 n.53
Rhône, river, 2, 144
Robertson, David, 43
rock formations, 72, 77, 79–80
Roeder, Karl, 33, 39, 43

Roghudi, Italy, 222, 230 n.35, 231 n.36
romances, medieval, 2, 59, 125, 146, 152 n.61, 199
Romania, 10, 174, 181, 189 n.2
Romans, 139
Romanticism, 57, 109, 112, 117, 160, 209
Rosalia (festival), 198
Ross, Ludwig, 219
Rudolstadt, Germany, 166
ruins, 57, 79, 80, 86 n.24, 122, 124, 130, 131, 203, 206
'Rumpelstiltskin' (tale type), 249
*rusalki*, 10, 197, 198, 199, 205, 244, 249–50, 252, 254, 255, 257, 260 n.29
Rushen, Isle of Man, 34, 45
Rye, Sussex, 53

Saale, river, 158, 162, 163, 164
Sabbat, Witches', 146, 177, 179, 201, 236
 'White Sabbath', 15 n.45, 200, 206
Sacheverell, William, 34
Sætrafjall (mountain), Iceland, 77, 78
sagas, 22, 88, 91, 92, 104 n.17, 113
Saint-Barthélemy, Mont, 145
St Elena, Guild of, 182
St George's Day, 176, 180
Sakcinski, Ivan Kukuljević, 209
Salamanca, Spain, 131
Sámi people, 88, 188
Samobor, Croatia, 201
San Juan, day of, 122, 128, 130
Sandwick Rigg, England, 55
Santa Claus, 200
Sapieha, Jan Stanisław, 236
satyrs, 34, 199
Scandinavia, 2, 3, 4, 10, 23, 59, 62, 87–106
 *see also* Iceland
*Scél Mongáin*, 19
*Scél Tuáin maic Cairill*, 22
Schönwerth, Franz Xaver, 156, 157, 159
Schrijnen, Josef, 108
Schwarz, Michael, 182–3
Scotland, 3, 7, 13 n.22, 16 n.58, 59, 187

Scott, Walter, 33, 111, 118
sea monsters, 79, 81
Sebastián de Covarrubias, 125–6, 127, 129
seers, fairy, 55–6, 64, 66 n.18, 67 n.30, 187, 194 n.57
seizures (strokes), 52, 62, 199, 204, 208, 221, 226
Serbia, 197, 198, 209, 210
*Serglige Con Culainn*, 21–2
sex, 25, 26, 56, 64, 129, 142, 157, 162, 179, 186, 205, 244–5, 246, 248
Shaftesbury, earl of, 61
Shakespeare, William, 63
shamanism, 56, 188
shape-changers, 5
Shetland, 42, 66 n.21, 90
Shevchenko, Taras, 243, 247
Shevchenko Scientific Society, 244, 245
Sicily, 10, 134 n.24, 181, 185, 192 n.35, 230 n.33
Silesia, 162
singing, 55, 73, 97, 165, 175, 177, 179, 184, 191 n.7, 205, 244, 246, 247, 248, 249, 250, 252, 253, 254, 256, 258
Sinninghe, J. R. W., 108, 118
sirens, 138, 199, 205
size of supernatural being, 1, 16 n.57, 55, 62–3, 196, 200, 201, 260 n.34
Skåne, Sweden, 100
skewers, 113, 114–16, 117–18
Sloet tot Oldhuis, B. W. A. E., 116, 117, 118, 121 n.48
*skogsrå*, 249
Slovaks, 197
Slovenia, 183, 197
smithing, 27 n.5, 97, 98, 159
Smollett, Tobias, 69 n.64
snakes, 130, 162, 196, 206, 229 n.28, 259 n.28
Snapper, Susan, 53
'social supernatural', definition of, 1–9
 geography of, 9–10, 199-200
 spectrum of, 9

'solitary supernatural', definition of, 3–6
Somerset, England, 53, 60
Sommer, Emil, 156, 162
Sopron County, Hungary, 177, 182
sorcery, 7, 88, 89, 91, 138
'soul battles', 182–3
South Barrule, Isle of Man, 38
Souvestre, Émile, 147
sovereignty, 19, 20, 25
Soviet Union, 245, 247
Spain, 2, 125, 129, 130, 133 n.3 *see also* Iberia
spinning, 6, 10, 98, 101, 113, 116, 128, 140, 146, 165, 207, 238, 239, 246, 252–3, 254, 260
Spiritualists, 1
Staffordshire, England, 54, 56
Staring, Anthony, 117–18
Stefánsdóttir, Erla, 71
Stockholm, Sweden, 98
storm genies, 133 n.3
storms (whirlwind), 35, 42, 113, 143, 176, 183, 186, 221
Stowmarket, England, 56
Strandir, Iceland, 71–86
Sturluson, Snorri, 92
succubi, 139
Suffolk, England, 52, 63
suicide, 248, 250, 251, 252, 260 n.38
Sussex, England, 63
Svealand, Sweden, 95, 105 n.35
Sveinsson, Einar Ólafur, 79
swan maidens, 196, 205, 208
Sweden, 2, 87, 88, 90–91, 92, 93, 94, 95, 97, 99, 100–101, 103 n.3, 103 n.4
SWFs ('small winged fairies'), 1, 226
swineherds, 20
Switzerland, 155, 161, 168
Sybil, 138, 146
Sydow, Carl Wilhelm von, 3, 4, 104 n.9
Sylt, island of, 160, 168
symbiosis with humans, supernatural, 2, 5–6, 7, 9, 197, 202

Szekler Land, Romania, 174, 175, 176, 183, 185, 186, 189 n.2
*szépasszony*, 2, 6, 10, 173, 174–7, 178–81, 183–4, 185, 186, 187, 189 n.2

taboos, 5, 52, 60, 61, 69 n.62, 103, 153 n.67, 157, 158, 178, 197, 238, 239
Tacitus, 107, 116
*Táin Bó Cúailnge*, 22
*Táin Bó Dartada*, 19
*Táin Bó Fraích*, 20
Tara, Ireland, 20
*tarroo ushtey* (water bull), 35
Taunton, England, 53
Tavistock, England, 56
Tchango communities, 174, 183
Teti, Vito, 222
theosophy, 1, 11 n.5, 71, 110
Thiesselin, Jeannette, 146
Thor (deity), 113
three (number), 22, 23, 25, 94, 114, 116, 128, 165, 175, 179, 203–204, 208, 222, 236, 237
Thuringian Forest, Germany, 156
time, experience of, 151 n.55, 199–200
Tinker Bell, 1–2, 200, 226
Tír Tairngire, 24
*Tochmarc Becfola*, 19
*Tochmarc Étaine*, 20
*Togail Bruidne Da Derga*, 20
torture, 178, 182, 250, 253
tourism, 71, 90, 109
trance, 56, 180, 181, 187, 188, 210
Transylvania, 174, 175
travel, supernatural, 85 n.16, 145, 150 n.36, 185
treasure, 52, 53, 54, 56, 113, 122, 129, 130, 166, 191 n.7, 238
trees, 19, 21–2, 125, 127, 129, 146, 157, 175, 178, 202, 203, 205, 206, 218, 221, 235
    alder, 43
    apple, 25

    beech, 112–13
    poplar, 229 n.26
    thorn, 57
Trékyllisvík, Iceland, 76, 77
trolls, 2, 3, 6, 79, 87–106
trooping fairies, 3, 63
Túatha Dé, 20, 22–3, 24, 25, 26, 27 n.7, 28 n.27, 29 n.44, 30 n.61, 30 n.62
*Tucait Baile Mongáin*, 21
*tündér*, 174
Tündér Ilona ('St Ilona'), 182, 191 n.7
Tynwald, 32
Typhon, 135 n.36
Tyrry, Joan, 53, 59, 60, 62

Úaine Buide, 24
Ukraine, 2, 6, 8, 9, 243–60
Ulster, Ireland, 19
'un-gods', 22
underground, as abode of fairies, 14 n.34, 23, 26 n.2, 54, 67 n.29, 97, 118, 122, 123, 129, 130, 132, 144–5, 158–9, 160, 163
Uppsala, Sweden, 98
Urth, 113

Valjevec, Matija Kračmanov, 209
Valkyries, 107, 114, 117, 200
vampires, 133 n.3, 187, 189 n.1, 217, 226
Värmland, Sweden, 97, 99, 100
Västergötland, Sweden, 94, 98, 99, 101
*vättar*, 92, 93
Velesniv, Ukraine, 243
Vesoul, France, 146
Viking Age, 90, 91
*vile*, 2, 9, 196–216
*vilenjaci*, 200–201, 206, 210
virginity, 244–5, 246, 247, 248–9, 259 n.13
Virje, Croatia, 204
*Vision of Paul*, 24
visions, 51, 54, 55, 142, 144, 176–7, 187
*vittra*, 92, 93

Vizcaya, lordship of, 127, 128
Vlachs, Serbian, 181
Vǫluspá (Old Norse poem), 92
Vrouw Holle, 108

Wacker, Michael, 182, 183
Waldron, George, 32–3, 34, 36, 37, 38, 39, 40, 43, 45
Wales, 16 n.58, 70 n.67
wands, magical, 126
*Warnmärchen*, 231 n.44
washing, 6, 8, 10, 64, 144, 147, 163, 205
water, spirits of, 6, 14 n.34, 35, 147, 153 n.69, 162–4, 165, 166, 167, 170 n.46, 201, 226, 235, 238, 239, 244
water horses, 35
wealth, 7, 52, 54, 59, 65, 73, 75, 95, 101, 198, 224
weather, 9, 42, 79, 93, 143, 163, 182
wells, 57, 125, 130, 162, 231 n.44
Werenskiold, Erik, 105 n.33
werewolves, 90, 138, 140, 187, 188 n.1, 193 n.45
West, Alice, 6, 51, 65
Wharton, Goodwin, 56, 64
Wichtel, 6, 155, 156, 158, 159–61, 168

Wild Hunt, 142, 157, 158, 169 n.10, 199
William of Auvergne, 139
Wilson, Jack, 55
wings, supernatural, 1, 196, 205, 221, 226
wish-fulfilment, 59
witchcraft, 39, 105 n.21, 186, 249
    trials for, 174, 177, 181
witches, 52–3, 66 n.23, 91, 109, 124, 130, 142, 146, 175, 178, 179–80, 182–3, 185, 187, 189 n.1, 189 n.2, 192 n.26, 201, 217, 230 n.33, 234, 236, 239, 240, 244, 253
*witte wieven*, 10, 107–21
Woden (deity), 110, 113
Wucke, Christian Ludwig, 156
Wüstefeld, Karl, 156

Yeats, W.B., 3, 4
Yorkshire, England, 64
youth, perpetual, 24, 25

Zakučac, Croatia, 207
Zamora, Spain, 127
Zárate, Tomás, 126
Zelenin, Dmitri, 250
*žemėpačiai*, 233
Zörnißberge, Germany, 164

Printed in the USA
CPSIA information can be obtained
at www.ICGtesting.com
JSHW020757280824
68893JS00001B/8

9 781804 131046